Justice for Some

JUSTICE
FOR
SOME

Law and the Question of Palestine

Noura Erakat

STANFORD UNIVERSITY PRESS
Stanford, California

STANFORD UNIVERSITY PRESS
Stanford, California

Printed in the United States of America on acid-free, archival-quality paper

Library of Congress Cataloging-in-Publication Data

Names: Erakat, Noura, author.
Title: Justice for some : law and the question of Palestine / Noura Erakat.
Description: Stanford, California : Stanford University Press, 2019. |
    Includes bibliographical references and index.
Identifiers: LCCN 2018054406 (print) | LCCN 2018055966 (ebook) |
    ISBN 9781503608832 (electronic) | ISBN 9780804798259 (cloth) |
    ISBN 9781503613577 (paper)
Subjects: LCSH: Palestine—International status—History. | Palestinian Arabs—
    Legal status, laws, etc.—History. | Israel-Arab War, 1967—
    Occupied territories. | Arab-Israeli conflict—History.
Classification: LCC KZ4282 (ebook) | LCC KZ4282 .E73 2019 (print) |
    DDC 956.04—dc23
LC record available at https://lccn.loc.gov/2018054406

Designed by Kevin Barrett Kane
Typeset at Stanford University Press in 10/15 Adobe Caslon
Cover design by Kevin Barrett Kane
Cover Art: The Balfour Declaration, 1917

For my parents,
Nahla, Saleh, and Asmahan

CONTENTS

MAPS

PREFACE

This book is a culmination of fifteen years of advocacy, struggle, disappointment, and enlightenment. As a human rights attorney and scholar, my advocacy for Palestinian rights quickly confronted political obstacles, which in turn inspired deeper questions about knowledge and practice.

Originally my research for this book focused on bias in U.S. federal courts, the limits of human rights advocacy at the United Nations, and the political incapacitation of international tribunals like the International Criminal Court. With time and experience, new questions expanded the scope of this research. As a result, this book examines the relationship between international law and politics in the question of Palestine over the course of a century. It explores the role and the potential of law in the pursuit of Palestinian freedom.

More specifically, *Justice for Some: Law and the Question of Palestine* surveys how occupation law (the body of international law that addresses enemy occupation of a territory) has failed to regulate Israel's settlement enterprise; the incongruence between the United Nations' attention to the question of Palestine and its inability to deliver any meaningful change; and finally, how the Oslo peace process ensured the failure of a two-state solution. It also addresses how Israel's devastating register of death and destruction in the Gaza Strip became permissible within the language of law. None of the conditions on the ground today in Israel and Israel-Palestine have been inevitable. The law has the capacity to dominate as well as to resist. Using international law to advance the Palestinian cause for freedom requires a praxis of "movement lawyering," where lawyers follow the lead of political movements to buttress their collective efforts. At most, the law can be a tool, and even then, its efficacy will depend on multiple factors. These include geopolitical power, national and international interests, personnel capacity, strategic cohesion, effective leadership, and most significantly, political vision. There is no lack of good Palestinian lawyers. There is a lack of a robust political movement to inform their legal advocacy and to leverage their tactical gains.

Justice for Some builds on a rich literature on the relationship between international law and Palestine. These works include Victor Kattan's *From Coexistence to Conquest: International Law and the Origins of the Arab-Israeli Conflict 1891–1949*, and John Quigley's *The Case for Palestine: An International Law Perspective*. I build on these texts by scrutinizing Israel's legal and political strategy following the 1967 War; analyzing the Palestine Liberation Organization's legal advocacy at the United Nations during the 1970s; tracing the peace talks in Madrid, Washington, and Oslo between 1991 and 1993; and examining how Israel's legal interventions shifted the legal framework from occupation to warfare between 2001 and 2017.

The formative literature on international law and the question of Palestine also includes the essays in *Beyond Occupation: Apartheid, Colonialism, and International Law in the Occupied Palestinian Territories*, edited by Virginia Tilley, and *International Law and the Israeli-Palestinian Conflict: A Rights-Based Approach to Middle East Peace*, edited by Susan M. Akram, Michael Dumper, Michael Lynk, and Ian Scobbie. These texts pay meticulous attention to the law, either to advance a legal argument or to suggest practical approaches for resolving the conflict. The works of George Bisharat, *Palestinian Lawyers and Israeli Rule: Law and Disorder in the West Bank*, and Lisa Hajjar, *Courting Conflict: The Israeli Military Court System in the West Bank and Gaza*, examine how Israel's legal regimes and Palestinian legal advocacy have shaped Palestinian subjectivity and social life. They highlight the simultaneous durability and vulnerability of Israeli structures of domination over Palestinians.

This book does not advance legal prescriptions nor make exhaustive legal arguments. It reveals how the law is working during consequential historical moments. It shows how the law's ability to oppress is evidence not of its failure but rather of the fact that it can be strategically deployed. This cynicism about the law is also found in volume four of Raja Shehadeh's *From Occupation to*

Interim Accords: Israel and the Palestinian Territories, which traces Israel's deployment of law to successfully consolidate its land takings and sanctify its system of domination in the negotiated peace agreement between Israel and the Palestine Liberation Organization (PLO). More recent titles, such as Lori Allen's *The Rise and Fall of Human Rights: Cynicism and Politics in Occupied Palestine*, and Neve Gordon and Nicola Periguini's *The Human Right to Dominate*, similarly examine the limitations of human rights law and the risks posed by invoking it.

Finally, *Justice for Some* benefits from researchers' resurgent use of a settler-colonial framework to understand the question of Palestine. The return of this analytical approach has made it possible for this book to delve into the settler-colonial nature of the Palestinian struggle. Ongoing struggles in the United States, Canada, Hawai'i, and Australia also offer instructive lessons on decolonization. Similarly, U.S.-based movements protesting state violence and the dehumanization of black communities—in particular—inform my optimism. Among the many lessons that black radical protest and knowledge production have offered is that there is no return to an optimal past. There are only optimal futures to shape.

While I build on and advance a skeptical analysis of the law's utility, I am not pessimistic. Change is possible. Our present is the culmination of people's triumphs. This work is intended to contribute to ongoing scholarly endeavors about the role of the law on behalf of progressive causes. It also intends to empower future advocates, legal and otherwise, to be more strategic in their efforts, tempering their faith in the law's capacity to do what only a critical mass of people are capable of achieving.

Justice for Some

INTRODUCTION

ON 23 DECEMBER 2016, the United Nations Security Council met to consider yet again an agenda centered on the "situation in the Middle East, including the Palestinian question."[1] The specific topic was Resolution 2334, which unequivocally condemned Israel's settlements in the Palestinian territories. These settlements, the resolution reaffirmed, including those in East Jerusalem, lack "legal validity and [constitute] a flagrant violation under international law and a major obstacle to the achievement of the two-State solution."[2] The Palestinian delegation to the United Nations (UN) had been lobbying the Security Council's fifteen members nearly all year.[3] When it came time for a vote, 14 members voted in favor, zero members voted against, and the United States abstained. The resolution passed. This was no small feat.

The Security Council had reached some sort of formal decision on these settlements only twice before this moment, and the last time was nearly four decades before, in 1980.[4] Since the passage of UN Security Council Resolution 242. U.S. administrations, from the Johnson administration on, have systematically undermined nearly all Palestinian efforts to internationalize its conflict with Israel. Between 1972 and 2017, the United States used its Security Council veto forty-three times to shield Israel from international censure.[5] In 2011, for example, the Obama administration had vetoed an anti-settlement resolution similar to Resolution 2334.[6]

In 2012, the United States had opposed the Palestinian National Authority's bid for statehood;[7] in 2014, it tried and failed to prevent the Palestinian

Authority from seeking the jurisdiction of the International Criminal Court;[8] and in late 2014, it quietly crushed an effort to have the Security Council set a deadline for ending Israeli occupation of Palestinian territories.[9] So in 2016, the United States' choice to refrain from using its veto to obstruct Resolution 2334 was remarkable. For the first time in nearly four decades, it removed a primary impediment to the application of international law, and this should have, in theory, signaled a shift in the diplomatic treatment and international regulation of Israel's settlement enterprise.

Two weeks later, in mid-January 2017, representatives from seventy countries convened in Paris for the Middle East Peace Conference, part of an ongoing effort to negotiate peace between Israel and Palestine. This marked the first opportunity the parties would have to leverage the newly established international consensus on the illegality of the settlements. Israel condemned the meeting and Resolution 2334 as threats to peace.[10] It argued that both efforts failed to fully appreciate Israel's position: Israel had not occupied East Jerusalem in 1967, the Israeli representative claimed, it liberated it.[11]

The conference closed with a commitment to the two-state solution and a reversion from an international and legal framework to a political one.[12] Not even three months later, and in accordance with the resolution's reporting requirement, the UN Special Coordinator for the Middle East Peace Process briefed the Security Council on Israel's intention to build thousands more housing units in the settlements.[13] The Council noted the development and did little more. The juxtaposition of the extraordinary passage of Resolution 2334 alongside the failure of an international conference to leverage it, as well as an increase in the number of settlement units in the resolution's direct aftermath, tells a familiar story.

Throughout the course of the Palestinian struggle for freedom, international law has seemed futile, if not irrelevant. Since the First World War, serious legal controversies, including the disputes over the settlements, have characterized the question of Palestine. Yet, it has been the use of force and the balance of power—not judicial decisions—that have fundamentally shaped the realities on the ground. Given how history has unfolded, does this mean that the law is indeed irrelevant? Israel's founding story and Palestinians' dispossession seem to indicate as much.

Time and time again, we see evidence of the law's assumed insignificance in the dispossession of Palestinians. Great Britain remained committed to establishing a Jewish national home in Palestine despite its legal duties as the Mandatory Power to shepherd local Arab peoples to independence.[14] The Permanent Mandates Commission remained committed to the incorporation of the Balfour Declaration into the Mandate for Palestine, in contravention of the Covenant of the League of Nations, which, in discussing the disposition of the "communities formerly belonging to the Turkish Empire" stated that "the wishes of these communities must be a primary consideration."[15] The United Nations proposed partition of Palestine without legal consultation and in disregard of the existing population's "well-being and development," which the same Covenant had declared to be a "sacred trust of civilisation."[16] Zionist militias established Israel by force, without regard to the Partition Plan's stipulated borders.[17] The United Nations accepted Israel as a member despite that state's violation of the nondiscrimination clauses of the Partition Plan and of the UN's own condition that Israel permit the return of forcibly displaced Palestinian refugees.[18]

The very origins of the Palestinian-Israel conflict suggest that it is characterized by outright lawlessness, and yet few conflicts have been as defined by astute attention to law and legal controversy as this one. Do Jews have a right to self-determination in a territory in which they did not reside but settled? Are Palestinians a nation with the right to self-determination, or are they merely a heterogeneous polity of Arabs eligible for minority rights? Did the United Nations have the authority to propose partition in contravention of the will of the local population? Are the West Bank (including East Jerusalem) and the Gaza Strip "occupied," as a matter of law, that is, are they recognized as such by the law? Does Israel have the right, in law, to self-defense against Palestinians living in the Occupied Palestinian Territories? Do Palestinians have the right to use armed force against Israel? Is the route of Israel's Separation barrier, built predominantly in the West Bank, illegal? Is Israel an apartheid regime?

Enumerating a comprehensive list of the legal questions surrounding this conflict could span the pages of an entire book. Indeed, concern with them has produced several specialized legal journals.[19] Significantly, however, none of these issues has been resolved by legal fiat, even as all parties have availed themselves of the law's moral, political, and intellectual logic. What explains this conundrum of excessive attention to law in the conflict and the law's seeming irrelevance in resolving it? What function is the law serving if not the expected one as an authoritative referee? This book's inquiry begins here, with the desire to better understand both the present conditions of the Palestinian struggle for liberation and the role that law has played in furthering and in stunting the realization of that liberation.

I argue that the law is politics: its meaning and application are contingent on the strategy that legal actors deploy as well as on the historical context in which that strategy is deployed. This does not mean that the law is a political fiction. To the contrary, it has a life of its own and the capacity to influence, though not command, the behavior of state and non-state actors. While the imbrication of law and politics in the case of Palestine is exemplary of a global system, the sovereign exception that produced the question of Palestine demands particular attention to the potential risks, and benefits, of appealing to international law. In order to serve an emancipatory function, the law must be wielded in the sophisticated service of a political movement that can both give meaning to the law and also directly challenge the structure of power that has placed Palestinians outside the law.

This book explores five critical junctures in the history of the Palestinian struggle for freedom. The first of these explorations is unique in its breadth and purpose. It spans five decades in the twentieth century and provides a historical overview critical for understanding the subsequent four junctures. Not coincidentally, each of these subsequent junctures has followed some confrontation that recalibrated the regional and international balance of power, creating key moments of "principled opportunism," or instances when actors were able to use international law as a tool; I refer to these moments as *legal opportunities*.[20] Each juncture demonstrates how legal work shaped the meaning of law as a site of resistance or oppression, and how law thereafter structured the political framework regulating the question of Palestine.

The junctures are organized chronologically over a century-long arc (rather than thematically by legal norms, such as self-determination, occupation law, and laws of war) for two reasons. First, the chronological narration demonstrates how the meaning of law is responsive to the legal work of state and non-state actors and also to the historical context in which that work is being done.[21] Looking at sequential episodes reveals that while the content of the relevant legal norms did not change across time and space, their meaning changed significantly. This variation can be attributed to the strategy of the actors doing the legal work as well as to the balance of military, economic, and normative considerations during each historical moment. It is for this reason that the book pays much closer attention to the details of these historical turns than to the content of the legal norms.

Second, the chronological narration helps to explain a history of the present of the Palestinian question. The legal work deployed during each juncture has had an enduring impact on how the international community diagnoses the conflict and imagines its proper remedy. These episodes demonstrate legal work's impact in shaping the normative conceptions and diplomatic treatment of the question of Palestine. Overall, this approach enables us to trace how legal work has facilitated these junctures leading up to the present day.

Against the Law

The casual observer may attribute injustice to a failure of law or to its nonexistence and thus prescribe more law, better law, and/or stricter adherence to law as the requisite corrective. The law's malleability, however, undermines any such promise and should make us wary of legal prescriptions. Nazi Germany and apartheid South Africa, for example, were both based on meticulous adherence to self-referential legalistic regimes yet were unequivocally oppressive. The rule of law is not synonymous with justice. For this reason, I have not sought to provide an alternative legal framework as a solution to the conflict, nor reform existing laws, nor suggest a better model for compliance. Instead, this book urges all involved to use critical analysis and strategic intelligence in the service of the Palestinian struggle for freedom.

International law is not always a site of contestation. Even strong states desire it to regulate some spheres of their relations, like economic trade, diplomatic immunity, maritime passage, and consular relations. In these spheres, international law engenders predictability and a mutually beneficial reciprocity that benefit weak and strong states alike. This logic of reciprocity and voluntary compliance fails, however, when discussing geopolitical conflicts—for example, state sovereignty, territoriality, war and peace—where interests and preferences diverge, as they do in the question of Palestine.

There are at least two reasons to be skeptical that international law has the capacity to overcome geopolitical realities and advance the Palestinian struggle for freedom. One is the sordid origin of international law as a derivative of a colonial order and therefore as a body of law that reifies, rather than unsettles, an asymmetry of rights and duties among international actors. The other is the fact that the international system lacks a global sovereign, thereby politicizing enforcement by leaving it to the discretion of states to decide when, how, and whom, to punish. Together, these critiques, regarding the content and the form of international law respectively, suggest that international law can be used as a tool against the least powerful international actors but is toothless when it comes to regulating the behavior of the most powerful ones, specifically in regard to geopolitical conflicts. The following two sections address each critique in turn to show, first, that the content of international law does not determine its final meaning, and second, that challenging the structural conditions giving rise to asymmetry in power requires political action—it cannot be accomplished by legal strategies alone. My purpose here is not to defend international law as it is, but to illuminate how its relationship with politics shapes its function in counterintuitive ways.

Content: International Law Is Derivative of a Colonial Order

Doctrinally, the term *international law* refers to treaties, customs, and general principles that define the rights of states, regulate states' behavior towards one another, and establish states' duties and responsibilities towards organizations and individuals within their jurisdiction.[22] The history of international law's development makes that law primarily a tool for powerful states.[23] International law as it exists today began in Europe among states that were colonial powers.[24] Positioned as universal in appeal and application, international law is the codification of exclusively European traditions. As Spain encountered the indigenous societies of the Western hemisphere, a Spanish theologian and jurist, Francis de Vitoria, articulated a body of law that made the rights of indigenous nations contingent on their society's resemblance to European society.[25] After establishing and projecting Europe's particular norms as universal, Spain then used these norms to justify the plunder and conquest of indigenous peoples and their lands.[26] The first seeds of international law were thus planted during a violent conquest to afford that conquest a veneer of objective legality.

These sordid origins continue to characterize international law. It has never been rewritten by an international community of the present. Instead, former colonial powers, newly independent states, and also movements and peoples have incrementally developed international law based on its first articulation. Moreover, since the sixteenth century, former colonial powers have been the principle progenitors of the international legal regimes governing trade,[27] refugees,[28] human rights,[29] and warfare.[30] International law can be accurately and fairly described as a derivative of a colonial order, and therefore structurally detrimental to former colonies, peoples still under colonial domination, and individuals who lack nationality or who, like refugees, have been forcibly removed from their state and can no longer invoke its protection.[31] It is inaccurate, however, to conclude that this law serves the interests only of the powerful and, then, only as a tool of oppression.

The belief that the law can be used only as a tool of oppression rests, in some part, on the false assumption that a legal statute or norm—including those developed by former colonial powers—has a fixed meaning impervious to interpretive manipulation. Under this assumption, once facts are established, a law will "apply itself" and produce a predictable outcome.[32] But the law is contingent and does not predetermine an outcome. It only promises the possibility of a contest over one. A legal norm is inherently contradictory and has no demonstrable meaning until it is applied. When it comes time to apply the law, it must be mediated, first by an adversarial process and ultimately by the vast discretionary powers of judicial interpretation.[33] In that process, there is little to limit the ways in which the law can be framed, deployed, interpreted, or suspended to produce a particular effect. The operative variable determining a law's particular meaning is not necessarily its content, though that is relevant.[34] Rather it is what legal scholar Duncan Kennedy describes as "legal work," or the work that the legal actor performs to achieve a desired outcome.[35] Legal work is undertaken strategically "to transform an initial apprehension of what the system of norms requires, given the facts, so that a new apprehension of the system, as it applies to the case, will correspond" to the extralegal preferences of the worker.[36] The same law can have a different meaning depending on the historical context, the balance of power, and the strategy of the legal worker. The legal work's success is a "function of time, strategy, skill, and of the 'intrinsic'... attributes of the rule that one is trying to change, as these appear in the context of the facts presented."[37]

Legal work embodies and evidences the imbrication of law and politics. For someone who believes that the law has an invulnerable core meaning, the idea that a jurist would deploy a legal norm in strategic pursuit of an ideological agenda is absolutely unfitting.[38] Such strategic work is better suited for a legislature, which can create the law, but not the judiciary, which can only interpret it. This conclusion rests on a fidelity to the law that it does not merit. The ways in which powerful states, for example, have deployed international law to achieve their policy objectives demonstrate as much. The most vivid examples in recent history include the Bush administration's legal argument that neither international humanitarian law nor U.S. constitutional law applied to the treatment of foreign detainees at the Guantanamo Bay military prison.[39] The Bush administration sought to evade external regulation of its treatment of the detainees so that it could, in the name of national security, hold them indefinitely, without charge or trial, and subject them to what amounted to torture for the purpose of extracting information.[40] The U.S. Supreme Court ultimately rejected this national security line of argumentation, but the U.S. attorneys' legal memos and adjudication advancing it were tantamount to legal work in pursuit of an ideological agenda and a particular outcome. While we may agree that those objectives were pure evil, it does not diminish the legal nature of the work performed or the possibility that, under different historical circumstances, the Supreme Court could have agreed with the Bush administration lawyers to realize those objectives.[41] This does not mean that any outcome of legal work is legitimate but that legitimacy is a function of political effect; it depends on the prevailing outcome and whether a political society accepts or rejects that outcome.[42]

States engage in legal work as a matter of fact.[43] This book will demonstrate, for example, how Israel's most enduring legal frameworks regarding the regulation of the Occupied Palestinian Territories and the conduct of hostilities towards them, especially in the Gaza Strip, are the products of legal work. Non-state actors engage in legal work as well. While states remain the most significant, and effective, actors in international law, subaltern studies (that is, the study of non-elite and hegemonic cultures, histories, and societies) have

demonstrated how nongovernmental organizations (NGOs) and social movements have also critically shaped international law from the bottom up.[44] These
subaltern movements mobilize various forms of coercive pressure, including
crude violence, massive uprisings, civil disobedience, and boycott, to shape the
content, purpose, and development of international law.[45]

The power of non-state actors in the international realm is especially relevant
to the question of Palestine, and to this book, since it is precisely the lack of a Palestinian state that has animated Palestinians' struggle for self-determination and
the conflict more generally.[46] In fact, Palestinian organizations and movements have
been pioneers in developing international law and applying it in the Arab world.[47]
As this book will show, for example, the Palestine Liberation Organization's legal
work during the 1970s successfully altered the international status of Palestinians
from a nondescript polity to a juridical people inscribed in international legal
instruments and institutions. If we were to accept that only states could deploy
law to achieve their desired objectives, this book would have no purpose. It is precisely because individuals and organizations can recalibrate, and have historically
recalibrated, an international balance of power and can shape the content and
application of international law that there is a story to be told.

Notwithstanding the universal engagement in legal work since the early 2000s
and even in the midst of the U.S.-led "war on terror," the United States and
Israel have framed legal challenges to their conduct of hostilities as illegitimate
legal warfare, or "lawfare."[48] Their contention is that the use of law by relatively
weak U.S. and Israeli adversaries is disingenuous and manipulative for its attempt to achieve an ideologically driven outcome.[49] Israeli leaders have described
Palestinian legal strategies at the UN Human Rights Council, at the Hague,
and at the UN Security Council as tantamount to political and legal warfare.[50]
The NGO Monitor, an organization dedicated to defunding NGOs that challenge Israel's domination, describes organizations engaging in legal advocacy on
behalf of Palestinians, such as the Center for Constitutional Rights and Defense
for Children International–Palestine Section, as the leading culprits in such
lawfare.[51] There is, of course, a blatant contradiction in the lawfare accusation:
it does not condemn the practice of legal work in general, it takes issue with it
only when it is directed at powerful states.[52] As put by one military lawyer, "the

reaction against lawfare turns out to be less about the law itself than with the broader question of the political and moral reaction to the application of forces that has the capacity to undermine military effectiveness."[53] In this way, lawfare, seen as a framework that delegitimizes legal work, functions much like terrorism, seen as a framework that delegitimizes political violence: its applicability is based on the identity of the perpetrator rather than the act in question.[54] Both frameworks accept the tactics of the strong, and neither is instructive in discerning legitimate violence or legitimate legal work.

Israel's legal opposition to UN Security Council Resolution 2334 is exemplary of legal work. As the following chapters will closely examine, Israel has insisted that the lack of a sovereign in the West Bank and the Gaza Strip in 1967 means that those territories cannot be considered *occupied*, as a matter of law. In this view, the body of international law known as *occupation law*, which includes a prohibition on civilian settlement in militarily occupied lands, does not strictly regulate Israel's administration of the West Bank and the Gaza Strip. Given this view, Israel has applied a modified legal framework it deems more appropriate. The discrepancy between the two legal frameworks is not one between law and no law, but reflects a contest over whose law.[55] Occupation law cannot apply itself. Its meaning and application has to be mediated by interpretation, leading in this case to two distinct accounts and a legal contradiction that cannot be solved by judicial resolution alone.

Resolution 2334 established an international consensus over the applicability of occupation law and rejected Israel's legal framework. Notwithstanding the international consensus, Israel's legal work has enabled it to advance its political goals of settlement in the territories under the veneer of law and the legitimacy that veneer affords. Meir Shamgar, the architect of Israel's legal regime in the West Bank and the Gaza Strip, boasted about it in 1982:

> Since those early days in the beginning of June 1967 the Israeli Military Government became a governmental system applying the norms of international law pertaining to the administration of territory taken over from hostile military forces more extensively and more diversely than most if not all military administrations in this century with regard to both the frequency and intensity of the application of these norms and the duration of time which passed since it was first established.[56]

This potential for international law's strategic deployment does not necessarily make the law good or bad but it does make its invocation a risk. This risk together with the fact that the law is biased towards the most powerful states has led some critical scholars to decry the law as central to the problem itself (it can be), and have prescribed that it be abandoned altogether.[57] This prescription incorrectly assumes that the law is avoidable. In the century-long arc traced by this book, international law has forced itself upon the question of Palestine—first in the form of the Mandate system, then in the regulation of the occupation, later in the affirmation of the right to self-determination and the legitimacy of violence, then in the form of binding treaties, and finally in the return to the question of political violence. In this way, legality is like all other structural asymmetries (that is, military, economic, and political): brutally unfair and inescapable. Overcoming these obstacles requires strategic and tactical ingenuity to leverage weaknesses into strengths and the adversaries' strengths into weaknesses.

Think of the law as like the sail of a boat. The sail, or the law, guarantees motion but not direction. Legal work together with political mobilization, by individuals, organizations, and states, is the wind that determines direction. The law is not loyal to any outcome or player, despite its bias towards the most powerful states. The only promise it makes is to change and serve the interests of the most effective actors. In some cases, the sail is set in such a way that it cannot possibly produce a beneficial direction, and the conditions demand either an entirely new sail, or no sail at all. It is this indeterminacy in law and its utility as a means to dominate as well as to fight that makes it at once a site of oppression and of resistance; at once a source of legitimacy and a legitimating veneer for bare violence; and at once the target of protest and a tool for protest.

Form: Anarchy Characterizes the International System

Even if relatively weaker international actors can sometimes shape the meaning of the law, the structure of the international system—with its lack of a reliable enforcement model and characterized by a material inequality among states—makes it nearly impossible to punish a powerful state and/or command its behavior in the face of a geopolitical conflict. This raises two questions: first, is international law meaningless if it fails to punish and command? And second, what does the question of Palestine's particular history tell us about the law's potential and limitations?

To the casual observer, the law is a known quantity, namely a set of rules that must be observed and whose violation is met with punishment.[58] That makes some, though not complete, sense in the domestic sphere where there exists a hierarchical regime, a supreme court, lower courts, branches of government, and law enforcement authorities that can pass binding judicial decisions and impose punishment when necessary.[59] However, it makes much less sense for the international community, where there is no global police, no hierarchical judicial system, nor a single lawmaking authority.

Some would argue that if there is no punishment, there is no law; there is only a state of anarchy wherein might means right.[60] This pessimist framework understands power as the ultimate determinant of both legitimacy and legality. Its adherents argue that the political framework regulating the use of coercive pressure by and against states renders international law a political fiction meant to maintain the privileges and supremacy of the most powerful states.[61] This argument is compelling since a state's behavior is only subject to external regulation by voluntary submission. Treaties are only binding on the states that ratify them and customary norms are only binding on the states that do not consistently violate or object to them.[62] Even in the case of a state's violation of an overriding principle from which no derogation is permitted, like slavery, torture, and genocide, punishment by the application of force or sanctions is still contingent on the political will of other states when their interests sufficiently converge.[63] The only case when a state can legally use force against another state is in individual or collective self-defense. While the question of whether force is defensive or not is a legal one, political exigencies, rather than judicial adjudication, usually settle that question. The UN Security Council is the ultimate arbiter of that inquiry, and its five permanent members have the authority to single-handedly oppose the will of the international community in order to protect themselves as well as their closest allies. These realities have given rise to a potent critique of international law in regard to conflict as a purely instrumental "tool of foreign policy, to mobilize support for . . . policies at home, and especially as a legal club with which to bash adversaries."[64]

While this pessimist approach makes a lot of sense for its matter-of-fact simplicity, it risks bludgeoning the complexity of state behavior, sacrificing a nuanced understanding of power, and worse, standing in as an apology for it.[65]

The belief that law is subservient to geopolitics rests on an assumption that anarchy, as a structure characterizing our global system, causally leads to competition between states wherein self-help is a guiding principle.[66] Accordingly, states produce international law to further their interests, but international law is incapable of either regulating state behavior or shaping state interests.[67] What this pessimist framework fails to consider, however, is the ways in which state interests and international law are mutually constituted, a claim advanced by constructivists.[68] Constructivism's adherents consider international behavior a function of social interactions among states, rather than a function of power and interests.[69] Any particular state interest reflects a process, rather than an attribute that existed prior to contact with other international actors.[70]

Constructivists contend that international legal norms can be internalized by states in the course of relational processes, thus influencing their choices and preferences. An internalized norm indirectly shapes state behavior in response to a state's inner logic, in contrast to a norm that directly regulates state behavior as a result of an external command.[71] Additionally, legal norms can indirectly shape state behavior by providing a discursive framework.[72] A legal framework has the ability to shape how policymakers and states understand a conflict, as well as imagine its proper remedies, thus ordering their diplomatic agendas. International law and norms may also be critical in justifying, organizing, and constraining a policymaker's decisions even though the law and related norms may not be directing an outcome.[73] International law can be doing a lot of work even as it explicitly fails to exact punishment or command state behavior. It is not merely at the instrumentalist disposal of the most powerful states for furthering their interests, though it certainly does that too.

An illustrative example of international law's counterintuitive utility is found in the story of Resolution 2334. While this resolution's inability to stem settlement construction suggests its futility, a closer examination reveals a quiet and lasting impact. Resolution 2334 includes a clause calling on states to distinguish in their dealings with Israel between the state of Israel and the territories it occupies. This established an obligation among states to alter their national policies in regard to Israel's settlement enterprise.[74] This clause mirrors and enshrines a European Union policy.[75] The EU does not recognize the legality of Israeli settlements and is, in theory, obligated to put this non-recognition policy into practice.[76] It has done this with a mix of incentives and disincentives, captured in a policy of differentiation that obligates the "EU and its member states to exclude settlement-linked entities and activities from bilateral relations with Israel."[77]

Differentiation is a policy under which states maintain relations with Israel while delegitimizing its settlement enterprise.[78] Unlike a boycott strategy, differentiation is inward looking in that it "seeks to protect the integrity and effectiveness of [the EU's] own legal orders by ensuring that they are not giving legal effect to internationally unlawful acts."[79] It is concerned with the EU's compliance with its own laws and less concerned with enforcing international law abroad, in this case upon Israel. Upon the mere publication of a 2015 report endorsing differentiation as a coherent policy in Europe, Tel Aviv's banking index dropped 2.46 points.[80] As of October 2016, eighteen EU member states had formally adopted advisories warning businesses against the legal repercussions of engaging with Israeli settlements.[81] This EU clause stipulating differentiation, together with Resolution 2334's quarterly reporting requirement, represents a tangible policy with the capacity to indirectly punish Israel for settlement expansion by directly taking issue with, and targeting, the policies of European states.

At a more abstract level, the resolution also reified the question of Palestine as a conflict within a peace process paradigm by focusing solely on Israel's violations of occupation law as an impediment to the establishment of a Palestinian state. This is significant because the facts on the ground indicate that the two-state solution has been long dead and that Israel is overseeing a singular regime based on racial and ethnic discrimination characterized by spatial and political separation, or apartheid, an international crime against humanity.[82] In fact, several months after the UN Security Council passed Resolution 2334, the UN Economic and Social Commission for Western Asia (ESCWA) published a report concluding that "Israel has established an apartheid regime that dominates the Palestinian people as a whole," that is, both the Palestinian citizens of Israel and the stateless Palestinians in the Occupied Territories.[83] ESCWA's report recommended that the United Nations and national governments adopt appropriate measures to prevent and punish this crime of apartheid, including prosecuting Israeli officials and endorsing the tactics of boycott, divestment, and sanction against Israel.[84] Whereas Resolution 2334 frames the problem as an intractable conflict between two parties, thus demanding that UN member states prod both

sides to compromise, the ESCWA report frames the problem as one of Palestinian subjugation and demands that states exert pressure upon Israel to upend its
regime of domination. The ESCWA report caused a diplomatic maelstrom. The
UN ultimately shelved it and maintained the primacy of Resolution 2334 and
the occupation law framework.[85] While neither the resolution nor the report
changed the reality on the ground, the fact that the international community
upheld Resolution 2334 and maligned a UN agency report indicates the capacity of legal frameworks to shape diplomatic understandings of, and remedies to,
a conflict. The story of Resolution 2334 highlights how international law can
perform legal work even when, on the face of it, it appears irrelevant.

    This leads to the second question—how does the international structure bear
upon the law's potential and limitations in regard to the question of Palestine?
This international structure encompasses both the historical conditions that transformed Palestine into a question and the present-day balance of power characterizing the ongoing struggle for freedom. The law's counterintuitive utility does not
diminish the relevance of the asymmetries distinguishing strong and, relatively,
weak international actors. Power remains determinative in regard to the law's
enforcement and especially the ability to declare a sovereign exception.

    The ability to suspend international law's application is a *sovereign exception*,
and it falls within the scope of enforcement authority. Only a sovereign has the
ability to declare an exception, and that decision is based on the sovereign's unencumbered assessment of what is necessary to preserve itself or its interests.[86]
It is a moral or political conclusion that is "undecidable in fact and law" and
therefore cannot be legally challenged or externally regulated.[87] It outlines a zone
of exceptional lawmaking wherein political necessity determines applicable law.
Examples include the domestic application of martial law during times of national
emergency or the expanded executive authority to detain civilians without charge
or trial during wartime.[88] While some would argue that an exception is a zone
of lawlessness and therefore not law at all,[89] legal doctrine views an exceptional
fact pattern as *sui generis* (Latin for "of its own kind").[90] If a fact pattern is *sui
generis*, or unlike anything else, then there is no applicable precedent or analogy,
thus creating the need to establish new law. Declaring a *sui generis* fact pattern
produces a lawmaking authority that empowers the sovereign to establish new
law wherein its claims of exception are legally regulated and internally coherent.

What would otherwise be a suspension of applicable law becomes a distinct modality of governance, and compliance with a *sui generis* regime is, in appearance and function, *lawful* not lawless. The ability to declare an exception in the international system is predicated upon the strength of the sovereign to withstand censure and punishment. This means that relatively weaker actors can be subject to a sovereign exception but are rarely able to declare one.[91] Overcoming this condition is not merely a matter of insistence on applicable legal norms, and is certainly not about compliance, but requires instead a direct confrontation with the geopolitical structure that maintains the framework of exception.

In the case of Palestine, Britain's decision to support the establishment of a Jewish national home in a territory where a native Arab population sought to govern itself constituted a sovereign exception. The 1917 Balfour Declaration was predicated on Britain's finding that the condition of the global Jewry and the history of Palestine rendered Palestine unique and distinct from all other former territories of the Ottoman Empire. This fact-based conclusion produced a lawmaking authority for the colonial power to establish a "special regime" in Palestine.[92] The Balfour Declaration enabled Britain, together with the Allied powers of the First World War, to legislate a unique framework for Palestine's regulation in the international proceedings following the close of that war, and culminated in the 1922 British Mandate for Palestine.[93] This Mandate incorporated the Balfour Declaration and declared the purpose of British tutelage in Palestine to be the establishment of a Jewish national home in that territory—even though the native community there, 90 percent of the population, was seeking to govern itself. This Mandatory regime was, by definition, *sui generis*, distinct from all the other Class A Mandates, where non-self-governing territories, comprising the existing local communities, would be ushered to independence. The exception, however, engendered its own rules, and according to these rules, the suppression of Palestinian self-determination constituted an international legal obligation—even though it required Palestinians' juridical erasure to achieve the self-determination of a settler population in their place. The sovereign exception and the rules it produced were co-constitutive: the exception authorized the creation of new rules and the new rules sustained the exception.[94] Thereafter, all Palestinian protest against Britain's colonial decision became a struggle against established international law and the international community seeking to uphold it. Palestinians have literally fought against their state of exception since this defining moment in 1922.[95] Moreover, Palestinians are not unique in this regard. While the suppression of Palestinian self-determination and the erasure of Palestinians' juridical peoplehood—their status as a legally recognized polity—is indeed the outcome of a sovereign exception, it is not an exception to the norm at work for other former colonies seeking their independence and especially as regards other cases of settler-colonialism.[96]

Since Israel's establishment in 1948, the sovereign exception that denied Palestinians their status as a juridical people and established the right to Jewish self-determination in Mandate Palestine has underscored Israel's claims that the facts of the Palestinian case are *sui generis* and not subject to strict legal regulation by any existing body of law. Israel has used its military and economic power, as well as its alliances to global superpowers in the past and present, to advance its claims so that it can create *alternative legal models* for regulating Palestinian life.[97] These legal models, predicated on claims of *sui generis* fact patterns, represent continuations of colonial era practices, and they have placed Palestinian natives outside the normal state of law. This book will demonstrate how these alternative models have permitted the ongoing settler-colonial elimination of Palestinians through removal, dispossession, assimilation, and containment, within Israel as well as the territories, by making them nonexistent in the language of the law.[98] Palestinian legal protest, alone, has been futile in altering this condition since it was being designated an exception that rendered Palestinians ineligible for normal rights in the first place. Any possible recourse for challenging this exclusion has been, and must be, based on challenging the political structure that declared and has sustained the sovereign exception.

As will be shown, in the 1970s and 1980s, the PLO had managed, through unconventional warfare, political mobilization, civil uprisings, and legal advocacy, to successfully challenge this exception. Upon entering the Middle East peace process in 1991, it willingly relinquished its political claims, which had with great effort been enshrined in UN resolutions as well as international treaties, and entered the interior of U.S. and Israeli governance. That position has neutralized its capacity to challenge the political structure that sustains an oppressive status quo, thereby diminishing the emancipatory potential of its most strident legal strategies. The story of Resolution 2334 is illuminating in this regard as well.

In the case of that resolution, the Palestinian interpretation that occupation law applied to Israel's governance of the West Bank triumphed over Israel's insistence that occupation law cannot regulate that territory because of its disputed status. The resolution passed because the United States did not use its veto to shield Israel from legal accountability, a break with the United States' decades-long policy. Nevertheless, the passage of Resolution 2334 failed to stem settlement expansion. This suggests that the previous U.S. provision of diplomatic immunity is an insufficient explanation for the law's historical inability to restrain Israel. The political context helps to resolve this conundrum. Only weeks before the successful passage of Resolution 2334, the Obama administration increased U.S. military aid to Israel from US$3 billion annually to $3.8 billion annually for a ten-year period. It did not condition this aid on Israel's compliance with occupation law.[99] Moreover, the United States did not alter its long-standing commitment, inaugurated in the aftermath of the 1967 War, to maintain Israel's qualitative military edge over all other Middle Eastern countries, individually or collectively, ensuring that it is not at risk of a military challenge. Finally, the administration abstained from taking a position on the resolution when it had only two weeks left in office and thus could not enforce its decision before the ascendance of the Trump administration. The incoming administration indicated its opposition to Resolution 2334 and its intention to go much further than any other U.S. administration to insulate Israel from international censure and facilitate its territorial ambitions.[100]

The balance of power, thus ensured by the United States, posed no threat to Israel's settlement policy. Moreover, the resolution itself contemplated the viability of Israel's settlement enterprise if the two parties agreed to "changes to the 4 June 1967 lines, including with regard to Jerusalem," in the course of negotiations.[101] This context represents a structural challenge that a legal strategy could ostensibly aim to unsettle. But according to the U.S. Ambassador to the United Nations at the time, the Palestinians' legal strategy was to appease rather than challenge the United States in order to ensure the resolution's success.[102] Outside the legal strategy, Palestinians made no indication of challenging the United States politically or taking any steps that would displace them from the interior of the U.S. sphere of influence.[103] Simply put, Palestinians did not mobilize a political strategy aimed at challenging U.S. policy. I contend that without such a strategy, the law's utility is at best limited and at worst harmful. In addition, even though

Resolution 2334 has the potential to alter EU policies towards dealing with Israel and the settlements, the EU, as evidenced by the resolution's content as well as the Paris Peace Conference proceedings, remains deferential to political negotiations, indicating the tenuous impact of the resolution's differentiation policy. Worse, Palestinian commitment to bilateral negotiations with Israel brokered by the United States implicitly enables Israel's settlement expansion. It also sustains a false parity between Israel and Palestinians that lessens the potential for applying more coercive pressure upon Israel.

Structural transformation is the purview of the strong. On its own, the law can neither undo the conditions that engendered the violation nor recalibrate the balance of power that sustains it; it can be used only as a tool in support of a political strategy that aims for this transformation.[104] Altering an oppressive structure requires coercive pressure, most effectively embodied by, but not limited to, military force.[105] Economic coercion deployed through the promise of various forms of aid (incentives) as well as the threat of sanctions and boycotts (disincentives) is also effective. Other forms of coercion are not material at all but are normative claims that target legitimacy. These can be marshaled through mass demonstrations, civil disobedience, literature, films, music, knowledge production, media work, and legal challenges.[106] The language of law should not displace, direct, or supplant politics because it does not possess a determinate meaning nor guarantee a particular outcome. Politics aimed at shifting the structure of an oppressive status quo should provide a strategic compass. When, in the course of that political endeavor, an opportunity arises to use the law to further those political goals, then law should be used as a matter of principled legal opportunism.[107] Recalling the analogy of the law as a sail, politics are the forceful winds that mobilize change and the law can be used in the service of those efforts; raise the sail when useful, drop it when harmful, and stitch together a new one when possible.

The junctures explored in this book indicate that Israel has appreciated this logic much better than Palestinians have. That, together with Israel's economic, political, and military prowess, has made international law, on balance, more beneficial to Israeli interests than it has been to Palestinian ones. Though stateless and lacking a standing army and modern weapons technologies, Palestinians have intermittently used the law in the service of their cause. When they have failed to do so, it has not simply been a tale of the oppressive force of law, but one of political blunders, foreign intervention, and/or personal aggrandizement, as well as plain and serious misfortune. Those factors are critical to understanding the relationship between law and politics, as well as how that relationship has helped to shape the present-day conditions and horizons of the Palestinian liberation struggle.

Self-Determination and Freedom

In 2017, the Palestinian demand remains the same as it was in 1917: to achieve national self-determination. In all of its many iterations in those intervening decades, that demand has appeared as some form of a state, be it truncated, bi-national, or the wholesale return of Palestinian sovereignty from the Mediterranean Sea to the River Jordan. Statehood has promised self-rule, equal access to the rule of law, security, and stability, as well as an international personality among other sovereign nations.[108] This particular articulation of the Palestine question as a search for national independence and sovereignty squarely implies a turn to international law because statehood is a juridical invention, in contrast to freedom, which is not.

Yet the call for self-determination among Palestinians has increasingly ceased to refer to the desired national state alone, and has come to encompass a more abstract demand for freedom. It is a call that implicates an attachment to the land as a means of memory, existence, and dignity. It upends the eliminatory logic that for so long has marked the Palestinian body as a site of expendability. Palestinian self-determination has come to signify an ability to pursue a future, collectively and individually, as a natural condition of possibility and not as a form of resistance to the condition of social death. Statehood and freedom are two distinct strands of Palestinian self-determination, though they can, and often do, intersect. One strand is legal and highly regulated, while the other is expressive and refers to a metaphysical aspiration.

The distinction between freedom and statehood in the case of Palestine and Palestinians is similar to the distinction between a life-long partnership and marriage. Two people can enter a life-long union without a state's recognition, but without such recognition, they remain individuals in the eyes of the state and can be denied the right to both be listed on birth certificates, to inherit property from each other, to benefit from certain forms of tax relief, to enjoy hospital visitations with each other, and even to have the right to some forms of privacy.[109]

Conversely, as a legal institution, marriage has the exclusive authority to confer state benefits and protections to committed couples, but it is not equivalent to partnership in other ways and is even a lesser guarantor of love.

The rights to independence, sovereignty, territorial integrity, and juridical recognition as a people are positive rights inscribed by international law and regulated by a state-centric international legal order. These rights are not equivalent to freedom, but do represent an aspirational guarantee against the brutality and violence of foreign and colonial domination. Indeed, so many of the challenges Palestinians have encountered, and which this book will explore, have revolved around their contested status as a nation, their political existence as an embryonic sovereign, and all the attendant rights that flow therefrom. Statehood continues to offer Palestinians permanent freedom from these violent negations. Becoming a state with meaningful sovereignty would effectively remove Israel's brutal rule and trigger the legal and political mechanisms available only to states. It would unequivocally establish Palestinian nationhood and would protect against Israeli settler-colonial encroachment and erasure, arbitrary arrest, systemic war, siege, and institutionalized deprivation based on Palestinian identity alone.

A state, however, is not the only path to freedom. It may not even be the optimal path. Regardless of scope and viability, a state does not promise Palestinians emancipation from the oppressive throes of exploitation and insecurity, nor from premature and arbitrary death. A nation has the capacity to cannibalize itself as well as the ingenuity to construct social, racial, and economic hierarchies that rationalize and legitimate such self-inflicted violence. Palestinians are not exceptional in this regard. Statehood can incapacitate an external threat but, alone, does not adequately treat the conditions of unfreedom.

In 1963, in his prescient and insightful writings on the Algerian war of liberation against French settler-colonization, the philosopher and revolutionary Frantz Fanon highlighted this unsatisfactory promise of nation-statehood. He appealed to his comrades in this struggle, saying,

let us not pay tribute to Europe by creating states, institutions and societies which draw their inspiration from her. Humanity is waiting for something other from us than such an imitation, which would be almost an obscene caricature. If we want to turn Africa into a new Europe, and America into

a new Europe, then let us leave the destiny of our countries to Europeans.
They will know how to do it better than the most gifted among us. But if
we want humanity to advance a step farther, if we want to bring it up to a
different level than that which Europe has shown it, then we must invent and
we must make discoveries. If we wish to live up to our peoples' expectations,
we must seek the response elsewhere than in Europe.[110]

Perhaps offering humanity a better model than it has been able to produce is
the current chapter of the Palestinian struggle. But the first chapter, so to speak,
of the Palestine question was much more typical of its time, when a native people
sought to steward their own future in an independent state on a land that a European colonial power designated for settlement by another people. One hundred
years of settler-colonial erasure and resistance to it have dramatically transformed
the conditions on the ground today, and urge us to look beyond the mainstream
understandings of this conflict in order to better appreciate how economics,[111]
labor,[112] gender,[113] and race[114] inform the struggle for freedom and its horizons.
However, insofar as we choose to frame the struggle as a nation lost, to be restored
only by the reestablishment of native sovereignty, the Palestine question remains
deeply informed by the mainstream narrative of two peoples fighting for one land.
International law significantly informs this particular approach.

While we may no longer choose to understand the Palestine question exclusively
in this way, it is how the story begins in the early twentieth century—in the context
of the First World War, the disintegration of imperial rule, and the crystallization
of national self-determination as a legal norm. In that context, international law
mediates the first set of exceptions and deployments of violence leading up to the
establishment of Mandate Palestine in 1922 and continuing through the end of
Israel's martial law regime imposed on Palestinian citizens of Israel in 1966.

Chapter 1

COLONIAL ERASURES

There was no such thing as Palestinians. When was there an independent Palestinian people with a Palestinian state? It was either southern Syria before the First World War, and then it was a Palestine including Jordan. It was not as though there was a Palestinian people in Palestine considering itself as a Palestinian people and we came and threw them out and took their country away from them. They did not exist.

—Golda Meir, "Golda Meir Scorns Soviets,"
(*Washington Post*, 16 June 1969)

IN APRIL 1936, Palestinians launched an open-ended general strike to protest Britain's designation of Palestine as a site of Jewish settlement. The strike followed nearly two decades of unsuccessful legal protest highlighting Britain's failure to fulfill its legal obligations as a Mandatory Power to render "administrative advice and assistance" to the native population until it was able to "stand alone" and practice self-governance.[1] The specialized legal regime enshrined in the Mandate for Palestine had trumped all Palestinian efforts to overturn a policy that negated Palestinian peoplehood and their attendant right to self-determination.

Ever since the turn of the twentieth century, British imperial policy had fostered a steady rise in Jewish immigration to Palestine. Growing tensions between native Palestinians and Jewish settlers had culminated in repeated riots, most notably in Jerusalem in 1920, in Jaffa in 1921, and near Jerusalem's Western Wall in 1929.[2] In Europe, the genocidal Nazi policies institutionalized following the rise of the Third Reich in Germany in 1933 led to Jewish flight on an unprecedented scale. After the First World War, Palestine's Jewish population tripled in less than two decades, going from one tenth of the population at the end of 1918 (some 66,000 out of 639,000 inhabitants) to almost one third by 1936.[3]

Palestinian protests rose in parallel, and so did British repression. In October 1933, British officials shot and killed twenty-six Palestinians, including women, demonstrating against British immigration and land sale policies that facilitated Jewish settlement.[4] But demonstrations, riots, and national self-organization did little to stem colonial determination to transform Palestine into a Jewish national home. By 1935, when British forces killed the nationalist rebel leader Sheikh 'Izz il Din Al Qassam in a firefight, Palestine had become a tinderbox. Al Qassam's death was the catalyst for direct mass resistance to British rule: 30,000 people attended the funeral, foreshadowing the national strike and uprising to come.[5]

Syrian in origin, Al Qassam began his revolutionary career leading an insurgency against French colonial rule in the former Ottoman province of Syria. Like the Palestinians, the inhabitants of Syria had been denied the self-determination promised them in the League of Nations Covenant in 1919. After French troops defeated that insurgency, in 1920, Al Qassam fled to northern Palestine, where he began organizing rebel forces against the British. The nationalist strike in Syria, which later transformed into a revolt, inspired a Palestinian general strike and marked the beginning of the Great Revolt (1936–1939) in Palestine.[6]

In support of this effort, dignitaries from notable Palestinian families formed the Arab Higher Committee (AHC). Serving as an umbrella organization for six Palestinian political parties, the AHC was headed by the Mufti of Jerusalem, Haj Amin al-Husseini, and it established several committees charged with organizing and mobilizing the population. With this consolidation of political power, the Palestinians presented a more or less unified front against British efforts to prevent Palestinian self-determination. The general strike lasted for six months and resulted in a complete halt in commercial, agricultural, industrial, and transportation activities, as well as a boycott of foreign goods and, eventually, of taxation.

The Palestinian press, which became the nationalists' bullhorn, helped to keep the movement accountable.[7] The twenty-six-year-old popular leader Akram Zu'aytir used his platform at the newspaper *al-Difa'* to hold the elite AHC to the revolutionary standards of the strike and revolt. In one appeal, he wrote:

We want the Arab Higher Committee to act as Gandhi acted in India when
he called for civil disobedience. We want the Committee members to be an
example to the sons of their nation, in the battle for the homeland.[8]

The mass strike prompted Britain to establish the Palestine Royal Commission, headed by Lord Peel, to investigate the unrest. Eight months later,
the six-member panel released its report, now commonly known as the Peel
Commission Report. Towards the end of the four-hundred-page document,
the commission recommended partitioning Palestine into a Jewish state and
an Arab state, with several British-administered areas.[9] Zionists rejected the
Peel Commission's proposal for partition but not the concept of partition itself.
Palestinians unequivocally rejected partition, not least because it designated
Transjordan as the sovereign of the proposed Arab state, and demanded full
independence. The partition proposal breathed new life into the revolt. By the
summer of 1937, the general strike had become an armed uprising—a development Zu'aytir had predicted:

The decision to stop paying taxes is the second step in the struggle, while
the prolonged strike was the first step. The time has now come to realize
the third step, which is the violent stage, the dangerous outcome of which
we cannot foresee.[10]

The nationwide uprising lasted until 1939, when British troops succeeded in
crushing the movement, using inordinate and brutal force. Britain commissioned
yet another study. The resulting 1939 White Paper concluded that unfettered
Jewish immigration and land acquisition with a view to the establishment of
a national home for the Jews was a mistaken policy.[11] It recommended against
partition and urged that Jewish immigration be severely restricted. Thus, the
three-year strike and armed uprising had yielded what two decades of legal and
diplomatic advocacy had failed to do: a reassessment of Britain's commitment to
Jewish, that is, Zionist, settlement in Palestine. The Great Revolt's achievement
was short-lived, however, and the sovereign exception, justifying the elision of
Palestinians' juridical status as a nation, endured.

First articulated in the 1917 Balfour Declaration and later in the 1922
Mandate for Palestine, the privileging of Jewish Zionist settler sovereignty over

Palestinian peoplehood remained dominant in international deliberations through 1939 and until Israel's establishment in 1948. The fallout from the revolt helps to illustrate the entwinement of law and politics with particular reference to settler-colonial settlement. The closest Palestinians came to realizing their right to self-determination during the Mandatory period was when they revolted against the geopolitical structure that rendered them nonexistent in the language of law.

The severity of the British response to the revolt also definitively undermined Palestinian capacity to resist the Zionist militias that would establish Israel by force less than a decade later. The uprising ushered in Britain's martial law regime, an exception to "normal" order that was predicated upon the existence of a state of emergency so as to justify the extraordinary amount of force deployed to quash the rebellion. Upon its establishment as a state and for eighteen years afterwards, Israel institutionalized this emergency regime under the thinly veiled pretext of security in order to dispossess, remove, and concentrate Palestinian populations that remained in Israel.[12] From its inception, Israel securitized the presence of Palestinian natives and perpetuated the legacy of repression established by Britain in Mandate Palestine. The discursive frameworks, racial tropes, and legal controversies deployed in the half century between Britain's issuance of the Balfour Declaration in 1917 and the end of Israel's (first) martial law regime in 1966 continue to shape the question of Palestine today. This chapter provides a survey of these formative five decades and serves as a foundation to the rest of the chapters, which cover the subsequent fifty-year period from 1967 to 2017.[13]

Colonial Erasures: The Balfour Declaration

In 1917, the British Foreign Secretary, Lord Balfour, committed Britain to establishing a Jewish national home in Palestine, without consultation with, or regard for, the wishes of its native inhabitants. As Balfour would comment in 1919, it did not matter what the natives thought because

> Zionism, be it right or wrong, good or bad, is rooted in age-long traditions, in present needs, in future hopes, of far profounder import than the desires and prejudices of the 700,000 Arabs who now inhabit that ancient land.[14]

Britain's Zionist commitment represented the culmination of efforts led by Theodor Herzl, an Austrian Jew, to secure territory for the purpose of establishing a Jewish state. In addition to articulating a vision for Jewish nationalism, Herzl led the political movement towards its realization in late nineteenth- and early twentieth-century Europe. He was convinced that Jews would never successfully assimilate into Europe or be accepted as European. Indeed, it would seem that European Enlightenment ideals agreed with him.

The European Enlightenment interrupted traditional social relations based on religious doctrine, advancing instead an ethnographic science that produced hierarchies of human existence based on secularism. While the Enlightenment's universal pronouncement of humans as bearers of reason opened the doors for Jews to pursue assimilation, it also conditioned their acceptance by European societies on the erasure of their difference. The process of assimilation was thus an effort to de-Orientalize the Jews, understood to have Asiatic origins. This discourse expressed revulsion at "Jewish poverty . . . their dark, disorderly ghettos," and their Yiddish language, which was "too under-developed to support high-powered thoughts."[15] Essentially, the Enlightenment removed both Christian and Jewish polemics from the debate about the status of Jews in European society, only to reformulate that status in Orientalist terms.[16]

Herzl became convinced that Jewish assimilation in Europe had failed after witnessing how violently the Dreyfus Affair unfolded in France.[17] This led him to argue that only an independent state for Jews could guarantee them freedom from institutionalized violence, both political and physical. But rather than challenge the disfiguring tropes that excluded and subjugated Jews in Europe, political Zionism—the movement whose genesis Herzl oversaw—internalized and reproduced them. Herzl came to believe that only the establishment of a Jewish state would transform the exilic Jew and render him eligible for acceptance within Europe.[18]

The problem with Herzl's conception was that Judaism—both a religion and an ethno-national identity—did not constitute a political community existing as a single polity in a bounded territory. In Europe, Jews lived across several territories, either as stateless persons or in possession of various nationalities. In order to establish a state, Zionists needed to do two things: first, transform many kinds of Jews into a homogenized national category so that civil law, and not religious doctrine, would define who was a Jew; and second, obtain from a colonial power a territory to settle. For Herzl and other European Zionists, this necessity was not controversial nor particularly cruel, as colonialism had yet to be discredited as an oppressive and immoral system of governance. The modus operandi of the time, whereby Europeans subjugated non-Europeans, was fundamental in shaping Zionist ambitions.[19]

At the turn of the twentieth century, and at the height of Herzl's efforts, fewer than forty sovereign states existed, and imperial powers governed the majority of the world's population. Ottoman, British, French, Dutch, Russian, German, Portuguese, Italian, and Austrian dominion spanned the globe. Even in Europe, a quarter of the population, approximately one hundred million people, lacked a nationality and lived under imperial rule.[20] During and after the First World War, nations everywhere demanded self-determination, conceived as the end of foreign domination and the right to self-government and national independence.[21] Such demands, however, only began to coalesce more than a decade after Herzl's death in 1904. Thus, under his leadership, Zionists sought to collude with, rather than resist, colonial domination in order to establish a Jewish state.

Herzl considered Argentina, Uganda, and El Arish in the Egyptian Sinai Peninsula as possible sites of settlement. Each of them fell under some form of European administration and could thus be marked for Jewish settlement by colonial fiat.[22] However, the great majority of Jewish Zionists in Europe coveted Palestine because of its religious and historical significance; as they would not settle for an alternative, Herzl appealed to German, Turkish, and English officials in an impassioned effort to secure Palestine. He framed Jewish settlement in Palestine as beneficial to imperial powers, explaining that Zionists would "form a portion of a rampart of Europe against Asia, an outpost of civilization as opposed to barbarism."[23] When Herzl approached Cecil Rhodes, the British businessman who infamously settled the south African territory named after him, Rhodesia, he wrote:

> You are being invited to help make history. . . . It doesn't involve Africa, but a piece of Asia Minor; not Englishmen, but Jews. How, then, do I happen to turn to you since this is an out-of-the-way-matter for you? How indeed? Because it is something colonial.[24]

Herzl did not live to witness the culmination of his efforts. Thirteen years after his death and one month before Britain captured Jerusalem from the Ottomans, the British government committed itself to establishing a Jewish national home in Palestine. In a letter to the head of the Zionist Federation in Britain in November 1917, Lord Balfour wrote:

> His Majesty's Government view with favour the establishment in Palestine of a national home for the Jewish people, and will use their best endeavours to facilitate the achievement of this object, it being clearly understood that nothing shall be done which may prejudice the civil and religious rights of existing non-Jewish communities in Palestine, or the rights and political status enjoyed by Jews in any other country.[25]

This statement, which became known as the Balfour Declaration, referred to Palestine's native inhabitants, who constituted 90 percent of the population, simply as "non-Jewish," and limited the rights they would enjoy to civil and religious liberties. It effectively negated their status as a political community and dismissed their demands for self-determination.[26] In contrast to Palestine's population, which naturally includes everyone, the Palestinian nation, as a concept, references an exclusionary entity whose members are bound by a common sense of history, language, culture, and solidarity.[27] Denying Palestinians' status as a legally recognized political community was tantamount to rejecting their sovereignty claims. This elision of Palestinian peoplehood flew in the face of the reality of a national consciousness among Arabs in Palestine. It also violated a promise to support Arab aspirations to national independence that the British Empire had made two years earlier.

In 1915, upon learning that the Ottoman Empire, spanning an area from North Africa to Southeastern Europe and across the Near East to the Arabian Peninsula, would join the war effort against the Allied powers, the Sherif of Mecca, Hussein bin-Ali, exchanged a series of letters with Britain's Colonial Secretary in Egypt, Sir Henry McMahon. Sherif Hussein offered the Allied powers Arab support in the war effort in exchange for Britain's support of Arab aspirations for national independence. McMahon responded favorably but insisted that some of the Arab territories in question should be excluded from the promise of independence.[28] The Hussein-McMahon correspondence never specified the scope of these exempt territories nor settled the disagreement over them. Although the correspondence was carried out secretly and ended abruptly, the Arabs joined the Allied side against the Ottomans on the grounds of their understanding of its contents. Britain provided them with materiel and logistical support, the Ottomans were defeated, and the British Empire emerged as the single most powerful force in the region, able to deliver on McMahon's promise of independence. However, the Great Powers, namely Britain and France, had no intention of relinquishing their newly established authority over former Ottoman territory.[29]

The Arabs who sought and expected independence began to organize themselves immediately. Prince Faysal, the son of Sherif Hussein, emerged as a leader of this effort and eventually established a constitutional monarchy known as the Syrian Arab Kingdom that set out to demonstrate Arab readiness for independence and the irrelevance of European tutelage.[30] While all of the formerly Ottoman territories were denied self-determination right after the end of the war and the dissolution of the Ottoman Empire, the struggle in Palestine would be distinct and more difficult. By November 1917, Britain had effectively promised Palestine both to its native Arab population, who sought to govern themselves and to Zionist leaders in Europe as a place to establish a national home for the Jews.

Britain's primary interest at this time was to maintain dominance in the Middle East in order to protect oil and trade routes, and also to counter French influence in the region.[31] Recognizing Palestinians as a people would extend the right to eventual independence to them, which contravened Britain's regional interests.[32] In contrast, Zionist settlement of Palestine promoted these interests: the Colonial Office did not envision the Jewish national home as a state but rather as a cultural mecca, which did not necessarily summon the specter of independence.[33] Moreover, Zionist settlement afforded Britain a pretext for its sustained presence and intervention in the region: "to support the self-determination of the European settlers, and to mediate the conflict that resulted as the settlers attempted to acquire Palestinian lands."[34] Britain's colonial logic was in line with a well-established practice since the late nineteenth century, whereby European powers, including Britain, Russia, France, and Austria, had justified their interventions across the Ottoman Empire on the grounds that they were protecting various Christian and Jewish minorities.[35]

Given its general disregard for non-European populations and faced with intense Zionist lobbying in Europe, Britain not only ignored Palestinian demands for independence, it suspended the principle that entitled native populations to self-determination. In a letter he penned to the British Prime Minister in 1919, Lord Balfour explained that

> in the case of Palestine we deliberately and rightly decline to accept the principle of self-determination. . . . Our justification for our policy is that we regard Palestine as being absolutely exceptional; that we consider the question of Jews outside Palestine as one of world importance, and that we conceive the Jews to have historic claim to a home in their ancient land; provided that home can be given to them without either dispossessing or oppressing the present inhabitants.[36]

Balfour's conclusion was arbitrary. It was not based on a legal inquiry finding that Palestinians did not constitute a political community. To the extent that a legal inquiry existed, its rules, established by Enlightenment ideals regarding nationalism, rendered Palestinians ineligible because they failed to "assume a natural and neat fit between identity and territory."[37] The earliest expressions of Palestinian nationalism reflected a broad Arab nationalist consciousness, whose vision of freedom from Ottoman rule took the form of a Greater Syria.[38] Although Palestinians established a congress to express their nationalist ambitions in 1919, it would be another year until they articulated their claims as Palestinians rather than as Arabs.[39] Talking about the nonexistence of a Palestinian people flies in the face of what was the regional reality at the time. The parallel pursuit of a Greater Syria among Levantine Arab populations in what are today Lebanon, Syria, and Jordan, did not similarly entail the negation of their existence as political communities nor make them ineligible for self-determination. Palestinians did not lack a particular attribute disqualifying them from being a juridical people. Simply put, British policy demanded that Palestinians not exist as a people in order to pave the way for Britain's colonial ambitions in the Middle East.[40]

British cabinet members understood the potential, and dismal, consequences of their decision but rested it, in part, on a conception of Palestinians as "a backward, Oriental, inert mass."[41] Further, Britain justified its policy by insisting that

Palestine was uniquely distinct and unlike any other former Ottoman territory
seeking independence. In June 1923, Lord Milner put this view to the House
of Lords in the following words:

> Palestine can never be regarded as a country on the same footing as the other
> Arab countries. You cannot ignore all history and tradition in the matter. You
> cannot ignore the fact that this is the cradle of two of the great religions of
> the world. It is a sacred land: to the Arabs, but it is also a sacred land to the
> Jew and the Christian; and the future of Palestine cannot possibly be left
> to be determined by the temporary impressions and feelings of the Arab
> majority in the country of the present day.[42]

Palestine's exceptional nature, as defined by Britain, would enable the colonial power to establish a specialized, or *sui generis*, regime for the territory's
administration. Unlike populations in other former Ottoman territories, Palestine's native population would neither be groomed for self-governance nor
forcibly removed. Instead, to balance its dual commitment—to Zionist policy
and to the Mandatory system—Britain would protect the civil and religious
rights of native Palestinians while fostering the growth of the settler Jewish
population both through immigration and by conferring economic and political advantages on the settlers.[43] At an unspecified point, a new arrangement,
yet to be conceived, could be established to govern all of Palestine's inhabitants.
This regime was as experimental as it was unique.[44] Its impact was nevertheless
real and consequential. Britain's Zionist policy justified the juridical erasure
of native Palestinians, and no amount of legal argument could overcome the
framework of exception that made it possible.[45] Palestinians became ineligible
for self-determination as a matter of British law as well as policy, rendering their
protest cumbersome but nonetheless immaterial.[46] This result was borne out by
the fate of the King-Crane Commission's findings, which supported Palestinian
demands but were essentially ignored.

In preparation for the 1919 Paris Peace Conference, which effectively carved
up the territories of imperial powers defeated in the First World War between
the Allies, U.S. President Woodrow Wilson had charged a commission of enquiry, known as the King-Crane Commission, with the task of inquiring into

the wishes of the peoples of the Middle East. This consultation reflected the principle, later included in the League of Nations Covenant, that native populations were to be consulted in regard to their Mandatory administration. This marked the first opportunity for Palestinians to express their nationalist ambitions to an international audience. In preparation for the commission's visit, political associations in Palestine worked diligently to present a united front, and they mobilized with various petitions and campaigns.[47] The core demand that Palestinian representatives brought before the commission was a definitive and absolute rejection of Zionism. When drafting its findings for review, the commission commented, "To subject a people so minded to unlimited Jewish immigration, and to steady financial and social pressure to surrender the land, would be a gross violation of [self-determination]." It concluded:

> In view of all these considerations, and with a deep sense of sympathy for the Jewish cause, the Commissioners feel bound to recommend that only a greatly reduced Zionist program be attempted by the Peace Conference. . . . This would have to mean that Jewish immigration should be definitely limited, and that the project for making Palestine a distinctly Jewish commonwealth should be given up.[48]

The commission's report was never given serious consideration and its findings were not made public until 1922.[49] By then, Wilson was no longer president, the Great Powers had already divvied up the former Ottoman Empire among themselves, French troops had crushed the Arab constitutional experiment in Syria, and the sovereign exception justifying the erasure of Palestinian peoplehood had been enshrined in international law and policy by being incorporated into the League of Nations Mandate system that emerged from the conference.

Enshrining Erasure in International Law and Policy: The Mandate for Palestine

The Paris Peace Conference convened with the intention of deciding the fate of the Ottoman and German Empires and that of the millions of people who constituted their former subjects and who were demanding independence. The victors acknowledged that they could not forcefully suppress the demand for the right to self-rule by a majority of the world's population, but they also did not want to relinquish control of former Ottoman and German territories. At that juncture, peoples under colonial domination understood self-determination as a promise of independence, but European powers viewed it otherwise: for them, it was a potential mechanism of control.[50] The indeterminacy of the concept of self-determination made it susceptible to legal work, and therefore potentially effective for achieving European aims.

More specifically, from the time of the principle's earliest iteration, there existed a gap between the concept of self-determination and its attachment to colonized peoples as rights-bearing agents.[51] It would take four more decades of direct revolt for that principle to become a claim to national independence as a matter of legal right.[52] In 1919, however, it was merely an emerging norm without a basis in law. U.S. President Woodrow Wilson, the individual most closely associated with the idea that self-determination was tantamount to national liberation, never used that term in his Fourteen Points speech, which articulated a basis for reconciliation and global interdependence after the First World War. Instead, he explained, the Allied powers had fought that war for the principle of equality among nations, and for their right to determine their own futures and be free from aggression.[53] For Wilson, then, the concept of self-determination meant the right to autonomy in a civic sense and "had nothing to do with the tradition of collective or ethnic nationalism."[54] Wilson himself later admitted that he had made his visionary speech "without a knowledge that nationalities existed," and he expressed anxiety about the possibility that he had raised the hopes of millions of people.[55] For the rest of the Great Powers, with the exception of the Union of Soviet Socialist Republics (USSR),[56] national self-determination was tolerable only insofar as it converged with their strategic and geopolitical interests.[57] The Mandate system, the international institution created to shepherd colonies to independence, advanced these interests.

The League of Nations established the Mandate system to lead the peoples of vanquished empires to stand on their own, with help from the resources and experiences of "advanced nations."[58] A people would become eligible for self-rule once their system of governance became more like that of European nation-states, thus creating a fiction of sovereignty arising along a linear continuum that European experience had charted.[59] Moreover, colonial powers would have to penetrate the interior of the Mandates, physically and administratively, in order to ensure this linear development. In effect, European powers deployed self-determination as a mechanism reflecting the consent of the governed in order to shift the cost and responsibility of governance onto peoples seeking independence, without disrupting colonial penetration in, or access to, those territories and their resources.[60] The Mandate system provided the infrastructure for this arrangement.[61]

Far from facilitating a movement toward self-governance based on local and particular ideals, customs, demands, or traditions, the Mandate system continued the task of "ensuring that the Western model of law and behavior would be seen as natural, inevitable, and inescapable."[62] It thus created a hierarchy wherein former colonies were tasked with the elusive challenge of replicating the social, political, and economic development of their former colonial overseers under their tutelage. World powers enshrined this hierarchy in their enumeration of three Mandate classes, A, B, and C, that reflected the proximity of each society to European ideals.

The League of Nations designated Palestine, along with the other territories of the former Ottoman Empire, as Class A Mandates (see the League of Nations Mandate System map). These societies enjoyed provisional recognition of the right to independence because of their advanced state of development, despite the fact that self-determination had yet to crystallize as a customary right.[63] In accordance with British and French preferences, outlined in the 1916 Sykes-Picot Agreement, Britain became the Mandatory Power for Palestine, Transjordan, and Iraq, while France became the Mandatory Power in Syria and Lebanon. The League of Nations Covenant authorized Britain and France to provide these embryonic sovereigns with "administrative advice and assistance . . . until such time as they are able to stand alone" and join the international system.[64] As a matter of international law and in the name of self-determination, British and French forces occupied the Mandates, established self-governing institutions comprised of natives, and steered the development of national law and policy to suit their colonial interests.[65]

Prince Faysal appealed to the Great Powers at the Paris Peace Conference to grant Arab states immediate independence.[66] Upon returning to Damascus in May 1919, he organized elections to the Syrian-Arab General Congress and authorized its one hundred members to draft a constitution. After British forces withdrew from Syria in exchange for French approval of the British Mandate for Palestine, the assembly of Arab elite men declared a constitutional monarchy in March 1920. The short-lived Syrian Arab Kingdom, which included Lebanon, Syria, Jordan, and part of Palestine and featured a monarch as well as elected representatives, was meant to highlight the level of local political sophistication and capacity for self-governance. However, French troops entered Syria and defeated the newly established Syrian-Arab army at the Battle of Maysalun, swiftly ending the constitutional experiment. Syria, Egypt, and Iraq would not enjoy unfettered independence for decades to come. Still, and despite the general denial of self-determination to all Arab peoples, the Mandate system's treatment of Palestinians remained a matter of exception.

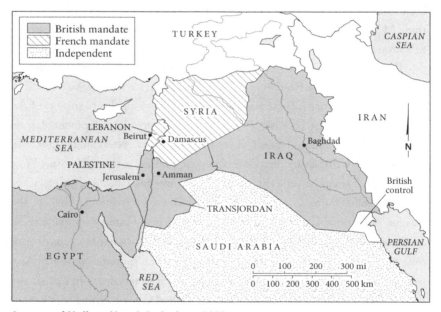

League of Nations Mandate System, 1922

After the First World War, the Great Powers convened at the Paris Peace Conference and established the League of Nations Mandate system to shepherd former Ottoman and German colonial territories to statehood and independence. The former Ottoman territories fell under British and French authority. Turkey, Iran, and Saudi Arabia became independent.

Britain led the effort to establish a specialized legal regime in Palestine that would regulate and enable the establishment of a Jewish national home while suppressing Palestinian self-governance. The ability to establish this regime was not merely a function of imperial power. Rather, Britain's efforts were fully within the scope of law and its internal logics. Britain saw Palestine as distinct because of its significance to the three monotheistic religions and, especially, because of the imperative to establish a Jewish national home. The insistence on unique distinction in fact engendered the lawmaking authority to create a specialized regime (a *sui generis* Mandate), and in turn, the specialized regime validated and sustained the unique fact pattern.[67]

The 1920 Treaty of Sèvres, for example, which delineated the fate of the former Ottoman territories, set Palestine apart from the others with the specific intent of realizing the Balfour Declaration's goals. While its stipulations regarding Iraq and Syria recognized their provisional independence, it did not recognize the provisional independence of Palestine—even though this concept was enshrined by the League of Nations Covenant as one of the characteristics of Class A Mandates—*in order* for a Jewish national home to be established there. When Palestinians protested that this violated paragraph 4 of Article 22 under the Covenant, requiring consultation with local populations, the British Secretary of State for the Colonies explained:

> There is no question of treating the people of Palestine as less advanced than their neighbors in Iraq and Syria; the position is that His Majesty's Government are bound by a pledge which is antecedent to the Covenant of the League of Nations, and they cannot allow a constitutional position to develop . . . which may make it impracticable to carry into effect a solemn undertaking given by themselves and their Allies.[68]

The Colonial Office acknowledged the similarity in status between Palestinians and the Arabs of nascent neighboring states marked for independence. It simply insisted that such facts were secondary, if relevant at all, in the establishment of self-governing institutions because Britain's commitment to the establishment of a Jewish national home in Palestine engendered a special regime. What at first appears to be a violation of the law becomes a firm commitment to it under this *sui generis* framework.

Similarly, Britain's 1922 proposal for the government in Palestine stipulated the establishment of a Legislative Council that was not representative, with only ten or eleven of its twenty-seven voting members representing the Palestinian population.[69] Britain understood that an overwhelming majority of Palestinians opposed the Balfour Declaration and that a representative national government would impede its realization. But Britain's specialized legal regime for Palestine rendered this transgression irrelevant and misplaced. Therefore, when a Palestinian delegation protested the unrepresentative nature of the proposal to Britain's Secretary of State for the Colonies, highlighting its contravention of the Covenant, the Colonial Office forthrightly responded that the Balfour Declaration mandated "a somewhat different interpretation" of the law in Palestine. The ideal path forward for Palestine, argued the Colonial Office, would be "combining a large measure of popular representation with the necessary degree of control to ensure that the policy of the Government is not thereby stultified."[70] Britain's hybrid model of governance sought to include Palestinians in form only to justify their exclusion in substance.[71] Palestinians understood this as "the strongest proof that the Jewish National Home undertaking is the cause of depriving us of our national right of establishing an independent government the same as Mesopotamia and Hedjaz."[72]

The logic of unique distinction paved the path to the Mandate for Palestine. During the international deliberations leading to its adoption, Lord Balfour, together with British Zionists including his confidant and president of the World Zionist Organization Chaim Weizmann, made a concerted effort to incorporate Britain's Zionist policy in the language of the document. Balfour's influence was pivotal in drafting the Mandate.[73] Other Great Powers strongly opposed his effort for fear it would hurt their regional interests and/or undermine the standing of Palestine's Christian population. Upon repeated assurances that Zionist policy would do no harm, and after four and half years featuring multiple interventions within the League, Balfour succeeded.[74] The final text of the Mandate for Palestine, adopted by the League of Nations in July 1922, incorporated the Balfour Declaration verbatim in its preamble, thereby transforming British colonial prerogative into international law and policy.

The Mandate explicitly mentioned Jewish national rights and a national home six times. It affirmed that Jews had a "historical connection" with Palestine, and it committed to establishing a Jewish national home as a matter of legal obligation. It made no mention whatsoever of Palestinian national rights or the right to self-determination of the native Arab Palestinians. Arab Palestinians appear by association only—as "non-Jewish" and "sections of the population"—even though they constituted the overwhelming majority, some 90 percent of the total.[75] The Mandate never describes Palestinians as a community nor affirms their presence in, or connection to, Palestine as a matter of right.[76] They do not even appear as natives of the land.[77] The World Zionist Organization successfully lobbied the League to refrain from referring to Palestinians as natives by insisting that Zionist Jews—not yet settled in Palestine—be regarded as natives as well.[78] With the stroke of a pen, a nascent international community institutionalized the framework of exception justifying the elision of Palestinians' juridical status as a people. In its capacity as the Mandatory Power, Britain thereby suppressed the Palestinians' right to self-governance and self-determination in order to fulfill the self-determination of a settler population in their place. Mandate Palestine became an exception to the rest of the Class A Mandates by design.

Every other Class A Mandate had a parallel, native governing authority alongside the High Commissioner of that tutelary state, an individual appointed by the Mandatory Power. In Palestine, however, there were no responsible Arab officials nor a recognized representative body or cabinet.[79] All British proposals for self-governing institutions were predicated on Palestinian acceptance of the Mandate's self-effacing terms. Meanwhile, Britain recognized and supported the Jewish Agency, a Zionist self-governing institution, within Mandate Palestine. Moreover, whereas organic laws were prepared for other Class A Mandates, no such authority was delegated in relation to Palestine.[80] The only similar exceptions in the Middle East and North Africa region, Algeria and Libya, at that time under the control of France and Italy, respectively, were also sites of European ambition for colonial settlement. The Mandate system had thus come to recognize the existence of nations with the eventual right to independence, except where a predominantly European settler community coveted that right for itself.[81]

In response to colonial erasure, Palestinians demanded their rights as a nation, pointing to the promises of self-governance in President Wilson's Fourteen Points and the Allied guarantees to the Arabs during First World War, as articulated in the Hussein-McMahon Correspondence.[82] They argued that based on their numerical majority and the fact that their presence preceded that of the Jewish minority, they were entitled to establish a national government.[83] They pointed to Iraq, Transjordan, Greece, Serbia, Montenegro, and Poland, where peoples were realizing their right to self-governance, and insisted that they were no less worthy. They highlighted their existing representative institutions and their impressive literacy rates, as well as the numbers of Palestinians who had completed advanced degrees in medicine, law, engineering, and agriculture—all in an effort to demonstrate their proximity to European standards for statehood.[84]

Britain was intransigent. It would grant Palestinians their right to self-governing institutions—although not independence—but only on condition that they accepted the Mandate for Palestine. This was the crux of the issue: to realize their national rights, the Palestinians had to formally accept "their own legally subordinate position [to the Jewish community], indeed ... their nonexistence as a people" as laid out by the Mandatory legal regime.[85] Rejecting this premise, Palestinians insisted that the Mandate itself was invalid. They made an astute legal argument, pointing to Article 20 of the League of Nations Covenant, which stipulated that if a Mandatory Power took on an obligation (such as the Balfour Declaration) that ran counter to an obligation in the Covenant (such as shepherding the Mandatory land to independence), it must free itself of those contradictory obligations. British officials retorted that there existed "a special situation in Palestine recognized by all the Allied Powers" that made acting on this contravention inapposite.[86] Britain was in compliance with the *sui generis* regime regulating the administration of Palestine. Legal argument alone would be insufficient to overcome the framework of exception embodied in the Mandate for Palestine.

Undeterred, Palestinians petitioned the Permanent Mandates Commission (PMC), created by the League of Nations to oversee the Mandate system, and argued that the Mandate for Palestine contradicted Article 22, stipulating that a Mandatory Power must consult the local population in establishing policy.

Britain insisted that the PMC did not have the authority to alter the Zionist project. The commission itself was split on this issue. One contingent insisted that the Zionist commitment enshrined in the Mandate for Palestine was supreme, while another insisted that it was secondary to ensuring the welfare of native inhabitants. The commission resolved this tension by distinguishing between the Mandate's long-term goals, namely establishing a Jewish national home and self-governing institutions, and the immediate objective of creating the conditions that could facilitate those outcomes. In practice, that meant prioritizing Jewish immigration as an immediate obligation and relegating the question of self-government to a more ambiguous gradual project. Thereafter, the PMC, on behalf of the international community, subordinated the national rights and needs of the Palestinian population in order to successfully establish a Jewish national home in Palestine.[87]

The Great Revolt Redefines British Colonial Policy

Palestinians launched the Great Revolt in 1936, nearly a decade and a half after the Mandate for Palestine institutionalized the state of exception that rendered their legal claims non-justiciable (that is, not open to legal redress). This armed uprising was massive, and it signaled the first direct challenge to the geopolitical structure marking Palestinians for exclusion. There were several periods during the rebellion when Britain "lost control of Palestine, including many major towns and, for about five days in October 1938, the Old City of Jerusalem."[88] Enraged by the challenge to their rule, the British Mandatory authorities responded brutally. They imposed martial law, which allowed the use of an extraordinary amount of force to achieve their policy objectives.[89]

Martial law was a tried and true British colonial tactic. It had been implemented as early as 1835 in South Africa, and it was predicated on the idea that the suspension of "normal" governance was acceptable in order to respond to a state of emergency.[90] However, since the meaning of *emergency* is subject to the sole discretion of the sovereign, who alone can decide what is a threat to its existence, declaring an emergency does not constitute an objective evaluation and thus remains beyond external and/or strict regulation.[91] Nevertheless, the concept of a state of emergency is embedded in a rule-of-law framework even when the rule itself is, by definition, outside a normal state of law.[92] As such, an emergency can be indefinite, despite its exceptional basis, and can come to constitute a permanent structure of political management.[93] This exceptional legal regime would also become central to Israel's governance of Palestinians, which would begin within a decade's time.

The 1937 Palestine (Defence) Order-in-Council bestowed on the Mandatory Power the authority to establish military courts, arbitrarily exclude persons from reentering Palestine, deport and exile Palestinian leaders, impose harsh punishments (including death or life imprisonment for the possession of firearms), destroy homes as a form of collective punishment, detain persons without charge or trial, impose curfews on entire villages and towns, and commandeer civil institutions such as the press, suspending newspapers viewed as agitating against the Mandate.[94]

In the early days of the revolt, the British arrested so many Palestinians that they ran out of space in the camps where the detainees were held. Akram Zu'aytir, a prominent figure in the revolt, wrote in his diary that he was "moved from the desert detention camp in Awja al-Hafir to Sarafand because the former could no longer accommodate the ever-increasing number of detainees, which had doubled in a matter of weeks."[95] Other Palestinian accounts relate the deaths of detainees, among them women and children, held outdoors for days at the height of summer and denied food or water. Restriction on Palestinian movement was a hallmark of the martial law regime. Physical barriers such as checkpoints and roadblocks were common, as were curfews and the military occupation of individual villages, dubbed "closures." In one instance, the British military placed Safad, a town in northern Palestine, under a dusk-to-dawn curfew for 140 days, and would regularly subject villages to twenty-two-hour curfews for days at a time.

At the height of the Palestinian uprising in 1938, the British deployed some 25,000 servicemen.[96] The following year, British forces were able to quash the Great Revolt and gut the Palestinian national movement, which had the effect of ensuring that it would not have the capacity to rekindle the revolt or to avert the wholesale dispossession caused by the 1948 War. In three years, British forces had killed 5,000 Palestinians, wounded 10,000, and detained 5,679 others. They blew up nearly 2,000 homes, destroyed agricultural lands, and exiled a significant portion of the Palestinian national leadership.[97] It is estimated that

British forces killed, wounded, detained, and/or exiled 10 percent of the adult male population at the time.[98]

Despite its devastating outcome, the Great Revolt made clear that partition of Palestine would have to be imposed by force, something that was anathema to the British Empire. As Malcolm MacDonald, Britain's Secretary of State for the Colonies, explained to the PMC in 1939, the Mandatory Power could not just "slay large numbers of Arabs" indefinitely, especially when the Covenant's terms for the Mandate clearly outlined its temporary nature and the global call for self-government had become a steady one.[99] Over the course of the revolt, Palestinians had established their own self-governing body, the Arab Higher Committee, without regard for the preconditions set by the British, and had further emphasized the imperative of self-governance.

More significantly, the Second World War was on the horizon, and Britain could not risk antipathy from Arab states.[100] Having agreed to withdraw its troops from Egypt, it now sought to secure an "unlimited presence in Palestine" to ensure its foothold in the region.[101] In the looming shadow of war and at the height of the Great Revolt, in March 1938, Britain established yet another Commission of Inquiry to examine the viability of partition as articulated in the Peel Commission Report. Eight months later, the British government reassessed its Zionist commitment and issued a White Paper setting out a new policy for Palestine.

The 1939 White Paper repudiated partition and opposed continued unregulated Jewish immigration. It set forth a proposal to limit Jewish immigration over the next five years, to regulate land sales more stringently, and to establish an independent Palestine government within ten years, albeit without the guarantee that self-government would amount to statehood.[102] The government would be neither fully Arab nor Jewish, notwithstanding the presence of Arab Jews or Jews who identified as Palestinians. Moreover, the White Paper conditioned Palestinian statehood on a Jewish referendum, and the future of Jewish immigration on an Arab referendum. While the White Paper was hotly debated and left much to be desired, the withdrawal of the partition option came in direct response to the revolt and, as such, was treated by the Palestinian and Arab publics as a major victory: "The bullets of rebel Palestine have torn up the Royal Commission's [partition] decision," wrote Zu'aytir in his diary.[103]

The Great Revolt directly targeted Britain's military regime and stretched its personnel to the breaking point at a time of impending war. Palestinians forced Britain to reevaluate its Zionist policy, not by the use of moral and legal persuasion but by changing the material conditions on the ground. In fact, during its deliberations leading up to the White Paper, the Royal Commission declassified the Hussein-MacMahon correspondence in order to revisit and unsettle a legal analysis that the Colonial Office had used to justify the suspension of Palestinian self-determination.[104] The conditions on the ground directly impacted the interpretation of the law in this instance. In addition to taking up armed resistance, Palestinians also created self-governing institutions on their own terms. They effectively challenged their exclusion from the promise of self-determination and the negation of their status as a political community by undermining the structure that upheld the framework of exception. In so doing, Palestinians also helped to further shape self-determination as a legal right tantamount to national independence.

Though a significant policy shift, the White Paper failed to definitively resolve the contest over national self-determination created by Britain's catastrophic policy.[105] Palestinians refused to compromise their demands for independence. Zionists felt betrayed by the British and vowed never to come under Arab governance.[106] The Jewish Agency began to mobilize its military wing, the Haganah, to confront the British, and the Irgun, a Jewish underground militia, began a series of bombing campaigns targeting Palestinian civilians.[107] In 1940, Winston Churchill assumed power in Britain as the Prime Minister, and resolved to postpone the establishment of a Palestinian government until the war with Germany and the Axis powers was over. By then, however, so much had changed that none of the White Paper's terms was ever fulfilled. The Palestinian victory in tearing up the partition plan was short-lived.

Normalizing the Exception: Israel Establishes Itself by Force

In 1947, two years after the end of the war, Britain referred the question of Palestine to the United Nations, the multilateral body established in 1945 that ultimately supplanted the League of Nations. By the end of the Second World War, the British Empire was waning and Mandate Palestine was an embarrassment to an exhausted Britain. The atrocities perpetrated by the Third Reich in

Europe, beginning with the denationalization of Jews and culminating in their mass annihilation using modern weapons technologies, were by now widely known. The Jewish refugee crisis was massive, and yet Western governments, including the United States and Britain, were averse to absorbing the refugees and were refusing them entry. To further advance its cause, the Jewish Agency entwined the refugee crisis with Zionism and did not lobby Western governments to accept the refugees. In some cases, it encouraged those governments to do just the opposite.[108] Indeed, Britain and the PMC, as well as the countries of Eastern Europe came to see the issue of Mandate Palestine as an opportunity to resolve the refugee crisis and, more generally, Europe's Jewish question.[109] In its referral, Britain explicitly asked the United Nations to incorporate the condition of the Jewish refugees into its deliberations on solutions to the problem of Mandate Palestine.[110]

The United Nations established the Special Committee on Palestine (UNSCOP) and charged it to prepare proposals for consideration. In its September 1947 report, the committee recognized that the principle of self-determination had not been applied to Palestine "obviously because of the intention to make possible the creation of the Jewish National Home there." The committee recognized that the "*sui generis* Mandate for Palestine" might in fact have been a violation of that principle, but it went on to justify the legal lapse by citing the co-constitutive relationship between the exception and the specialized regime it engendered. Drawing on the Peel Commission Report, it explained that Article 22 of the League of Nations Covenant did not *command* the "recognition of certain communities formerly belonging to the Turkish empire as independent nations" but only *permitted* such recognition should the League choose to confer it—and, in the case of Palestine, it had chosen not to do so in order to fulfill the terms of the Balfour Declaration.[111] UNSCOP concluded its report by outlining three possible solutions: a unitary state with strong protections for minorities, a unitary bi-national state, or partition into two states for two peoples. The eleven-member committee was divided. In particular, Iran, India, and Yugoslavia highlighted that the Mandate for Palestine and partition violated Palestinian self-determination, and they recommended a unitary state, but a majority of the committee concluded that two states, one for Jews and one for Arabs, was the optimal choice.[112]

UNSCOP's partition proposal vexed the General Assembly. One of the subcommittees charged with reviewing it preferred a unitary federal state, and pointed out that the partition proposal raised several legal issues. The subcommittee recommended placing the question of the legality of partition, and the General Assembly's authority to recommend it, before the International Court of Justice (ICJ). It was to no avail; the broader committee defeated the request for an ICJ advisory opinion.[113] The political imperative to use the Mandate for Palestine as a means to resolve the Jewish refugee crisis overrode the questions of law.

On 29 November 1947, the General Assembly, after intense pressure, and some cajoling, by the United States, endorsed the UNSCOP proposal for the partition of Palestine (see the Plan of Partition map). It passed Resolution 181 with a vote of 33 in favor, 13 against, and 10 abstentions.[114] Much like the UNSCOP proposal, Resolution 181 did not consider the will of the local population, nor the legality of the UN's authority to propose partition, nor the legality of partition itself. It was, unabashedly, a political solution.[115]

Although Jews comprised only 30 percent of the population and owned 6 percent of the land at this point, Resolution 181 apportioned the Jewish community 55 percent of Palestine. It allocated 45 percent of the territory to native Palestinians, who constituted 70 percent of the population and owned the vast majority of the land.[116] The resolution designated Jerusalem an international zone under international trusteeship, and envisaged that neither state would be purely Jewish or Arab, stipulating religious and minority rights in each. It mandated that individuals be given the right to "become citizens of the State in which they are resident and enjoy full civil and political rights" upon independence, with a choice to opt for citizenship of the "other State." Resolution 181 prohibited discrimination on grounds of "race, religion, language or sex"; it entitled "all persons within the jurisdiction of the State . . . to equal protection of the laws," and prohibited land expropriation.[117]

The UN Partition Plan required a "radical territorial redistribution in favor of Zionists" yet did not articulate the means of its implementation.[118] The status quo favored the Palestinians, who together with the Arab states, rejected the resolution. They argued that such an arbitrary redistribution of land and the suppression of the native majority's right to self-governance violated the principle of self-determination. But internal Palestinian rivalries undermined a unified strategy: moderate leaders urged restraint while others vied for control

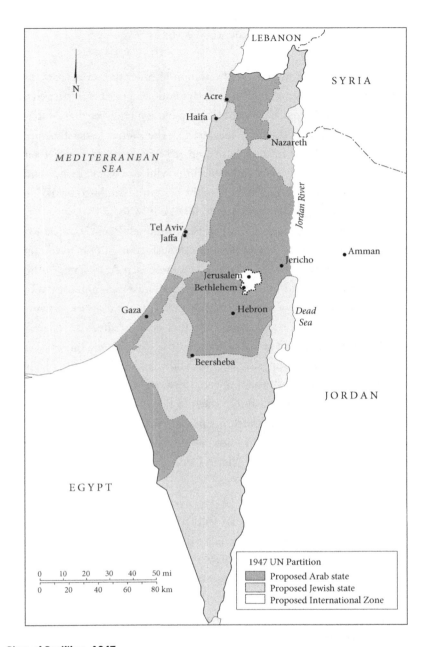

Legend:

1947 UN Partition
- Proposed Arab state
- Proposed Jewish state
- Proposed International Zone

Plan of Partition, 1947

In 1947, the United Nations proposed the partition of Palestine into a Jewish and an Arab state. Its plan did not envision that either state would be exclusively Arab or Jewish. It allotted 55 percent of the land to Jews, who constituted 30 percent of the population and owned 6 percent of the land, and 45 percent to Arab Palestinians, who constituted 70 percent of the population and owned the majority of the land. Jerusalem was to be placed under an international regime.

and authority to lead a military confrontation in order to prevent partition.[119] The Jewish Agency was not pleased with Resolution 181 either: it desired more territory than was allotted, but accepted the resolution knowing that Arab rejection diminished the chances of its realization.[120] The Zionist leadership, superior in "both quality and organization," also prepared for a confrontation to establish a Jewish state by force.[121] They understood that violence would be necessary to implement partition, especially in light of the hesitation exhibited by the United Nations and individual member states to impose it by force.[122]

Initial Zionist plans, laid out in their Plan Gimmel (Plan C), aimed to suppress a Palestinian offensive as well as to establish contiguity between Jewish settlements that were located in areas of the proposed Arab state.[123] Though framed in defensive terms, the plan instructed Zionist paramilitaries to inflict "forceful and severe blows" against not only militants but also "those who provide them with assistance" and shelter. The attacks "must affect large areas" and include both warning and strike operations, the plan stated. Targets were to include "clubs, cafes, meetings, assemblies, and the like." Execution of Plan C featured explosions in Palestinian residential areas and raids against communities in the middle of the night, to induce them to flee.[124] In February 1948, David Ben-Gurion, the head of the Jewish Agency and the first Prime Minister of the State of Israel, traveled to the emptied and destroyed village of Lifta, a suburb of Jerusalem, and reported to the Mapai Council, a major Israeli Labour party, that same evening:

When I come now to Jerusalem, I feel I am in a Hebrew (*Ivrit*) city. . . . It is true that not all of Jerusalem is Jewish, but it has in it already a huge Jewish bloc: when you enter the city through Lifta and Romema, through Mahaneh Yeuda, King George Street and Mea Shearim—there are no Arabs. One hundred percent Jews. Ever since Jerusalem was destroyed by the Romans—the city was not as Jewish as it is now. . . . And what happened in Jerusalem and in Haifa—can happen in large parts of the country. If we persist it is quite possible that in the next six or eight months there will be considerable changes in the country, very considerable, and to our advantage. There will certainly be considerable changes in the demographic composition of the country.[125]

Ben-Gurion's satisfaction with the demographic shifts reflected his conviction that "only a state with at least 80 percent Jews is a viable and stable state."[126] Zionist leaders admitted that increased immigration alone would never counterbalance the Palestinian majority resident in the proposed Jewish state.[127] One way to achieve a Jewish demographic majority, Ben-Gurion suggested, was to transfer, or expel, Palestinians.[128] In a letter he penned to his son in October 1937, he justified this as follows:

> We must expel Arabs and take their places ... and, if we have to use force—not to dispossess the Arabs of the Negev and Transjordan, but to guarantee our own right to settle in those places—then we have force at our disposal.[129]

The concept of transfer had been embedded in mainstream Zionist thought for at least a decade. It also appeared in U.S. and British proposals for resolving the challenges posed by the Mandate for Palestine at the end of the Second World War.[130] While there is no single "smoking gun" indicating that Ben-Gurion gave Zionist troops an explicit order to forcibly expel Palestinians as a comprehensive plan—with some notable exceptions[131]—this was the outcome of the Zionist military campaigns in practice.[132]

By early 1948, the level of violence and the specter of foreclosing Palestinian self-determination were such as to move the United States to abandon its support for Resolution 181. Thus, when the question of partition came up for reconsideration at the Security Council in March 1948, the United States suggested that the General Assembly establish a trusteeship over Palestine to shepherd its transition from a British Mandate to independence.[133] The U.S. policy shift, considered a betrayal by Zionists, proved a turning point in the war and precipitated the launch of Plan Dalet (Plan D).[134]

This plan was more aggressive and ambitious than its predecessor, Plan C. Its geographic scope exceeded the parameters of the proposed Jewish state and, if fully implemented, would have extended Jewish-Zionist sovereignty across the whole of Mandate Palestine.[135] Like Plan C, Plan Dalet also took direct aim at Palestinians, under the pretext of military necessity. It authorized targeting Palestinian villages that provided assistance to Palestinian militants or could be used as bases for attacks. In the name of achieving a "defensive system," it authorized:

Destruction of villages (setting fire to them, by blowing up, and planting mines in the debris), especially those population centers which are difficult to control continuously; mounting combing and control operations according to the following guidelines: encirclement of the village and conducting a search inside of it. In the event of resistance, the armed forces must be wiped out and the population expelled outside the borders of the state.[136]

This military strategy, featuring both excessive use of force and the logic of collective punishment, was not unfamiliar to Zionist forces. During the Great Revolt, Britain had recruited thousands of troops from the Jewish community to help put down the Palestinian armed uprising.[137] These men became the nucleus of Zionist paramilitary forces, and adopted British colonial military technologies and tactics.[138] In possession of significant armaments, they used devastating violence against Palestinians, even in cases where they posed no military threat.[139]

In one notable operation, in early April 1948, Palestinian forces cut off much needed supplies to Zionist forces by capturing the road connecting Jerusalem to Tel Aviv. To recapture the passage, the Zionists targeted Deir Yassin, a village located on this road. Village leaders had entered into a nonaggression agreement with the Haganah, signaling that they had no capacity to be a threat, and that should have protected these Palestinian civilians. Yet, when the Irgun attacked the village, the operation not only had the support of the Haganah's commander in Jerusalem, but he provided them with rifles and ammunition.[140] Over the course of one night, Zionist paramilitary forces killed at least one hundred unarmed villagers. Fahim Zaydan was twelve years old at the time of the massacre, and recalls that night:

> They took us out one after the other; shot an old man and when one of his daughters cried, she was shot too. Then they called my brother Muhammad, and shot him in front of us, and when my mother yelled, bending over him—carrying my little sister Hudra in her hands, still breastfeeding her—they shot her too.[141]

Zaydan was also shot, while standing in a row of children whom the soldiers had lined up against a wall. The Zionist paramilitaries sprayed them with bullets, "just for the fun of it," before they left.[142] As the news of the Deir Yassin massacre spread, in part through a "whispering campaign" initiated by Zionist leaders, many Palestinians fled from other localities in order to escape a similar fate.[143]

By early May 1948, the Zionists had launched thirteen full-scale military operations, resulting in the forced displacement of 250,000 Palestinians from their homes.[144] On 14 May, Israel declared its independence, on 15 May, Great Britain relinquished its Mandate, and seven Arab armies declared war on the State of Israel.

The Arab armies were no match for the newly established state.[145] Israel's troops outnumbered Arab ones, both regular and irregular, and in the wake of the first truce and consequent break in fighting, Israel was able to increase its firepower decisively. That was not all; the Arab armies failed to coordinate their efforts, as each country pursued its own interests in the war. King Abdullah of Jordan, who had been given nominal command of the Arab forces in Palestine, was more concerned about annexing the partitioned Arab state than he was with preventing partition. Before the war, he had been in direct contact with the Jewish Agency in an effort to reach agreement on dividing Palestine upon termination of the Mandate. Under Abdullah's command, Arab forces "made every effort to avert a head-on collision and, with the exception of one of two minor incidents, made no attempt to encroach on the territory allocated to the Jewish state by the UN cartographers."[146] More significantly, there was no coordinated military or diplomatic Arab plan of action. Israel roundly prevailed in the war.

Israeli forces continued the forced transfer of Palestinians throughout the hostilities. Spiro Munayar recounts their attack on al-Lydd in July 1948:

> During the night the soldiers began going into the houses in areas they had occupied, rounding up the population and expelling them from the city. Some were told to go to Kharruba and Barfilyya, while other soldiers said: 'Go to King Abdullah, to Ramallah.' The streets filled with people setting out for indeterminate destinations.[147]

The Palestinians, both those forcibly expelled and those who fled voluntarily, took refuge in Lebanon, Syria, and Jordan, as well as in the areas of Mandate Palestine not conquered by Israel. Between the start of hostilities in December 1947 and the end of the first Arab-Israeli War in March 1949, Zionist paramilitary and, later, conventional Israeli forces had reduced the Palestinian population from 1 million to 160,000, and destroyed and/or depopulated more than 400 Palestinian villages.[148] The newly established state had realized Ben-Gurion's vision of a decisive Jewish demographic majority. Palestine was lost.

Within six months of its declaration of independence, Israel applied for membership at the United Nations. The Security Council rejected its first application over concerns that it had not declared its borders, remained at war with Arab states, and refused to allow Palestinian refugees to return to their homes.[149] In response, Israel established armistice agreements with Egypt, Jordan, and Lebanon. It began talks with Syria, and it declared temporary borders and a truce by 1949 (see the Armistice Lines map). Seventy-eight percent of Mandatory Palestine was now formally under Israel's control, and the remaining 22 percent of Palestine that Israel did not conquer—the West Bank, including East Jerusalem, and the Gaza Strip—came under the control of Jordan and Egypt, respectively.

In March 1949, Israel resubmitted its application for UN membership. It had not resolved the Palestine refugee crisis nor established permanent borders. With a vote of 37 in favor, 12 against, and 9 abstentions, the General Assembly endorsed the Security Council's referral of Israel's membership.[150] Although the newly passed Resolution 273 noted the earlier conditions that had been set for Israel's membership, namely resolving the Palestinian refugee problem in accordance with UN General Assembly Resolution 194 and the internationalization of Jerusalem in accordance with Resolution 181,[151] it recognized Israel's "declarations and explanations" in regard to those conditions.[152]

The new state was delighted that it had reduced the Palestinian population to less than one fifth of its original size, and it had no intention of disrupting its Jewish majority by permitting refugees to return. It rebuffed responsibility for the mass exodus of Palestinians and insisted that their return should be predicated on permanent peace with the Arab states.[153] But Prime Minister Ben-Gurion had already rejected peace overtures from Jordan, Egypt, and Syria. He believed that the return of the newly created refugee population and the relinquishment of territory acquired by war were too high a price to pay for the permanent peace they offered.[154]

Israel's establishment in 1948 realized Jewish-Zionist settler sovereignty in Palestine, and its acceptance as a UN member-state normalized the sovereign

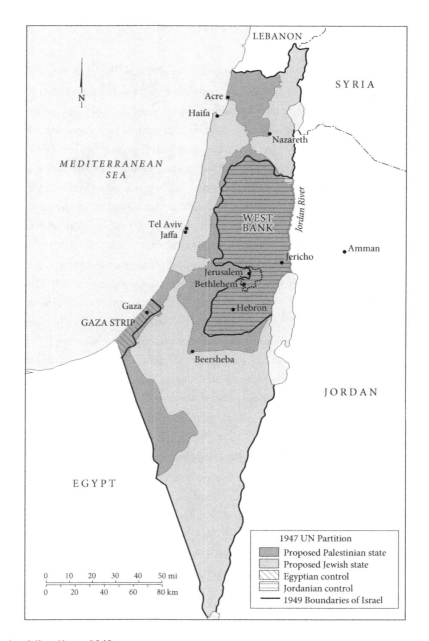

Armistice Lines, 1949

In March 1949, Israel established armistice agreements with Syria, Egypt, Jordan, and Lebanon. The agreements ended the Arab-Israeli War that began on 15 May 1948 but did not establish permanent peace. Israel established itself on 78 percent of the land that had constituted Mandate Palestine, 23 percent more of the territory than the Partition Plan had allotted for the establishment of a Jewish state.

exception justifying the erasure of Palestinian peoplehood. The 1948 War and the demographic and territorial shifts it engendered were the culmination of a process that had begun at least three decades before. The transformation of Palestine into Israel helps illustrate international law's utility in advancing settler-colonial ambitions and in consolidating their gains. What began as British prerogative (establishing a Jewish national home in Palestine) and was later enshrined into international law and policy (in the Mandate for Palestine) now became embodied in the legitimacy and legal standing of the Israeli state. In a state-centric global order, the territorial integrity of a state, its domestic governance, and its right to be free from external interference are sacrosanct.[155] The state's establishment retroactively legitimated Israel's founding violence because, not only was the violence used in the service of a public interest defined by the nascent settler sovereign, it also embodied a claim of new lawmaking authority.[156] Therefore, once diplomatic recognition was extended to Israel, its actions in pursuance of its statehood become beyond legal and diplomatic challenge. And what it does to preserve its national interests, however it defines them, becomes a matter of state sovereignty.[157] Statehood, as a juridical invention, erected these fault lines and produced these claims. Israel has availed itself of this sovereignty framework as well as the legal fiction of Palestinian nonexistence to pursue its settler-colonial ambitions to the present day.

Permanent Emergency: Racialized Exception as a System of Governance
After the 1948 War, an estimated 160,000 native Palestinians who had not fled or been expelled during the war remained either in their homes or internally displaced within the new state. Though small in number, they posed an existential and demographic challenge to Jewish-Zionist settler sovereignty.[158] Israel thus sought to remove, dispossess, or contain them. It incorporated the structure of exception into its everyday system of governance, placing them outside the law by racializing their presence as a threat, physically (in terms of demographics) and metaphysically (to, for instance, the claim of Jewish temporal and spatial continuity), thus justifying their exceptional and distinct treatment in law under the pretext of emergency.[159]

Upon its first convening, Israel's Provisional National Council, its first legislative body and the precursor to the Knesset, declared a state of emergency and adopted the Defense Emergency Regulations (DERs), the same emergency provisions the British had introduced to crush the Great Revolt.[160] The new Israeli government maintained the British Mandatory legislation regarding emergency with "limited adjustments."[161] The National Council's declaration of a state of emergency served to legitimize the adoption of the martial law regime.[162] The government justified the policy on security grounds, but Israel maintained the emergency regulations for seventeen years after the armistice that brought to an end hostilities with Arab states in March 1949.[163]

Shortly after establishing the 1949 truce with the Arab states, Ben-Gurion commissioned a review of military rule to determine when it should end. The review concluded that military rule was the state's optimal mechanism for preventing the return of Palestinian refugees and forcibly removing remaining population concentrations, expropriating their lands, and replacing them with Jewish settlers. In addition, the Israeli government wanted to be prepared to seize the opportunity to forcibly remove the remaining Palestinian population in the event of renewed war with neighboring Arab states. Regulating the population under an exceptional legal framework "not subject to the rules of normal procedure" would facilitate such a massive population transfer.[164] Ben-Gurion plainly explained that "the military regime came into existence to protect the right of Jewish settlement in all parts of the state."[165] With this, Israel institutionalized the emergency regime to advance its settler-colonial ambitions still further.

In December 1948, the National Council laid the groundwork for mass Palestinian dispossession with the passage of the Emergency Regulations regarding absentees' properties law.[166] This legislation authorized the Israeli government to confiscate land under a temporary framework. It marked the advent of a legal process that would effectively transform Palestinian lands into "Israeli Lands" for Jewish settlement within a span of twelve years.[167] The second phase of this transformative process began in 1950, when the government passed a new law making the expropriation of Palestinian lands and properties permanent.

The Absentees' Property Law of 1950 established four categories of so-called absentee individuals and rendered absentee property eligible for confiscation and possession by a custodian of state land.[168] Ironically, the "absentees" included approximately 750,000 Palestinian refugees to whom Israel had denied the right of reentry to claim their lands,[169] as well as those who remained in Israel as internally displaced persons. Israel legislated the latter group as "present-absentees." Palestinians in Israel existed insofar as they constituted a physical and metaphysical threat, but did not exist as far as legal rights were concerned; they could harm but not be harmed.[170] The law thus normalized the removal of the native population and enabled the confiscation of Palestinian lands without compensation to their owners.

The third phase of the legal transformation process aimed to seize the properties of non-absent Palestinians. It included a tactic whereby, under the emergency powers, certain Palestinian lands could be declared "closed areas" at the discretion of military commanders. This arbitrary edict prevented Palestinians from cultivating their agricultural holdings, rendering those areas "waste lands," which were liable to seizure under another emergency regulation, Cultivation of Waste Lands (1948). In 1953, the Land Acquisition Law retroactively legalized these land seizures.[171] From 1948 to 1953, the five years following the establishment of the state, 350 (out of a total of 370) new Jewish settlements were built on land owned by Palestinians. By 1954, "more than one third of Israel's Jewish population lived or worked on Arab 'absentee' property."[172]

The power to declare entire villages and towns closed areas bolstered the legal framework reifying Palestinian displacement. Often, the original residents were only miles from their homes. This was the case of the inhabitants of Iqrit and Kufr Bir'im in the Galilee, for example. Israel forcibly removed the villagers in the fall of 1948 and declared them present-absentees. The localities were then declared closed areas, and the lands seized and given to Jewish settlers. The Palestinian villagers used the Israeli legal system to file for the right to return to their homes. Iqrit's villagers won their case, and the Israeli Supreme Court issued a return order in their favor to the minister of defense, who promptly refused to enforce it and ordered the Israeli army to demolish the village. The army destroyed the village on Christmas Day in 1951.[173] In 1953, as Kufr Bir'im's case remained pending, the Israeli army leveled that locality also in order to prevent its inhabitants from returning. As the Palestinian residents proceeded with both a legal challenge and popular campaign, the military repeatedly extended the closure orders for the two villages, making an example of them. As Ben-Gurion explained, "These are not the only villagers living a long way from their home villages. We do not want to create a precedent for the repatriation of refugees."[174]

Between 1953 and 1960, Israel embarked on the final phase of the process to transform the legal status of Palestinian lands. Now, appropriated Palestinian lands were consolidated into a new category designated as national lands (along with other state holdings). With legislation it passed in late July 1960, the Knesset established a unified land administration department that successfully dispossessed Palestinians and transferred their property rights to the state. Excluding them as a matter of law and policy, the legislation prohibited Palestinians from "owning, leasing, or working on 97 percent of state-held land."[175] These measures, together with a series of other regulations, dispossessed Palestinians of their homes, businesses, and approximately two million acres of cultivable land without discrimination, whether they were refugees who had fled or those who had remained inside Israel.[176]

Israel's racialized deployment of martial law enabled the new state to dispossess, displace, and above all, contain its native population. The martial law regime aimed to "terrorize [the Palestinian] politically and economically, to kill the will to resist, to prevent the formation of political parties and to prevent free literary activities."[177] Mistreatment and violation of human rights was an endemic feature of the martial legal regime. In Dayr Hanna, located in central Galilee, for example, residents lodged a complaint about ill treatment at the hands of two military governors, including beating, extortion, theft, urinating on residents, and compelling residents to sign documents that threatened their legal status as well as the legal status of others.[178]

The emergency regulations did not fully achieve the permanent exile of Palestinian refugees, however, nor did they adequately preserve the right to immigration and permanent residence as a privilege for Jews only. After the close of hostilities in 1949, it was not uncommon for Palestinian refugees to make their way back to their homes across the patrolled but unsealed border. This was a dangerous endeavor. In June 1948, Chief of Staff Yigal Yadin gave orders to prevent return of refugees "by every means,"[179] and thus in the span of twelve years, an estimated 3,000 to 5,000 Palestinian returnees were killed by Israeli troops along the 1949 armistice lines. Still, many Palestinian refugees did manage to return to their homes and lands. The State of Israel considered the returnees "infiltrators," and initiated sweeps through Palestinian villages suspected of harboring them. Israel had distributed IDs to Palestinians who remained after

1948, and it used these to identify which village inhabitants were returnees. It conducted ID sweeps to flush out so-called infiltrators.

The ID system was not foolproof, and Israel needed a more systematic way to distinguish those Palestinian natives who had never left from those who had left and returned. Extending universal citizenship to all Israel's inhabitants would immediately mark out Palestinian returnees but would fail to treat Jewish Israelis with distinct privilege. To achieve that distinction, Israel adopted the Law of Return (1950) and the Nationality Law (1952).[180]

The Law of Return created a juridical category of Jewish nationality, entitling Jews, the world over, to immediate Israeli citizenship as well as some financial benefits upon immigration.[181] It also consecrated Palestinians' forced exile by dismissing even an attenuated commitment to resolving the Palestinian refugee crisis through the combination of UN mediation and a political solution.[182] The Nationality Law repealed the Palestinian Citizenship Order of 24 July 1925, a Mandatory regulation that had granted both native Palestinians and Jewish immigrants the status of citizens and nationals of Palestine, resulting in the de facto "denationalization" of this entire population.[183]

Under the 1952 Nationality Law, becoming a "citizen of Israel" was possible only for Palestinians and their descendants who were present in Israel between 1948 and 1952, effectively excluding all those who were expelled and/or who fled between December 1947 and March 1949.[184] Palestinians who could not meet the criteria of the 1952 Nationality Law were consequently rendered stateless.

The Nationality Law, together with the Law of Return, differentiated between Jewish and Palestinian Israelis by bifurcating Jewish nationality from Israeli citizenship. Although titled the Nationality Law, there is no such thing as Israeli nationality or an Israeli national established by it. Instead, nationality came to be based on religious affiliation. The Law of Return bestowed the automatic right of "Jewish nationality" on every Jewish person in the world, and defined a Jewish national as someone who is "born of a Jewish mother or has become converted to Judaism and who is not a member of another religion." The law provided that the rights for acquiring nationality and citizenship were also vested in "a child and a grandchild of a Jew, the spouse of a Jew, the spouse of a child of a Jew and the spouse of a grandchild of a Jew, except for a person who has been a Jew and has voluntarily changed his religion."[185]

Under this legal framework, Palestinian Muslims and Christians were excluded from becoming nationals of Israel because they were not Jewish. Palestinians obtained the right to be juridical citizens of the state but never members of the nation, a bifurcation between citizen-only and national-citizen that enabled the state to provide basic rights to land residency, housing, movement, and employment on a discriminatory basis with the explicit purpose of privileging Israel's Jewish population.[186] The legal matrix rendered the "citizen of Israel," the "citizen-only," a category of second-class citizenship. It also enabled the state to maintain a Jewish majority, facilitated the ongoing forced population transfer of Palestinians, and enshrined Palestinians' subordination within a civil law framework.[187] Together, the Law of Return and the Nationality Law effectively placed Palestinians inside the law only to ensure their exclusion.

One manifestation of the Palestinians' subordination was their forced participation in the very national celebrations that symbolized their erasure. Fathiyya 'Awaysa was forcibly displaced from her town of Saffuriyya near Nazareth and remained internally displaced within the State of Israel. She recounts the precariousness of being Palestinian during this time:

> The military regime was still there, and no one dared to speak out. . . . I remember as a girl how we were told never to take down the Israeli flag or we would be arrested and taken to prison. The mukhtars said that we had to carry out the government's orders.[188]

The martial law regime subjected Palestinian citizens of Israel to severe physical and psychological violence for eighteen years. In 1966, the Israeli government lifted martial law, viewing the Palestinian population as sufficiently controlled by then. Israel was keen to remove the taint of racism with which it had become associated as anticolonial liberation movements worldwide had brought into disrepute policies of unabashed racial segregation and domination. By this time also, Israel had established an ethno-religious hierarchy that could facilitate continued Palestinian dispossession and removal entirely within a civil law framework, and it could afford to abandon the military regime.

The martial law regime had established a stark native-settler binary, articulated in security terms. The Palestinian native presence constituted an active frontier of, and challenge to, Jewish-Zionist settler sovereignty. Israel's structure of permanent emergency securitized Palestinian natives because their existence negated the spatial and temporal continuity of Jewish dominion in Palestine. Similarly, Palestinian refugees claiming the right to return threatened to disrupt Israel's Jewish demographic majority, as well as the Jewish-Zionist settler mythology that justified the conquest of Palestine and recast it as redemption; refugee claims thus constituted an existential threat. This condition was not, objectively, a military threat. However, as established by British imperial practice, the ability to define a national threat and declare an emergency is within a sovereign's exclusive purview. In effect, Israel successfully declared an eighteen-year national emergency and oversaw a military legal regime that ensured the forced exile of refugees and removed, dispossessed, and contained the Palestinians that remained in situ. Upon ending its martial law regime, though maintaining its state of emergency, Israel internalized this racialized structure within a civil law framework that entrenched Palestinian exclusion within the state.

One year after dismantling the military regime that subjugated Palestinian citizens of the state, Israel applied it to another set of Palestinians: those residing in territories that Israel had not conquered during the 1948 War but would overrun in 1967. However, the challenge of establishing a permanent emergency proved much more difficult beyond Israel's then undeclared borders, where it could not claim sovereign jurisdiction. It overcame this challenge through political evasion and the strategic deployment of law. Using the framework of permanent emergency together with the legal fiction of Palestinian nonexistence, Israel would continue to pursue its settler-colonial ambitions in the West Bank, including East Jerusalem, and the Gaza Strip.

Chapter 2

PERMANENT OCCUPATION

History has taught us all that seeds of past wars were sown in every unjust peace imposed by force. A lasting peace cannot be imposed by force. One does not open the way for it by seizing another's property and demanding certain concessions before that property is given back to its legal, lawful owner.

—Syrian Representative speaking to the
UN Security Council, 22 November 1967.

WHEN, IN MID-SEPTEMBER OF 1967, Israeli Prime Minister Levi Eshkol sought to establish a civilian settlement in the West Bank near Bethlehem, he was aware of international law's proscriptions on such settlements in occupied territory. He thus asked Theodor Meron, then Legal Adviser to the Ministry of Foreign Affairs, whether occupation law, a military legal regime meant to regulate the governance of an occupied territory on a temporary basis until civilian authority can be restored, applied to the West Bank. Although Israel did not say so publically yet, its position was that the territories it had occupied as a result of the 1967 War were "not 'normal.'"[1] As far as the Israeli government was concerned, Palestinians were not a juridical people, and therefore did not constitute the rightful sovereign of the West Bank in 1967. Moreover, only Britain and Pakistan had recognized Jordan's unilateral annexation of the West Bank in 1950, rendering Jordan's sovereign claims invalid. The resulting sovereign void in the territory, in Israel's view, nullified the application of occupation law and freed Israel from the law's strict regulation.

In a "Top Secret" legal memo submitted to Eshkol, Meron rejected this argument, and concluded that Article 49 of the Fourth Geneva Convention categorically prohibited the establishment of permanent civilian settlements in the West Bank and the Gaza Strip.[2] Meron pointed out that Israel's own actions contradicted its claims that the territories were not subject to occupation law, because Military Proclamation Number 3, issued on 6 July 1967, instructed Israeli military courts in the West Bank to apply the Fourth Geneva Convention, under which occupation law is subsumed.[3] Meron also reminded Eshkol that international policy rejected Israel's expansionist ambitions. Meron advised that

> any legal arguments that we shall try to find will not counteract the heavy international pressures that will be exerted upon us even by friendly countries which will base themselves on the Fourth Geneva Convention.[4]

Meron's legal findings did not derail Eshkol; in fact, they gave him a way forward. In his memo, Meron had indicated that occupation law permits temporary encampments established by the occupying power to meet a pressing military need. Therefore, should Israel choose to build a civilian settlement, Meron advised, it should be built "in the framework of camps and [should be], on the face of it, of a temporary rather than permanent nature."[5]

Heeding Meron's advice, Eshkol instructed the army to establish paramilitary outposts, to create the veneer of temporality. When settlers arrived in the West Bank at the end of September, the government publicly referred to them as soldiers despite their civilian status.[6] This afforded Israel the appearance of being law-abiding, sparing it diplomatic censure while not hampering its expansionist ambitions. Israel's strategic deployment of law enabled it to successfully expand its territorial holdings while maintaining its Jewish demographic majority under a rule-of-law framework. Its ability to mobilize the law to fulfill its settler-colonial ambitions in the West Bank and the Gaza Strip is exemplary of effective legal work.

Israel planned from the outset to hold onto the Palestinian territories it had occupied during the 1967 War. There was one problem however: it wanted the land but not its Palestinian inhabitants. If it annexed the territories, it would have to absorb the Palestinian population, thereby disrupting the demographic majority it had achieved as a result of the 1948 War and transforming Israel into a bi-national state. It preferred to empty the territories of their Palestinian natives and to replace these Palestinians with Jewish nationals.[7] However, by 1967, colonialism and conquest had become delegitimized, and the principle of self-determination had crystallized into positive law guaranteeing independence and self-rule; Israel's settler-colonial ambitions were now anachronistic and controversial. Consequently, Israel constructed a legal and political machinery to overcome these obstacles.

Predicating its argument upon the fiction of Palestinian nonexistence enshrined by Britain's Mandate for Palestine and normalized by Israel's establishment, Israel claimed that the lack of a sovereign in the West Bank and the Gaza Strip made the territories *sui generis*, or exceptional as a matter of law. Whereas occupation law requires maintaining the status quo ante until the establishment of peace enables the reversion of a displaced sovereign's authority, Israel insisted that there was no sovereign to restore in the West Bank and Gaza and that it would apply the humanitarian provisions of occupation law as a matter of discretion. This was not a benevolent scheme. Applying only the humanitarian provisions of occupation law, and none of those pertaining to national rights, conferred sovereign authority in the territories upon Israel, while relieving it of occupation law's obligations to respect the sovereignty of the displaced power. Finding themselves under this specialized legal regime, the Palestinians would be suspended in limbo as non-citizens of Israel and as non-sovereigns under occupation, completely subject to Israel's discretionary whims. Under the pretext of achieving security, recognized as a military necessity under occupation law, Israel could incrementally remove, dispossess, and contain Palestinian natives in the West Bank and the Gaza Strip while implanting Jewish nationals in their place.

This legal framework represents a colonial continuity. Israel's martial law regime had enabled it to similarly dispossess, remove, and contain Palestinian natives within the 1949 armistice lines, from the time of its establishment in 1948 until 1966. Whereas Israel had used sovereign authority within its own undeclared borders to proclaim an emergency, in the West Bank and Gaza it now used the veneer of occupation law to establish an exceptional regime based on security. The fact that Israel now sought to incrementally expropriate land outside its putative borders, however, presented significant obstacles as a matter of law and policy.

In particular, Israel had to overcome the political will of the international community, which quickly moved to resolve the conflict at the United Nations. The outcome was Security Council Resolution 242, mandating Israel's withdrawal from Arab lands in exchange for permanent peace. Rather than stem Israel's territorial ambitions, however, the resolution proved instrumental to fulfilling them. Resolution 242's final text provided Israel with a legal loophole that it has since strategically deployed to legitimate its colonial takings. By itself, however, the legal argument would have been ineffective had the United States not aggressively intervened on Israel's behalf. Ever since the June 1967 War, the United States has used its political, economic, and military prowess to systematically shield Israel from international legal accountability, helping it to normalize its legal arguments into a tenable political framework.

This U.S. political intervention completed a legal and political machinery that has enabled Israel to poach Palestinian lands without serious consequences. International law did not just fail to regulate the occupation of Palestinian lands, it provided the legal framework for their incremental colonization. It is precisely law's susceptibility to legal work that made such a perverse outcome possible, and it was the power politics shaping the Middle East that gave occupation law and Resolution 242 the meaning they assumed under Israel's interpretive model. This outcome would not have been possible without the legal opportunity that the 1967 War engendered.

The 1967 War Creates a Legal Opportunity

In April 1967, cross-border disputes had escalated on the Syrian-Israeli border. Established under Israel's 1949 Armistice Agreement with Syria, the border proved tenuous. Israel insisted its sovereignty extended over the demilitarized zone that fell on its side of the border.[8] Syria protested that any sovereign claims violated the temporary nature of the Armistice Agreement, meant to facilitate a permanent peace yet to be established.[9] The UN Security Council agreed with Syria, but Israel continued to build up its presence in the contested zone.[10] Syria attacked Israeli installations and Israel responded. At the request of Syria and with the encouragement of the Soviet Union, Egypt prepared itself for war were Israel to attack Syria. Egypt's President, Gamal Abdel Nasser, who at the time was aware of his own military's weakness after a war in Yemen, was concerned that Israel would make good on its threats to overthrow the regime in Damascus for the sake of its security.[11]

Nasser, who championed the cause of nationalist socialism across what came to be known as the Global South, closed the Straits of Tiran, a significant sea route for Israel, and mobilized Egyptian forces on the Egyptian-Israeli border in the Sinai. Israel insisted that Egypt was preparing to attack first, but Cairo demonstrated restraint. Formal and informal intelligence reports to U.S. President Lyndon B. Johnson's administration confirmed that Egypt was not prepared to go to war against Israel and that its actions were aimed at garnering political concessions from the United States (as well as enhancing Nasser's standing in the Arab world).[12] Convinced it could resolve the tensions politically, the Johnson administration urged Israel to refrain from war.[13] The United States had supported Israel's decision to go to war but on condition that Israel "not fire the first shot."[14] To its consternation, Israel attacked Egypt on 5 June 1967 without warning.[15] Seizing an opportunity to undermine Egypt's vulnerable military position, Israel launched an air strike and destroyed Egypt's entire arsenal of air power, which lay bare and exposed in the Sinai Peninsula.[16] It completed the attack in less than two hours and the rest of the war was expedited equally swiftly.[17] It lasted only six days and indelibly changed the balance of power in the Middle East.

Israel emerged as the unequivocal victor. It established itself as a formidable military power—the most strategic ally for the United States in its Cold War struggle for hegemonic influence in the Middle East—and as the military occupier of sovereign Arab land. Its military jurisdiction now extended across Egypt's Sinai Peninsula and Syria's Golan Heights, as well as the West Bank and the Gaza Strip (see the Occupied Territories map). In a gesture that transpired to be only symbolic, Nasser resigned from the presidency in humiliation.

For the nineteen years since 1948, Arab states had regarded Israel as a foreign colony established thanks to the collusion of imperial powers. In the anticolonial fervor that animated much of the Global South at the time, these states had refused to recognize Israel. They demanded that Palestinian refugees be allowed to return to what had been Mandate Palestine until Israel's establishment on 15 May 1948, and be given the right to govern themselves as promised by Britain, the League of Nations Mandate system, and also the United Nations Charter.

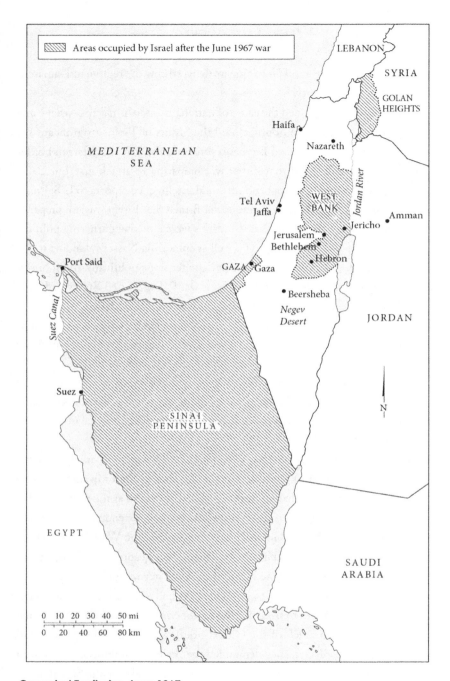

Occupied Territories, June 1967

By the end of the June 1967 War, Israel occupied the West Bank, including East Jerusalem, formerly under Jordanian control; the Gaza Strip, formerly under Egyptian control; the Golan Heights of Syria; and the Sinai Peninsula of Egypt.

The 1967 War not only blunted these demands, it also created new claims of Arab dispossession. Israel's most recent occupation of Arab territory obscured, and helped to further normalize, its establishment by war on 78 percent of what had been Mandate Palestine.

The 1967 War jolted the entire world. Within two days, the international community began to organize itself to draft a resolution to establish "peace and justice within the area."[18] The UN General Assembly convened in an emergency special session to draft a resolution, but could not come to an agreement even after four weeks of deliberation. The debate revolved around whether Israel should immediately withdraw from occupied Arab territories without preconditions or, instead, should withdraw in exchange for permanent peace with Egypt, Syria, and Jordan. This debate could have been settled by resolving a legal question. If Israel had not launched the war in self-defense, then it would have to withdraw its forces immediately because of the illegality of its use of force. If, by contrast, it had acted in self-defense, then it could legitimately set up a military occupation regime until a permanent peace could be established. Legally speaking, whether the attack was preemptively defensive or an act of aggression can be debated,[19] but as a policy matter, historiography has settled that Israel's attack was not a measure of final resort.[20]

Israel much preferred to have no resolution at all.[21] Intoxicated by its overwhelming victory, it now sought to keep the territories for a variety of reasons—religious, military, and political—and was fully prepared to do so. Israel had contemplated the scope of its military jurisdiction ever since its four-month occupation of the Gaza Strip a little over a decade before the 1967 War. In 1956, Nasser had nationalized the Suez Canal Company, and Israel joined Britain and France in launching a military attack and occupying Egyptian territory, which at the time extended to the Gaza Strip. In the context of the Cold War, U.S. President Dwight D. Eisenhower urged the occupying powers to withdraw in an effort to mitigate the impression of Western aggression against the Arab world as well as to avoid a direct military confrontation with the Soviet Union.[22] The occupying forces withdrew without concession.

Lyndon B. Johnson, then the U.S. Senate majority leader, believed that Israel should have been able to retain the territories as leverage for establishing peace with Egypt. In 1967, with Johnson now U.S. president, the Israelis were adamant they would not withdraw from Arab territory without reliable guarantees that their frontiers would be protected. Only hours after the 1967 War ended, President Johnson's envoy in Tel Aviv cabled Washington saying, "We would have to push [the Israelis] back by military force, in my opinion, to accomplish a repeat of 1956; the cut-off of aid would not do it."[23] For the mass majority of Israelis, however, security was incidental.

Although Israel framed its action as a defensive one, it became clear that in the weeks preceding the war (and in the subsequent policy of aggressive attacks that followed), Israel had welcomed hostilities in its efforts to obtain more territory.[24] Notwithstanding such ambitions, even Israel was surprised by the extent of the territory it was able to capture. Initially, the cabinet had only approved conquest of the West Bank's high grounds and minor border modifications for strategic military purposes.[25] Upon discovering the weakness of Jordan's armed forces, however, the army "rolled forward all the way to the Dead Sea and the Jordan River, taking the entire West Bank."[26] Defense Minister Moshe Dayan, who oversaw the military operation, considered the territory "part of the flesh and bones—indeed the very spirit—of the Land of Israel."[27] Dayan's attachment to the Whole Land of Israel or Greater Israel, a vision of Israeli jurisdiction extending over all of Mandate Palestine as well as parts of Jordan, similarly motivated a majority of Israelis. When the war ended and the dust settled, revealing Israel's expanded holdings, 90 percent of those Israelis polled supported the retention of the West Bank and the Gaza Strip.[28]

Israel's political establishment did not need much cajoling. Although it gave repeated assurances to the United States that it had no territorial ambitions, Israel began planning for its permanent settlement of the newly occupied territories on the fourth day of the war.[29] This was no simple task, as its claims of Jewish sovereignty over the territories had no legal or political legitimacy.[30] For Israel to acquire these lands without provoking formidable international censure required overcoming the international legal prohibitions on conquest and colonialism that had coalesced in the aftermath of the Second World War.

Occupation, Conquest, and International Law

International law had recognized a victor's right to territorial conquest into the late nineteenth century.[31] The right was diminished and ultimately extinguished as the dual international norms of self-determination and the prohibition on the use of force crystallized and were enshrined in the first two articles of the

UN Charter, drawn up in 1945.[32] In the years following the Second World War, international law continued to develop in ways that challenged Israel's colonial aspirations in the West Bank and the Gaza Strip.

The Second World War had exposed the inadequacy of existing law to protect civilians and guard against colonial conquest.[33] After the end of hostilities, state plenipotentiaries convened in Geneva in 1949 and drafted four conventions, international agreements, in an attempt to fill that legal lacuna. The Convention Relative to the Protection of Civilian Persons in Time of War (commonly known as the Fourth Geneva Convention), in particular, enhanced protections for civilians by classifying them as protected persons under international humanitarian law, thus shifting attention "from the rights of the ousted sovereign to the rights of the civilian population under occupation."[34]

Article 49 of the Fourth Geneva Convention proscribed the individual or mass forcible transfer of protected persons from an occupied territory "regardless of the [occupying power's] motive."[35] It also forbade an occupying power from transferring or deporting civilian populations into the territory that it occupies. The plenipotentiaries drafted Article 49 in response to Nazi atrocities during the Second World War, when Germany's Third Reich had forcibly removed local populations from lands it occupied—primarily Jews, who were sent into exile or to labor and concentration camps.[36] The Third Reich had also transferred its own nationals into the territories it occupied, in pursuit of non-military ambitions, including settlement. The International Committee of the Red Cross commentary on Article 49 indicates that states sought to

> prevent a practice adopted by certain Powers, which transferred portions of their own population to occupied territory for political and racial reasons, or in order, as they claimed, to colonize those territories.[37]

The Fourth Geneva Convention, the Hague Regulations (1907), and customary law, together constitute the broader body of law known as occupation law, whose purpose is to facilitate the transition from wartime to peacetime. Occupation law vests temporary authority in an occupying power pending a political solution.[38] It also imposes a duty upon the occupying power to protect the local population and maintain the territory's political and geographic integrity. In fulfillment of these goals, occupation law empowers an occupier to exercise law enforcement authority until such time as it withdraws from the territory and authority reverts to the rightful sovereign.[39] In such a framework, occupation is viewed as short-term and utilitarian. The law considers the occupying power a trustee and thus forbids it from altering the territorial, legal, and demographic status quo in place before the onset of the occupation. The only exception to this prohibition is in limited circumstances of military necessity. In no circumstances can the occupying power acquire legal ownership or sovereignty of the territory over which its military jurisdiction extends, since that would be tantamount to conquest.[40] Occupation law, together with Articles 1 and 2 of the UN Charter, affirmed a global consensus that the conquest of territories by war was no longer to be tolerated.

Alongside these legal developments, national liberation and decolonizing movements also helped to shape customary and treaty law regarding self-determination and the sovereignty of colonized peoples. The Mandate system, established after the First World War to advance colonial interests under the veneer of protectionism, continued to unravel during the mid-twentieth century as colonized peoples used force to demand national independence.[41] By 1955, sixteen newly independent nations had joined the ranks of the United Nations, bringing the total number of member states to seventy-six.[42] Five years later, another nineteen followed suit. In mid-December 1960, the UN General Assembly passed the Declaration on the Granting of Independence to Colonial Countries and Peoples, and established self-determination as a customary norm equivalent to independence.[43] Still, colonial domination endured, as did resistance to it. Algeria did not gain independence from France until 1962, after 132 years of settler-colonization, and that event breathed new life into the anticolonial movement, inspiring ongoing struggles in Mauritius, Mozambique, Guinea, Cape Verde, Rhodesia (now Zimbabwe), Namibia, and South Africa.

By 1967, when Israel occupied the West Bank and the Gaza Strip, colonialism had become both passé and illegal. Israel knew it faced a serious challenge to its territorial aspirations. It could not legally annex these territories. Nor could it remove the Palestinian population from, nor implant its own civilians into, the West Bank and the Gaza Strip. Not only were Israel's goals out of step with global developments, but its argument that it was restoring Jewish sovereignty over the territories had no political value. Moreover, the UN Security Council, which happened to be in session during the 1967 War, immediately turned its attention to Israel's occupation of Arab territories. The Council had the authority to mandate Israel's withdrawal, thereby eliminating any prospects Israel might have had of retaining the territories. Legal strategies and political evasion enabled Israel to overcome the first significant hurdle within the Security Council and to embark on its campaign to acquire the land without the people.

Deliberating UN Security Council Resolution 242

As the Security Council deliberated Resolution 242, which would not pass until several months later, Israel pursued its settlement enterprise. By September 1967, it had unilaterally annexed East Jerusalem, established two civilian settlements in the West Bank and the Golan Heights, respectively, and passed a secret measure in the cabinet declaring the Gaza Strip as falling within its territorial boundaries.[44] Cognizant of the Security Council resolution's potential to undermine its expansionist objectives, Israel diligently worked to ensure that if it did pass, the measure would not be unequivocally prohibitive. The leading figure in this effort was Abba Eban, Israel's Foreign Minister.[45] Although Eban failed to thwart the resolution altogether, his work yielded a positive outcome for Israel. The final text provided Israel with enough wiggle room to pursue its territorial ambitions in disregard of the policy objectives of its two primary allies, Britain and the United States.

A scholar and a politician, Eban established close relationships with central figures in the Johnson administration, which staunchly supported Israel's position throughout the UN deliberations. During the Middle East hostilities, the United States was embroiled in Vietnam, a hot war in the Cold War against the Soviet Union. Like Eisenhower, Truman, and Kennedy before him, Johnson believed that Communist victory in the Vietnam war would be a watershed for the spread of Communism throughout the region.[46] His administration drew up U.S. Middle East policy within this Cold War context. Thus the United States had continued a 1950s policy of competing with the Soviet Union as they both sought to fill the power vacuum created by diminishing European colonial influence in the Middle East. Johnson's primary concern was to contain Communism and, to this end, his support for Israel aligned with his support for pro-Western Middle Eastern states, including Jordan, Saudi Arabia, Lebanon, and Iran. This dualistic stance constituted the logic of Washington's stalemate policy: arming both Israel and the conservative Arab regimes in order to stave off Soviet influence.[47] The 1967 War revealed the futility of this approach and informed the revision of Johnson's Middle East policy in two ways.

First, Israel's overwhelming victory in the war demonstrated its ability to secure its interests without U.S. intervention and vindicated Johnson's valuation of the country as a Cold War asset. Going forward, U.S. policy would aim at ensuring that Israel maintained a qualitative military edge over neighboring militaries. This would guarantee that Israel had "the ability to counter and defeat any credible conventional military threat from any individual state or possible coalition of states or from non-state actors, while sustaining minimal damage and casualties, through the use of superior military means."[48]

Second, Johnson sought to provide Israel with negotiating leverage to normalize its relations in the Middle East without alienating pro-Western Middle Eastern allies. In an address to the U.S. State Department on 19 June 1967, the president articulated "five principles for peace in the Middle East": "the recognized right of national life, justice for the refugees, innocent maritime passage, limits on the wasteful and destructive arms race, and political territorial integrity for all."[49] In line with his stance during the Suez crisis, Johnson believed that Israel should not be made to withdraw as a matter of legal obligation from Arab lands it had occupied but should instead be able to use those lands as leverage to establish peace with Egypt, Syria, and Jordan. Thus, what Johnson proposed was that Israel return Arab lands in exchange for the promise of peace, and not because international norms required it. His quid pro quo framework clashed head-on with Arab demands for the restoration of the occupied territories without precondition, thereby vexing and prolonging UN deliberations.

The Soviet Union, the Arab states, and the Non-Aligned Movement (NAM) —mostly former European colonies in Asia and Africa that had joined forces to resist Western domination[50]—pressed for a resolution that condemned the war as an act of "aggression" and an unjustified use of force, demanding Israel's immediate withdrawal from the territories it had occupied without precondition. If the United Nations framed Israel's initial attack on Egypt as an act of aggression, Israel was legally obligated to immediately withdraw from the territories it had occupied.[51] While omitting language of aggression would not sanction Israeli conquest, it *would* permit Israel's occupation of the territories. The United States together with Britain lobbied for the latter, endorsing a text that framed Israel's use of force as legitimate in order to enable Israel to maintain the territories as consideration, as something of value to be exchanged for permanent peace. In addition, the United States believed that the parties should negotiate minor border modifications to rectify what it considered tenuous truce arrangements established in 1949.[52] All the competing parties, with the exception of Israel, agreed that Israel should withdraw from *all* the territories it occupied in 1967. They just disagreed on the precise terms of the withdrawal.

This monumental legal debate took for granted the circumstances surrounding Israel's establishment, namely the removal and forced exile of nearly 80 percent of Palestine's native population from the territory that became Israel during the period surrounding that nation's establishment in 1948.[53] There was a lot at stake as the UN debate raged, but with the political separation of the events of 1967 from those leading up to 1948, Palestinians could not possibly redress their juridical erasure and as yet unfulfilled demands for self-determination. According to Johnson's five principles, Palestinians were refugees necessitating humanitarian concern but not a dispossessed people in need of a political solution.[54]

Palestinians themselves had very little say in the debate, as the Palestine Liberation Organization (PLO), which had been formed in 1964, was not yet empowered to represent their national interests. Egypt's Nasser had helped to establish the PLO as a way to control the rising influence of Palestinian-led groups in exile. The early PLO deliberately excluded those groups, including the Arab National Movement (established in 1951 in Beirut) and Fatah (established in 1958 in Kuwait).[55] The defeat of the Arab armies in 1967 came as a rude awakening to Palestinian popular and organized forces and made evident that, alone, the Arab armies would not liberate Palestinian lands. The war catalyzed a process resulting in the ascendance of Palestinian-led groups and their takeover of the PLO in 1969. During the UN deliberations in 1967, however, Arab interlocutors continued to represent Palestinian interests and speak on their behalf. As a result, the war and the debate surrounding Resolution 242 further normalized Israel's establishment and indelibly reconfigured legal claims and political grievances regarding the conflict. The main issue in 1967 was whether Israel would withdraw from Arab territories with or without precondition.

The United States and the Soviet Union each proposed a resolution, and their drafts starkly articulated the two competing positions.[56] Aware that their drafts would not garner majority support, neither state submitted its resolution for a vote. Subsequent draft resolutions reflected these competing stands, albeit less starkly. In late June 1967, a Latin American bloc submitted a resolution emphasizing Israeli withdrawal from all the territories occupied.[57] The Latin American text also mandated the establishment of permanent peace but did not specify the sequence: that is, whether withdrawal would precede or follow a peace agreement. The relevant text urgently requested:

(a) Israel to withdraw all its forces from all the territories occupied by it as a result of the recent conflict;

(b) The parties in conflict to end the state of belligerency, to endeavor to establish conditions of coexistence based on good neighborliness and to have recourse in all cases to the procedures for peaceful settlement indicated in the Charter of the United Nations.[58]

The ambiguity on the sequence tempered Arab and Soviet support for the Latin American resolution and divided the General Assembly. In contrast, the United States voted for it.[59] While the vote reflected the controversy over the terms of a permanent peace, it expressed unequivocally that Israel's withdrawal had to be to the 1949 armistice lines.

Following the failed Latin American resolution, Arthur Goldberg, the U.S. Ambassador to the United Nations, and Andrei Gromyko, the Soviet Foreign Minister, proffered a compromise text. Arab states rejected it because it required recognizing Israel's right to exist without addressing the national rights of Palestinians or the right of refugees to return. Israel rejected it because it mandated the return of all the territories. Eban described the proposal as a "terrifying moment" and argued that the inadmissibility of territory by conquest was "a doubtful principle."[60] No one agreed with him, not even Israel's staunchest allies.

In late June 1967, and just before Israel's unilateral annexation of East Jerusalem, British Foreign Secretary George Brown warned Israel that "if [the Israelis] purport to annex the Old City or legislate for its annexation, they will be taking a step which will not only isolate them from world opinion, but will also lose them the sympathy that they have."[61] Brown added that any peace settlement must be based upon UN Charter principles, particularly Article 2, which prohibits the use of force against the territorial integrity of other states. He explained:

> Here the words "territorial integrity" have a direct bearing on the question of withdrawal, on which much has been said in previous speeches. I see no two ways about this; and I can state our position very clearly. In my view, it follows from the words in the Charter that war should not lead to territorial aggrandizement.[62]

The Johnson administration for its part contemplated minor border adjustments to the 1949 armistice lines to rectify what Johnson considered as "only fragile and violated truce lines for 20 years."[63] Johnson also gave credence to repeated Israeli assurances that it would withdraw from the territories in exchange for peace.[64] It was on this basis that the United States vehemently opposed Soviet and Arab demands for a comprehensive withdrawal from the territories as a matter of fiat in Security Council negotiations. Although the United States received several early indications that Israel would retain the territories, Johnson believed that "Israel would become more moderate and flexible once the euphoria of victory had worn off."[65]

When Israel annexed East Jerusalem on 28 June 1967, in full daylight and in the midst of international deliberations, the General Assembly unanimously passed two resolutions condemning the annexation and demanding that Israel rescind all actions taken to alter the status of Jerusalem.[66] Britain voted for both resolutions and the United States abstained, indicating opposition to territorial expansion. In protest, both the United States and Britain refused to move their embassies from Tel Aviv to Jerusalem. Eban tried to deflect criticism by claiming that Israel's actions did not amount to annexation, but were merely administrative measures to ensure the smooth functioning of municipal services.[67] As to Britain's harsh warnings and the biting General Assembly resolutions, Israel simply ignored them.

In November 1967, Britain introduced a new draft resolution in the Security Council that sought to achieve a compromise.[68] Lord Caradon, then Britain's Ambassador to the United Nations, described it as a balanced formulation that was "both fair and clear."[69] It sought to restore Arab lands to their rightful people and to ensure Israel's existence in the Middle East based on negotiations to be overseen by a UN envoy. UN member states responded positively to the draft resolution, although controversy persisted on the question of Israel's withdrawal. The draft mandated that Israel withdraw "from territories occupied in the recent conflict," excluding the definite article "the" or the phrase "all the" to describe the scope of the territories in question. The omission was deliberate and reflected U.S. and British support for minor rectifications to the 1949 armistice lines with a view to establishing "viable" borders. To ensure that the omission not be read as sanction for Israeli territorial expansion, and in order to achieve Arab support, Lord Caradon emphasized the "inadmissibility of the acquisition of territory by war" in the resolution preamble.[70] Caradon also added the qualifying words "in the recent conflict" after "territories occupied," to specify the scope of the territories referenced.[71] This concerned Eban, who lamented in a diplomatic cable the qualifying words "convert the principle of eliminating occupation into a mathematically precise formula for restoring the June 4 Map," which, he explained, Israel would not do under any circumstance.[72]

During the final stage of Security Council proceedings, a considerable number of states clarified their support for the British resolution as being predicated on their understanding of it as a quid pro quo formula that mandated Israeli withdrawal from *all* the territories in exchange for peace. The proceedings indicate the noncontroversial nature of the definite article's omission. The French ambassador highlighted the French text of the resolution, explaining that it

> is equally authentic with the English and leaves no room for any ambiguity since it speaks of withdrawal '*des territoires occupés*,' which indisputably corresponds to the expression "occupied territories." . . . We were likewise gratified to hear the United Kingdom representative stress the link between this paragraph of his resolution and the principle of inadmissibility of the acquisition of territories by force.[73]

In French, an official language of the United Nations, the definite article is included. France's insistence on the comprehensive scope of withdrawal was not exceptional. State after state repeated the same point. India, which along with Mali and Nigeria had proposed its own draft resolution, explained that its delegation

> has studied the United Kingdom draft resolution in the light of these two policy statements of the British Foreign Secretary. It is our understanding that the draft resolution, if approved by the Council, will commit to the application of the principle of total withdrawal of Israel forces from the territories—I repeat, all territories—occupied by Israel as a result of the conflict which began on 5 June 1967.[74]

Israel, eager to evade strict legal regulation, made its position known from the beginning and responded to the critiques forthrightly. "For us, the resolution says what it says. It does not say that which it has specifically and consciously avoided saying."[75] Israel's legal work, aimed at using the ambiguity of the English text to achieve that state's expansionist ambitions, was not lost on the state parties. Syria, particularly, expressed vehement opposition. The Syrian delegate explained

> It is inconceivable to Syria that this draft resolution be accepted because it ignores the roots of the problem, the various resolutions adopted by the United Nations on the Palestine question and the right of the Palestinian people to self-determination, and goes farther than that; it crowns all those failures by offering to the aggressors solid recognition of the illegitimate truths of their wanton aggression when it speaks of 'secure and recognized boundaries.' . . . While the Arabs are being asked to surrender, the Israelis who ought to withdraw their forces, on the contrary are consolidating their grip more and more on the occupied territories.[76]

The omission of the definite article in Britain's draft resolution did not split the Security Council. With the exception of Israel, the parties understood it as providing negotiating room to modify the 1949 armistice lines, not to establish entirely new borders. In fact, four days after Britain had introduced its text, the Soviet Union submitted another draft resolution that did include the definite article.[77] The addition made little difference to the voting states. President

Johnson, eager to pass a resolution favorable to both Israel and the United States' pro-Western Arab allies, successfully solicited Soviet support for the British draft.[78] At the Arab summit held in Khartoum in September 1967, Arab states had adopted the position, "no peace with Israel, no recognition of Israel, and no negotiation with Israel," indicating an aversion to the land-for-peace framework.[79] However, Egypt's President Nasser and Jordan's King Hussein felt that Israel was there to stay and were ready to support a draft resolution that ensured their interests.[80] Confident that the British text guaranteed complete withdrawal with minor border modifications, they lent their support to the initiative. The resolution passed by unanimous vote on 22 November 1967.[81]

Palestinians rejected the resolution. The ambiguity of the terms of withdrawal and the nonreciprocal terms of recognition made it unacceptable. Worse, the resolution did nothing to rectify the elision of Palestinian peoplehood set in motion by the Mandate for Palestine and normalized by Israel's establishment. In line with President Johnson's formulation, Resolution 242 referred to Palestinians merely as "the refugee problem."[82] Walid Khalidi, Palestinian historian and adviser to the Iraqi delegation during the UN proceedings, explained that the "dictates of power were already being displayed." Palestinians had no input of any kind, and the resolution gave

> Israel a free hand and allowed it to dictate the terms of withdrawal at the pace that it wanted. It made the fate of the Occupied Territories, whether the Golan Heights or the West Bank, a hostage to the balance of power. . . . The PLO could not accept it because it even allowed for the occupation of Jerusalem . . . after its passage, we clung to the preamble that prohibited the acquisition of territories [by force]. Like a drowning person, we clung onto it and exaggerated that.[83]

Palestinian insight proved correct. Israel would soon justify its settler-colonial expansion into the West Bank and Gaza on the basis of the definite article's absence from the English text. In a significant example of legal work, it would strategically exploit this semantic loophole to achieve its territorial interests notwithstanding the resolution's compelling drafting history, which documents the noncontroversial omission of the definite article "the" in the resolution's final

English text. Resolution 242 provided Israel with a way forward, enabling it to formalize its legal argument regarding the *sui generis* status of the West Bank and Gaza and turn it into a viable and specialized legal regime.

Sui Generis: Annexing the Land Without the People

In 1968, Hebrew University Law Professor Yehuda Zvi Blum articulated Israel's *sui generis* legal argument in a scholarly article consecrating what the government of Israel had hitherto established, albeit informally. In the article, Blum went to great lengths to demonstrate that Jordan, which had annexed the West Bank in 1950, was not a rightful sovereign in the West Bank. He concluded, "the legal standing of Israel in the territories in question is thus that of a State which is lawfully in control of territory in respect of which no other State can show better title." He continued, "the rules protecting the reversionary rights of the legitimate sovereign find no application,"[84] thus relieving Israel of the duty to maintain the sovereign rights of a nation under occupation.

Blum argued that the West Bank and Gaza were not occupied as a matter of law. Accordingly, Israel only had a legal obligation to apply the humanitarian provisions of occupation law, such as access to food, water, and sanitation, but none of the law's provisions intended to protect a sovereign's rights, such as the preservation of the territorial, legal, and demographic status quo in place prior to the 1967 War.[85] However, since, according to Blum, there was no sovereign and no one could show better title than Israel, why apply occupation law at all? Because without it, Israel could not lawfully fulfill its territorial ambitions and maintain its demographic objectives.

Blum's argument was based on the following logic. Absent occupation, Israel as the nominal sovereign in the West Bank and Gaza, would need to extend its civil authority to all of the territories' inhabitants, granting them citizenship, which would then disrupt its Jewish demographic majority. Whereas if there were an occupation, Israel would be obligated to maintain the status quo ante in the territory for a limited time until the establishment of peace and the restoration of sovereign authority, which would nullify its expansionist goals. If, however, the status of the territories was *sui generis*, one of a kind or unlike any other, Israel could exercise its authority therein without *either* preserving the sovereign rights of its inhabitants *or* absorbing them under its civil jurisdiction. As for the

Palestinians, under this specialized legal regime they become suspended in a legal vacuum with only attenuated legal claims to humanitarian relief.

Blum's conclusion stood in marked contrast to Theodor Meron's earlier findings, but Israel had classified its Legal Adviser's memo, which prevented its release to the public. When the Likud Party's Menachem Begin assumed the premiership almost a decade later, he adopted Blum's argument as official policy and appointed him to be Israel's Ambassador to the United Nations, where Blum assiduously propagated this legal framework during his tenure from 1978 to 1984. Israel's *sui generis* argument represents the epitome of legal work, shaping the meaning of law to suit a client's needs. As a legal matter, however, the argument has not withstood analytical scrutiny.

To start with, Blum's argument does not consider that sovereign rights in the West Bank vest in the Palestinians themselves. The sovereign void argument rests on the assumption that when, in 1947, Palestinians rejected UN General Assembly Resolution 181, the Partition Plan stipulating the establishment of an Arab and a Jewish state, they forfeited their right to national self-determination.[86] This conclusion disregards empirical and legal evidence demonstrating Palestinian sovereignty claims, as discussed in Chapter 1. Under Ottoman rule, Palestinians had an effective system of governance featuring taxation as well as "a system of land registration, political parties, a judicial system, hospitals, and a railway," not to mention national newspapers and schools.[87] The Mandate system designated Palestine as a Class A Mandate, owing to its advanced level of social, political, and economic development, in a classificatory scheme that reserved this top level for colonial territories with the highest capacity for self-governance.[88] All other Class A Mandates had become independent by 1946; only Palestine had not. Although it lacked formal statehood, Palestine had all the attributes of a state and Palestinians the attributes of a juridical nation. The Mandate system denied them independence in order to facilitate the establishment of a national home for Jews in Palestine, not because Palestinians lacked any objective features qualifying them for self-determination.[89]

Moreover, Palestinians had successfully inscribed their right to self-determination in the White Paper of 1939, in the UN Partition Plan (1947), and in the UN draft Trusteeship Agreement (1948). Thus, when the British Mandate for Palestine expired in May 1948, sovereignty vested in the people of Palestine.[90] Arguing otherwise would make the territory vulnerable to conquest by whoever could invade it first and thus contradict "the whole raison d'être of the mandates system."[91] To argue that Palestinians were merely a polity of Arabs who happened to be in a territory to which no sufficient title could be shown, and not a nation with a right to self-determination because they rejected partition, belied this evidence.

Even if Palestinian sovereignty claims had no legal validity, international humanitarian law protected the rights of civilians under occupation. The drafters of the Geneva Conventions were well aware of historical attempts made by invading armies to negate a territory's sovereignty and justify their conquest. These plenipotentiaries deliberately aimed to close that loophole during the drafting process by stating that the Conventions should apply "in all circumstances" regardless of a territory's status.[92] The Conventions regulate conflict arising between two or more High Contracting Parties, and apply to any territory occupied in the course of conflict. Accordingly, since Israel, Jordan, and Egypt were parties to the Geneva Conventions during the 1967 War, Convention provisions applied to their respective territories.[93] The purpose of the Fourth Geneva Convention is to protect civilian populations caught in conflict.[94] Even before the adoption of the Geneva Convention in 1949, the drafters of the 1907 Hague Regulations had defined occupation in a way that did not condition the application of the military legal regime on de jure title, precisely in order to stem territorial acquisition by force.[95] Blum also made an argument for "defensive conquest," but that concept has no basis in modern international law.[96]

Beyond the legal arguments, Israel's policies are also rife with contradictions. In the Egyptian Sinai and the Syrian Golan Heights, where sovereignty was not in question, Israel also ignored occupation law. In the case of those territories, Israel made no attempt to rebut the relevance of the Geneva Conventions because its ambitions for civilian settlement there were less pronounced at the time.

Had this been merely a legal matter, it would have had no consequence. Leading international and multilateral legal institutions, including the UN Security Council, the UN General Assembly, the International Court of Justice, and the International Committee of the Red Cross, as well as several international human rights organizations, have all rebuffed Israel's argument and repeatedly affirmed the de jure applicability of occupation law to the West Bank and the Gaza Strip. As explained by George Washington University Law School

Professor W. T. Mallison at a U.S. Congressional hearing on the settlements in 1977, the

> thesis developed by Dr. Blum and acted upon by Mr. Begin is defective in law, although no one can doubt its effectiveness, thus far, as a matter of power politics. As a substantive matter, it does not merit serious consideration but, because it has been acted upon by the Government of Israel, it will now be considered.[97]

Mallison's observation highlights the significance of state action in international law. There is no general enforcement mechanism in the international sphere. There is no hierarchical order and no international police force dissociated from the state system. State compliance is almost always voluntary and noncompliance is met with sanctions as a result of political will, not legal obligation. Collective enforcement lies within the limited purview of the UN Security Council. Chapter VI of the UN Charter allows the Security Council to impose sanctions on a state, and Chapter VII empowers states to use force as a measure of coercion. Strong states, chiefly the Security Council's five permanent members, will not allow such remedies to be used against themselves or their allies. In effect, enforcement of occupation law reflects the measure of political will and the prevailing balance of geopolitical power. In the case at hand, the balance has been settled largely by U.S. intervention on Israel's behalf.

While the United States has remained opposed to Israeli settlement expansion as a matter of law and policy, it has remained simultaneously committed to maintaining Israel's qualitative military edge and to achieving a negotiated settlement. This dual commitment has driven it to shield Israel from meaningful international censure on the grounds that the imposition of external legal obligations would diminish Israel's negotiating hand in a land-for-peace framework. Additionally, the U.S. commitment to Israel's military superiority in the region has impeded the application of any meaningful pressure on this U.S. ally.[98]

Within this framework, if Israel makes a legal argument that is rejected by international consensus, the international community's opposition does not change the political value of Israel's claims. So long as it faces no meaningful censure, Israel can wage a long-lasting challenge to the law and simultaneously deploy its own legal framework to advance its political goals. It has done precisely that in its own domestic courts with great efficacy.

Israeli Courts Provide Legal Reasoning for Colonization

During his tenure as Israel's Military Advocate-General between 1961 and 1968, Meir Shamgar fleshed out Yehuda Zvi Blum's argument, making it an expedient legal regime. As the Israeli army's top lawyer, in 1963 Shamgar had overseen a process inside the military's legal establishment to formulate a proposal in the event that Israel were to "find itself in control of a civilian population." The military lawyers he supervised created a comprehensive occupation framework "that left nothing to chance." According to Shamgar, "everything was done with foresight," and thus in 1967, the army pulled out the plans for military occupation that it had prepared four years earlier.[99]

While Shamgar endorsed Blum's *sui generis* framework, unlike the legal scholar, he believed that the customary provisions of occupation law should also regulate the territories.[100] By this logic, Israel should have applied the Fourth Geneva Convention, which enjoyed customary status. Moreover, Israel ratified all four Geneva Conventions in 1951, indicating its support for them. And in 1971, before the state's *sui generis* argument had fully crystallized, the Israeli Supreme Court ruled that the Fourth Geneva Convention applied to the Occupied Territories as a matter of custom.[101] But Shamgar repudiated this application and argued that the Convention was not binding on the state because Israel's legislature had never incorporated the Geneva Conventions into domestic law.[102] This is, however, an inaccurate assessment of customary law's binding force. Custom is a form of tacit consent and is binding irrespective of a state's taking domestic legislative action.[103] Insisting that Conventions are not binding because they lack domestic incorporation is simply a legal tactic.[104]

In contrast, Shamgar concluded that the Hague Regulations did apply as a matter of custom. Like the Fourth Geneva Convention, the Hague Regulations clearly stipulate that an occupying power must maintain the status quo that prevailed before the onset of hostilities, prohibit the confiscation of private property, and impose limits on the use of public property.[105] Unlike the Convention, however, the Hague Regulations are silent on the issue of civilian settlement. Therefore, they posed no impediment to Israel's expansionist goals.[106] Although it constituted a blatant contradiction, observing the Hague Regulations allowed Israel to technically adhere to customary occupation law, and appear law-abiding, while circumventing the Convention's absolute prohibition on civilian settlements.

In 1975, Shamgar became Israel's Chief Supreme Court Justice and served on the Court for two decades. Under his leadership, the Court developed, in piecemeal fashion, the legal framework for regulating Israel's presence in the West Bank and Gaza. It opposed the state in several instances, thus demonstrating judicial independence and enhancing the law's legitimating force.[107] Notably, however, it has refused to rule on the legality of civilian settlements in the Occupied Territories.[108] When presented with a case challenging the entire settlement enterprise, Shamgar concluded that this was a political, not a legal question, better suited for other branches of government.[109] In the majority of cases, however, the Court has addressed difficult legal questions, and in the majority of those cases, it has interpreted the law in ways that have facilitated the state's interests, including its expansionist ambitions.

In order to retain the veneer of legality and to avoid having to absorb the Palestinian population, the legal system was careful to never treat the territories as Israel's holdings. Instead, the Supreme Court insisted that Israel was administering the territories until such time as a political settlement was reached. At that point, the state would remove its settlers where demanded by the political agreement.[110] But what limits were there on achieving a political resolution? Whereas under occupation law, occupation is seen as being short-term, Shamgar claimed that the law did not speak to that question. He argued that factual conditions determined the length of the occupation, and that absent a political resolution, there was no end to the occupation but also no territorial annexation. The occupation could be indefinite so long as it was not permanent.[111] A situation without a definite end does not have to end, in contrast with a temporary situation, which must end.[112] This legal fiction has allowed Israel to continue its civilian settlement under the auspices of temporality, demonstrating intent *not* to annex the land, without imposing on the state any duty to withdraw.

Occupation law has provided a further legal basis for Israel to claim that it could acquire land for civilian settlements: military necessity.[113] Occupation law permits an occupying power to alter the status quo ante where military necessity requires. Thus, the phrase "required for essential and urgent military needs" became a recurring refrain the Israeli military used to justify the requisition of land in the West Bank between 1968 and 1979.[114] The Supreme Court acted as a steady force in the creation of the legal fiction of military necessity, while simultaneously blocking any Palestinian efforts to challenge the contradictions posed by the requirements of humanitarian law.[115] This was the case until 1979, when the Supreme Court ruled that the Elon Moreh settlement did not enhance the state's security objectives and established a precedent prohibiting the confiscation of private Palestinian lands.[116] However, this ruling proved not to be an insurmountable challenge.

A primary mechanism facilitating confiscation of private Palestinian property was the change in the meaning of the term "non-registered property." Under the Ottoman land regime, non-registered property was a broad category referring to lands held by villagers communally and/or for future use, a condition that eliminated the need to register them. In contrast, "state land" belonged to the government for public use. This was the case under Ottoman, British, and Jordanian rule in the territories. In 1967, Israel's military administration passed Order 59, which empowered a military commander to assume control of state property in the West Bank and Gaza for use at his exclusive discretion. Originally, the order had conferred authority on Israel's military to manage Jordanian government property during the occupation. But in 1979, the military administration amended this order to "declare non-registered property state land and to transfer it to the exclusive use of Jewish settlers."[117] Israel amended the definition of non-registered property the same year that the Israeli Supreme Court ruled that private Palestinian land could not be seized. The amendment made non-registered land, claimed by Palestinians as their own commons, equivalent to state land in order to facilitate its confiscation under a military pretext.

Order 59 was one of an avalanche of orders that transformed otherwise private property into "state land," in the language of Israel's military law.[118] The Order Regarding Abandoned Property of 1967, for example, expanded the concept of state land to include lands that were lying fallow and/or whose claimants were "absent."[119] Similar to the legal tactics employed by Israel with the Palestinian natives inside its undeclared borders, this order prohibited Palestinian

landowners who had fled the 1967 War from returning to establish their presence and thus their title.[120] It then authorized the Commissioner of Abandoned
Property to regulate and manage the "absentee"-owned land, including for the
purpose of establishing civilian settlements.[121] Israel's land scheme successfully
removed, contained, and dispossessed Palestinians in the West Bank and Gaza, as
a similar scheme had previously done with the Palestinian natives who remained
inside Israel after 1948.

Israel's judiciary was integral in advancing these ambitions.[122] The Supreme
Court explicitly ruled that Jewish-Israeli settlers should be considered part of the
public to whom the Israeli military owed a duty to protect.[123] This was a radical
proposition, because under occupation law, a military power is obligated to balance
its security needs against the humanitarian concerns of the occupied population,
also known as "protected persons." The Court's legal finding contravened the
Fourth Geneva Convention, which explicitly excludes an occupying power's own
nationals from the category of "protected persons."[124] Israel could circumvent this
prohibition, however, because Shamgar's legal framework gave the military regime
the discretion to cherry-pick applicable provisions of the Convention.

Thus, judicial aversion and innovative legal argumentation together paved the
path for a series of decisions that have justified the expropriation of Palestinian
lands to construct roads connecting settlers to the state's interior,[125] the deportation of Palestinians from the Occupied Territories,[126] and even the extraction
of natural resources that should have been reserved for Palestinian national
benefit.[127] Under a rule-of-law framework, Israel's Supreme Court has enabled
the state to achieve colonial expansion. While the judicial branch has justified
Israel's actions in the territory based on occupation law, it has simultaneously
invoked the *sui generis* argument to block Palestinian legal redress under the
same framework. As a result, Israel has enjoyed "both the powers of an occupant
and a sovereign in the [West Bank and Gaza], while Palestinians enjoy neither
the rights of an occupied people nor the rights of citizenship."[128]

The Court and also other branches of Israel's government have insisted that
all such measures—which have steadily dispossessed Palestinians, confiscated
their lands, and concentrated them in fragmented land clusters while implanting Jewish-Israeli settlers in their place—have not amounted to creeping annexation. This condition could be reversed, or endorsed, by a political solution

under Resolution 242's land-for-peace framework, they have argued.[129] In effect, Israel was not a colonial power taking the land; it was merely an administrator of disputed lands that belonged to no sovereign until such time as Israel could enter into a political agreement to resolve the conflict. This was a legal strategy deployed in the pursuit of a political objective.

Retooling UNSC 242: Retroactive Cover for Colonial Takings
In addition to the legal fiction of temporality and military necessity that allowed Israel to steadily poach Palestinian lands under the *sui generis* framework, Israel strategically deployed Resolution 242 to justify its territorial encroachments. The logic was that if Jordan (or the Palestinians) ceded any part of the territories in a peace agreement, then Israel had never acquired title to that land through conquest: the countries would simply be exchanging some of the land for peace, as mandated by the resolution. Rather than shepherding peace, however, Israel has retooled the resolution to retroactively legitimate its colonial takings.

Despite the international consensus on withdrawal expressed throughout the drafting of Security Council Resolution 242, Israel used the text's lack of the definite article to justify its settlement expansion. Arguing that the omission left open to interpretation and political negotiation which territories were to be exchanged for peace, Israel took the position that it was under no obligation to return all of the West Bank and the Gaza Strip but could, theoretically, return a fraction of them. Moreover, its security needs should dictate the scope of the territory to be returned.

Yigal Allon, who was the Israeli Deputy Prime Minister during the 1967 War, developed the doctrine of "defensible borders" to justify Israel's expansionist posture in security terms. In a 1967 article published in the U.S. journal *Foreign Affairs*, he described the development of his approach. Building on Resolution 242's deliberate lack of specificity (to allow for minor border rectifications, as discussed above), Allon explained that "[t]he purpose of defensible borders is . . . to provide Israel with the requisite minimal strategic depth, as well as lines which have topographical strategic significance." This necessitated

> absolute Israeli control over the strategic zone . . . that lies between the
> Jordan River to the east, and the eastern chain of the Samarian and Judean

mountains to the west . . . [as well as retention of the Golan Heights and
full control of] the strategic desert zone from the southern part of the Gaza
Strip to the dunes on the eastern approaches of the town of El Arish, which
itself would be returned to Egypt.[130]

Israel's defensible borders amounted to control over almost the entire
West Bank and the Gaza Strip, as well as the Golan Heights (see the Allon
Plan map). Adherence to the Allon doctrine, ipso facto, undermined the
land-for-peace framework. Assuming, for the sake of argument, that Israel
retained those territories as an incentive to negotiate a peace agreement, the
proliferation of civilian settlements belied its claim that its presence in the
territories served a temporary and military function. Not only do civilian
settlements suggest permanency, but the use of civilians to achieve a military
goal amounts to human shielding, an outright prohibition under humanitarian
law.[131] Nonetheless, Israel effectively deployed this security framework even
in the face of direct opposition from its primary patron, the United States.

In July 1977, upon Prime Minister Begin's return from Washington, Israel's
Ministerial Committee on Settlements conferred legal status on three settlements.[132] The Carter administration immediately expressed its disappointment
and stated in unequivocal terms that

> the establishment of settlements in the occupied territories is not only con-
> trary to the Fourth Geneva Convention, but also constitutes an obstacle to
> progress in the peace-making process.[133]

In response, Begin delivered an address at the Knesset denouncing the U.S.
charge, saying:

> Jewish settlement does not in any way or under any circumstances do harm
> to the Arabs of Eretz Yisrael. We have not dispossessed, and will not dispos-
> sess, any Arab from his land.[134]

Using the cover of occupation law, Begin justified the presence of the settlements as temporary and therefore not a seizure of land. Rather than combat

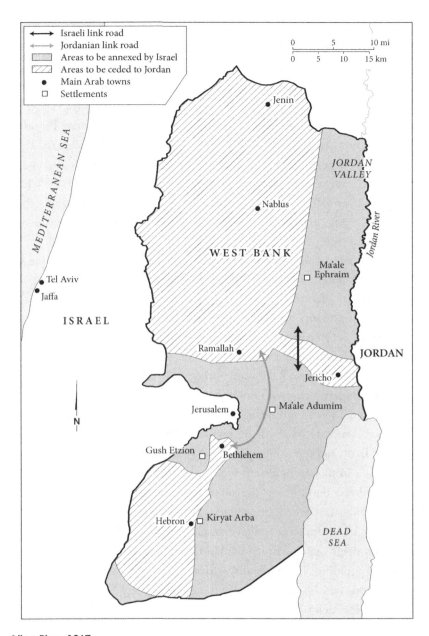

Allon Plan, 1967

In July 1967, Yigal Allon, Israeli Deputy Prime Minister, proposed a scheme for defensible borders in the West Bank and Gaza. The Allon Plan created an Israeli corridor from the Mediterranean Sea through Jerusalem and to the Jordan River; it divided the West Bank into two parts, and allocated territories within the West Bank for Jewish settlement.

these maneuvers as altogether illegitimate, the United States engaged in a narrow legal inquiry about Israel's compliance with occupation law, reducing the debate to detailed technicalities that lost the forest in the face of a single tree. Indeed, at a press conference two days after Begin's remarks, President Carter reiterated the illegal nature of the settlements and characterized them as an obstacle to peace, adding, however, that they were "not an insurmountable problem." Carter went so far as to defend Begin, and furthered Israel's legal framework by insisting, "the Israeli Government has never claimed that these settlements are permanent. What they have done is to say that they are legal at the present time."[135]

Resolution 242's drafting history unravels Israel's legal work, but the law is only as meaningful as the political will underpinning its enforcement. The backing of the United States, whether diplomatically through the provision of near-total immunity inside the Security Council, or materially through the unequivocal provision of financial and military aid, has impeded any significant action to hold Israel accountable.[136] Still, successive U.S. administrations, beginning with that of Lyndon B. Johnson in 1967, have insisted that Israel withdraw from all of the territories, with minor border adjustments.

Following the end of hostilities in 1967 War, the United States felt particularly obligated to its ally King Hussein of Jordan, who had laid claim to the West Bank and repeatedly pressured Israel to enter into talks with him. The Johnson administration went so far as to promise the King that he would regain the West Bank in a matter of six months. Israel had no such intent, however: at most, it would return noncontiguous Arab population blocs surrounded by Israeli military and civilian jurisdictions. Still, because it had become exclusively dependent on the United States for military aid after the war, Israel could not be so blatantly dismissive of U.S. demands. Instead, it embarked on what historian Avi Raz has described as a "consistent policy of deception." Raz describes it as

> a series of cabinet resolutions and ad hoc government decisions and actions ...
> the aim of which was to mislead the international community—first and
> foremost the US—into thinking that Israel was seriously seeking a peaceful
> settlement with its Arab neighbors.[137]

Immediately following the war and for several years thereafter, King Hussein made repeated overtures to establish peace with Israel. In response, Israel maintained what Eban described as a "futile discussion" with him. In 1969, Eban explained that Israel's political strategy was "to insert a sufficient number of obstacles into any American document [about an Arab-Israeli settlement] so that Arabs could not accept it."[138]

Israel also rebuffed Palestinian peace advances made by self-organized Palestinian elites in the territories. Within days after the close of the 1967 War, fifty elite Palestinians in the West Bank requested that the Israeli government recognize them as representatives of the Palestinian people and enter into negotiations with them to establish a Palestinian state along the outlines of the 1947 Partition Plan. Prime Minister Eshkol's office rejected this offer outright.[139] Israel could reject Palestinian peace overtures with much greater ease than Jordan's similar requests because the United States had not yet endorsed the idea of a Palestinian state and the PLO had not yet accepted Resolution 242. But Israel nevertheless maintained the appearance of weighing a Palestinian option, propagating the idea that it remained in compliance with the Security Council's mandate to return the territory in exchange for peace.[140]

In 1969, as Israel's ambitions to retain the West Bank and the Gaza Strip became undeniable, the United States confronted Israel about its repeated disavowal of territorial ambitions. Eban shrugged his shoulders and simply told his baffled U.S. counterparts, "We changed our minds."[141] The Johnson administration did not take this lightly but was constrained at the time by its deep involvement in the Vietnam war. It did not have the capacity to pursue a vigorous Middle East policy. President Johnson's personal commitment to protect Israel, the Soviet Union's mounting penetration in the region, and the rise of Palestinian guerilla attacks resulted in the United States doing little more at that juncture than issuing a series of empty condemnations and frustrated diplomatic cables.[142] When subsequent U.S. presidential administrations sought to take Israel to task, the U.S. Congress proved to be a critical impediment.[143] But the United States did not just stand on the sidelines: as we shall see, it remained an active and critical element in Israel's setter-colonial expansion, whose role cannot be overstated.[144] Aggressive U.S. intervention has been a cornerstone of Israel's legal work, enabling Israel to deploy international law to fulfill its territorial ambitions.

Shifting Tides: The Rise of the PLO and the 1973 War

In the aftermath of the devastating outcome of the 1967 War and the lack of meaningful protest from the international community that followed, Palestinians emerged as a force to represent themselves. The defeat of the Arab armies together with Egypt's and Jordan's endorsement of Resolution 242 emboldened Palestinian revolutionary groups to take their fate into their own hands by way of a national liberation movement. They saw the displacement of Jordanian and Egyptian jurisdiction over the West Bank and the Gaza Strip as an opportunity to set up a revolutionary authority and base in these territories. Fatah began to transfer cadres and operatives to the territories in the hope "that a new, undisputed national leadership could emerge on Palestinian soil, free from Arab control."[145]

In December 1967, Fatah, the Arab National Movement, the General Union of Palestinian Students, and several other Palestinian groups protested against the PLO leadership for its lack of accountability, forcing its then chairman, appointed by Egypt's Nasser, to resign. Yahya Hammuda, a left-leaning lawyer and a member of the PLO's Executive Committee took over in his place. In January 1968, Fatah convened a conference in Cairo alongside seven out of the eleven existing Palestinian guerilla groups, with the goal of either taking control of the PLO or dissolving it altogether. Fatah's efforts would yield tangible results only two months later, when it helped lead the Battle of Karama.[146]

The Karama refugee camp, located in the Jordan Valley, had become a site of increased Palestinian guerilla activity. In March 1968, the Israeli army attacked the camp, and although it militarily defeated the guerillas, who were supported by the Jordanian army, it also suffered significant losses. The battle "turned overnight into a resounding political and psychological victory in Arab eyes." Although credit for the tactical victory was owed to Jordan's armed forces, "it was the guerillas whose reputation soared. Their decision to stand and fight, militarily disastrous, catapulted them into a position of political pre-eminence." In a televised speech, Jordan's King Hussein reinforced this perception saying, "we are all guerillas" (*fida'iyyun*).[147] The battle was the sea change that consecrated the idea of guerilla warfare against Israel as a legitimate tactic, and it transformed Fatah's status. The group named Yasser Arafat as its leader and official spokesman, "offering an identifiable public figure after years of clandestinity."[148] One year later, in 1969, Fatah gained control of the PLO and Arafat became the PLO's chairman.[149]

Major transformations of power in the Arab world in the subsequent four years would redirect the region as a whole. In 1970, King Hussein consolidated his power in Jordan by administering a crushing defeat to the PLO, which had threatened to wrest control of the kingdom. Black September, as the operation came to be known, forced the PLO to relocate to Beirut, in Lebanon. That same year, Egypt's President Gamal Abdel Nasser died and was replaced by Anwar al-Sadat; and Hafez al-Assad became president of Syria in 1971.[150] Sadat was determined to regain the Egyptian territory taken in the 1967 War, either by force or by diplomacy. President Assad wanted to recover the Golan Heights as well.[151]

Egypt and Syria took the Israeli army by surprise when they attacked Israel on Yom Kippur in October 1973, which allowed them to score important victories in the first days of hostilities.[152] The Arab armies were so successful that Israeli Defense Minister Moshe Dayan concluded that the existence of Israel itself was endangered. The Israelis were soon able to block the threat on both fronts and conduct counterattacks.[153] The United States provided Israel with critical assistance, enabling its army to go on the offensive and win several decisive battles.[154] The Israeli army crossed the Suez Canal, creeping towards Cairo, and also captured Mt. Hermon, coming within 40 kilometers of Damascus.[155] The parties agreed to a ceasefire after a few weeks. Although Israel had come close to losing in the initial days of the war, it ultimately emerged as the military victor.

The 1973 War demonstrated that Arabs could work together when needed and that Israel was not as invincible as it had believed. The war left its scars on Israel, which suffered over 2,500 dead, US$4 billion in direct monetary losses, and deflated confidence. Although the Arabs technically lost the war, they won psychologically and diplomatically as the world once again focused on the ongoing conflict.[156] In 1973, the UN Security Council passed Resolution 338, affirming the land-for-peace framework enshrined in Resolution 242 and setting into motion what was to become known as the Middle East peace process. Palestinian control of the PLO and the rise of guerilla warfare, together with the shift ushered in by the 1973 War, would lay the groundwork for the PLO's political agenda and aggressive legal strategy throughout the decade that followed.

Chapter 3

PRAGMATIC REVOLUTIONARIES

> If *racial discrimination* against the "inferior natives" was the motto of race-supremacist European settler-regimes in Asia and Africa, the motto of the race-supremacist Zionist settler-regime in Palestine was *racial elimination*.
>
> —Fayez A. Sayegh, 1965

ON 14 NOVEMBER 1974, Yasser Arafat, Chairman of the Palestine Liberation Organization (PLO), stood at the podium in the United Nations General Assembly before an audience of nearly every member state. The U.S. and Israeli Ambassadors were conspicuously absent. This was a tremendous victory for the Palestinian cause and for the global anticolonial movement more generally. This international rostrum had been historically reserved for member states, as a matter of privilege and right. UN rules of procedures mandated that non-state organizations, including liberation movements, address specialized committees. The passage of General Assembly Resolution 3210 (1974), extending an invitation to the PLO, signaled a remarkable precedent and demonstrated the potential of the Global South as a united voting bloc and thus as a source of international lawmaking.

In 1974, formerly colonized nations and nations still seeking liberation constituted a critical mass in the United Nations and threatened to unravel the hegemony of former and existing colonial powers. Between the establishment of the United Nations in 1945 and Arafat's visit in 1974, the number of UN member states had increased from 51 to 138.[1] The new states were mostly former colonies, and many had achieved their independence through wars of liberation. Meanwhile, several liberation movements continued armed struggles with the goal of independence. Newly independent states and national liberation movements had consolidated their interests in the Non-Aligned Movement (NAM) and were now closely collaborating in an effort to usher in a new world order, both within and beyond the United Nations; they considered the PLO's militancy necessary and justified.

In the course of Arafat's five years at the helm of the PLO, and since the Battle of Karama (in 1968), the PLO had unified the most active Palestinian movements and parties. It served as a political umbrella for various armed factions, each of which oversaw and launched its own military activities. These groups included Fatah, the dominant party in the PLO and led by Arafat, and the Popular Front for the Liberation of Palestine (PFLP), the leading opposition party, led by Dr. George Habash. Between 1967 and 1970, Fatah and the PFLP took Jordan as their main base of operations. They subsequently became centered in Lebanon, where the PLO had established a firm base after Jordan expelled it in 1970 and from where it was launching cross-border reconnaissance and armed operations.[2] Israel breached the Lebanese border frequently in both offensive and reprisal attacks on PLO positions as well as on Lebanese civilian targets. These attacks included kidnappings, assassinations, and disproportionate use of force that intensified tensions between the Palestinian fighters and some sectors of Lebanon's ruling elite. Armed resistance defined the PLO and resonated with similar national liberation struggles across the African continent and East Asia. This did not reflect an international consensus, however.

Several powerful states and colonial powers condemned all use of non-state force as criminal and terroristic. This group included the United States, which was mired in war in Vietnam, along with Portugal, which was fighting to maintain its colonial domination of Mozambique and Angola. It also included Israel, which clung to its occupied Arab territories and denied the Palestinians' right to self-determination, as well as South Africa, which obstinately maintained its apartheid regime in south and southwest Africa. In 1974, these powers constituted a minority and were losing the battle to define what constituted legitimate violence. Their failure to delegitimize the PLO and to thwart the PLO Chairman's address to the United Nations was a significant blow to the

United States and Israel, in particular.[3] The General Assembly's invitation to the PLO represented a victory for the NAM.

That same year, in another NAM victory, the General Assembly unanimously elected Algeria's Foreign Minister, Abdelaziz Bouteflika, to be its President. During the course of its liberation from 132 years of French colonization, achieved in 1962, Algeria had established several diplomatic and military milestones, making it an unequivocal reference for all other liberation movements.[4] Bouteflika paid homage to this anticolonial sentiment when he introduced Arafat to the United Nations as the General Commander of the Palestinian Revolution.[5] Arafat began his address by recognizing the significance of the PLO's presence at the UN and its commitment to the NAM's political aspiration to "end racism and imperialism" and achieve "freedom and self-determination."[6] He spoke on behalf of all nations seeking liberation from enduring colonial domination and the fulfillment of the League of Nation's long ago promise of independence.

Arafat's appearance marked one of the most meaningful junctures for the Palestinian liberation movement as well. Though hailed as a victory, the PLO's presence at the United Nations was full of ambiguity. On the one hand, it embodied the culmination of a struggle to achieve recognition as a people entitled to self-determination, thereby reversing the juridical erasures first enacted by the Balfour Declaration (1917) and later by the Mandate for Palestine (1922), Israel's establishment (1948), and most recently, Security Council Resolution 242 (1967). Arafat captured this strategic interest when he explained the value of recounting the story of Palestine beginning before the onset of the Israeli occupation in 1967:

> If we return now to the historical roots of our cause we do so because present at this very moment in our midst are those, who, while they occupy our homes as their cattle graze in our pastures, and as their hands pluck the fruit of our trees, claim at the same time that we are disembodied spirits, fictions without presence, without traditions or future. We speak of our roots also because until recently some people have regarded—and continued to regard—our problem as merely a problem of refugees. They have portrayed the Middle East Question as little more than a border dispute between the

Arab states and the Zionist entity. They have imagined that our people claims rights not rightfully its own and fights neither with logic nor valid motive, with a simple wish only to disturb the peace and to terrorize wantonly.[7]

The PLO's efforts at the United Nations represented a strategic effort to inscribe the juridical status of the Palestinian people in international legal instruments and institutions. This legal strategy complemented a political one aimed at challenging the hegemonic control that former colonial powers maintained over the majority of the globe. Using this approach, the PLO contested the order shaped by the United States and Israel, who together had sustained the sovereign exception regulating the question of Palestine. The PLO's strategic deployment of the law during the 1970s marked an apex in its legal advocacy and yielded a series of fundamental legal achievements. The value of affirming the status of Palestinians as a nation possessing an international legal personality, rather than a motley bunch of Arab refugees, could not be overstated; indeed, this was tantamount to a proclamation of existence.

On the other hand, the PLO's inscription of Palestinian nationhood suggested the acceptance of a state-centric global order and a bid to establish a Palestinian state. In fact, for Arafat, as well as for official leadership organizations belonging to the PLO, such as Fatah, the Democratic Front for the Liberation of Palestine, and al-Sa'iqa, the move to the United Nations enhanced the possibility of establishing a state and "joining the [international] club."[8] This embodied a significant risk for the Palestinian struggle. In 1968, the Palestinian National Council (PNC), PLO's parliament in exile, had defined the political purpose of the movement as the "liberation of the whole land of Palestine and the establishment of the society which the Palestinians aim for on that land."[9]

In line with this position, the PNC rejected UN Security Council Resolution 242 as a framework because it necessitated accepting Israeli control over 78 percent of historic Palestine and then trying to regain the remaining 22 percent through negotiations. It also failed to articulate clear principles for resolving the forced exile of Palestinian refugees. The PNC affirmed that armed struggle was the only means by which to achieve liberation. As to the possibility of establishing a Palestinian state in the West Bank and the Gaza Strip, the PNC explicitly rejected "Imperialist and Zionist plans for establishing a false Palestinian entity on the territories occupied in the June war of 1967."[10]

By articulating its demands for peoplehood in the framework of international law and pursuing this goal at the United Nations, the PLO drew upon the same legal and institutional norms that legitimated Israel's establishment, naturalized its existence, and protected its territorial and political sovereignty. A turn to international law included the possibility of establishing a truncated Palestinian state in the West Bank and the Gaza Strip and normalizing Israel's Zionist settler sovereignty. The regional and international balance of power following the October 1973 War made this possibility even more acute.

This reality catalyzed a schism within the PLO between a "pragmatic" camp that sought a state as an interim, or even final, step to full liberation and the "Rejection Front," led by the PFLP, that insisted upon revolution in order to upend Zionist settler sovereignty. Arafat's appearance before the United Nations did not resolve these issues. His momentous speech was a revolutionary call for liberation imbued with pragmatic ambitions for a statist solution.[11] He articulated a demand for a single democratic state for all peoples on the land while pursuing a direct channel with the United States in order to be brought into the fold of the Middle East peace talks.

The United States, however, took a rejectionist line, obstinately opposing the PLO's participation and foreclosing the diplomatic possibility of negotiating a state. This left the PLO's pragmatists with nothing to lose by pursuing a revolutionary course of action.[12] Moreover, the rejection camp within the PLO blocked any attempts to dilute the demands for revolutionary liberation. To bypass rejectionist opposition and to create leverage to enter into peace negotiations, the so-called pragmatists strategically amended the PLO's mandate. Thereafter, the PLO embarked on a program of liberation diplomacy within the United Nations to cement its legal status as a national liberation movement.

The PLO's legal work at the UN throughout the 1970s would successfully transform the Palestinian question from a humanitarian crisis, punctuated by the overwhelming presence of an exiled refugee population across the Arab world, into a political crisis marked by the failure of current and former colonial powers to deliver sovereignty and independence to a colonized people. The PLO's legal work left open to question whether a Palestinian state would be established in place of Israel or alongside it in the occupied territory.[13] The tension between the competing agendas embodied by the PLO—the revolutionary movement for national liberation of all Palestine and the establishment of a state in the West Bank and the Gaza Strip as an interim, or final, step towards liberation—would not be resolved until nearly a decade and a half after Arafat's UN address. The October 1973 War provided the impetus for this series of shifts.

The October 1973 War Creates a Legal Opportunity

In early September 1973, Egyptian President Anwar Sadat summoned senior Fatah leaders, including PLO Chairman Arafat, to inform them of his plans for a limited war against Israel.[14] He intended to participate in a postwar peace conference to recoup the territories occupied in 1967.[15] Egyptian and Syrian plans for a limited war dashed Palestinian hopes for a war of liberation. Palestinian guerilla fighters understood that while their military contributions enhanced the efforts of Arab conventional armies, on their own, they were insufficient to militarily defeat Israel.[16]

The 1973 War ended the six-year status quo of "No Peace, No War" following the 1967 War, and upon its cessation presented new diplomatic possibilities in the region. The UN Security Council passed Resolution 338, under the binding authority of Chapter VII of the UN Charter, and laid the groundwork for the first Arab-Israeli peace conference.[17] This resolution, introduced hastily by the United States and the Soviet Union, called for the implementation of Security Council Resolution 242 and emphasized its clause stipulating peace negotiations.[18] On its face, the diplomatic process was a joint Soviet-U.S. initiative, but in practice, it was "designed to preserve U.S. dominance in the region."[19]

Henry Kissinger, U.S. President Richard Nixon's National Security Adviser and Secretary of State, saw the 1973 War as an opportunity to diminish Soviet influence and ensure that Israel could retain as much of the Palestinian territories as it had captured in 1967.[20] Kissinger believed that compelling Israel's withdrawal necessitated a more confrontational U.S. policy that, in his view, would threaten the country's very existence.[21] He sought to shield Israel while steadily currying favor with each of the Arab states for the sake of undermining their coalescence as well as to "demonstrate the limitations of Soviet influence."[22] He was careful not to portray the U.S. position in such hardened terms, and objected to full-scale withdrawal on procedural grounds (it should be achieved through negotiations, not compulsion), thus maintaining the image of the United States as a credible broker. Sadat welcomed U.S. involvement, even at such great risk. He believed that while Europe had provided diplomatic support and the Soviet Union had provided arms, "only the United States could create the political momentum for a return of Arab territory."[23]

Sadat insisted that the PLO participate in the nascent peace process on behalf of Palestinians to negotiate the return of the Occupied West Bank, including East Jerusalem, and Gaza.[24] He sought to moderate the Palestinian demand for the liberation of all of Palestine, in order to make the PLO a more tenable negotiating partner, at least to the United States. Egypt was not alone in its entreaty. In the war's aftermath, the Soviet Ambassador in Beirut handed the Palestinian leaders a memo urging them "to adopt a realistic and constructive attitude which consists in claiming the recovery of the territories lost in 1967."[25] In mid-November 1973, Moscow issued its first public endorsement of a Palestinian state in the Occupied Palestinian Territories and urged the PLO to phase its struggle into stages towards liberation.[26]

That same month, the Arab League convened in a summit meeting in Algiers and quietly endorsed the PLO as the sole and legitimate representative of the Palestinian people. The summit did not make its endorsement official in consideration of Jordan's position. The Kingdom of Jordan maintained its territorial claims over the West Bank as well as representational rights over Palestinians on both banks of the Jordan River. These diplomatic gestures generated a momentum within the PLO and among an international community aimed at instating the PLO as an authoritative body capable of representing Palestinian interests in negotiations. Palestinians in the West Bank, organizing themselves under the banner of the Palestinian National Front, urged the PLO to participate in the negotiations, for fear that if it did not, Jordan would take its place.[27]

The pragmatists within the PLO were amenable to this strategic course. During the 1973 War, leaders of Fatah and Sa'iqa, a Syrian-affiliated political and military formation, indicated their willingness to cease their guerilla activities if Israel publically recognized the Palestinian right to self-determination.[28] Fatah had been signaling its eagerness to enter the U.S. sphere of influence since early 1970.[29] These gestures were all made in secret, however, as they contravened the PLO's official position of liberating the whole land of Palestine through armed struggle.

Despite the pragmatists' flexible position as well as ardent advice from his national security advisers, Kissinger adamantly refused to involve the PLO in the peace negotiations. To exclude the PLO and diminish Arab leverage in negotiations, Kissinger sought to initiate bilateral negotiations between Israel, Jordan, Syria, and Egypt respectively and to disaggregate an Arab bloc. He wanted to establish peace with each of the Arab regimes and then bring in the PLO at the very end in order to impose a peace settlement upon the Palestinians.[30]

In November 1973, the regional and international balance of power constrained the PLO's strategic options. Its parliament opposed any negotiations and any settlement short of complete liberation. Egypt and Syria, with two of the most significant Arab armies, had made it clear that they had no intention of entering a war of liberation against Israel. The PLO's Arab and superpower allies urged it to modify and moderate its political position in order to recoup the occupied territory, in accordance with Security Council Resolutions 242 and 338. Meanwhile, Sadat's Egypt was marching towards bilateral negotiations with Israel, brokered by the United States. And the United States remained intent on excluding the PLO and, instead, had recognized Jordan as the sovereign to which the West Bank should be returned.

When the Peace Conference on the Middle East, commonly known as the Geneva Peace Conference, convened in December 1973, only Egypt and Israel attended. Syria declined the invitation, and the PLO was not invited. Though it lasted only two hours, the conference planted the seeds of a regional peace process. The PNC convened its Eleventh Summit and its first meeting since the 1973 War the following month, in January 1974. It reiterated Palestinian opposition to Resolution 242, to a negotiated settlement, and to recognition of Israel, as well as the Palestinian commitment to revolutionary armed struggle. Despite the PNC's institutional resolve, leaders of the most significant Palestinian political and military groups continued to deliberate the import of the new balance of power upon the PLO's strategy. They could not agree. Ultimately, the pragmatist camp would find a way to appease the rejectionists and establish a legal mandate to pursue a diplomatic strategy. This was the outcome of legal work.

Internal Shifts Within the PLO

Following the Palestinian National Council's summit, the PLO publication *Palestine Affairs*, together with the Palestine Research Center, convened a public roundtable in Beirut, moderated by Palestinian poet and icon Mahmoud Darwish. Shafiq al Hout, the Director-General of the PLO's Beirut Office and a self-proclaimed independent, urged the PLO to take a clearer position, because standing aside after a military battle is "an approach reserved for a historian, not a revolutionary political militant."[31] Al Hout appealed for moderation, explaining:

> When man begins to struggle, out of oppression, he will of course be compelled to pronounce unrealizable slogans. But when he, in concert with others, begins to apply pressure to influence events, it is bound to result in willingness by the other side to amend its position.[32]

PFLP leader George Habash cautioned that while the October War had altered the balance of power, it did not ensure that Palestinians could establish a democratic authority over historic Palestine. Establishing a mini-state in the Occupied Territories would simply make Palestinians hostage to the whims of "American-Hashemite-Zionist" control. Habash was mindful of the political costs associated with rebuffing Soviet and Arab appeals for moderation, and urged the PLO to strategically dodge moderation "in a way which does not harm our mutual friendship. The Soviets ask us to take our own position; they have theirs and are not prepared to compromise." He insisted that "political struggle alone will not be sufficient," as demonstrated by the inability to force Israel's withdrawal from Arab territories between 1967 and 1973. "Fighting," Habash explained, "is the only way."[33]

Nayef Hawatmeh, Secretary-General of the Popular Democratic Front for the Liberation of Palestine, a splinter group of the PFLP, agreed with Habash that fighting was necessary, because all forms of negotiated settlement are "products of the sword's edge."[34] Nevertheless, Hawatmeh urged the PLO to modify its strategy and adopt a phased approach that began with a national authority and culminated in a single, democratic state.

> Now we are beginning to deal with our problem out of a belief in our ability to effect changes, rather than out of incapacity to accomplish anything. . . .

What is demanded under conditions of defeat, of course, incites fear and sarcasm. After the war, we are, more than ever before, in a position to continue the struggle and to change the balance of power in our favor. Planning a strategy based on successive stages has become very realistic.[35]

Habash seemed to be in the minority as Salah Khalaf of Fatah also endorsed a phased approach. Like the rest of the leaders, he remained committed, rhetorically, to the complete liberation of Palestine but insisted that "the October War brought us face to face with the necessity of devising a policy that would be oriented in terms of stages" and that Palestinian leaders of the past made a mistake "in adhering to our people's historical rights without adopting stage-by-stage programs of struggle under the obtaining conditions."[36]

In private, Khalaf and the pragmatists within Fatah were much more conciliatory to a compromise agreement.[37] According to Khalaf's memoirs, Fatah's Central Committee first contemplated a phased program as early as July 1967.[38] In 1973, Fatah continued to receive arms from the Soviet Union and, more than any other political party, tied its fate to Egypt.[39] According to William Buffum, then U.S. Ambassador to Lebanon, leaders of Fatah and other PLO factions were "prepared to participate in peace talks and settle for [a] rump Palestinian entity."[40] Arafat personally endorsed the concept of a two-state solution, but despite his position as the PLO Chairman, he could not act unilaterally on its behalf.[41] The Popular Democratic Front for the Liberation of Palestine and Sa'iqa joined Fatah in the quest to modify their strategic approach and enter the peace conference. Meanwhile, the Popular Front for the Liberation of Palestine, the Popular Front for the Liberation of Palestine–General Command, the Arab Liberation Front, the General Union of Palestinian Students, and the General Union of Writers and Journalists remained opposed to participating in the peace process.[42]

In February 1974, Fatah, Sa'iqa, and the Popular Democratic Front for the Liberation of Palestine submitted a working paper to the PLO Central Committee that outlined a compromise position between the PLO and the parties that opposed negotiations. The document reiterated the PLO's key positions but added that it should adopt a phased approach to liberation by ending "the occupation and forc[ing] the enemy to withdraw unconditionally from the West

Bank and the Gaza sector without making any political concessions to him in return."[43] This would be an intermediate stage, wherein the PLO would establish its authority on any liberated Palestinian lands in the long-term effort for the complete liberation of Palestine. The Popular Front for the Liberation of Palestine responded by submitting its own proposal that reaffirmed its rejection of any national authority framework based on Resolution 242 and a commitment to sabotage any ensuing peace conference. Having reached an impasse, the PLO Central Committee convened a national dialogue among the leaders of the armed organizations in May 1974. They reached an agreement about a phased approach but did not agree on the details.[44]

The PNC commenced its twelfth meeting in Cairo in order to flesh out and finalize the agreement proposed by the Palestinian leaders shortly thereafter, in June 1974. In a vote of 187 to 183, the PNC adopted the Ten Point Program, also known as the Phased Political Program. It provided the pragmatists the wiggle room to participate in the Middle East peace process without relinquishing the vision of liberating all of Palestine. This program would spark a serious rupture within the PLO. Its second point stipulated:

> The Palestine Liberation Organization will employ all means, first and foremost armed struggle, to liberate Palestinian territory and to establish the independent combatant national authority for the people over every part of Palestinian territory that is liberated.[45]

Point Two signaled a significant departure. It was the first time the PLO had affirmed the liberation of "Palestinian territory" rather than the liberation of Palestine. On the day of the Ten Point Plan's adoption, the PNC separately issued a recommendation to the PLO Executive Committee endorsing the committee's participation in negotiations as long as it did so in a "framework other than that of resolution 242."[46] Although Habash participated in the PNC's twelfth meeting and endorsed the Ten Point Program, he believed that the final outcome involved deception. The Popular Front for the Liberation of Palestine argued that Point Two (authorizing an authority on any liberated land) was meant to be read together with Point Three, which rejected recognition of Israel, conciliation, and secure borders. The PFLP claimed it had assumed that Point Three also stipulated a rejection of entering the peace conference and that its exclusion from the final text was a tactic aimed at "misleading fellow comrades and the masses, rather than the enemy."[47] It issued a statement explaining that it had

> reached the profound, certain and unshakable conviction that the settlement which is being prepared for the area can only be an imperialist liquidation settlement. Its only consequence could be, on the one hand, the expansion and extension of American imperialist influence in the area and, on the other, the establishment of Israel's legality and the safeguarding of her future and her security.[48]

The PFLP stepped down from the PLO's Executive Committee in protest and established the Rejection Front, along with the Popular Front for the Liberation of Palestine–General Command, the Arab Liberation Front, and the Popular Struggle Front to oppose the PLO's participation in the negotiation process. Rejectionist opposition was formidable but still left room for maneuver. The Ten Point Program afforded Arafat, together with the PLO's pragmatist forces, the right to establish a national authority on Palestinian territory recouped through diplomacy. They had to do so, however, without recognizing or negotiating with Israel, on a basis other than Resolution 242, and in a framework of a phased strategy towards the complete liberation of Palestine.

The PLO remained committed to revolutionary struggle while also pursuing a diplomatic track. Diplomacy itself was not controversial; rather the PLO's lack of clear diplomatic objectives imbued its strategic course with uncertainty and conflict. On its face, the PLO sought to establish a base for itself in the West Bank and Gaza as an interim phase towards the liberation of all of Palestine through armed struggle. The framework for ending Israel's occupation, however, was based on the formula achieved in 1967 and captured in Security Council Resolution 242, which limited the horizon of Palestinian liberation to the occupied territory. The land-for-peace framework allowed for supporting Palestinian self-determination and opposing Israel's 1967 occupation, but it did not clearly object to Israel's Zionist settler sovereignty. It at once provided the PLO with its political advantage but also constituted the primary challenge to its vision for liberation. The PLO sought to shift the international balance reflected in this framework through a combination of guerilla warfare on the ground and legal work on the international stage, including at the United Nations. It did this primarily by pursuing every opportunity to establish the juridical status of the Palestinian nation as well as to demonstrate and exercise its embryonic sovereignty.

Embryonic Sovereignty and the "Right to Fight"

The PLO's pursuit of diplomatic recognition as the sole and legitimate representative of the Palestinian people directly challenged the elision of a Palestinian people and their characterization as a nondescript "refugee population." This tactical approach edified the status of Palestinian peoplehood as a matter of law while armed resistance worked to achieve the same goal as a matter of fact.[49] In September 1973, the Non-Aligned Movement recognized the PLO and invited it to join NAM as an observer organization along with other African liberation movements. In February 1974, the Organization of Islamic Cooperation, comprising fifty-seven states, similarly recognized the PLO. And the Organization of African Unity followed suit after the PNC's Twelfth Summit. Around this same time, the PLO was also making a different kind of diplomatic bid, one that aimed to legitimate its use of armed force and reify its status as a nation.

In the early seventies, only states could legally participate in war. However, between the Second World War and the early seventies, the primary forms of armed conflict were nonconventional wars: that is, wars between non-state actors and states (i.e., wars of liberation) or within states (i.e., civil wars). These wars had concerned the international community, and yet the legal framework available to regulate them was limited to a single article common to the four Geneva Conventions of 1949; it was demonstrably insufficient.[50] In March 1974, an international conference was convened to review two Additional Protocols to the Geneva Conventions that sought to expand the legal lexicon regulating nonconventional armed conflicts and, by extension, legitimating the use of force by non-state actors, or guerilla fighters.

The United States and Israel led the march to delegitimize such armed force on the grounds that it was terrorism. In 1972, the United States attempted to achieve a UN declaration condemning terrorism but faced significant opposition, especially from African states, which supported national liberation movements within the African continent and especially in Namibia and South Africa. The apartheid government in South Africa had recently condemned Nelson Mandela—a member of the African National Congress and co-founder of Umkhonto we Sizwe, an organization committed to using revolutionary violence—to life imprisonment. During his 1964 trial, Mandela explained this organization's resort to arms as critical precisely to avoid terroristic violence:

> Firstly, we believed that as a result of Government policy, violence by the African people had become inevitable, and that unless responsible leadership was given to canalize and control the feelings of our people, there would be outbreaks of terrorism which would produce an intensity of bitterness and hostility between the various races of this country which is not produced even by war. Secondly, we felt that without violence there would be no way open to the African people to succeed in their struggle against the principle of white supremacy. All lawful modes of expressing opposition to this principle had been closed by legislation, and we were placed in a position in which we had either to accept a permanent state of inferiority, or to defy the Government. We chose to defy the law. We first broke the law in a way which avoided any recourse to violence; when this form was legislated against, and then the Government resorted to a show of force to crush opposition to its policies, only then did we decide to answer violence with violence.[51]

The United States did not want to alienate the African bloc for fear of enhancing a Soviet sphere of influence. Still, it could not endorse the use of force by liberation groups. In turn, African states could not accept a blanket condemnation of the use of force because violence was considered a primary and necessary element for political transformation.[52] The outcome was a document that explored the underlying causes of terroristic violence.[53] This marked an achievement for the liberation movements, which insisted that their nonconventional tactics were symptomatic of broader, structural violence. In November 1973, the UN General Assembly passed a more pointed resolution that reaffirmed "the legitimacy of the peoples' struggle for liberation from colonial and foreign domination and alien subjugation by all available means, including armed struggle."[54]

The effort to enshrine the right to fight for non-state actors had begun in early 1969, when the UN Secretary-General published a report examining the applicability and relevance of humanitarian law in these new contexts.[55] Georges Abi Saab, an international law scholar who prepared the report for the Secretary-General explained that the International Committee of the Red Cross (Red Cross), an independent organization responsible for ensuring humanitarian protections during armed conflict, "did not like the UN dabbling in their expertise so they took up the banner themselves."[56] The Red Cross, in consultation with government experts, drafted two Additional Protocols that it now sought to review at the Diplomatic Conference on the Reaffirmation and Application of International Humanitarian Law Applicable in Armed Conflicts (Diplomatic Conference). The first Additional Protocol sought to elevate the status of wars of national liberation to international armed conflicts, thus recognizing the embryonic sovereignty of the liberation movements and affording them the right to use armed force.[57]

The first Diplomatic Conference meeting lasted for three months and proved contentious because it wanted to admit liberation movements as participant observers.[58] Abi Saab, who was now representing the Group of 77 (G77), a coalition of seventy-seven Third World actors who proposed a different model for economic development,[59] has explained how admittance of national liberation movements into the Diplomatic Conference meetings is tantamount to recognition of their embryonic sovereignty: Whereas individuals and unaffiliated groups use force for a private purpose, "the definition of sovereignty is the exclusive use of legitimate force. And legitimate force is the force used in the name of the community as a source of order not disorder."[60]

The PLO was among the movements seeking admittance into the conference. It had established an irregular army in 1966, and its various political factions also had their own military wings. Its campaign to bring its guerilla warfare against Israel within the regulatory scope of international law sought to achieve two things: first, to challenge the criminalization of its armed struggle as criminal and terroristic by creating new law "to accommodate wars of their [the combatants'] own making";[61] and second, to establish itself as an embryonic sovereign with the ability to exercise a monopoly on violence and a right to use it on behalf of an entire people.

While the PLO's bid to join the Diplomatic Conference was beneficial to Palestinian interests, it also embodied a risk. The Additional Protocols stood to disadvantage national liberation armed struggles by entrenching the asymmetries of power between a state, which has significant military technological capabilities, and guerilla formations, which depend on irregular combat tactics to achieve a military advantage.[62] Western states that supported the initiative saw it as a way to better restrain the use of force by non-state actors. Opponents to it, like the United States and Israel, rejected it because, they insisted, it would restrain only the states engaged in nonconventional warfare while failing to discipline the military engagement of non-state actors. The PLO was cognizant of these legal impositions.[63]

Daoud Barakat, who represented the PLO's delegation to the conference, explains that there was no contradiction for the organization. The PLO had a formal army with a clear chain of command. According to Barakat, its "position was very clear that Palestinians were moving towards a state and there was a willingness to comply with the laws of war."[64] Nabil Shaath, a strategic consultant to the PLO Chairman at this time, cautions that in reality, "the PLO did not have a team of experts to handle all these efforts." Its strategy was to enter into every available space in order to enhance its international standing.[65] Abi Saab agrees with Shaath and adds, "at that time, the PLO's primary concern was achieving legitimacy of their organization and their cause, rather than the technical aspects of it."[66] By the close of the first Diplomatic Conference in June 1974, the PLO had succeeded in gaining admittance as a participant observer.

Over the next three years of proceedings, the narrow applicability of the Additional Protocols to nascent states resisting colonialism, as opposed to liberation movements in general, became increasingly clear.[67] Abi Saab explains that the original draft of the Protocols referred to foreign domination, rather than occupation, in order to avoid redundancy with the Geneva Conventions. The Fourth Geneva Convention, in particular, had already contemplated military occupation as a continuation of an international armed conflict and thus had triggered the application of the laws of war in that situation. Referring to military occupation in the Additional Protocols could create a legal loophole, allowing a combatant to evade the application of the laws of war to situations of occupation by rebuffing the supplementary proceedings to the Geneva Conventions.

But Latin American and Arab members of the G77 were concerned that the Additional Protocols would provide legal sanction for dissidents to take up arms against the state in the name of fighting any foreign domination, including excessive foreign influence, for example. The United States, which participated in the conference proceedings and simultaneously aimed to undermine them, capitalized on this concern, and argued that it would ultimately threaten the sovereignty of newly independent states.[68] Abi Saab tried to assuage the fears of reticent states by changing the draft language to make clear that the domination must be there forcefully. His efforts failed and the final text of Protocol I refers to "armed conflicts in which peoples are fighting against colonial domination and alien occupation and against racist regimes in the exercise of their right of self-determination."[69]

The final text of the Additional Protocols I and II expanded the applicable scope of the laws of war to those armed conflicts not of an international character,[70] characterized wars of national liberation as international in character, reduced the stringent standards requisite upon combatants to distinguish themselves from civilians,[71] and expanded those violations considered war crimes.[72] By 1977, a sufficient number of states had ratified the Protocols. The United States and Israel refused to do so and continued to characterize such force as criminal and terroristic.[73] The adoption of the Additional Protocols successfully created new law where none existed in order to legitimate the resort to arms by national liberation movements, including the PLO.

This legal work at once legitimated the PLO's revolutionary violence against Israel and further affirmed the existence of a Palestinian nation with the right to self-determination. It thus exacerbated the tension between its vision for revolution and vision for statehood. If a state does not yet exist, diplomatic recognition builds the political momentum to bring it into existence.[74] And by 1974, the PLO possessed several critical elements of sovereign governance: it had a parliament, national portfolios, a national budget, armed forces, and diplomatic representatives across the world, including Western European capitals.[75] The move to affirm its juridical status and embryonic sovereignty indicated the PLO's ambitions to establish a state even as it insisted on liberation of Palestine through armed struggle. At the outset of its diplomatic efforts, these ambitions did not appear to be in controversy, since the PLO sought to establish a

Palestinian state over all of Palestine wherein Jews could remain as enfranchised citizens rather than settler sovereigns.

The PLO had deliberately avoided establishing a government in exile and declaring itself a state under foreign domination for fear that such a declaration would delimit its territorial authority and undermine its quest for a single and democratic state.[76] Demanding a state would also risk signaling de facto recognition of Israel and make the PLO more vulnerable to political demands by its allies.[77] Strategically, the organization considered a government in exile to be a negotiating chip and did not want to squander it prematurely. Arafat, who supported the concept of a state, for example, saw the establishment of a government as "linked to a political solution."[78] To circumvent this challenge, the PLO did not include a state as part of its diplomatic appeals. It could not, however, unilaterally contain nor define the significance of its formal recognition by states and regional organizations. The campaign to obtain an international personality thus remained filled with strategic uncertainty.

This suited the pragmatists' ambitions for a state in the West Bank and Gaza. Arafat could not pursue those ambitions because he understood that the political consensus within the PLO was against him.[79] The ambiguity that inhered in a turn to international law and diplomacy therefore served the pragmatists' vision because it implied the creation of a state without specifying its borders, the means of its establishment, or its relationship to Israel. It was a grey area that authorized the PLO's pragmatists to pursue a political, rather than military, settlement to the conflict without conceding the PLO's hardline position of nonrecognition and nonconciliation. However, the United States, which continued to lead the diplomatic effort, had no intention of including the PLO in the peace process. In an effort to earn a seat at the negotiating table, and as a secondary option, Arafat set his eyes on the United Nations.[80]

The PLO Goes to the United Nations: A *"Feda'i* Operation"

Arafat considered UN recognition as providing two tangible benefits: first, it would further consecrate the representative status of the PLO; and second, recognition would generate the requisite political pressure for the PLO to join the negotiations on its own terms. Nabil Shaath, Arafat's strategic consultant and a professor at the American University in Beirut, as well as the Director-General of the Palestine Planning Center, a strategic think tank for the PLO, explains that no one in the PLO's top leadership agreed.[81] They believed that the UN was the source of Palestinians' problems; after all, it had proposed partition of Palestine, failed to realize Palestinian self-determination, normalized Israel's Jewish-Zionist settler sovereignty, failed to compel Israel to allow Palestinian refugees to return, and then reified Palestinian erasure in Security Council Resolution 242. The UN seemed unable to politically resolve the very obstacles to Palestinian self-determination that it had engendered. Still, and despite its political failures, the United Nations had managed to deliver humanitarian aid and relief to Palestinian refugees through the UN Relief and Works Agency (UNRWA).

Undeterred, Arafat called Shaath to discuss his diplomatic ambitions. Shaath was reluctant. He believed that while the UN had the "capacity to feed refugees, it could not ensure their return." Moreover, he thought the cost of entering negotiations was too high for what could be achieved through diplomacy. According to Shaath, Arafat insisted, telling him: "You are a *feda'i* (guerilla) and I demand you go to the United Nations, you will get me an invitation, and you will join me when I go there. This is a *feda'i* operation."[82]

In August 1974, Shaath traveled to New York to lobby the United Nations. His goal: to obtain an invitation for the PLO to participate in UN meetings. Though he diverged with Arafat on the question of negotiations, he believed the UN provided a platform where the PLO could establish a record that could enhance the Palestinian cause globally.[83] The PLO's New York information office having been recently closed after Zionist vigilantes physically assaulted its representative, Sa'adat Hasan, Shaath set up shop in the Arab League's New York office. From there, for the next two months, he curried support for this brief but pointed resolution:

The General Assembly
Considering that the Palestinian people is the principal party to the question of Palestine,
Invites the Palestine Liberation Organization, the representative of the Palestinian people, to participate in the deliberations of the General Assembly on the question of Palestine in plenary meetings.[84]

Though only one-sentence long, the proposed resolution introduced several unprecedented elements. It affirmed the Palestinian people, and not Arab refugees, as central to the question of Palestine. It also established the PLO, and not Jordan or the Arab League, as the representative of the Palestinian people. The resolution put the question of Palestine, as opposed to the Middle East, on the UN General Assembly's agenda for the first time in that body's history.[85] This effectively shifted the conflict from one about tenuous armistice lines between Israel and Arab states to one about the colonial condition afflicting a Palestinian people. Finally, it invited the PLO to address the Assembly in a plenary meeting, a right reserved only for states. In fact, the invitation represented an explicit attempt to change the UN's procedural rules.

Each week, Shaath met with an Arab ambassador to discuss strategy. He used well-established relationships to obtain more difficult endorsements. Fiji, for example, did not usually attend UNGA meetings because travel to New York was a prohibitive expenditure. Knowing that a robust Yemeni community existed in Fiji, Shaath convinced the Yemeni Ambassador to invite Fiji's UN diplomatic representatives to the Assembly and to pay for their travels. Similarly, Shaath worked with Iraq to bring Bhutan and Nepal on board and with Lebanon to bring on Brazil and Argentina, where the Lebanese diaspora had a significant presence. He kept track of his progress with a map of the world and indicated yes votes with a green thumbtack, no votes with a red one, and undecided states with orange. Shaath describes his efforts as "the most effective lobbying in my life."[86] His efficacy had much to do with the balance of power at the United Nations in 1974.

When Algerian Foreign Minister Abdelaziz Bouteflika assumed the presidency of the Twenty-Ninth General Assembly, he presided over an automatic majority of nonaligned states in a global context of ongoing, armed liberation struggles. These included wars of liberation in Namibia, South Africa, Mozambique, Angola, and Cape Verde, as well as the proxy war between the Soviet Union and the United States in Vietnam. Algeria emerged as a leader of the Global South during and after its own struggle for independence. In 1964, the newly independent state succeeded in establishing a development-oriented agency in the UN. Three years later, it convened the first major meeting of the G77. The G77 as well as the Non-Aligned Movement unabashedly criticized

Western powers' exploitation of the Third World, which these powers had pillaged and to which they owed their exceptional wealth.[87] Algeria strove to lead the nonaligned bloc in the movement to establish a new world order.

Bouteflika carried the flag of this mandate and found resonance within the General Assembly. Karma Nabulsi, a PLO cadre who later represented that organization at the UN, explained that the nonaligned ambassadors to the multilateral body "were leadership cadres who had been trained in their national battles and were now at the UN . . . they weren't diplomats and lawyers, they were fighters."They considered the United Nations as another "locus of battle."[88] The ascendance of the nonaligned bloc within the General Assembly threatened to unravel Western hegemonic control. The PLO entered the diplomatic fray in this context.

The nonaligned bloc had consistently endorsed Palestinian self-determination since the Bandung conference in 1955, where it established the Non-Aligned Movement.[89] The PLO itself had allied with revolutionary movements in Vietnam and Cambodia as well as across Africa.[90] Nabulsi explains that this bloc embraced the PLO and guided its cadre on how to "approach the UN as a battleground."[91]

In contrast, Israel allied itself with the West, particularly the United States. Concerned that the United States would drag them into a war in the Middle East, European states had begun to shift to a position of neutrality. This left the United States, which waged war on Vietnam, stymied the fall of apartheid, and vied for hegemonic control of Southwest Africa, as Israel's sole ally.[92] On its own, Israel had entrenched economic, military, and diplomatic relations with South Africa and Portugal. Israel's alliances with imperial powers helped to consecrate African-Arab solidarity. As early as 1973, the General Assembly condemned "the unholy alliance between Portuguese colonialism, South African racism, zionism, and Israeli imperialism."[93] When Shaath lobbied to pass his bold resolution, more than half of the UN's member states had no diplomatic relations with Israel.

On 14 October 1974, the General Assembly deliberated the resolution, which had successfully garnered seventy-two co-sponsors. Member states overwhelmingly supported extending an invitation to the PLO and affirming the centrality of the Palestinian people to the conflict. Although some supportive states remained reticent and insisted that the PLO should address the First Committee, in order to comply with UN procedures,[94] their protest was minimal, and Resolution 3210 passed with 105 votes in favor, 20 abstentions, and 4 votes against: from Israel, Bolivia, the Dominican Republic, and the United States.[95]

With UNGA Resolution 3210 in hand, Shaath returned to Lebanon, where Arafat appointed him to lead the committee to draft his UN speech. The committee included Mahmoud Darwish, Salah Khalaf, Farouq Kaddoumi, and Shafiq al Hout among others. Together, they reviewed several drafts before finalizing the text. Simultaneously, the PLO continued its efforts to obtain recognition. It was particularly concerned about the Arab League.[96]

The national liberation movement had yet to achieve official recognition from the regional body where Jordan sustained its challenge to the PLO's representational mandate. Jordan thought it should be responsible for returning the West Bank and that the PLO should be brought in later to negotiate the rights of the refugees. As for representation, it wanted to put that question, in the form of a referendum, to the Palestinians on both banks and let them decide, after liberation. The PLO had enhanced its political edge on this question in September 1974, when the head of its Political Department together with the Egyptian and Syrian Foreign Ministers convened in Cairo. These three parties had issued a tripartite communiqué affirming that

> an independent Palestinian authority is to be established in the Palestinian territory that is liberated by political or military means . . . [and the parties to this statement agree] to continue to support the Palestine Liberation Organization as being the sole legitimate representative of the Palestine people, and to help it to ensure steadfastness in the occupied territories.[97]

The terms set out in this communiqué represented a victory over Jordan's opposition and laid the groundwork for the Arab League's summit in Rabat in late October 1974. There, the Arab states, now with Jordan's acquiescence, recognized the PLO as "'the sole legitimate representative of the Palestinian people in any Palestinian territory that is liberated,' and reaffirmed the right of the Palestinian people under the PLO's command to establish an 'independent national authority.'"[98]

The League's endorsement crowned the PLO's international campaign for recognition and equipped PLO to represent the Palestine question on the international stage. Together with the endorsements of the Diplomatic Conference, the Non-Aligned Movement, and the Organization of Islamic Cooperation, as well as the Organization of African Unity, it meant that Arafat could go to the United Nations to address the international community on behalf of the Palestinian people.

The Dream of a Single Democratic State

The UN General Assembly hall brimmed with energy. Arafat's address to a plenary session marked the first time a non-state actor had taken the international podium. He captured this unique moment by placing the Palestine question within a global framework and on behalf of all struggles against imperialism, colonialism, and economic exploitation. He opened with words of welcome and reverence for newly established states:

> In the name of the people of Palestine I take this opportunity to congratulate three States that have recently been admitted to membership in the United Nations after obtaining their national independence: Guinea-Bissau, Bangladesh and Grenada. I extend our best wishes to the leadership of those Member States and wish them progress and success.[99]

Arafat then used his UN platform to rehearse the history of Palestine and to directly address the removal of its native inhabitants and their attendant erasure as a people. In doing so, he also set up an argument that Palestine should be a home to all faiths and not just to Judaism. He primed the audience for the concept of a single, democratic state:

> It pains our people greatly to witness the propagation of the myth that its homeland was a desert until it was made to bloom by the toil of foreign settlers, that it was a land without a people, and that the colonialist entity caused no harm to any human being. No: such lies must be exposed from this rostrum, for the world must know that Palestine was the cradle of the most ancient cultures and civilizations. . . . Our people continued to pursue

this enlightened policy until the establishment of the State of Israel and their dispersion. . . . Our people cannot but maintain the heritage of their ancestors in resisting the invaders, in assuming the privileged task of defending their native land, their Arab nationhood, their culture and civilization, and in safeguarding the cradle of monotheistic religion.

He then asked the audience:

Why therefore should I not dream and hope? For is not revolution the making real of dreams and hopes? So let us work together that my dream may be fulfilled, that I may return with my people out of exile, there in Palestine to live with this Jewish freedom-fighter and his partners, this Arab priest and his brothers, in one democratic State where Christian, Jew, and Muslim live in justice, equality, and fraternity.[100]

Fayez Abdullah Sayegh, a Palestinian scholar who earned his PhD degree at Georgetown University in 1949, had inspired the use of "dream" in this speech to describe the vision of a single state.[101] Sayegh, who had taught at Yale, Oxford, the American University, and Stanford, moved to Lebanon and established the Palestine Research Center in Beirut in 1965. He was deeply affected by the U.S. civil rights movement and developed a series of analytical texts exploring the settler-colonial and racial dimensions of Zionism.[102] He encouraged the drafting committee to use Dr. Martin Luther King Jr.'s framework of a dream for racial justice and equality in the United States to frame the Palestinian dream and better appeal to a U.S.-based audience.[103] Arafat drove this point home directly when he said:

Let us remember that the Jews of Europe and the United States have been known to lead the struggles for secularism and the separation of Church and State. They have also been known to fight against discrimination on religious grounds. How then can they continue to support the most fanatic, discriminatory and closed of nations in its policy?[104]

Arafat brilliantly made the appeal for a secular democracy. But according to Shaath, this was a compromise for the Chairman who believed the two-state solution, while not optimal, was more pragmatic.[105] In some ways, Arafat laid the groundwork for that option as well.

Arafat framed the emancipatory vision for Palestine as the legal right to national self-determination that has been "consecrated in the United Nations Charter and has been repeatedly confirmed in resolutions adopted by this august body since the drafting of the Charter."[106] Arafat's invocation of the UN Charter also implied Israel's right to enjoy territorial integrity and freedom from external intervention, as captured in the Charter's first two articles. By going to the United Nations and turning to international law, the PLO sought to leverage the very same legal framework and principles that also enshrined and protected Israel's sovereignty. Placing the dream of a single state in the framework of UN principles created enough ambiguity for the PLO to pursue its ambitions without alienating potential allies or defying the PNC's mandate for the liberation of Palestine.

International legal norms regarding self-determination and state sovereignty at once embodied the rights of Palestinian freedom and the competing rights of Israel's viability, and on its own, legal doctrine could not resolve this conflict. The question would have to be settled politically. Salah Salah, a political leader of the Popular Front for the Liberation of Palestine, had cautioned that the PLO should approach the United Nations only if it was "willing to fight more and militarily resist, otherwise the law will be used against us [Palestinians]."[107] In November 1974, that military context existed both among Palestinian guerilla fighters based in Lebanon as well as other fighters throughout the globe in armed liberation movements.[108] Accordingly, Arafat ended his rousing speech by emphasizing his role as a militant and the threat of the use of force:

> Today, I have come bearing an olive branch and a freedom fighter's gun. Do not let the olive branch fall from my hand. I repeat: do not let the olive branch fall from my hand. War flares up in Palestine. And yet it is in Palestine that peace will be born.[109]

The General Assembly erupted in thunderous applause. Arafat's reception unsettled the United States and Israel. Henry Kissinger was furious and warned that the energy curried by the PLO Chairman was likely to turn into a massive onslaught on [the United States] in another year or two. . . . That is totally wrong of the United Nations to treat the head of the liberation movement with so much respect.[110]

Israel was in an even worse position. The General Assembly had voted to limit its Ambassador's right of reply to Arafat's speech to a single intervention at the end of the day (with 75 votes in favor to 23 against and 18 abstentions).[111] Arafat flew to Cuba on that same day, leaving Shaath and Farouq Kaddoumi to reap the rewards of the momentum he generated.[112] Together, they laid the groundwork for two additional fundamental UN resolutions that edified the juridical status of Palestinian peoplehood and affirmed Palestinians' right to self-determination.

Resolution 3236 was a remarkable piece of legal work. It established an alternative legal framework for achieving a diplomatic settlement for the Palestinian question, thus circumventing the constraints imposed earlier by Security Council Resolution 242. General Assembly Resolution 3236 affirmed the Palestinian right to self-determination and to "national independence and sovereignty," as well as the right of refugees to return to their homes and property.[113] Whereas Resolution 242 had negated the existence of a Palestinian nation and predicated Israeli withdrawal from Arab territories on Arab nations' establishing permanent peace with Israel, Resolution 3236 affirmed Palestinian self-determination without preconditions. It also left the geographic scope of that self-determination vague, in order to achieve legal sanction for restoring Palestinian sovereignty over the entirety of what had been Mandate Palestine, and not just the West Bank and the Gaza Strip. This legal tactic was not lost on other states.

Some supporters of Palestinian self-determination clarified that their vote did not negate Israel's sovereign rights. Liberia, for example, voted for the resolution but its Ambassador explained that

the basic principles in Security Council resolutions 242 (1967) and 338 (1973) still stand. . . . We believe the draft resolution lays the groundwork for self-determination or independence for the Palestinian people with a view to both the State of Israel and a Palestinian state existing within recognized and secure boundaries in the area.[114]

The Norwegian Ambassador began by affirming Palestinian aspirations and their centrality to resolving the conflict, but explained that Resolution 242 "must be the point of departure for a [peace] settlement." It is essential, he explained, "because it contained . . . the principle of respect for and acknowledgment of the sovereignty, territorial integrity and political independence of every State and its right to live in peace within secure and recognized boundaries, free from threats or acts of force," which applies to every state including Israel.[115] Norway voted against the resolution.

The Ambassador representing Barbados understood that the Palestinian people exist, but raised concerns about whether "Palestine" referred to the West Bank and Jordan or to the "geopolitical area, which is now occupied by the State of Israel." Jamil Murad Baroody, the Saudi Arabian Ambassador, raised a point of order, reflecting the position of many Afro-Asian countries. He explained that Palestine refers to "that geographical entity which was defined by the League of Nations in the Covenant and placed under a British Mandate."[116] Baroody's remarks contradicted claims that Resolution 3236 designated the Occupied Territories as the site of Palestinian self-determination. The General Assembly never resolved this ambiguity. It passed the resolution with 89 votes in favor, 8 against, and 37 abstentions.

Whereas Resolution 3236 provided a legal route for the PLO to pursue a diplomatic resolution on its own terms, Resolution 3237 definitively settled the question of Palestinian peoplehood and representation. It invited the PLO to be a nonmember observer in the United Nations and authorized it to participate in all "work and sessions of the General Assembly."[117] This resolution afforded the PLO all rights of a member state with the exception of the right to vote. Such a status had hitherto been limited to nonmember states, like the Vatican, and to certain regional organizations, like the Organization of African Unity. As such, Resolution 3237 also espoused the tension between the PLO's revolutionary mandate and its pursuit of a state. The United Kingdom protested because the PLO

is not the government of an existing State; it has not been recognized by anybody as the government of a State; it does not purport to be one . . .

. . . [And yet] the PLO is being treated as though it were a Member State of the United Nations.[118]

The British Ambassador cautioned that the precedent would "bring into question the nature of the United Nations as it has hitherto been accepted."[119] The overwhelming majority of the General Assembly disagreed. As put most succinctly by the Philippines delegation, UN recognition of the PLO followed a series of significant precedents. These included the PLO's participation as an observer delegation to the UN Conference on the Law of the Sea in August 1974 and its recognition by the League of Arab States as the sole and legitimate representative of the Palestinian people.[120] The Assembly passed Resolution 3237, demonstrating, once again, the lawmaking authority of the Global South.

The PLO successfully created new law to establish its legal status as a nation entitled to self-determination, without specifying whether it would be realized in place of Israel or in the territories it occupied. Together Resolutions 3236 and 3237 provided the PLO, and particularly its pragmatic elements, the legal framework to participate in a peace process without having to recognize or negotiate with Israel and on a basis other than Security Council Resolution 242.

South African Legacies: Zionism Is a form of Racism

Following its momentous achievements in 1974, the PLO embarked on a multifaceted strategy that sustained its policy of revolutionary struggle and statist appeals. McMurtrie Godley, then the U.S. Ambassador to Lebanon, described the PLO's approach as borrowing from the North Vietnamese model of "talk[ing] while] fight[ing]."[121] On the diplomatic plane, the PLO continued to establish its presence in all UN specialized agencies as well as multilateral organizations, including the International Telecommunications Union, the World Health Organization, the International Labor Organization, the Universal Postal Union, the International Civil Aviation Organization, and the UN Economic and Social Council (ECOSOC).[122] It also embarked on a campaign to exclude Israel.

On the heels of the PLO's strong showing at the United Nations, the United Nations Educational, Scientific and Cultural Organization (UNESCO) voted to withhold aid from Israel and to exclude that state from its European regional group.[123] Exclusion as a strategic tactic imbued Resolutions 3236 and 3237 with substantive meaning as a bid to supplant, rather than complement, Israeli sovereignty. The United States withheld its funding of the UN agency in protest but failed to reverse the decision. The PLO's move within UNESCO was the beginning of a much bolder campaign to unseat Israel from the General Assembly, following the South African model.

In November of 1974, under Abdelaziz Bouteflika's leadership, the General Assembly had suspended South Africa as a member state. Doing so required changing the rules of the United Nations. Since 1965, the General Assembly, led by African states, had rejected South Africa's UN credentials owing to that state's violation of UN Charter principles, failure to represent the majority of South Africans, and institutionalized racial discrimination.[124] The General Assembly could not, however, expel South Africa from the UN, as questions of membership are within the exclusive purview of the Security Council.[125] In 1974, the Security Council considered expelling South Africa from the UN at eleven of its meetings, but the United States, the United Kingdom, and France opposed the initiative, arguing that expulsion should be an absolute last resort. To overcome the Council's intransigence, Bouteflika put forward the interpretation that the rejection of a state's credentials effectively suspended its membership. Western states protested that this decision violated the UN Charter. The General Assembly, led by a coalition of African, Asian, and Arab states, sustained Bouteflika's decision by vote of 91 to 22, with 10 abstentions. In effect, Bouteflika established a precedent that the General Assembly could suspend a member state by an UNGA presidential ruling, without a recommendation from the Security Council.[126] Daniel Moynihan, then U.S. Ambassador, noted that while the General Assembly decision contravened UN law, no one wanted to defend apartheid, and so the other member states accepted the defeat.[127]

The PLO took inspiration from South Africa's suspension, and began to mobilize a similar move against Israel. In July 1975, it developed the momentum for this campaign at the Islamic Conference of Foreign Ministers in Jeddah, with thirty-nine heads of state in attendance.[128] The Organization of Islamic Cooperation endorsed the move. The PLO next set its sights on the Organization of African Unity summit that was to be held in Kampala, Uganda, in early August. The issue proved extremely contentious.

Egypt, which had raised no objections to the proposal in Jeddah, emerged as the primary force of opposition within the Organization of African Unity meeting. Egypt had entered into its first interim peace agreement with Israel, negotiated by the United States, in early 1975. It feared that an Arab-led initiative to unseat Israel would undermine its ability to recoup the Sinai through diplomacy and, more generally, would sour its relations with the United States.[129] In addition to Egyptian opposition, several Black African states withheld their support in protest of limited Arab aid to the continent's poorest countries, whose financial crisis had deepened as a result of the quadrupling of oil prices.[130] As a compromise position, the Organization of African Unity adopted a resolution to "reinforce the pressure exerted on Israel at the United Nations and its specialized agencies, including the possibility of eventually depriving it of its membership."[131] The expulsion of Israel nevertheless remained a real possibility as the Non-Aligned Movement planned to address it at its conference in Lima, Peru, in late August.[132]

In Peru, the ministerial meeting of eighty developing states granted full membership to the PLO and welcomed it to the NAM Coordinating Committee. Peru's President, who was chairing the NAM meeting, "told three-hundred cheering delegates that he hoped the Palestinians would soon have their own state."[133] Despite this enthusiasm, the body failed to endorse a resolution to expel Israel. In addition to internal conflicts, Egypt once again emerged as the primary force of opposition.

The PLO's pragmatist camp viewed the expulsion initiative as enhancing its chances of being invited to negotiate for the return of Palestinian lands. To that end, the mere threat of Israel's expulsion was beneficial. The problem, according to Anis Fawzi Kassem, a legal scholar and later adviser to the PLO, was that "no one could answer the question of how the PLO should translate its legal achievements into diplomatic victories."[134]

The PLO's pragmatists tried to do just that by indicating the movement's readiness for a compromise and its eagerness to open a direct channel with the United States.[135] In a May 1975 meeting with Democratic Senator Howard Baker, Arafat tried to assuage U.S. concerns about the PLO by explaining that the goal for a single, democratic state for Jews and Arabs was not a short-term dream and that Palestinians would be willing to establish a state on any land "Israel can be gotten to give up ... even Gaza."[136] U.S. State Department and National Security Council officials urged the Gerald Ford administration to enter into negotiations with the PLO, but Kissinger remained firmly opposed to its inclusion.

In September 1975, Kissinger entered into an agreement with Israel that directly rebuffed the threats embodied by Resolution 3236. In preparation for the second Egyptian-Israeli interim peace agreement, Kissinger oversaw the establishment of the Memorandum of Understanding (MOU) between Israel and the United States. The MOU conditioned negotiations with the PLO on the PLO's acceptance of three demands: recognition of Israel, renunciation of armed violence, and acceptance of Resolutions 242 and 338. Moreover, the United States conditioned the participation of "any possible additional state, group, or organization" on the acquiescence of the "initial participants," effectively giving Israel veto power over the PLO's participation should it accept the terms of the 1975 MOU.[137]

On the same day, Egypt and Israel signed their second Interim Peace Agreement, or Sinai II. It reaffirmed a commitment to a comprehensive ceasefire and stipulated that neither side would resort to military force, the threat of the use of force, or a military blockade against the other side.[138] The agreement effectively neutralized Egypt as a potential military threat. The following month, Egypt entered into a large-scale economic aid package with the United States that cemented its shift from Moscow to Washington. Egypt's military neutralization and pivot towards U.S. tutelage indelibly transformed the geopolitical balance of power and further reduced pressure on Israel to deal with the PLO.[139]

The regional euphoria evident in the aftermath of the 1973 War was quickly fading. In the year since the triumphant passage of Resolution 3236, Israel contractually secured U.S. assurances to maintain its regional prowess and significantly diminished its regional military threats. In an effort to recalibrate the balance of power, the PLO together with the nonaligned bloc intensified their UN activities when the General Assembly reconvened in September 1975. In response to intransigent U.S. opposition to the PLO's participation in negotiations, the General Assembly passed Resolution 3375, calling for PLO inclusion "in all efforts, deliberations, and conferences on the Middle East which are held under the auspices of the United Nations, on an equal footing with other parties on the basis of resolution 3236."[140] Gravely concerned that no progress had been achieved to fulfill Palestinian rights in the intervening year, the Assembly also established the UN Committee on the Inalienable Rights of the Palestinian People.[141]

Within a year, the committee submitted a proposal of implementation to the UN Security Council. It included a two-phase plan for the return and restitution of Palestinian refugees displaced in 1948 and 1967; a timetable for the withdrawal of Israeli forces from the West Bank and Gaza; the presence of a temporary peacekeeping force to protect Palestinian civilians; the temporary stewardship of the West Bank and Gaza by the UN and the Arab League, until these territories could be handed over to the PLO; the cessation of all Israeli settlement activity; the recognition by Israel of the applicability of the Fourth Geneva Convention to the Occupied Territories; and the creation of all means necessary to establish the self-determination and independence of the Palestinian people. The United States would exercise its Security Council veto to quash this resolution in June 1976.[142] All of the NAM's collective power and all the momentum of the global anticolonial movement failed to alter the geopolitical realities that the United States engendered and sustained.

The NAM did not relent. During a UN General Assembly session in 1975, Cuba, South Yemen, Libya, Somalia, and Syria jointly introduced an amendment to a resolution regarding the Decade for Action to Combat Racism and Racial Discrimination (Decade Against Racism), in a meeting of the Third Committee. African states had initiated the Decade Against Racism to further delegitimize the apartheid regime in South African and Namibia. Other efforts included the drafting of the Convention on the Suppression and Punishment of the Crime of Apartheid, which was approved by the UN General Assembly in 1973 and came into force in 1976.[143] The nonaligned coalition sought to amend the Decade Against Racism so that wherever the terms apartheid, racism, colonialism, racial discrimination, and alien domination appeared, the word "Zionism" would be inserted into the text as well. They also proposed to add a new operative paragraph that considered "Zionism as a form of racial discrimination to be included in the Decade."[144] Having failed to achieve the requisite support to unseat Israel from the United Nations, the nonaligned bloc strove to delegitimize Israel's constitutive ideology and expel it by other means. This would lead to tabling Resolution 3379 declaring that Zionism is a form of racism and racial discrimination.

The PLO did not lead this initiative but did approve it.[145] Palestine Research Center founder Fayez Sayegh, who now represented Kuwait to the United Nations, suggested the idea to the Kuwaiti Foreign Minister, Sheikh Sabah Al

Ahmad. The Minister encouraged him and pledged full support.[146] As part of his scholarly pursuits, Sayegh had developed a rigorous racial analysis and legal argument demonstrating the applicability of the 1965 UN International Convention on the Elimination of All Forms of Racial Discrimination to Israeli policies, and more generally, Zionism.[147] Sayegh participated in the committee deliberations on the resolution, making his case in these words:

> Zionism, essentially, vests certain rights—very important rights—in some people and denies them to others. For example: it says that a Jew, simply by virtue of being a Jew, has a "right" to "return" to the Palestinian territories occupied by Israel, even if he had never been there before! But it also says that his compatriot, a non-Jew, has no such right; and that the indigenous Palestinian Arab, dislodged in 1948 or 1967, also has no such right—because he is not a Jew. Here we have a clear-cut case of "distinctions," "preferences," exclusions" and "restrictions"—that is to say, of "discrimination"—based solely on the basis of whether a person is or is not a Jew. And Jewishness, all Zionists would agree, is a national/ethnic bond; it is, under Israeli law, determined—for the vast majority of the persons involved—by birth and ancestry. Therefore, in accordance with the authoritative United Nations definition, the discrimination which is inherent in Zionism is incontestably a form of racial discrimination—for it is based on "descent" or "national origin" or "ethnic origin," all of which are subsumed under the generic concept of "race."[148]

Sayegh did not limit his racial analysis of Zionism to the distinctions between Jews and non-Jews but explored how Zionism produced racial stratification among Jews themselves. He explained:

> Like a cancer, racism has a propensity for expansion: it defies containment. Having adopted a racist approach towards non-Jews, Zionism soon came to draw a color-line or a racial line among the Jews themselves. The Zionist myth of "one Jewish people" was exploded as soon as Jews from different cultural, ethnic and racial backgrounds were assembled together. Oriental Jews and Black Jews found themselves subject to discrimination by other Jews—i.e., by the Jews of the "White Jewish Establishment."[149]

The proposed resolution caused a tremendous uproar. Declaring Zionism to be a form of racism would reconfigure the Arab-Israeli conflict from a peace-making imperative aimed at reconciling Israel's establishment and Palestinian national self-determination to an antisubjugation imperative wrought by Zionist settler-colonization as a structure. In the latter case, it would no longer be sufficient to reform Israel and call upon it to withdraw from Arab territories; instead, Zionist laws, policies, and institutions would have to be dismantled. Resolution 3379 sought to dismantle Jewish national supremacy as a political structure predicated upon the removal, forced exile, dispossession, second-class status, and elision of the Palestinian people. Unlike Resolution 3236, which was ambiguous as to the future of Jewish-Zionist settler sovereignty, Resolution 3379 unequivocally rejected it.

Western states saw this move as unnecessarily aggressive and divisive.[150] Livid, the UK Ambassador exclaimed, "it risks bringing this whole organization into disrepute. It is exactly the wrong issue raised in the wrong way and at the wrong time, and we will have none of it at all."[151]

Of the thirty-eight Black African UN member states, five opposed the resolution, and twelve abstained. They espoused reasonable concerns that the resolution undermined global support for the Decade Against Racism. The resolution on Zionism was a single part of a three-part proposal. Part one condemned the apartheid regime in South Africa and part two supported a world conference against racism to be convened in Ghana. Introduction of part three, which condemned Zionism as racism, dramatically diminished Western support for the entire resolution. Western states were prepared to condemn antiblack racism, especially in South Africa and Namibia, but were reticent in regard to the question of Zionist domination of Palestinian Arabs. In fact, inclusion of the question of Palestine in the Decade Against Racism provided a useful pretext for Western states to withdraw their support entirely. This concerned African states, especially. For example, Zambia had no diplomatic relations with Israel and condemned its "expansionist policies" and "the racial overtones of its activities in the occupied Arab territories." Despite its support of the resolution's substance, Zambia abstained on the resolution because of its dedication "to the total success of the Decade and does not therefore welcome anything that would detract from this."[152]

The General Assembly passed Resolution 3379 with a vote of 72 for, including Egypt, 35 against, and 32 abstentions. The United States and Israel were shaken; members of the U.S. Congress introduced dozens of bills to reduce U.S. financial contributions to the United Nations.[153] The nonaligned bloc's intervention in the multilateral institution on behalf of Palestinians was so successful that the Jewish Telegraph Agency commented, for Israel, "1975 could not have ended too soon."[154] The resolution on Zionism was a hard-won victory, but in the shadows of a failed attempt to unseat Israel from the United Nations, it demonstrated the potential as well as the limits of UN advocacy.

The Limits of UN Advocacy

At the end of 1975, the PLO continued its precedent-setting strides and became the first non-state entity to formally participate in a UN Security Council discussion. The Security Council invited it to participate after Israel launched an aerial bombing campaign against Palestinian refugee camps in southern Lebanon that killed over fifty civilians.[155] The PLO's participation contravened UN Charter procedures, demonstrating, yet again, the nonaligned bloc's ability to rewrite UN rules.[156] The move infuriated Western powers, which considered that bloc's lawmaking capacity a destabilizing threat to their dominance. Kissinger alleged that "ideological confrontation, bloc voting, and new attempts to manipulate the Charter to achieve unilateral ends threaten to turn the United Nations into a weapon of political warfare."[157] Nonetheless, the PLO and its allies failed to leverage these gains to their ultimate advantage because of geopolitical developments.

Matters had become worse for the PLO upon Syria's intervention in the Lebanese civil war. In April 1975, tensions between some sectors of the Lebanese government together with its Christian militias on the one hand and the radical left Lebanese National Movement and the PLO on the other reached a head. The PLO had succeeded in pushing the Lebanese Army out of the Palestinian refugee camps in 1969, and in 1975, the Lebanese National Movement seemed to be on the cusp of grasping control of the state.[158] Its success had the potential to significantly enhance Palestinian efforts to militarily confront Israel and/or apply the requisite pressure to enter negotiations. Then Syria intervened to crush the radical insurgency. Syrian President Hafez Asad was intent on leveraging Syria's control over various forces within Lebanon, in the service of his broader goal of a "comprehensive strategic balance" with Israel.[159] Asad's control ensured that neither the Lebanese right nor the left would enhance the risk posed by Israel. In the former scenario, the right-wing alliance risked paving a path for an Israeli offensive. In the latter, uncalculated moves by a radical, militant Lebanese and Palestinian coalition allied with Iraq and Libya "could drag Syria into a premature and costly confrontation with Israel."[160] Acting with U.S. and Arab approval, Syria launched a military campaign that reestablished the rule of a delegitimized Lebanese state.[161] The Syrian intervention compounded the fracturing of Arab solidarity that was already a reality, with such events as Egypt's turn to the United States and Jordan's expulsion of the PLO in 1970. Arafat was personally disturbed and signaled an even greater willingness to compromise than in the past.[162]

The Thirteenth Session of the Palestinian National Council convened in March 1977 and formally endorsed the PLO's participation in negotiations based on Resolution 3236; this signaled a victory for the PLO's pragmatist camp, which sought to achieve a diplomatic resolution.[163] In June 1977, things appeared more hopeful for the PLO, as U.S. President Jimmy Carter's administration affirmed the right to a "homeland for the Palestinians." In a brief diplomatic détente, the United States and the PLO agreed to enter into negotiations based on Security Council Resolution 242 so long as it was amended to reflect Palestinian national rights. The Carter administration proposed that rather than amend the resolution, the PLO should accept it with reservations. The PLO insisted on an amendment, and Arafat instructed a committee to draft various formulations.[164] Anwar Sadat's surprise visit to Jerusalem in November 1977 would abruptly halt this diplomatic breakthrough. Without securing a resolution to the Palestinian question in his negotiations with Israel, Sadat directly addressed the Israeli Knesset and told its members, "We really and truly welcome you to live among us in peace and security."[165]

Arab states reacted severely. They convened in Tripoli and established a diplomatic and economic boycott of Egypt.[166] The regional backlash placed intense pressure on the PLO to align itself with an Arab coalition opposed to Egypt, and limited its ability to pursue an independent diplomatic resolution. These shifting tides signaled a retreat from the pragmatist platform and a win for the Rejectionist Front.[167] At the United Nations, in response to yet another

U.S. veto in the Security Council, the General Assembly established a permanent secretariat for Palestinian rights.[168] Thus the tug-of-war between the nonaligned bloc and the West at the United Nations continued but failed to alter the regional balance of power that sustained Palestinian subjugation. The Camp David Accords reached in 1978 and 1979, which established a permanent peace between Egypt and Israel, cemented this political impasse.

The Egyptian-Israeli peace process fleshed out an autonomy framework for limited Palestinian self-rule in the West Bank and the Gaza Strip. The first part of the Accords, The Framework for Peace in The Middle East (1978), proposed a five-year interim phase in which to establish a self-governing authority and a permanent status phase to be inaugurated by the third year of the interim arrangement. The final status agreement would be consecrated in a peace treaty between Israel and Jordan.[169] The stipulation of establishing a treaty with Jordan, acting as the Palestinians' representative, reflected Israel's enduring denial of Palestinian claims of a right to national self-determination.

In its agreement with Egypt, Israel contemplated dealing with Palestinians but not a Palestinian people. The latter would imply the establishment of an independent state, whereas the former implied dealings with a scattered polity with whom a host of arrangements could be conceived, including a self-governing authority. In line with this logic, the Framework for Peace deliberately excluded reference to Palestinians in the diaspora, and to the PLO in particular. Instead, it refers to representatives of the "inhabitants of the West Bank and Gaza."[170] Resolutions 3236, 3237, and 3379 were seemingly impotent in the face of Egyptian-Israeli bilateral arrangements.

Menachem Begin, the Israeli Prime Minister negotiating this peace with Egypt, was not coy about his intentions. He made it known that he did not believe Palestinians were a people, rather, they were just "Palestinian Arabs residing in Judea, Samaria, and the Gaza District."[171] Moreover, should the Framework for Peace be implemented, he planned to announce Israeli sovereignty over the West Bank and the Gaza Strip at the end of the five-year transition period and to refuse a return of East Jerusalem, a return to the 1967 borders, and the establishment of a Palestinian state. In a speech to Jewish leaders in New York in September 1978, Begin repeated Israel's legal argument for rejecting Resolution 242's prohibition on the acquisition of territory by force. He explained that because the prohibition is found in the resolution's preamble, it has no binding force. Moreover, in a war of self-defense, Begin continued, it is 'the Golden Rule, under international law, [that] territorial changes are not only permissible, but necessary.'[172]

In October 1978, in response to the Framework for Peace, Palestinians in the West Bank and the Gaza Strip convened national congresses in their respective territories. Both congresses, deploying the slogan "No to self-government, yes to the PLO," formally rejected and condemned the Camp David agreement.[173] In November 1978, the PLO, along with the participants at that year's Arab League summit in Baghdad, also categorically rejected the Framework for Peace. While rejecting the autonomy framework, the summit participants did gesture positively towards conciliation with Israel. They endorsed Israeli withdrawal from the West Bank and the Gaza Strip and the establishment of a Palestinian state, thereby signaling de facto recognition of Israel.[174]

Nothing came of the summit's conciliatory overtures or of the Camp David agreement. Sadat signed the peace treaty without exacting assurances regarding the West Bank and the Gaza Strip, though he demanded them in an exchange of letters with Begin.[175] Shortly thereafter, an Egyptian member of the Islamic Jihad assassinated Sadat, leaving Israel to implement its version of autonomy in the territories.

The Begin government was determined to establish limited Palestinian autonomy in order to mute Palestinian claims of a right to self-determination and to undermine the PLO. It embarked on plans to establish a civilian administration in the Occupied Territories. Menachem Milson, who was an adviser on Arab affairs to the Israeli military government in the West Bank and Gaza and later headed the civil administration of Judea and Samaria, headed these efforts and offered local Palestinian leaders the responsibility of assuming all civil functions of the administration. Hanan Ashrawi, a comparative literature scholar who had established the Department of English at Birzeit University in the West Bank and was a prominent activist, was among the leaders Milson approached. She recalls rejecting his invitation by explaining:

> We are perfectly capable of running our lives. You can leave and we can
> run our lives. We want to be free and not under the employment of the

occupation. What we want is for you to leave us alone . . . we are not col-
laborators. We are not going to accept any functional responsibilities while
you maintain the power.[176]

In addition to appointing moderate local leaders to lead these administrative bodies, the Begin government established Village Leagues, Palestinian
local councils empowered by Israel to govern and suppress Palestinian protests
alongside the Israeli army. Palestinians in the territories revolted against the
Village Leagues and the civil administration, leading to violent and deadly confrontations between March and April of 1982. Begin's efforts to install limited
autonomy led by a moderate and collaborator class of Palestinian local leaders
had failed.[177]

In June 1982, Israel invaded Lebanon with the aim of destroying and routing
the PLO.[178] Israeli forces marching from southern Lebanon arrived at Beirut
within eight days and established a peace treaty with Syria, ending the hostilities. Israel then remained in Lebanon, however, and laid siege to Beirut in areas
where the PLO and Lebanese national paramilitary forces remained and where
they withstood a concerted attack for nearly three months. Israel did not succeed
in crushing the PLO, but did force its withdrawal. By 30 August 1982, Arafat
and approximately 4,000 Palestinians were evacuated from Beirut, under the
supervision of a multinational force, and taken to Athens, Greece. The PLO
eventually established a new headquarters in Tunis, Tunisia.

The impact of this juncture cannot be overstated. Several Palestinian political
parties, and primarily the Popular Front for the Liberation of Palestine, believed
that the evacuation from Beirut was merely a setback that did not require a
reevaluation of strategy. However, the mainstream PLO leadership considered
it a more decisive blow to its banner of armed struggle.[179] The evacuation from
Lebanon deprived the PLO of its territorial base and, with it, a vast sociopolitical
structure. This included the 300,000 to 400,000 Palestinian refugees who had
fulfilled the PLO's military and administrative demands and had constituted a
vibrant political base that animated the national liberation movement.[180] Forced
removal from Beirut gutted the organization of its structure, fractured its base,
and spread its leadership across nine countries.[181] Additionally, despite several
notable exceptions, armed struggle fell into abeyance; Egypt, Syria, and Jordan

posed no risk of a conventional war against Israel, and, with the PLO removed to Tunis, its ability to launch cross-border attacks was all but extinguished. Significantly weakened, the mainstream PLO leadership began to pivot towards Arab governments that enjoyed friendly relations with the United States, in an effort to establish their own direct contacts. From late 1982 onwards, the PLO's primary activity, led by Arafat himself, became diplomatic in nature, with the goal of negotiations.

The beginning of the first Palestinian uprising, or *intifada*, in December 1987, would consolidate the resolve of the PLO's mainstream leadership to establish a diplomatic resolution. This massive civil uprising shifted the locus of Palestinian authority from the diaspora to the West Bank and Gaza and threatened the relevance of the PLO. A series of other developments in the late eighties and early nineties would increasingly unravel the PLO's authority and diminish its leverage.

Within less than four years of the start of the intifada, the United States and the Soviet Union presented an almost identical version of the failed autonomy framework, originally proposed by Begin and Sadat, to the Palestinians again. This time, the Palestinians agreed to entertain the proposal, thus planting the seeds for the Oslo peace process and finally resolving the uncertainty and tension regarding the PLO's strategic vision and the geographic scope of Palestinian self-determination.

Chapter 4

THE OSLO PEACE PROCESS

So first of all let us call the agreement by its real name: an instrument of
Palestinian surrender, a Palestinian Versailles. What makes it worse is that
for at least the past fifteen years the PLO could have negotiated a better
arrangement than this modified Allon Plan, one not requiring so many
unilateral concessions to Israel.

—Edward Said, "The Morning After," October 1993

ON 8 DECEMBER 1987, an Israeli driver of an Israeli tractor-trailer ploughed
head on into two vans transporting Palestinian workers on their way back from
Israel to Gaza, killing four Palestinians.[1] The next day, Israeli forces shot dead
Hatem Abu-Sisi, a seventeen-year-old protestor among the crowd of Palestinians mourning the dead and protesting the arbitrary nature of their killing.[2]
These lethal confrontations unfolded in the twentieth year of Israel's military
occupation and in the context of mounting confrontations between Palestinians
and the Israeli army across the Gaza Strip and the West Bank. Israel's attempts
to forcefully quell the protests backfired. The clashes across both territories
escalated, culminating in a sustained grassroots uprising, known as the intifada.

Civil disobedience strategies, including the boycott of Israeli economic goods
and institutions, characterized the broad-based protest movement. Though seemingly spontaneous, the eruption of the uprising came on the heels of a decade
of mass-based organizing. Students, women, professionals in many areas, and
laborers responded to Palestinian ambitions for independence by combining
national and social liberation. The Palestinian civilians under occupation made

themselves ungovernable. Decentralized popular and national committees organized communities to meet their own needs, from creating alternative economies, schooling, day-care centers, and ways of ensuring food security to promoting "social and political consciousness to sustain the intifada."[3] Broad-based and inclusive, the uprising featured boys and girls as well as young men and women throwing stones, burning tires, and hurling Molotov cocktails.

The Israeli army responded forcefully. Yitzhak Rabin, then Israel's Defense Minister, instructed soldiers to break the bones of children caught throwing stones.[4] The Swedish branch of Save the Children documented that by 1989, nearly 30,000 children had required medical treatment.[5] Israel's response to Palestinian resistance highlighted the asymmetry of power and violence between the state and the people under its occupation, and this response took place before the watchful gaze of international news cameras and reporters.

The intifada proved to be a watershed in the Palestinian struggle for freedom. Israel's systematic and decades-long domination of Palestinians was revealed as not viable. This shift compelled Israel and the United States to reevaluate their trenchant opposition to negotiations with Palestinians. In the midst of the uprising, U.S. Secretary of State George Shultz developed a proposal for a short timetable for negotiations based on UN Security Council Resolutions 242 and 338.[6] Shultz made repeated appeals to Palestinian leaders in the territories, who consistently responded that the proper channel for discussion was the Palestine Liberation Organization.[7] In his capacity as Defense Minister, Rabin's mandate was to find ways to end the intifada. His attempts to use brute force and offer Palestinians limited autonomy, as opposed to national liberation, failed. His inability to squash the uprising brutally, together with diminished army morale, eventually softened Rabin's harsh stance towards direct negotiations with Palestinians, and he proposed entering into talks with a Palestinian delegation to be determined by local elections. In May 1989, Israel subsequently amended and adopted this plan, marking the first time Israel had recognized that the future of the territories had to be determined with Palestinians and not other Arab states.[8]

Initial Israeli and U.S. overtures resulted in track two negotiations between Palestinian and Israeli representatives. The meetings at this informal level revealed the vast gap between the parties. Palestinians demanded recognition of their right to self-determination and independence. The most Israel was willing to concede was the establishment of limited self-rule and truncated political and economic rights. The 1990 Gulf War helped break this impasse and catalyzed the Middle East Peace Conference.

In early August 1990, Iraqi President Saddam Hussein led his country's invasion and occupation of Kuwait, claiming that the Mandate system had arbitrarily separated this territory from the rest of Iraq.[9] The United States established an international coalition to defend Kuwait, with thirty-nine countries, including Egypt, Bahrain, Morocco, Oman, Qatar, Saudi Arabia, Syria, and the United Arab Emirates, taking part.[10] Believing that the international coalition would not intervene, Arafat supported Iraq. The U.S.-led coalition's swift defeat of Iraqi forces and the liberation of Kuwait left the PLO financially vulnerable and politically isolated. Kuwait expelled 400,000 Palestinians in retaliation for their leadership's support of the Iraqi occupation, diminishing a significant source of remittances to Palestinians in the territories as well as to the PLO.[11] The coalition's victory in the Gulf War also enhanced U.S. status in the Middle East, although it left the United States with a diplomatic debt owed to those Arab states that had joined the coalition against Iraq.[12] The United States sought to leverage this heightened influence and pay its debt by embarking on a regional peace process.

By the end of the war, the U.S. Navy had come to directly control the Persian Gulf, thus diminishing Israel's value as a military force and a U.S. proxy in the region.[13] The Soviet Union had also collapsed, and Israel's Prime Minister at the time, Yitzhak Shamir, sought U.S. support to absorb nearly one million Russian Jews.[14] The Bush administration threatened to withhold 10 billion USD in loan guarantees to support Israel's absorption of Russian Jews if Israel did not initiate a settlement freeze. It would be the only time the United States applied pressure on Israel throughout the peace process. Believing that it stood to lose more than it could gain if it opposed U.S. efforts, Shamir signaled his willingness to participate in the peace process.[15]

The United States, together with the Soviet Union, formally initiated the Middle East Peace Conference with a letter of invitation to the parties to convene in Madrid in late October 1991. The objective of the process was "real peace" between Israel, Syria, Lebanon, Jordan, and the Palestinians. Just as Henry Kissinger had disaggregated the Arab-Israeli talks in 1978, intending to establish separate treaties between each country and Israel in order to then impose a peace agreement on the Palestinians, none of these negotiations between Israel and each of the other countries would be linked. Moreover, Palestinians would be allowed to join the proceedings only as part of a joint Jordanian-Palestinian delegation.[16] According to the Madrid Letter of Invitation, the process with the Palestinians would proceed in two stages: the first would establish "interim self-government arrangements" in the occupied territory over the course of five years. The second would commence no later than the beginning of the third year of autonomous self-governance and would decide the permanent status of more controversial issues, such as Palestinian refugees, Israeli settlements, and Jerusalem.

These terms were disadvantageous to Palestinian interests. Indeed, the contours for Palestinian-Israeli peace talks articulated by the United States in 1991 reflected, nearly verbatim, the 1978 Framework for Peace in the Middle East Agreed at Camp David between Egypt and Israel, including the two-stage process consisting of an interim agreement followed by permanent peace. More significantly, the renewed overtures for peace did not correct the fundamental elision of Palestinian peoplehood. Like the Framework, it excluded the PLO as the national representative body and sought to enter into negotiations with Palestinians from the West Bank and Gaza, but only as a derivative of a Jordanian delegation. In addition, despite Israel's repeated and repeatedly failed attempts since the late seventies to establish local self-governing Palestinian institutions, at the height of the intifada, the United States once again offered this arrangement to Palestinians via the peace talks in Madrid.

Palestinians accepted the invitation to Madrid as did Israel. The United States sent each party a Letter of Assurances establishing the terms of the peace talks. The terms exacerbated the structural imbalance of power that encumbered the Palestinian people. Although they stipulated that the talks be based on UN Security Council Resolutions 242 and 338, this was no guarantee of Palestinian independence. Recall that since 1967, Israel had insisted that Resolution 242 did not mandate complete withdrawal from the territories to the 1949 armistice lines. Instead, based on a legal loophole in the text, Israel had claimed it could establish new borders based on its security interests and withdraw from a mere fraction of the territories so long as its negotiating partner agreed. The United States accepted Israel's interpretation as legitimate. Now, in its 1991 letter to Israel, the United States explained that in accordance with its "traditional policy, [the United States] does not support the creation of an independent Palestinian state. . . . Neither [does it] support the continuation of the Israeli rule or annexation of the occupied territories."[17]

In its letter to the Palestinians, the United States put this issue another way, stating that it believed the Israeli occupation should end and that "Palestinians should gain control over political, economic, and other decisions that affect their lives and fate."[18] In both iterations, the United States sought an end to Israeli domination that did not necessarily result in the establishment of a Palestinian state; it sought to establish Palestinian autonomy.

The limited horizon of U.S. peace efforts was not lost on the Palestinian people or on their formal leadership. Still, the Palestinian National Council (PNC), the body responsible for decision making on behalf of the PLO, voted to participate in the negotiations at its twentieth session in September 1991. Why would the PNC endorse a dismal autonomy framework it had fervently rejected since the late seventies? Simply put, by the late eighties the PLO had become relatively weak. The rise of alternative Palestinian leadership in the West Bank and Gaza together with several regional shifts had severely diminished the PLO's authority. The decision to enter into the negotiations represented the vulnerability of the national body but not necessarily of the Palestinians or their cause. The PLO strove to save itself.

Over the course of these negotiations, it managed to do that, but at a very high cost. The intifada provided the PLO with a legal opportunity to leverage international law and norms, including those it had helped to establish, in its pursuit of Palestinian self-determination. It could have used those legal instruments to demand better negotiating terms and/or as a defensive tool to resist Israel's demands; it did neither. Due to a lack of appreciation for the law's utility and risk, as well as a general political miscalculation, the PLO failed to take advantage of this juncture and surrendered some of its most significant legal achievements attained throughout the 1970s. Instead, Israel successfully used the peace process to consolidate its control of the West Bank and the Gaza Strip with Palestinian acquiescence.

The PLO's Steady Decline

The expulsion of the PLO from Lebanon in 1982 marked the beginning of the organization's steady decline. This monumental juncture geographically fragmented its leadership, gutted its sociopolitical apparatus in Lebanon, and limited its ability to launch cross-border raids into Israel. The advent of the intifada then shifted the nucleus of Palestinian authority to the site of the mass civil uprisings in the West Bank and Gaza, and this further diluted the PLO's relevance. Palestinian leaders in the territories included Hanan Ashrawi, a prominent activist and scholar who established the Department of English at Birzeit University; Faisal Husseini, the son of Abd al-Qadr al-Husseini who had led Palestinian armed forces until his death in 1948 and had established himself as a leader in his own right in Jerusalem; and Haidar Abdelshafi, a physician based in the Gaza Strip and a highly revered national leader. Eager to diminish the PLO's role, Israel, the United States, and now, several Gulf monarchies sought to create an alternative leadership structure that these individuals and others in the Occupied Territories would head.[19] In addition, several Arab regimes sought to diplomatically isolate and exclude the liberation movement in response to its support for Iraq's occupation of Kuwait.[20] Mounting external overtures to supplant the PLO troubled its mainstream leadership.[21]

Individual leaders in the West Bank and Gaza were not the only Palestinians who threatened the PLO's authority. In early December 1987, shortly after the beginning of the intifada, leaders of the Muslim Brotherhood in Gaza—including Sheikh Ahmed Yasin, who took the Brotherhood's helm in 1965, and Abdel Aziz al-Rantisi, who led its Islamic Center—held an emergency meeting at which they established Harakat al Muqawama al Islamiyya, better known by its acronym Hamas, in order to join the intifada.[22] This decision marked a dramatic break for the Islamic organization. Between its establishment in 1946 and up until that evening in December 1987, the Brotherhood in Gaza had explicitly avoided entering the national liberation movement, and had instead committed itself wholly to nurturing an Islamic spiritual revival.[23]

When Fathi Shaqaqi, a former member of the Brotherhood, established the Palestinian Islamic Jihad in the early 1980s, he directly challenged the Brotherhood's apolitical program. While Shaqaqi knew he could not compete against the Brotherhood for adherents, he sought to embarrass and outdo them where they had no agenda at all: the resistance of Israel's occupation regime. Islamic Jihad and PLO armed attacks against Israeli military installations inspired the young members of the Brotherhood and the Islamic Center in particular. In response to their entreaties to adopt a resistance platform, Sheikh Yasin insisted it was premature and that all attempts would be doomed to failure.[24] Instead, during this time, the Islamic Center, the embryonic organization of Hamas, competed with secular and nationalist Palestinian parties to control the Palestinian political scene in Gaza and the West Bank. The Brotherhood's focus remained internally centered until 1986. By then, the number of mosques that the Islamic Center controlled had doubled, from 77 in 1967 to 150.[25] In response to pressures resulting from Islamic Jihad's mounting attacks, Sheikh Yasin began to build a security apparatus, to enhance the Brotherhood's domestic standing as well as to directly confront Israel. The beginning of the Palestinian intifada in 1987 became the opportunity for the Islamic Center to launch its military campaign under the auspices of Hamas.[26] Its entry into the political fray in the context of the intifada was swift and resolute, taking aim at Israel as well as the PLO.

In August 1988, Hamas adopted a national charter and committed itself to a holy war, or jihad, against Israel for the sake of recovering custodianship of Palestine, which it described as "an Islamic Waqf consecrated for future Moslem generations until Judgment Day."[27] Hamas made no secret of its aversion for the PLO, which it refused to join. In its charter, it acknowledged the national structure but criticized the PLO for its secular character:

> The day the Palestinian Liberation Organization adopts Islam as its way of life, we will become its soldiers, and fuel for its fire that will burn the enemies. Until such a day, and we pray to Allah that it will be soon, the Islamic Resistance Movement's stand towards the PLO is that of the son towards his father, the brother towards his brother, and the relative to relative, suffers his pain and supports him in confronting the enemies, wishing him to be wise and well-guided.[28]

Meanwhile, the ongoing intifada and the asymmetries of power on display between Israel and the Palestinian people forced the United States and Israel to reconsider their obstinate position on the Palestinian question. In the summer of 1988, U.S. Secretary of State Shultz finally relented and began an indirect dialogue with the PLO on the possibility of a peace conference. He again emphasized the United States' three preconditions for embarking on negotiations, established in the 1975 Memorandum of Understanding with Israel: recognition of Israel, negotiations with Israel, and a renunciation of armed violence.[29]

This U.S. overture represented a new and welcome opportunity to demonstrate the PLO's relevance. In November 1988, the PNC convened its Nineteenth Summit in Algiers, where it conceded to all three preconditions. It disavowed armed struggle, accepted Israel as geopolitical reality, and endorsed negotiations with Israel. This endorsement was one in a series of similar decisions that reflected a "profound transformation in Palestinian thinking."[30]

In the same week, the PNC also adopted the Palestinian Declaration of Independence, authored by the Palestinian poet Mahmoud Darwish, endorsing the establishment of a Palestinian state in the West Bank and the Gaza Strip, with East Jerusalem as its capital.[31] The declaration drew on two elements of international law: Article 22 of the League of Nations Covenant (1919), promising independence to the Palestinian people, and UN Resolution 181 (1947), recommending the partition of Palestine into a Jewish and an Arab state.[32] From 1947 until that moment, Palestinians and the PLO had rejected the Partition Plan as an injustice.

More significant than this PNC endorsement of a truncated Palestinian state based on Resolution 181, was the PNC's endorsement of Resolution 242. As discussed earlier, the PLO had consistently rejected this resolution since its adoption in 1967, because of its elision of Palestinian peoplehood and its normalization of Israel's existence. In 1974, the PLO had adeptly legislated an alternative legal framework, captured by Resolution 3236, specifically to avoid Resolution 242's conditions and to legitimate PLO participation in negotiations. As recently as April 1987, when the PNC convened its eighteenth session, its Political Committee had reiterated the PLO's rejection of Resolution 242, commenting that it was not a "good basis for a settlement of the Palestine question because it deals with it as if it were an issue of refugees and ignores the Palestinian people's national inalienable rights."[33] Now, the PNC's endorsement of Resolution 242 marked a victory for the PLO's pragmatic elements and a culmination of their efforts. Following the October 1973 War, the PLO had embodied a revolutionary agenda, committed to the liberation of Palestine through armed struggle, as well as a self-described pragmatic position, aimed at establishing a truncated Palestinian state in the West Bank and Gaza as an intermediate, or final, step towards liberation. The PLO's decision at its Algiers summit together with the Palestinian Declaration of Independence definitively resolved this tension. However, not all Palestinians supported this shift, including Hamas, which remained outside the PLO's structure.

In 1989, Hamas launched its first military operation and captured and killed two Israeli soldiers, whose bodies were found buried. Such operations increased Hamas's influence among Palestinians and the movement used that growing support to challenge the PLO's representative authority and, more specifically, Fatah's dominance in the territories. In January 1990, Arafat invited Hamas to join the PLO and to attend the forthcoming PNC meeting. Hamas was willing to join so long as the PNC leadership could be chosen through an election. Alternatively, if an election was not feasible, Hamas proposed it should be allotted 40 percent of the PNC's seats, equal to the cross-section of Palestinian support for the movement. The most Arafat and the PLO were willing to offer Hamas, however, was about 5 percent of the seats (twenty-four seats in all).[34] Hamas also insisted on disavowing the political platform endorsing Resolution 242 and the two-state solution that the PNC had adopted in November 1988.

Hamas's rapid rise and bold demands threatened to undermine the achievements of Arafat and the PLO's pragmatic elements. Arafat did not take this lightly. He responded in a "lengthy tirade" in Fatah's publication *Filastin al-Thawra*. He admonished Hamas for attempting to sidestep the PLO structure and present itself as an alternative to a broad section of the Palestinian nation. The Gulf War both diminished this internecine rivalry and enhanced Hamas's political and financial position relative to the PLO. Even before the Gulf War, the PLO had revealed that it had received only 30 percent of the amount pledged by Arab states in the previous year and very few funds appeared to be forthcoming. Traditional PLO donors had begun to divert their funds to other Palestinian institutions, most notably among them Hamas. The Gulf War exacerbated this trend as Arab states financially "cut off" the PLO and rewarded Hamas "with continued financial assistance" for its cautious support of Kuwait's independence.[35]

By 1991, the deleterious terms of the autonomy framework outlined in the Letter of Invitation to Madrid as well as the Letter of Assurance to the Palestinians paled in significance to the opportunity of salvaging the PLO itself. With its financial crisis, its geographic isolation in Tunisia, the challenge to its primacy by individual leaders, the rise of Hamas, and the limited strategic options available to it, the PLO was vulnerable and weak. As explained by Camille Mansour, a legal scholar and an adviser to the Palestinian negotiating team in Washington, though the U.S. terms were "bleak," staying out of the peace process risked ending "the post-1965 Palestinian national movement itself."[36]

Negotiators Go to Madrid and Washington

The PLO accepted the U.S. terms based on the 1978 autonomy framework, but it also tried to strategically leverage those grim conditions. Its first challenge was to overcome the enduring negation of Palestinian peoplehood. Israel did not recognize the General Assembly resolutions legislated by the PLO during the seventies, including Resolution 3237 affirming its status as the sole and legitimate representative of the Palestinian people. With backing from the Bush administration, Israel excluded the PLO, Palestinians from East Jerusalem, and also Palestinians in the diaspora from the negotiations. This exclusion entrenched Israel's geographic, legal, and social fragmentation of Palestinians and the denial of their legal status as a people. Israel insisted that the Palestinian delegation to the peace talks could include only Palestinians from the West Bank and Gaza and only those who had no explicit ties to the PLO, and that the delegation itself must be part of a Jordanian-Palestinian negotiating team.[37]

To overcome this hurdle, the Palestinians established the Palestinian Steering Committee, made up of Palestinians from East Jerusalem and the diaspora who would accompany the Palestinian delegates but who would not formally participate in the talks. In his capacity as PLO Chairman, Arafat handpicked this committee, which was led by Faisal al Husseini and included Hanan Ashrawi, Camille Mansour, Yezid Sayigh, and Anis Fawzi Kassem. U.S. Secretary of State James Baker implicitly accepted this arrangement when he officially welcomed the Palestinian delegation, headed by Haidar Abdelshafi, to Madrid on 31 October 1991. Baker warned the Palestinians, however, that they should make no explicit mention of the PLO because it would risk compelling Israeli Prime Minister Yitzhak Shamir to walk out and abandon the process.[38]

Ashrawi, the committee spokesperson, responded, "Shamir can walk out, but we cannot give a speech without mentioning the PLO."[39] In his opening remarks, Abdelshafi, who was only permitted to attend the opening ceremony as part of the joint Jordanian-Palestinian delegation, boldly asserted the PLO's central role in the negotiating process when he reminded the audience that the "Palestine Liberation Organization launched its peace initiative based on Security Council Resolutions 242 and 338, and declared Palestinian independence based on Resolution 181 of the United Nations, which gave birth to two states in 1948: Israel and Palestine."[40] Shamir remained seated.[41]

The Steering Committee's fidelity to the PLO reflected an overall understanding that attempts to undermine its authority and divide the Palestinian polity amounted to an attack on the Palestinian right to self-determination. Ashrawi explains: "They were trying to turn the Palestinian people into inhabitants and orphans. And we wanted to insist on keeping a leadership because there was a history and a people."[42] Mansour adds: "A people without a leadership is not a people."[43] The Palestinians achieved their first victory and overcame a fundamental hurdle when, in coordination with the Jordanian delegation, they established that negotiations in Washington would proceed on two fronts: a Palestinian-Israeli one and a Jordanian-Israeli one. This did not elevate the status of the Palestinian delegation as representative of a nascent state, but it did distinguish Palestinian national interests from Israel's relations with Jordan.[44]

The issue of representation continued to dominate the talks when they commenced in Washington in December 1991. The Israeli team was chaired by Elyakim Rubinstein, a legal adviser and diplomat who had participated in earlier peace talks, and the Palestinian team continued to be led by Haidar Abdelshafi. The Israelis arrived with a desire to revert to the original arrangement of a Jordanian-Palestinian delegation whereby subcommittees would address either "Palestinian-related issues" or "Jordanian-related issues."[45] After seven days of discussions, disagreement persisted. The representation issue was not resolved until the next round of talks. The parties then resumed negotiations on a two front approach, delineating Palestinian interests, and began deliberating an agenda.

The Palestinian delegation now embarked on a strategy to deal with the second and related challenge: to overcome the autonomy framework laid out in the Letter of Assurances and ensure that the negotiations would result in Palestinian independence. The negotiators sought to deploy Resolution 242 to ensure Israel's complete withdrawal from the territories and the dismantlement of its settlement enterprise; Palestinians engaged in legal work to restore the resolution, only recently condemned as a tool of dispossession, into a tool of resistance. The negotiators also insisted on the immediate halt of settlement activities and the application of the Fourth Geneva Convention to the territories.[46] The Palestinian team preferred to present these issues as preconditions but was in no place to do so. Palestinian demands contravened the original conception of a two-stage process that relegated the question of settlements, Jerusalem, and final borders to the second stage of negotiations after a first two-year interim stage.[47] Moreover, the Palestinian team lacked an overall strategy for overcoming the severe power imbalance that plagued the negtiations.[48]

In an attempt to circumvent these challenges, Raja Shehadeh, a Jerusalem-based attorney and co-founder of Al Haq, one of the largest and most significant Palestinian human rights organizations, suggested that the delegation pursue a piecemeal strategy. Shehadeh proposed embedding the delegation's demands as part of a plan to elect an interim self-government.[49] The delegation thus proposed that the interim government would have

> legislative, executive, and judiciary powers, and its jurisdiction would extend to the OPT [Occupied Palestinian Territories]in their entirety, including its land, water, and natural resources . . . [and that] the Israeli military government and its civil administration would be abolished and their powers transferred to the Palestinian Interim Self-Government Arrangement (PISGA).[50]

Mere discussion of Palestinian self-government, even without any Israeli commitments, prompted the resignation of several ministers from Shamir's cabinet, undermining his majority government in the Knesset.[51]

When the negotiations resumed once again in late February 1992, the negotiating teams exchanged position documents. Israel's new position marked a significant retreat. It did not mention the election of a Palestinian authority to replace Israel's military government, it no longer referred to Resolution 242 at all, or even to the initiation of final status talks during the interim period. Israel would retain jurisdiction over the territories and delegate specific powers and responsibilities to "organs of the Interim Self-Government (ISGA) arrangements" across twelve administrative bodies. The ISGA would only have jurisdiction over some Palestinians in the Gaza Strip and the West Bank, excluding Jerusalem, and no territorial jurisdiction. Israel would retain all responsibilities not delegated, retain control over internal and external security, and have the "right" to reside in and settle the territories.[52] Israel's new approach sought to ensure its enduring control of the West Bank and Gaza and let Palestinians govern themselves in limited areas.

The Palestinian delegation refused to enumerate the spheres of operation that would fall within ISGA's authority, for fear of falling into the trap of limited autonomy without the promise of sovereignty. Palestinian obstinacy infuriated both the Israelis and the Americans. U.S. interlocutors wanted the Palestinians to take whatever the Israelis were offering.[53] According to Rashid Khalidi, then a University of Chicago professor and an adviser to the Palestinian delegation, the United States "essentially told us, you are allowed to decide on the decoration of your prison cell."[54] This fourth round ended without resolution.

The fifth round began in late April 1992, just before the Israeli elections. At this time, the Israelis attempted to further dilute Palestinian demands. Whereas Palestinians sought to establish elections across the West Bank and the Gaza Strip, Israeli negotiators proposed a plan for municipal elections as well as the transfer of authority over all health services in the territory.[55] The Palestinians perceived this proposal as a substitute for an interim self-government, and responded with a series of written questions and requests. Shehadeh explains that the Palestinian team employed a legal strategy "in order to bring the negotiations to focus on the issues of land and water and consequently the Israeli settlements." Their requests included calls to abolish particular laws, like the 1982 authorization allowing the Israeli National Water Company to control all water in the West Bank. They also requested access to public records, like land registration records, land use planning documents, and the Israeli budget for its "civil administration" in the territories. After the Israeli team responded, Abdelshafi tasked Shehadeh with rebutting their arguments, but the Israeli delegation refused Shehadeh's participation. He could advise but not participate in the negotiations because of his East Jerusalemite status; Israelis adamantly refused to recognize the holistic national character of a Palestinian people, and Palestinians from East Jerusalem exceeded the narrow bounds of what Israelis accepted as Palestinian. The United States did not intervene. The self-proclaimed, honest broker, stood by and allowed the Palestinian delegation to proceed without adequate legal representation, thus exacerbating the asymmetries between the parties and reifying Israel's overall framework.[56]

Between the fifth and sixth rounds, Yitzhak Rabin replaced Yitzhak Shamir as Israel's Prime Minister and Shimon Peres became Rabin's foreign minister. Rabin took full responsibility for bilateral negotiations and Peres for multilateral ones, and they would meet regularly to discuss them. Moreover, the Israeli center-left parties established a majority in the Knesset, affording Rabin greater latitude in the negotiations.[57] While Rabin was more inclined than other Israeli leaders to achieve an agreement, he remained opposed to Palestinian independence and continued to pursue an autonomy agreement with the Palestinian leadership within the territories. Accordingly, Rabin and Peres maintained the preexisting Israeli negotiating team.[58]

To appear flexible, Rabin agreed to entertain proposals for limited PLO involvement. Yair Hirschfeld, an Israeli scholar at Haifa University and member of Israel's negotiating team, was instructed to work with Ashrawi to draft a proposal on the PLO's role. Hirschfeld and Ashrawi proposed that Palestinians living in the diaspora and supported by the PLO could officially participate in multilateral working groups established to discuss specific issues like economics, refugees, land, and water. Arafat initially rejected the proposal for PLO participation in multilateral working groups. He preferred that Israel talk directly to the PLO. According to Hirschfeld, "it was also clear that if [Arafat] were allowed to control the negotiations, the positions he would offer would be more forthcoming."[59]

In early May 1992, the PLO Central Council, an intermediary body responsible for making decisions when the Palestinian National Council is not in session, convened, and for the first time included the Palestinian negotiators from the territories in an official capacity. The Central Council endorsed continuing the negotiations and approved PLO participation in the multilateral working groups. This decision made it explicit that the PLO was not merely advising the Palestinian team but instructing them.[60]

Though the Central Council's meeting made this dynamic official it had existed from the beginning of the negotiating process. Arafat and the PLO leadership in Tunis were kept abreast of all developments through daily reports. Arafat would respond with directives to the delegation via telephone and fax, yet this was not enough to alleviate Arafat's concerns. He regarded the Palestinian delegation, and Faisal al Husseini in particular, as a threat to his authority. The PLO Chairman did not trust anyone from the West Bank and Gaza Strip leadership because he feared external plans to supplant the PLO. Arafat considered the entire Palestinian delegation to Washington "contaminated."[61] At one point, he lamented to several PLO leaders in Tunis that negotiations had entered the stage of "cancelling out the PLO and liquidating this leadership. . . . Faisal and the delegation are the Trojan Horse." Beyond Arafat's personal concerns, the PLO leadership in general wanted to take control of the negotiations. They deliberately intervened to ensure that the Washington delegation appeared inflexible so that the "PLO in Tunis is viewed as more flexible," and thus could succeed in its efforts to achieve "recognition as a full partner in the negotiations."[62]

During the middle of the sixth round in late August 1992, Rabin announced an amendment to the settlement freeze that would permit the development of up to 2,000 settlement units to account for "natural growth."[63] The Palestinian delegation understood this as a clear provocation, demonstrating the futility of Palestinian demands. Together with concerns that Israel was buying time with the Palestinians in order to achieve an agreement with Syria, the Palestinian team shifted its strategy. It returned to negotiations with a simple priority: to establish the application of Resolution 242 to the interim process and not just the final status agreement.

This was a legal strategy that sought to link the interim and final stages of the process to immediately address the question of settlements and Jerusalem. Applying Resolution 242 from the outset of the negotiations would imbue it with a prescriptive function: to legally mandate withdrawal in exchange for peace. In contrast, applying Resolution 242 only to the final status agreement would afford Israel room for maneuver by insisting that the factual terms of the final agreement would fulfill the resolution's legal mandate. In this latter scenario, the resolution would have a descriptive rather than a prescriptive function.[64] For the Palestinians, the two stages were linked and facilitated an incremental but inevitable Israeli withdrawal and Palestinian state sovereignty. For the Israelis, the two stages did the exact opposite in order to definitively achieve autonomy in the first stage and to enshrine the indeterminacy of the final status issues.

The Palestinians had a useful precedent to draw on. Israel had accepted an understanding of Resolution 242 as mandating its withdrawal and the restoration of Egypt's sovereignty during the Israeli-Egyptian negotiations.[65] Later, it would establish a similar understanding with Jordan during their peace talks.[66] In stark contrast, Israel rejected the Palestinian demand and insisted it was willing to apply Resolution 242 only during permanent status negotiations, which would necessarily involve Jordan because "242 deals with states."[67] It had no intention of withdrawing to the 1967 borders. The refusal to establish an understanding of Resolution 242 and apply it to the interim agreement was a deliberate effort to retain as much of the West Bank and Gaza Strip as possible. Yitzhak Rabin declared, "I'll never, I'll never agree to any peace if it will be preconditioned on withdrawal to the pre-67 lines."[68] If there was to be a Palestinian state it would be in a series of self-governing territories that did not exercise meaningful sovereignty.

To achieve Israel's goals, Israeli negotiators pursued a strategy that permitted maneuvering around international law and human rights norms regarding the Palestine question. Rather than derive a settlement refracted through established international law, the Israeli delegation crafted political solutions that could be reconciled with legal principles. As explained by Daniel Reisner, a legal adviser to the Israeli Army between 1995 and 2004 and an Israeli negotiator in the peace process:

> One school of thought believes that we should begin by establishing legal principles before discussing substance. Another school of thought says, let's solve the problem in practical ways and then couch it in the law. It's a matter of substance and form.[69]

Israel's negotiating team sought to "legalize those existing arrangements" it had unilaterally imposed on Palestinians and their lands since 1967.[70] It had achieved that policy through state practice, legal work, and obstinate disregard of international censure. It was now attempting to achieve this arrangement through contractual agreement with the Palestinians themselves.

The Bush administration supported the Israeli approach. It acknowledged that Resolution 242 applied to both stages of the agreement, but accepted Israel's demands that in practice it only be applied to the final status stage. The United States adopted this approach, of limiting the application of law, in 1967, when the Lyndon B. Johnson administration introduced the land-for-peace framework. Since then, it had shielded Israel from the law's prescriptive demands in order to facilitate an unencumbered political resolution. The Bush administration's disavowal of international law as a negotiating framework departed from the U.S. approach to all other peace talks, including the Israeli-Egyptian negotiations in the late seventies and those with Syria, Lebanon, and Jordan in the current phase of Middle East peace talks. The United States had applied relevant law in every negotiating context other than Israel's negotiations with the Palestinians.

In response to Palestinian appeals to apply international law as a framework, Secretary of State Baker and his staffers insisted the Palestinians avoid discussing the law. According to Khalidi, Baker told the delegation to "stay within the confines which you voluntarily accepted in the Letter of Assurances." The limitations of the negotiations were clear: the existing balance of power would dictate the terms of agreement without the recalibrating potential of established law, and the United States would reify that imbalance by supporting Israel's positions. Not only could the Palestinians not challenge Israel's Jewish-Zionist settler sovereignty over 78 percent of former Mandate Palestine, they were now being forced to negotiate the remaining 22 percent that Israel had not conquered in 1948. Ultimately, Khalidi explains, the Palestinians understood that "what was Israeli belonged to Israelis and what was Palestinian would be negotiated."[71]

The Palestinian delegation was unsettled. Ashrawi protested to Secretary Baker, saying "everything you are asking to do is illegal because you are forcing a people under occupation to negotiate with their occupiers—this is duress."[72] The PLO leadership in Tunis did not agree. As the Palestinian delegation in Washington struggled to expand the framework established in the Letter of Assurances through legal tactics, the PLO leadership adopted a narrow political strategy that mirrored Israel's approach. It insisted on achieving the best possible agreement within the existing confines dictated by the United States and Israel. Shehadeh, one of the three legal advisers on the Steering Committee, resigned at the conclusion of this round of negotiations; he saw "no role for a legal adviser, or indeed legal strategies."[73]

By the end of the seventh round of negotiations in late November 1992, there was a deadlock. The Israelis wanted to negotiate details of the arrangements for interim self-government, while the Palestinians insisted on obtaining assurances on the applicability of Resolution 242. The Palestinian delegation sent a letter to the Israeli negotiators that described the Israeli model as

> "complicated," "impractical," "unworkable," likely to "create more problems than it would solve," to keep alive "the sources of friction and conflict" and the continuation of "violations of human rights," and to result in a self-government whose authority would be "unable to pass the test of time, and ultimately devoid of legitimacy."[74]

During the eighth round, which ran through December 1992 and was the last one to be convened during the Bush administration, the Israeli negotiators clarified and entrenched their position. They insisted that there existed only a "time-frame interlock" between the two stages of negotiations. This meant that final status agreements would inevitably follow interim ones but the interim stage would not predetermine or in any way impact the final status. Israeli negotiators also clarified that while Israel's military jurisdiction covered all of the territories, without distinction as to nationality or geography, the Palestinian interim government would be responsible for a patchwork of Palestinian constituents and lands. Moreover, Palestinian governance of those select populations would be contingent on coordination with Israel. The settlements fragmenting Palestinian lands and communities, as well as the settlers living within them, would be beyond Palestinian control. Israel would maintain jurisdiction over the settlements and Jerusalem, including sovereign legal jurisdiction over criminal cases involving Israelis in the territories.[75]

The eighth round ended more abruptly than Israel's revised position threatened. In mid-December 1992, a Hamas cell captured an Israeli policeman and sought to exchange him for Sheikh Ahmed Yasin, held in Israeli captivity for his suspected involvement in the intifada. Hamas's condition for the release of the Israeli hostage included broadcasting that release on television and establishing an international presence to ensure that Yasin would not be rearrested. In an effort to compel Hamas to release the policeman without concessions, Israel television interviewed Yasin, providing him his first opportunity to speak directly to the world and to the Israeli public. When asked about the threat of death posed to the policeman, Yasin responded, "The killing of the policeman, the killing of the Palestinian, and the killing of the soldier are all part of a cycle created by the occupation. When the causes are removed all these problems will be solved."[76]

In his interview, Yasin indicated that Hamas's increasing visibility reflected broader agreement among Palestinians that the "Islamic solution is the alternative," prompting a question about the utility of the ongoing peace negotiations. Yasin emphasized that Palestinians desire peace but criticized the negotiations: "Thus far they have achieved nothing. I expected right from the start that they would be unable to achieve anything because of the lack of balance."[77]

Israel refused to release Yasin, and Hamas executed the Israeli policeman. Within a few days, Israeli forces arrested nearly 2,000 Palestinians, including 415 suspected leaders of Hamas and Islamic Jihad. Israeli armed forces handcuffed and blindfolded these 415 detainees and drove them to the Lebanese border where they dumped them in the middle of a freezing night and relinquished any responsibility for them. The international community responded swiftly and harshly; the UN Security Council, with U.S. support, condemned the mass, forcible deportation as a breach of international law.[78] Israel's reprisal against Hamas turned into an unexpected boon for the movement, which received international media attention for the first time. In order to protest Israel's actions, the Palestinian negotiating team, with the PLO's backing, suspended its participation in the negotiations.

The Palestinian delegation in Washington understood what was at stake in the negotiations and avoided the traps erected by Israel's negotiating team. It both resisted Israel's legal tactics and deployed its own. None of this was enough to overcome the severe power imbalance that afflicted the negotiations. Worse, the PLO leadership in Tunis did not appreciate the risks posed by Israel's proposed terms. Upon its formal inclusion in the peace talks, the PLO would fail to consolidate its historic achievements, including the moral authority Palestinians had cultivated in the course of the intifada, and thus would lose the opportunity to enhance its negotiating leverage. It would also fail to wield the law as a defensive tool to resist Israel's demands. In secret negotiations conducted later in Norway, the PLO would fall into the very trap of autonomy the Palestinian delegation in Washington had so resolutely dodged.

Opening a Back Channel in Norway

The decision to deport Palestinians in flagrant violation of humanitarian law and in the face of diplomatic protest came at an especially awkward time. In early December 1992, Rabin and Peres had indicated a greater willingness to negotiate directly with the PLO. They wanted to open a direct channel with the liberation movement, but "had every interest in playing this card carefully, making Israel's quid pro quo for recognizing the PLO the conclusion of a peace agreement."[79] They preferred to open a back-channel track that would afford them full deniability.

To facilitate a direct channel with the PLO, Ashrawi and Husseini urged Yair Hirschfeld, the Israeli negotiating team member who had met previously with Ashrawi, to begin track two negotiations with Ahmed Qurei, a senior PLO leader heading the Palestinian delegation in the multilateral working groups.[80] Hirschfeld and Qurei agreed to meet in London in early December 1992.[81] Hirschfeld came to the meeting with Ron Pundak, his co-founding partner in the Economic Cooperation Foundation and an Israeli scholar and journalist. Yossi Beilin, the Deputy Minister of Foreign Affairs to Shimon Peres, gave Hirschfeld and Pundak the green light, in spite of Israeli law prohibiting contact with the PLO.[82] Despite this governmental approval, Hirschfeld and Pundak attended the meeting in their capacity as scholars and peace activists, without any semblance of officialdom. This concerned the PLO representatives and shaped their participation in the back-channel talks. Qurei attended the meeting with Afif Safieh, a PLO representative and the General Delegate to the United Kingdom. They had the backing of Arafat and Mahmoud Abbas, a deputy to Arafat responsible for the PLO's overall administrative function. The initial meeting in London led to a series of meetings in Sarpsborg, Norway, facilitated by Terje Larsen, a sociologist heading the Fafo Institute in Oslo.

Qurei attended the subsequent meetings with Hasan Asfour, a PLO official and agricultural engineer, who did not speak fluent English, the language
in which all the negotiations took place. Hirschfeld and Pundak continued to
represent Israel. At first, Qurei submitted positions that reiterated the Palestinian
delegation's demands and unyielding position in Washington. But the Israelis
presented a new element that created space for maneuver.

In January 1993, Peres suggested to Rabin that Israel offer Arafat the opportunity to return to the Gaza Strip, where the PLO could stand for elections
and, if successful, could negotiate directly with Israel.[83] Qurei's interest in the
Gaza-first approach as well as an economic development plan created a breakthrough in the meetings. Although Qurei feared that the framework could mean
"withdrawal from Gaza 'first and last'" he accepted the "formula in principle as
a preliminary first step, on the condition that it would also be applied at a later
stage to one or more cities in the West Bank, once withdrawal from Gaza had
become acceptable to the Israeli public."[84]

The outcome of these meetings in March 1993 was a document known as the
Sarpsborg Principles. The Palestinian positions had departed significantly from
the ones established in Washington. Indeed, within three months, the PLO had
relented on several of the key issues for which the Palestinian delegation fought so
hard. These included relinquishing the demands that Resolution 242 apply to both
stages of negotiations and that Palestinian jurisdiction cover all lands across the
West Bank and the Gaza Strip.[85] Hirschfeld explains that the Sarpsborg Principles

> maintained all the necessary control mechanisms for Israel; the source of
> authority and all residual power remained with Israel; and there was no need
> for any immediate withdrawal of the military government and/or the Civil
> Administration for a redeployment of the Israeli Defense Forces.[86]

The negotiators in Norway adopted the Sarpsborg Principles in secret and
without consulting the Palestinian delegation in Washington. During this time,
the Palestinian delegation was refusing to resume talks in Washington unless
the return of the Palestinian deportees could be negotiated. Rabin rejected this
condition. The United States, together with Russia, invited the parties to return

to negotiations in late April 1993. The Palestinian delegation refused. This created an obstacle for the back-channel process as well. The Israelis wanted to incorporate the outcomes of the Norway talks into the bilateral channel in Washington, and thus conditioned resumption of the back-channel process on resumption of the Washington talks. Moreover, Rabin wanted to test whether Arafat was willing to act in clear opposition to Hamas, which, like the Steering Committee, opposed resumption of the talks until the deportee issue was resolved. According to Hirschfeld, Arafat forced the Palestinian team to return to Washington in order to allow the back-channel talks to continue.[87]

Israeli delegation leader Elyakim Rubinstein then resumed the ninth round of talks in Washington by presenting terms very similar to those in the Sarpsborg Agreement. This frustrated Qurei, who wanted to maintain control and secrecy of the back-channel process.[88] In Washington, the Palestinian delegation continued to insist on clear terms of reference as the parties attempted to negotiate a Declaration of Principles. The team paid astute attention to details and the possible legal manipulation of the proposed language.

For example, in a May 1993 meeting with U.S. State Department officials Aaron Miller and Dan Kurtzer (who represented the President Bill Clinton's administration), the Palestinian delegation highlighted that there was no guarantee against an Israeli interpretation of Resolution 242 that permitted annexation. Kurtzer insisted that this could not be guaranteed, "If you are trying to lock in your interpretation of 242 in this document, it won't work. You can protect but not lock it in." Exasperated, Miller chastised the Palestinian delegation, saying, "it is illogical to expect [the United States] to give [its] preferred position on 242. You are thinking in idealized positions.... You didn't address it for 30 years.... You discovered 242 ..."[89]

The Palestinian delegation did not relent. They emphasized that Israel evaded the resolution in order to remain in the West Bank and Gaza. The negotiating team continued to highlight legal loopholes that could harm them, including insisting that every mention of territories in the document be preceded by the adjective "occupied."[90]

Despite being outflanked in terms of expertise, public records, and relative power, the Palestinian team demonstrated adept negotiating skills. Ultimately, none of that mattered. The entire process in Washington frustrated Arafat. He considered the Palestinian delegation's determination and staunch positions an impediment to reaching an agreement. Camille Mansour recalls one furious encounter when Arafat berated the team when it presented him with a draft document on agreed principles, exclaiming, "What do you want me to do with this piece of paper? Frame and mount it on my wall? I want action."[91]

Meanwhile, the back-channel talks had also resumed and had been moved to Oslo. The PLO regarded this a "legitimation" phase. It sought to make the Norway channel official rather than informal, which meant obtaining Israeli endorsement from the highest levels of government. Until May 1993, the PLO leadership had no assurances that the Norway back channel had any official endorsement. Qurei and the PLO leadership believed this was the most pressing issue. Qurei explained this later:

> Involvement of an official Israeli representative in the talks had in fact been one of our original objectives even before our arrival in Oslo. . . . We felt it was of the highest importance to induce Israel to abandon its long-held policy of refusing to deal with the PLO. Sooner or later, Israel had to accept that the PLO was in practical control of all aspects of the Palestinian-Israeli conflict, both inside and outside the territories. We knew if we could achieve this it would be a significant victory.[92]

In mid-May, the PLO leaders got what they wanted.[93] Rabin authorized Uri Savir, the Director-General of the Ministry of Foreign Affairs, to lead the Israeli delegation in Oslo. The teams began to discuss plans for initial withdrawal. As a result of talks with Egypt's President Hosni Mubarak, Peres agreed to include Jericho in the Gaza-first plan, to demonstrate incremental change in the West Bank and not just in Gaza. Although located in the Jordan Valley, the eastern-most border of the West Bank, coveted by Israel for security purposes, Jericho was negotiable because it lacked settlements. This transformed the concept of Gaza-first to Gaza-and-Jericho first. Qurei insisted that control over Jericho include control over the Allenby crossing, which connects the West Bank and Jordan. The Israelis rejected this out of hand for contradicting their fundamental position that Israel retain power over all external security and that Palestinians have only limited internal security.[94] Qurei consistently made demands and just as consistently retreated to the confines of the autonomy framework to establish an interim government.

For example, in June 1993, Qurei insisted that an international trusteeship be established over Gaza to ensure its successful transition from military occupation to independence. Peres strongly rejected this because, according to a legal memo submitted by an Israeli adviser, UN trusteeship was a formal step to independence "equivalent to the process of decolonization in cases such as Namibia."[95] This contradicted Israel's outstanding policy against Palestinian statehood. Hirschfield asked for five minutes to convince Qurei to drop the demand for trusteeship, and he explains that

> in practice, it took one minute. I simply asked [Qurei] if it would be better if the PLO obtained direct control over Gaza instead of handing it to a trusteeship managed by foreign actors. He asked me if this was what Israel wanted, and after I answered in the affirmative, he consented—and the concept that Peres so fervently opposed was eliminated from the equation.[96]

In July 1993, Rabin added Yoel Singer, a legal adviser to the Israeli army for nearly two decades and an attorney in a Washington, DC, law firm, to the negotiating team to strengthen the Oslo channel and achieve an agreement that solidified Israel's interests. Singer was very aggressive and subjected the PLO representatives to no less than 200 questions.[97] At first, Qurei was upset about the hostile approach, but took comfort upon learning that Rabin had instructed Singer to pose the questions.[98] In that case, according to Qurei, Singer's hostility was an "examination" to test the PLO's readiness to consent to the terms of the agreement and coordinate with Israel. The PLO responded with demands for further concessions, including expanding the understanding of the Jericho district to include the Jordan Valley and to delegate authority of the West Bank immediately to the Palestinians. Israel had established these as red lines and abruptly broke off the negotiations. The talks resumed within a month, after "the Palestinians informed [the Israeli negotiators] that they have reviewed their demands and wanted to adjust them according to Israel's needs."[99] Even Rabin was surprised by how much the PLO was willing to concede.[100]

The PLO delegation also threatened to quit the negotiations and, on several occasions, refused to agree on points in the draft Declaration of Principles. However, their power to shape the Declaration was negligible relative to that of the Israeli negotiators. As Qurei recalled, the Israelis seemed to believe

> that it was for [Palestinians] to accept or not the documents which they produced, but they did not see any reason why they should be expected to look seriously at our ideas. I felt they should remember that while we were seeking land, they were just as eagerly seeking peace.[101]

Indeed, despite the PLO's relative weakness, Palestinians and their cause possessed significant negotiating leverage in 1993. Images of the intifada engendered unprecedented global awareness that Palestinians endured an oppressive regime. Moreover, in 1988, the United States negotiated South Africa's withdrawal from Namibia, and in 1990, South Africa released Nelson Mandela from prison, generating significant momentum against racist and colonial domination.[102] Ultimately, this leverage may have been insufficient to recalibrate the severe asymmetry of power between Israel, backed by the United States, and the PLO, but that organization also failed to effectively wield it.[103] Instead, its leadership exacerbated the asymmetry by accepting the autonomy framework. In part, the PLO's failure reflected its leadership's lack of appreciation for the law, and particularly for the law's strategic malleability. It also reflected the PLO's lack of other options. Most significantly, the leadership's single-minded goal of obtaining de jure recognition for the liberation movement blinded it to the deleterious terms of the agreement it was drafting.

Israel used these weaknesses to secure its territorial ambitions with Palestinian consent. Shehadeh observed that "for Israel the negotiations were the culmination of a legal process that began at the end of the 1970s and that they sought through them to consolidate the arrangements made as a consequence of this process."[104] Singer successfully lobbied Rabin to recognize the PLO. Israel and the PLO agreed to conclude the Declaration of Principles first, then to negotiate mutual recognition afterward. While Qurei feared that accepting official recognition as the principal gain in the negotiations was giving "away too much for too little," the PLO leadership in Tunis saw it as an "exceptional victory," since recognition of a national liberation movement "by their enemy [is] a great achievement."[105]

Lingering disagreements over the exact details of the Declaration of Principles—concerning issues such as "control of the crossing points, security and movement of the settlers, the timetable for Israel's withdrawal, and the transfer of authority from the Israeli military government"—threatened to unravel the entire back-channel process. Peres, who saw the peace process as his legacy, traveled to the Swedish Ministry of Foreign Affairs in Stockholm in mid-August 1993 to salvage it himself. The Israeli Prime Minister, flanked by Singer as well as his assistant Avi Gil, joined Swedish Foreign Minister Johan Joergen Holst, Mona Juul from the Ministry, and Terje Larsen in Holst's office. They asked Holst to phone Chairman Arafat to finalize the agreement on the principles. Rabin and Savir were on the line from Jerusalem. Holst called Arafat, and that night, Qurei led the discussion on behalf of the PLO with an audience that included Mahmoud Abbas and Hasan Asfour, listening in from PLO headquarters as well. The mediated discussion lasted for six hours, until four in the morning in Tunis.[106] At the end of it, the parties agreed on the Declaration of Principles (DOP).

Only after reaching an agreement, did the PLO leadership consult a legal expert to review the documents. They consulted Taher Shash, an Egyptian diplomat and lawyer who was involved in the Camp David negotiations. According to Shash, Qurei and Asfour were both surprised by how long it was taking him to review the agreement. He then realized that his "arrival in Oslo was one day too late and there was nothing more for [him] to do but make a quick reading of the project which is now in its final form. There was no possibility of making any amendments to it."[107]

Shortly thereafter, on 19 August 1993, Qurei and Savir initialed the document in Oslo, in complete secrecy.[108] The PLO would finally obtain Israel's recognition of its juridical status. In exchange, it accepted ghettoized sovereignty across the West Bank and Gaza without any guarantee of independence.

PLO Gains Recognition in Exchange for Palestinian Independence

The final document was an agreement to agree. It reified Israel's control and did not guarantee a single national right for Palestinians. It did not mention the right to Palestinian self-determination nor the possibility of establishing a

Palestinian state. The only mention of eventual Israeli withdrawal from the territories in the DOP was a vague commitment that the transitional period shall lead "to a permanent settlement based on Security Council Resolutions 242 and 338."[109] The PLO considered this language a victory because Israel wanted to decide on particular terms for withdrawal later. However, Israeli negotiators in Washington had agreed that the resolutions would apply in the permanent status negotiations so long as they neither defined the scope of the interim agreement nor created more than a time-frame interlock between the two stages. The Israelis had succeeded in limiting Resolution 242's function to being descriptive and not prescriptive. The final terms mirrored the very ones that the Palestinian negotiating team had rejected in the bilateral talks.

In Washington, the Palestinian team had also insisted on extending Palestinian territorial jurisdiction over all of the West Bank and the Gaza Strip.[110] This would give the interim Palestinian government authority over the land and everything on it including Israeli settlers. However, the final DOP stipulated, "Jurisdiction of the Council will cover West Bank and Gaza Strip territory, except for issues that will be negotiated in the permanent status negotiations."[111] The permanent status issues referenced in the clause are enumerated elsewhere and include Jerusalem, Israel's military installations, and Israel's settlements in the West Bank and Gaza. Accordingly, Palestinian jurisdiction extended over land that Israel did not already claim or *intend* to claim. Read together with the explicit rejection of Resolution 242 as a legal mandate as well as reference to Palestinian self-determination, the DOP placed no outer boundaries on Israel's existing or future territorial ambitions. The DOP paved the way for the de facto legitimacy of Israel's settlement enterprise.

Nabil Shaath, who headed the bilateral negotiations on behalf of the PLO, disagrees. He insists that the DOP's clause stipulating that "the two sides view the West Bank and the Gaza Strip as a single territorial unit, whose integrity will be preserved during the interim period," was meant to cease settlement expansion. According to Shaath, the clause proved ineffective because of the lack of adequate enforcement. The United States was meant to oversee the agreement, but, Shaath explains, "it could not adequately enforce these terms because it acted as Israel's lawyer."[112] As a legal matter, however, the clause was poorly written and displayed excessive faith in the United States' ability to fulfill the arbitration role.

The clause could be read as referring to either of two things: one, the integrity of the territorial unity of the West Bank and the Gaza Strip, or two, the integrity of the territorial status quo. The former meaning simply guaranteed that the two territories would not be disaggregated, while the latter suggested that neither party, namely Israel, would unilaterally alter the territory. Without greater specificity and attention to legal detail, Israel could expand its settlement enterprise in the territories while maintaining the integrity of the unity between them and claim to be in compliance with the clause stipulating "integrity." Moreover, and assuming for the sake of argument that the PLO is right in its assessment that the lack of adequate enforcement, rather than inadequate treaty terms, is what allowed settlement expansion to continue, the clause's arbitration mechanism bears closer scrutiny.

The PLO agreed to place the peace process under the sole trusteeship of the United States, in spite of that country's explicit bias, which was manifested during the bilateral talks. Rather than ameliorate this severe power imbalance, the DOP further entrenched it in a dispute resolution clause stipulating that "[t]he parties may agree to submit to arbitration disputes relating to the interim period, which cannot be settled through conciliation."[113] The clause also gave the parties veto power over the arbitration mechanism, thereby giving Israel latitude to reject the potential role of third parties. In contrast, in its peace treaty with Egypt in 1979 and with Jordan in 1994, Israel agreed to a dispute resolution clause without deference to the negotiating parties' wishes.[114] Notably, none of the treaties have an arbitration mechanism referring the dispute to the International Court of Justice, thereby diminishing the ability of weaker parties to enforce each treaty in the face of intransigence. This omission was most detrimental to Palestinian interests and reflected their willingness to make significant concessions for the sake of entering into an agreement. Daniel Reisner, an Israeli negotiator, explains that the discrepancy in the agreement with the Palestinians is due to the fact that "Egyptians and Jordanians did not want to take us to arbitration every morning."[115] The Israelis ensured that they would be able to control enforcement of the agreement on their own terms and without interference.

Moreover, while the Palestinian negotiators in Washington refused to accept a framework of delegated scopes of authority, or functional jurisdiction, the PLO agreed to that very arrangement. The DOP established that authority would be transferred to the Palestinians only in a select number of enumerated spheres, including "education and culture, health, social welfare, direct taxation, and tourism." The DOP also established that even after withdrawal from Jericho and Gaza, Israel would maintain responsibility for "external security, and for internal security and public order of settlements and Israelis," meaning that the Palestinians would be left to police only themselves in coordination with the Israeli army. In effect, Palestinians could not protect themselves from settlers or Israeli military offensives, they would never be able to prosecute Israelis, and they would have no control over their own movement into and out of the territory.[116] By agreeing to these terms, the PLO accepted a patchwork arrangement over Palestinian civil affairs and natural resources.

Thus, in 1993, the Palestinian Liberation Organization signed onto the autonomy framework it had rejected for fifteen years, ever since Menachem Begin and Anwar Sadat introduced it in negotiating the Camp David Framework. There are only two differences between the DOP and the 1978 Framework for Peace. First, whereas the Framework stipulated that the Palestinians will have jurisdiction over individuals only, the DOP expanded that to include some fragmented lands as well.[117] Second, in 1978, Israel sought to co-opt Palestinian individuals to take the helm of this autonomy framework, but in 1993, the PLO itself assumed that responsibility.

In response to Israel's negotiating demands, the PLO also agreed to amend its National Charter to remove the commitment to armed struggle. It also rescinded the 1975 resolution finding that Zionism is a form of racism. In addition to these concessions, the PLO accepted Israel's preference to exclude reference to any international law or norms, not just Resolution 242 but also Resolutions 181 and 194, the Fourth Geneva Convention concerning occupation, and all of the PLO's remarkable legal achievements at the United Nations during the 1970s. Besides the cursory reference to Resolutions 242 and 338, the DOP only vaguely mentions law, in its preamble, as recognition of the "mutual legitimate and political rights" of both parties.[118] This was the cost of entering the U.S. sphere of influence; it meant uncritically accepting the U.S. understanding of the law as an impediment to a political agreement, as well as Israel's understanding that the law should fulfill a descriptive, rather than a prescriptive, function. By accepting the U.S. and Israeli approach to the law's relationship to the conflict, the PLO inadvertently endorsed a new exception in the question of Palestine. Like the sovereign exception in the Mandate for Palestine—which was seen as justifying the elision of Palestinian self-determination, thus rendering irrelevant the consultation of the native population in establishing the Mandate as well as the legality of partition deliberated by the United Nations—this exception engendered a specialized legal framework. In effect, it suspended all applicable international law and norms in order to achieve an unfettered political resolution.

The PLO willingly abandoned the law as one of its primary tools of struggle. More generally, it surrendered a politics of resistance. While that makes sense upon establishing peace, it made no sense in this case, where the DOP stipulated derivative Palestinian sovereignty contingent on Israeli prerogatives without any guarantees that the interim stage would culminate in independence. According to the PLO, the negotiators accepted this arrangement "on faith" that the United States would usher in Palestinian independence, and Israel would withdraw from the West Bank and Gaza.[119] However, without a resistance framework, Palestinians would not be able to recalibrate the balance of power to compel Israel to relinquish its control.

The Palestinian negotiating team had met for the last time in Washington in June 1993, two months before the secret signing in Oslo. They were deliberately kept in the dark the entire time. Upon seeing the final document, Rashid Khalidi was "disgusted. . . . Every pitfall, every trap, every Israeli scheme we had avoided, they walked blindly into. They made every single mistake. They made every single one."[120] Haidar Abdelshafi was furious. In a final meeting with U.S. State Department officials Ed Djerdian and Dennis Ross, he said, "You have taken advantage of our leadership. You allowed them to negotiate in secret while we were negotiating here in good faith." The State Department officials implored him to attend the signing ceremony in Washington and attempted to woo him with front row seats. George Salem, a Washington, DC–based attorney and legal adviser to the Palestinian delegation who was taking notes at the meeting, recalls that Abdelshafi told them, "I am going home to Gaza," and when Salem looked up from his notes all he saw was the back of the delegation chairperson as he walked out the door.[121]

Hanan Ashrawi was similarly disappointed. Despite her initial disappointment, however, Ashrawi continued to support the outcome because it salvaged the PLO's status.[122] Her contradictory position was not unique. Aside from a handful of advisers and negotiators who resigned from the negotiating team because of the Oslo agreement, most of the participants remained a part of the peace process. At the top levels, there was no revolt within the PLO. Despite the fact that the DOP fell far short of the PLO's 1988 Declaration of Independence, the Central Council of the PLO convened in Tunis in October 1993 and endorsed the DOP by a vote of 63 to 8, with 9 abstentions. Of the 107 council members, only 25 did not attend, in protest.[123]

Several key Palestinian figures did protest. Their concern was not the acceptance of a truncated Palestinian state but the DOP's dismal terms that did not guarantee that state. Mahmoud Darwish, the author of the Declaration of Independence, resigned from the PLO Executive Committee, explaining that "there was no clear link between the interim period and the final status, and no clear commitment to withdraw from the occupied territories. I felt Oslo would pave the way for escalation."[124] Edward Said, the renowned Columbia University professor of comparative literature who had translated the Declaration into English, wrote a series of scathing articles denouncing the DOP as "an instrument of Palestinian surrender, a Palestinian Versailles." Said's commentary, also used as a fitting epigraph for this chapter, continues:

> What makes it worse is that for at least the past fifteen years the PLO could have negotiated a better arrangement than this modified Allon Plan, one not requiring so many unilateral concessions to Israel. For reasons best known to the leadership it refused all previous overtures.[125]

But for the PLO this was not a decision made between a good and a bad agreement but one made between an agreement and no agreement at all.

The PLO calculated that the most it could obtain was de jure recognition and a foothold in Palestine. The agreement made possible the return of the PLO's exiled leadership, as well as 9,000 Palestinians who would become part of the territory's police force. This was more than the PLO had been able to achieve through armed resistance and legal advocacy alone. Moreover, Arafat did not fully appreciate the legal, and binding, consequences of the DOP. He believed that once inside the Palestinian territories, he could resuscitate the PLO and begin a new chapter of the Palestinian struggle.[126] According to Rashid Khalidi, he also believed that he "would be able to outsmart the Israelis."[127] On several occasions Arafat did exactly that.

Israel and the PLO signed letters of mutual recognition on 9 September 1993, a month after signing the DOP. The parties had agreed to sign an identical copy of the DOP on the White House on 13 September 1993, wherein the parties are shown as the "Government of the State of Israel and the Palestinian team (in the Jordanian-Palestinian delegation to the Middle East Peace Conference) ('the Palestinian delegation')." Before the signing ceremony, Arafat demanded that the text be changed to refer to the PLO as the official negotiating partner; he prevailed. The move infuriated Rabin, who considered canceling the ceremony, but ultimately, he and Arafat shook hands.[128] Upon entering the Gaza Strip in June 1994, Arafat smuggled in his confidante, Mamdouh Nofal, to whom Israel had denied entry.[129] On another occasion, Rabin instructed the Palestinian Interim Government to arrest Muhammad Deif, a Hamas operative accused of terrorist activity by Israel. Although Israeli intelligence indicated that Deif and Arafat had been together, Arafat refused to arrest him and denied he had seen him at all.[130]

These maneuvers yielded little more than occasional and tangential victories. Still, Arafat believed that if he were inside the territories, with the Palestinian people emerging from a momentous popular uprising together with international support, that the PLO would be able to build the momentum to establish better terms in the permanent status agreement. Mahmoud Abbas, a leading advocate of the DOP, believed that it was the only possible outcome. Neither of them believed that the interim stage of the agreement would in fact be interminable. Shaath comments that they thought, "with the collapse of the Soviet Union and the ascendance of the Clinton Administration and a Democratic Party in the United States supportive of peace, that this was a changing world. But their assumption was wrong."[131]

The Permanence of Interim Status

Fundamentally, this 1993 peace agreement, which became known as the Oslo I Accord, shifted global perceptions and diplomatic understandings of the Palestinian struggle. From at least 1974 to 1991, the PLO had successfully framed its struggle as one against settler-colonial subjugation, necessitating pressure on Israel to cease its expansionist and eliminatory project. In coalition with the Non-Aligned Movement, the PLO established new law on behalf of colonized people and marginalized Israel globally by emphasizing that nation's alignment with imperial powers, including Portugal, South Africa, and the United States, that sought to maintain their domination. The peace process reframed the struggle as a conflict between two equal parties that required compromise by both sides to achieve a resolution. Yet the framework of peacemaking also obfuscated the power imbalance that continued to characterize the relationship between Israel, a state with exceptional military and economic power, and the Palestinians, a stateless people. In effect, this diminished pressure on Israel and enhanced its global standing. Hirschfield explains that the Declaration of Principles

> paved the way for much more intense U.S.-Israeli security cooperating and the upgrading of Israel's technological capacities. It also contributed largely to the opening of worldwide markets, enabling a substantial increase in Israeli gross national product per capita in only a few years.[132]

The agreement also eased Israel's relations with other Arab states, with whom it normalized its economic relations. These new relationships diminished any inclinations among these states to aggressively intervene on behalf of Palestinians.[133]

The PLO benefited as well. In addition to achieving juridical status and the right of return to the territories for nearly 9,000 exiled Palestinians, it also acquired a governance authority it did not previously enjoy. This included jurisdiction over culture, social welfare, tourism, education, and health.[134] The Palestinian economic elite finally achieved some territorial stability, enabling their free market enterprises to flourish and providing them with access to foreign investment.[135] Together, these benefits constituted significant incentives for a Palestinian political and economic elite to exalt and perpetuate the Oslo framework.[136]

In addition, the terms of the DOP shaped the framework of subsequent negotiations. This was particularly true in regard to the Interim Agreement on the West Bank and the Gaza Strip, signed on 28 September 1995 (also known as the Oslo II Accord). Whereas the DOP had fleshed out an agreement to agree, Oslo II fleshed out the agreement terms in detail. Like the DOP, Oslo II made no mention of a future Palestinian state, addressing only "the legitimate rights of the Palestinian people and their just requirements," as well as the "establishment of Palestinian institutions."[137] The agreement stipulates that upon establishment of a Palestinian council, which would later come to be called the National Authority, the Israeli civil administration shall be dissolved and Israel's military shall be withdrawn. But Oslo II did not ensure the dissolution of Israel's military government. Instead, that government would remain intact and retain all responsibilities not delegated to the Palestinian Authority.[138]

Among the agreement's most significant consequences was the division of the West Bank into three areas of jurisdiction: Areas A, B, and C. Israel would transfer all civil and security authority to the Palestinian Authority in Area A, which amounted to 18 percent of the West Bank. In Area B, 22 percent of the territory, it would transfer civil powers and retain security authority (see the Oslo Accord–West Bank Areas map). Finally, Israel would retain full civil and security authority over Area C, or 60 percent of the West Bank. The parties agreed that Israel would gradually transfer civil and security authority over all territory to the Palestinian Authority, within eighteen months of its establishment, "except for issues that will be negotiated in the permanent status negotiations"—an exception that preserved Israel's exclusive control over settlements, Jerusalem, borders, and the question of refugees. Additionally, the Palestinian Authority's police force would only be responsible for incidents involving Palestinians, thus limiting Palestinians' ability to protect themselves from Israeli settlers who remained in the territories under Israel's jurisdiction. Israel would maintain

> the responsibility for defense against external threats, including the responsibility for protecting the Egyptian and Jordanian borders, and for the defense against external threats from the sea and from the air, as well as overall security of Israelis and Settlements, for the purpose of safeguarding their internal security and public order, and will have all the powers to take the steps necessary to meet this responsibility.[139]

In short, rather than improve the terms outlined in the DOP, Oslo II reified the patchwork authority delegated to Palestinians, enshrined Israel as the sole source of all authority, and did not enhance the prospect of Palestinian independence.

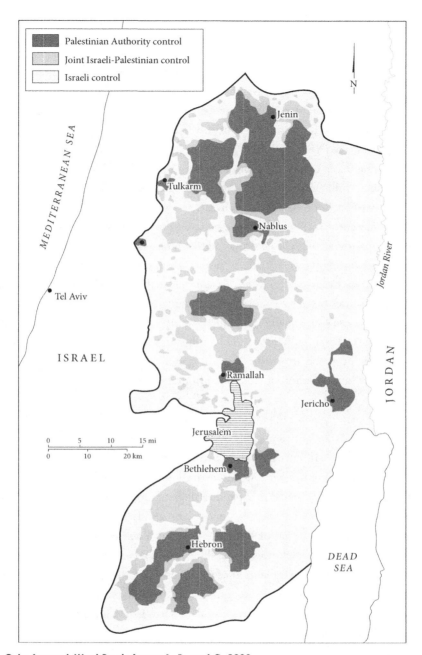

Legend:
- Palestinian Authority control
- Joint Israeli-Palestinian control
- Israeli control

N

MEDITERRANEAN SEA

Jenin

Tulkarm

Nablus

Jordan River

Tel Aviv

ISRAEL

Ramallah

Jericho

JORDAN

Jerusalem

| 0 | 5 | 10 | 15 mi |

| 0 | 10 | 20 km |

Bethlehem

Hebron

DEAD
SEA

Oslo Accord–West Bank Areas A, B, and C, 2000

The 1995 Oslo II Accord carved the West Bank and Gaza into three areas of jurisdiction. Area A came under full Palestinian control; Area B was under joint Israeli and Palestinian control; and Area C, the largest jurisdiction, came under full Israeli civil and political control.

Despite this favorable outcome for Israel, the Interim Agreement infuriated the Israeli right, which sought to establish Jewish sovereignty over the territories in its pursuit of a Greater Israel. In November 1995 and amid the right-wing Likud Party's incitement to protest, a twenty-five-year-old Israeli law student, Yigal Amir, assassinated Yitzhak Rabin.[140] Rabin never supported Palestinian statehood, but his pragmatic calculus led him to believe that Israel's domination was not sustainable. Unlike his hard-line counterparts and predecessors who believed in a Greater Israel, Rabin saw the settlements as a security, not an ideological, issue. Palestinian and Israeli analysts alike believed that Rabin was necessary to the further progress of the peace process and that his assassination marked its end.[141]

Several attempts were made to resuscitate the process and move on to a permanent status agreement. None of them yielded meaningful outcomes. Meanwhile, hostilities between Palestinians and Israel and its vigilantes intensified. In February 1994, an Israeli settler killed twenty-nine Palestinians as they were praying in the Ibrahimi Mosque in Hebron at dawn.[142] Hamas responded with its first suicide attack, in April 1994, killing eight Israelis in Afula.[143] These attacks set off an escalation of violent confrontations and further entrenchment of Israeli control. Under the leadership of Prime Minister Benjamin Netanyahu, elected to that top office for the first time in 1996, the peace process effectively stopped, and Israel's settlement activity, including Jewish settler takeovers of Palestinian homes in East Jerusalem, increased.[144]

Ehud Barak, considered a moderate in support of peace, succeeded Netanyahu in 1999 and continued to expand settlements and delay Israeli withdrawal from the Palestinian territories. By 2000, Likud and Labor Israeli governments had increased the number of settlements in the West Bank by 100 percent. Unlike his predecessors, however, Barak endorsed a two-state solution, marking the first official Israeli mention of the prospect of a Palestinian state.[145] At the urging of U.S. President Bill Clinton, Arafat and Barak convened at Camp David in July 2000 for negotiations over final status issues, including statehood, Jerusalem, and borders.

The Peace Process Collapses, A New Palestinian Intifada Begins

Israeli Prime Minister Ehud Barak broke with long-standing Israeli policy by endorsing a Palestinian state, but stayed in line with the right's hawkish vision of preserving the largest settlement blocs in the West Bank, controlling the territory's eastern most border, and consolidating Israeli jurisdiction over East Jerusalem. Israeli and U.S. officials mythologized Barak's negotiating position at Camp David as Israel's "most generous offer." Indeed, relative to previous Israeli offers that offered truncated self-autonomy, it was. But in light of established international policy, law, and certainly Palestinian demands, it fell severely short of being adequate, let alone generous.

At Camp David, Israeli negotiators sought to maintain Israel's unilateral annexation of East Jerusalem and to offer Palestinians nominal control over the city's Arab parts, amounting to what Barak himself described as a symbolic "foothold" in Jerusalem.[146] They also refused to return to the 1949 armistice lines because they wanted to annex 10 percent of the West Bank in order to retain its most significant settlement blocs, home to 150,000 settlers.[147] Worse, the settlement blocs would divide the West Bank into several cantons, and the Gaza Strip would form its own canton, rendering a nascent Palestinian state unviable.[148] *The Guardian*'s Ewen MacAskill explained that the proposed Palestinian state

> would have been in about half-a-dozen chunks, with huge Jewish settlements in between—a Middle East Bantustan. The Israeli army would also have retained the proposed Palestinian state's eastern border, the Jordan valley, for six to 10 years and, more significantly, another strip along the Dead Sea coast for an unspecified period: so much for being an independent state.[149]

In addition to making this territorial proposal for ghettoized sovereignty, Barak refused to accept any Israeli responsibility for the creation of the Palestinian refugee problem and refused to acknowledge the principle of the "right of return," enshrined in General Assembly Resolution 194 and upon which the UN had conditioned Israel's membership in 1949. Instead, Israeli negotiators offered to support and contribute to an international fund to compensate Palestinian refugees, and also to accept a limited number of refugees for repatriation. As the Camp David talks were intended to definitively resolve final status issues, acquiescence to these terms would have left no room for modification at a later date.

Arafat, who already conceded so much in the Oslo I and II Accords and had realized how little room there was for maneuver in their aftermath, could not politically afford to accept these terms. He refused to sign the agreement, and the Camp David peace talks collapsed in late July 2000.[150] Palestinians celebrated Arafat's resistance to Israeli and U.S. pressure, but the collapse of the talks exacerbated Palestinian frustration with the failure of the DOP to ease Israeli domination. In the seven years of the peace process, the number of settlements had doubled, while conditions wrought by military domination did not yield. The Oslo framework had curtailed Palestinian movement further, fragmented Palestinian society into a series of discontiguous areas, and did not show any promise of resolving the most vexing final status issues. As Nabil Shaath put it, "The Israelis used the interim state to steal the land and quadruple the number of colonial settlers ... all of what we know since Oslo is more Israeli control of our land."[151]

During this time, violence also significantly increased. Israel viewed its incremental withdrawal from the Occupied Territories and the transfer of limited control to the Palestinian Authority, stipulated by Oslo II, as a security matter. The redeployment of Israeli troops from Area A of the West Bank was accompanied by a perception that, once no longer governed by the heavy hand of Israel's martial law, Palestinian civilians had become a military threat. For every inch the state relinquished, it bolstered its military capacity to respond to that perceived increased threat. Israeli forces operationalized this by encircling the Palestinian towns now enjoying nominal sovereignty and preparing "detailed contingency plans for rapid intervention, involving heavy machinery, should Palestinian hostility indeed erupt."[152]

Barak had approached the Camp David negotiations with the anticipation that a conflict with Palestinians was on the horizon.[153] He had prepared the Israeli public for a more intense military confrontation by presenting Camp David as a "moment of truth" that would show that the Palestinians never wanted peace. During the negotiations, Barak explained to Israelis that only by exhausting all diplomatic options could "we look the parents of our soldiers in the eye and tell them we did everything in our power to search for peace before we sent their children to battle." Israel's withdrawal from southern Lebanon in July 2000 further complicated this calculus. Concerned that the army's withdrawal would be seen as a sign of military vulnerability, the members of the Israeli political right sought to reassert Israel's authority. They got that opportunity "in the only active military frontier still available for them—the Occupied Territories."[154]

On 20 September 2000, Israeli Defense Minister Ariel Sharon, flanked by 1,000 Israeli troops, entered Haram Al Sharif, the third holiest Muslim site, in a demonstration of power intended to lay Jewish claim to all of Jerusalem.[155] The provocation sparked a heated response from Palestinians, who clashed with armed soldiers, injuring one soldier and three Palestinians. Following Friday prayers the next day, clashes erupted again. Israeli troops responded with live fire and tear gas, killing five Palestinians. What ensued was a series of confrontations that culminated in sustained clashes between Palestinians and Israeli forces and marked the beginning of the second Palestinian uprising, also known as the Al Aqsa intifada.

Less than six weeks into the renewed uprising, and before Palestinian military force became a more salient factor, Israel dramatically increased its use of force against Palestinians. In doing so, it began a process that would affect the substance and meaning of international law regulating a state's use of force against non-state actors and indelibly shift Israel's relationship to Palestinians in the Occupied Territories.

Chapter 5

FROM OCCUPATION TO WARFARE

I am not the one who initiated the violence. I am not the one who is attacking Israelis. My tanks are not [be]sieging Israeli towns. I did not order my tanks, my air force, my artillery, my heavy weapons, my navy. . . . We are a nation with one airplane.

—Yasser Arafat, November 2000

ON 9 NOVEMBER 2000, Hussein 'Abayat and Khalid Salahat were visiting the seven homes partially damaged or completely demolished by Israeli airstrikes the night before in Beit Sahour, a predominantly Christian suburb of Bethlehem. Thirty-four-year-old 'Abayat was a member of Fatah's youth movement and an officer in the Palestinian Authority's General Intelligence Service. These political formations constituted "the leading political and military force behind the Al-Aqsa Intifada" and comprised a new Palestinian young guard.[1] These rising leaders saw this second intifada as an opportunity to undermine the traditional Palestinian leadership, which they viewed as corrupt and inept for their stewardship of the negotiations that led to the binding and deleterious terms of the Oslo Accords.[2] Though committed to the two-state solution, this new cadre opposed negotiations and sought to militarily force Israel to withdraw from the Occupied Territories.[3] Over the years since the signing of the Declaration of Principles, they had gained domination of the Al Aqsa intifada and enabled its militarization.

In the wake of the Oslo Accords, the PLO's leadership had returned from exile to the Occupied Territories, where they constituted the new Palestinian National Authority, supplanting the organic leaders and structures that had emerged during the first popular uprising. The transition to self-autonomy under the Oslo Framework for Peace marked a shift from the informal politics of mass mobilization to the formal politics of state building, where an elite leadership derived its symbolic legitimacy from "the people" without being directly accountable to them.[4] Together, these shifts marginalized Palestinian civil society and "meant that public space in the transitional era was virtually monopolized by the Authority (and particularly by its security services)."[5] The security forces included 40,000 men who carried light arms, provided to them to police the Palestinian population under Oslo's security coordination terms.[6]

The reorganization of public space also contributed to the militarization of the renewed uprising. After Israel departed from Area A, it classified the Palestinians there as latent threats and securitized the area's population; it also redefined the frontiers of confrontation between Israeli forces and Palestinians (see the Oslo Accord–West Bank Areas A, B, and C map in Chapter 4). Whereas, in the first intifada, "the site of struggle was the community, its streets, neighborhoods and homes," in the second intifada, the struggle became confined to the area frontiers, rendering the majority of Palestinian society, men and women alike, spectators of military clashes rather than participants in a mass uprising.[7] The confluence of these elements worked to sustain an intense and violent confrontation, ultimately characterized by Israeli airstrikes, Palestinian suicide attacks, and armed clashes between Israeli soldiers and Palestinian militants. By early November, when 'Abayat and Salahat visited Beit Sahour, the intifada had entered its sixth week and had claimed the lives of 180 people, 90 percent of whom were Palestinian.[8]

Less than a minute after the two men left one of the damaged homes, an Israeli helicopter gunship launched four antitank missiles at 'Abayat's Mitsubishi pickup truck as he and Salahat drove along a residential road in broad daylight. One of the missiles struck the vehicle, catapulting its blazing parts into the air. The attack killed 'Abayat and injured Salahat. Two women in their fifties who were standing nearby died from shrapnel wounds caused by the explosion, and six other bystanders were critically wounded.

Israel took responsibility for the attack, explaining that "the action was based on intelligence information."[9] Israel had targeted 'Abayat for his role in armed attacks on army posts and Israeli settlements in the Bethlehem district in the course of the nascent uprising.[10] On the same day 'Abayat was assassinated, Yasser Arafat was in a meeting with U.S. President Bill Clinton in Washington and he took the opportunity to describe the attack as a "very dangerous development."[11] Although Israeli armed forces and Palestinian militants had been engaging in intense clashes for several weeks, Israel's use of aerial snipers in the Occupied Territories signaled a deliberate escalation in hostilities. Palestinian gunfire, suicide attacks, and rocket fire had not yet become a salient feature of the struggle. Additionally, this assassination was the first Israeli public attack against a known leader, and the first time Israel had launched an airstrike without warning.[12]

Fatah declared revenge. Marwan Barghouti, a senior Fatah official and a political prisoner since 2002, described the assassination as a "cowardly aggression" and vowed that Israel would be held responsible for any response from Palestinian forces.[13] Israel understood this as well. Lieutenant General Shaul Mofaz told Israeli radio that although the military establishment expected a wave of Palestinian violence to follow the assassination, "in the long run, everyone who wants to harm Israeli army soldiers and citizens of Israel must know that he won't be spared."[14]

While the public nature of Israel's assassinations was new, the assassinations themselves were not. Israeli forces had engaged in covert assassinations of Palestinian political and military leaders since the early seventies.[15] In one attack, Ehud Barak, who was later to approve the strike on 'Abayat in his capacity as Prime Minister, dressed as a woman and led a group of Israeli commandos into Beirut to assassinate a group of senior members of Fatah.[16] In the late eighties, Moshe Ya'alon assassinated Khalil al-Wazir (Abu Jihad), the leader of the PLO's military wing, in Tunis. Israel's assassination policy continued into the nineties, even after the return of Palestine's exiled leadership to the Occupied Territories. Until November 2000, however, Israeli officials had vehemently denied responsibility for the willful killings. In 1992, for example, a government spokesman claimed:

> There is no policy, and there will never be a policy or a reality, of willful killing of suspects ... the principle of the sanctity of life is a fundamental principle of the IDF. There is no change and there will not be a change in this respect.[17]

The fact that Israel took full responsibility for its assassination of 'Abayat and vowed to assassinate others it deemed a threat was novel and proved to be a game changer for the conflict as well as for international law. In authorizing military force against Palestinians and the deployment of assassinations and other prohibited tactics, Israel's legal institutions embarked on two fundamental and interlocking shifts. The first was to unsettle the applicable legal framework regulating the Israeli state's relationship to Palestinians. The second was to change the laws of war that regulated a belligerent's right to use force more generally. Together, these shifts, achieved through legal work, enabled Israel to expand its use of force against Palestinians and to extinguish the specter of Palestinian military resistance. Israel literally created new law for colonial dominance, international law that in the past had been contemplated and rejected.[18]

Regulating "Almost War"

In late 2000, when Israel publicly embraced its assassination policy, it argued that it could use lethal force as a first resort against individuals it deemed terrorists. When it did so however, it was challenging existing international law, which regarded terrorism as a criminal issue of domestic concern. The proper response to such criminal activity is law enforcement authority, meaning a criminal suspect is entitled to a trial and can be executed only after a conviction of guilt. Under this framework, Israel cannot shoot to kill Palestinians suspected of terrorism. Such killings constitute extralegal, arbitrary, and summary executions, which are prohibited in law.[19] Similar prohibitions are operative under the framework of occupation law.

Military occupation may be part of an international armed conflict. During a military occupation, the occupying power assumes a sovereign's authority and retains effective control of the territory and its population. Only one state possesses jurisdiction and, therefore, the power to control the inhabitants and all their means of survival.[20] Since the occupied population does not have the means to protect or police itself, the occupying power must limit its force to law enforcement.[21] It cannot wage war or invoke self-defense against a population over whom it exercises effective control, and can use lethal violence only as a measure of last resort. When Israel assassinated 'Abayat, it laid claim to a broader use of force unavailable to it as an occupying power. Citing the militarized nature of the second intifada, the Israeli government argued that it is engaged in an *armed conflict short of war*. his is not a civilian disturbance or a demonstration or a riot. It is characterized by live-fire attacks on a significant scale both quantitatively and geographically. . . . The attacks are carried out by a well armed and organized militia under the command of the Palestinian political establishment operating from areas outside Israeli control.[22]

Israel asserted its right to use lethal force but refused to classify the conflict as war, neither a civil war ("non-international armed conflict," NIAC) nor a war against a liberation movement ("international armed conflict," IAC). States, national liberation movements, and regional organizations had contemplated both scenarios during the Diplomatic Conferences held between 1974 and 1977, and developed legal frameworks to regulate them, as captured in Additional Protocols I and II to the Geneva Conventions. Israel never ratified those treaties. Recognizing the confrontation as a NIAC or an IAC would recognize the Palestinian use of force as legitimate if deployed within the bounds of applicable law. So, instead, Israel claimed it could wage almost war against a population (Palestinians) that had no legal right to fight back.

Israel refused to recognize its confrontation with Palestinians as a civil war, or NIAC, because that would unravel the false partition separating Israel from the Occupied Territories. Such recognition would acknowledge Israel's maintenance of a singular, discriminatory government, thus exposing it to more pointed claims of pursuing a policy of creeping annexation and overseeing an apartheid regime. While Israel has denied that Palestinians are part of Israel's civilian jurisdiction, it simultaneously continues to insist they are not sufficiently outside it to be recognized as sovereign and independent.[23]

In a case where a state is fighting irregular forces that claim to be part of a state under colonial domination or occupation, as Palestinians have historically claimed, the conflict is known as an IAC. In these cases, colonized peoples have the right to use force in pursuit of their self-determination.[24] The laws of armed conflict recognize the embryonic sovereignty of these irregular forces and treat them as being nearly the same as a state.

If Israel recognized the conflict as an IAC, that would confer belligerent status on Palestinian militants, and Palestinian fighters would have the right, under an international legal regime, to use lethal force against Israeli military targets and installations. The Israeli civilian casualties of those attacks would be considered collateral damage. And, if captured, Palestinian fighters would be held as prisoners of war, to be returned at the end of hostilities or swapped in negotiations. This status would also permit other states to legally intervene, with military and/or financial assistance, upon a request by the Palestinian leadership. Israel has rejected any Palestinian claims of having the right to use force, whether through the defunct Palestine Liberation Army or any other organized apparatus. It does not recognize Palestinian claims to statehood in any part of what was Mandate Palestine and rejects the idea that Palestinians as a people constitute an embryonic sovereign with the right to use armed force. Israel insists that any Palestinian use of force is terroristic and criminal.

It is important to recognize that neither of the legal frameworks regulating irregular wars would adequately protect Palestinians or decisively enhance their ability to confront a technologically advanced state. Although the law would regulate Israel's conduct of hostilities and legitimate the Palestinian resort to arms, it would not be a game changer. In fact, the Palestine Liberation Organization rejected Israel's claim of engaging in an "armed conflict short of war," and emphasized that there was no armed conflict at all.[25] The PLO insisted that Palestinian militancy was erratic and unorganized and did not constitute collective armed resistance. It also demanded that Israel revert to an occupation law framework that would limit its use of force to law enforcement.[26] The point is that by avoiding available legal frameworks for armed conflict, Israel deliberately exceptionalized its in fact nonexceptional confrontations with Palestinians in order to expand its right to use force and delegitimize any responsive force.

Israeli officials and military lawyers understood that Israel's assassination policy contravened existing law. First, these assassinations constituted a disproportionate use of force against an occupied population, people who should only be policed with law enforcement authority. Second, extrajudicial assassinations are illegal under any circumstances except for warfare, in which case the targets also have a belligerent privilege to kill.[27] Israel wanted to use lethal force against the population it had a duty to protect under occupation law and which, it claimed, could not use lethal force in any circumstances. To overcome these legal hurdles, Israeli leaders charged the International Law Division (ILD) in the Military Advocate General's office with the task of developing a legal framework that would sanction the assassination of Palestinians in the Occupied Territories. Colonel Daniel Reisner, who headed this division at the start of the second intifada explained:

> Effectively, the question was whether we could treat terrorists like an army and use our force against them openly. We wrote a revolutionary opinion, stating that above a certain level, fighting terrorism is analogous to war and that, subject to very specific rules, we will authorize such attacks.[28]

Reisner's definition of the battle as *analogous* to war was no mistake. The state could not declare war against suspected criminals and it did not want to acknowledge the juridical status of Palestinians either as an oppressed minority or as a people struggling for self-determination. Israel also understood that as an occupying power, it maintained jurisdiction over the territories wherefrom Palestinian threats emerged, and was therefore responsible for order within them.[29]

To get around this circumstances, Israel argued that its military no longer had effective control where administrative authority had been transferred to the Palestinian interim government as a result of Oslo II.[30] Specifically, it was referring to Area A, the 18 percent of the West Bank and Gaza Strip that had come under the full civil and military control of the Palestinian Authority after the peace process. Israel was trying to make the case that it could maintain an occupation in 82 percent of the Occupied Territories and simultaneously be in an armed conflict against its occupied population in the remaining 18 percent where its control had been diminished. These arguments were absolutely novel in existing law.

Working with its legal advisors, Israel had devised the new category, "armed conflict short of war," out of necessity, but this category did not have a coherent framework; Israel developed it in piecemeal fashion. In a 2005 interview with the *Jerusalem Post*, Shavit Matias, then Director of the Department for International Agreements and International Litigation, captured the ambiguity and rashness of the new legal category when she commented, "Clearly the situation between the Palestinians and us during the intifada was almost a state of war or a state of war or whatever term you want to use."[31] Menachem Finkelstein, then head of the Military Advocate General, an office supplying legal expertise to the armed forces, explained that while "the scale and intensity of the events justifies the classification as an armed conflict," the condition that war be fought between "the military organizations of two or more states" was not met in this scenario.[32]

Israel's High Court of Justice moved in lockstep with the state's military and political establishment. In a series of decisions, beginning in 2001, the Israeli High Court began to implicitly recognize the existence of a conflict short of war.[33] By early 2002, the Court held that Israel was exercising its right to self-defense as defined by the UN Charter.[34] Later in 2002, it explicitly held that "this is not police activity. It is an armed struggle."[35] In 2004, in *Beit Sourik Village Council v. the Government of Israel*, the High Court described the situation as an "armed conflict," effectively recognizing the application of the laws of armed conflict to territories where Israel continued to exercise its military authority.[36]

Israel scrambled to find legal justification for its use of force against Palestinians. In avoiding available legal frameworks, Israel also claimed that no existing body of law had adequately contemplated the conflict between states and terrorists. Therefore, existing laws of armed conflict codified in treaties and custom were outdated and insufficient to regulate this new form of warfare. It argued that the situation was *sui generis*, or unlike anything else, and thus not subject to strict legal regulation. Instead, it said that its army and political establishment should have greater latitude to decide the appropriate course of action in combat on an ad hoc basis.[37] Israel would make these decisions for itself, using the law as a clear reference but not as a strict guide, and it claimed the right to do so because its challenges were unique and unprecedented.

This was not the first time, nor would it be the last, that Israel would claim its circumstances to be *sui generis* in order to achieve policy goals arguably prohibited in law. As described earlier, upon its establishment in 1948 and for eighteen years thereafter, it applied a martial law regime almost exclusively to its native Palestinian population to facilitate their removal and dispossession. And since 1967, it has insisted that the West Bank and Gaza do not have a rightful sovereign, thereby negating the de jure application of occupation law, in order to facilitate its settler-colonial encroachments. Israel could achieve its policy goals by mere reliance on its military prowess, but as a liberal settler state, it has sought the legitimating force of the law as well.[38] *Sui generis* is a category of exception, like necessity and martial law, and affords Israel room for maneuvering.[39] Israel deploys the *sui generis* framework as a sovereign act compelled by a unique circumstance, and thus insists it is within the bounds of law. In doing so, Israel is not merely claiming that it is justified in violating the law in this one instance but also asserting that its unprecedented conditions authorize it to create new law for itself and everyone else. A *sui generis* framework maintains the veneer of legality while producing a violence that "shed[s] every relation to law."[40]

Israel's *sui generis* claims were not without significant controversy as they belied a rich history of international legal regulation of its occupation of Palestinian territories and its relationship to Palestinians more generally. When Israel began applying its assassination policy, the United States as well as the United Nations responded with harsh disapproval. The question then is, how did Israel's radical propositions and legal transgressions lead to change rather than disapprobation and sanction? The answer is found in the nature of international law as a living instrument that is continually made, implemented, broken, and remade.

The Malleability of Law: A Violation Can Also Be a Proposition

Customary law is one of three primary sources of international law.[41] Unlike treaties, which are a form of explicit consent, customary law is not written and is therefore tacit. It is made up of state behavior, literally what states do, and *opinio juris*, what states believe is legal. When deciding what the law is, the International Court of Justice (ICJ) considers "judicial decisions and the teachings of the most highly qualified publicists of the various nations, as subsidiary means for the determination of rules of law."[42] That means that national jurisprudence as well as the production of knowledge among legal scholars shapes the content of international law.

Treaties mean what they say and can be changed only by the establishment of a new treaty or the explicit rescindment of the existing treaty. In contrast, customary law changes consistently—sometimes overnight, sometimes over a number of decades—and reflects state behavior, norms, and circumstances. There is no single, scientific approach to determining custom. Instead, there are diverging approaches that reflect different beliefs regarding the nature of law. Traditionalists place greater emphasis on state practice and believe that custom reflects law's descriptive accuracy and that it corresponds to reality.[43] In contrast, those taking a more modern approach place greater emphasis on what states say or believe even absent actual facts and practice. This includes considering the attitudes of states as found in multilateral treaties, General Assembly resolutions, and state declarations. The comparative utility of each approach remains an outstanding debate, and even the ICJ does not strictly adhere to only one approach.[44]

Given this reality, in war the law is also a battlefield, and the contest is to define what is legal and what is not.[45] When a state does not want to comply with international law, it can either contest the applicability of a treaty and/or argue that a custom has not crystallized. States that disagree can push back and argue for the application of a treaty and/or insist that the law has been established as custom. There is no easy way to settle this contest. Unlike domestic law, international law lacks a hierarchal enforcement model. That means there is no international supreme court, and no single body that has a monopoly on violence so as to enforce judicial decisions. Therefore, there was no authoritative way to determine whether a state's behavior is in violation of the law. Instead, there are specialized areas of law, such as environmental, business, maritime, refugee, human rights, and humanitarian law, and each has its own institutions and mechanisms with varying degrees of enforcement authority.[46] Moreover, these institutions and mechanisms are inflected with competing national interests and the balance of power among states.

As concerns the laws of war, these enforcement mechanisms and institutions include the International Criminal Court (ICC), the ICJ, regional institutions, and above all, the UN Security Council (UNSC). The ICC is a product of a multilateral treaty, the Rome Statute (1998), and membership is voluntary; state parties must ratify the treaty to be bound by its terms and subject to its jurisdiction. The ICJ is a subsidiary organ of the United Nations, and thus all UN member states are party to it. However, the ICJ has enforcement authority only when state parties voluntarily submit to it, and, when they do not, the ICJ can only issue a nonbinding "advisory opinion" declaring what the law is in a certain conflict. Chapter VII of the UN Charter empowers the UNSC to use force when necessary to restore international peace and security.[47] Security Council members can activate Chapter VII authority to enforce a judicial decision, but this rarely happens because of the veto power afforded to the Council's permanent members.

This mosaic of fragmented legal regimes, the distribution of power, and the nature of each existing international tribunal means that the enforceability of the laws of war largely depends on voluntary state consent and compliance or on robust state protest against a noncomplying state. In cases where there is no political will to compel a state to comply with the law, violations can become the norm rather than the exception.

Israel understood this, and deliberately worked to change the laws of armed conflict in order to accommodate its confrontations with Palestinians during the Al Aqsa intifada. Israel argued that it would have to develop new law based on its operational state practice because it was fighting a war no one had fought before. It insisted that its violations of existing laws were propositions for how the war should be fought. The nature of the laws of armed conflict made them susceptible to this legal work.

As part of international law, the laws of armed conflict are made up of treaty law and custom and reflect both when a state can initiate a war (*jus ad bellum*) and how a state should conduct itself in war once it is initiated (*jus in bello*). *Jus in bello* includes the Geneva Conventions and their Additional Protocols, which define how classes of people should be treated in conflict, while the Hague Regulations (1907) regulate the overall means and methods of warfare. Throughout the development of international law, both preceding and following its codification in the nineteenth century, it has failed to adequately limit wartime atrocities.[48]

This failure reflects inherent flaws and limitations in the laws of war. In order to achieve voluntary state buy-in, these laws must be adaptable to state needs. That very adaptability that makes legal regulation of warfare possible also makes the law an inadequate vehicle for constraining state behavior. First, the laws are established by the most powerful states, which are most interested in protecting their national interests. Thus, they will limit their use of force only insofar as they deem force unnecessary to achieving their goals.[49] Second, and as a result of this reality, new forms of warfare have been allowed to develop without the restraint of law.[50] Together with the fact that customary law is based on state practice and what they deem to be legal, if enough states adopt a particular practice and there is no significant protest in response, that practice can become an accepted norm. In contrast, if a state does something that is harshly condemned by other states, that behavior faces the specter of being found illegal. The global response to Israeli and U.S. force against Iraq, in 1982 and 2003 respectively, demonstrates this point.

In 1982, Israel struck and destroyed the Osirak nuclear reactor in Baghdad, before it was complete but when it was close to operational. Israel justified its attack as a measure of preemptive self-defense. The Security Council unanimously "condemn[ed] the military attack by Israel in clear violation of the Charter of the United Nations and the norms of international conduct."[51] As a result of the global protest and a Security Council rebuke, the argument of preemptive self-defense was rejected by other nations and such actions remained illegal. In 2003, the United States invaded Iraq, preempting Saddam Hussein's use of (supposed) weapons of mass destruction. Despite popular and national protest, no significant consensus emerged, thus bringing preemptive self-defense out of the realm of the categorically illegal and into a grey area of dispute.

Then, in the context of the Al Aqsa intifada, Israel attempted to move the question of preemptive self-defense further into the realm of legality. This process was described by ILD head Daniel Reisner:

> What we are seeing now is a revision of international law. . . . If you do something for long enough, the world will accept it. The whole of international law is now based on the notion that an act that is forbidden today becomes permissible if executed by enough countries. If the same process occurred in private law, the legal speed limit would be 115 kilometers an hour and we would pay income tax of 4 percent. So there is no connection between the question "Will it be sanctioned?" and the act's legality. . . . International law progresses through violations. We invented the targeted assassination thesis and we had to push it. At first there were protrusions that made it hard to insert easily into the legal moulds. Eight years later it is in the center of the bounds of legitimacy.[52]

This shift was not inevitable. Instead, a confluence of factors militated in favor of Israel's attempts to change the applicable legal framework and existing laws of war.

The United States: From Opposition to Collaboration

At the advent of Israel's assassination policy in November 2000, the United States responded with condemnation, describing Israel's behavior as "too aggressive."[53] This amounted to a state protest that put Israel's legal claims and military policies into dispute as a matter of law. Also in late 2000, the United States in consultation with the United Nations, as well as Israeli and Palestinian leaders, established the Sharm el-Sheikh Fact-Finding Committee aimed at ending the clashes that characterized the Al Aqsa intifada and resuming peace negotiations. U.S. President Bill Clinton appointed Senator George Mitchell to chair the committee. The committee published its report, commonly known as the Mitchell Report, in April 2001, only a few months after President George W. Bush had assumed office and one month after Palestinian groups had launched the first Palestinian mortar attack from Gaza into Israel, striking an army base.[54]

In its final recommendations, the committee rejected Israel's characterization of the second intifada as a *sui generis* one. It recommended that Israel "abandon the blanket characterization of the current uprising as 'an armed conflict short of war,' for failing to discriminate between terrorism and protest."[55] The report concluded that Israel's characterization was "overly broad, for it does not adequately describe the variety of incidents reported since late September 2000."[56] The committee explicitly recommended that Israel revert to the concept of law enforcement.[57] It also recommended that Israel reinstate "as a matter of course, military police investigations into Palestinian deaths resulting from IDF actions in the Palestinian territories in incidents not involving terrorism."[58] The Mitchell Report unequivocally rejected Israel's attempts to change the nature of the conflict as well as the heightened use of military force against Palestinians. The committee's conclusions and recommendations reflected the PLO's analysis of the applicable legal framework, as captured in the PLO's submissions to the committee. The committee's adoption of the PLO's legal analysis demonstrates law's utility as a defensive tool.[59]

In June 2001, under a directive from the Bush administration, CIA Director George Tenet published a plan for establishing a ceasefire and renewed security arrangements between Israel and the Palestinians.[60] Widely known as the Tenet Plan, the document affirmed the Mitchell Report's findings as well as its insistence that Israel abandon its militarized approach to the Occupied Palestinian Territories.[61] Notwithstanding these high-level U.S. objections, Israel continued its assassination policy and, with that decision, its defiance of existing law.

Less than two months after the release of the Tenet Plan, in August 2001, Israel assassinated two Hamas leaders in the West Bank city of Nablus, Jamal Mansour and Jamal Salim Damouni, also killing four bystanders. U.S. Secretary of State Colin Powell, speaking on CNN, condemned the attack as "too aggressive" and reminded viewers that "this was a targeted killing of the kind we have spoken out and condemned in the past, and we did so yesterday, both at the White House and in the State Department."[62] The State Department issued its own statement and described the attack as "excessive" and "highly provocative."[63]

The following day, U.S. Vice President Dick Cheney appeared on Fox News, where he was asked about Israel's assassination policy. Cheney's response signaled quiet consent, in contradiction of the State Department's position as well as that of the Mitchell Report and the Tenet Plan. While he did not defend Israel's policies, Cheney commented:

> If you've got an organization that has plotted or is plotting some kind of suicide bomber attack, for example, and they have evidence of who it is and where they're located, I think there's some justification in their trying to protect themselves by preempting.[64]

Cheney's remarks revealed a still nascent policy within the Bush administration that would come to full bloom in the course of its war on Iraq in 2003 as well as in its update of the National Security Strategy in 2006. Both this document and the war itself embodied the concept of preemptive self-defense, the central legal argument upon which targeted killing is based. Whereas state force is justified in response to an armed attack, the concept of preemptive self-defense claims that a state can use force against a latent, but certain, threat.[65] However, in August 2001, none of that thinking was in play, and Cheney's contradictory remarks caused a media maelstrom. The White House attempted to address the embarrassing schism during its daily press briefing. White House spokesperson Ari Fleischer emphasized U.S. opposition to Israel's assassination policy. He framed Cheney's remarks as speculation about the way Israel might justify its actions but not reflective of the U.S. position. Upon incessant grilling from one journalist, Fleischer doubled down on his comments, to put the controversy to rest by reiterating U.S. disapproval:

Q: Do you stand by your statement when you said that the Administration at all levels deplore the violence there and that includes the targeted killings?

MR. FLEISCHER: There is no doubt. That is the position of the Administration and is shared by all members of it.[66]

This stalwart U.S. resistance began to dissipate after 11 September 2001. Al Qaeda's attacks on the United States brought the once unacceptable within the realm of possibility and marked a significant juncture in states' understanding of non-state force. Following Al Qaeda's attacks, the UN Security Council passed Resolutions 1368 (2001) and 1373 (2001) declaring the operation against the United States tantamount to an armed attack, thus triggering Article 51 of the UN Charter permitting the use of force in self-defense. Prior to this moment, only states were recognized as capable of launching an armed attack. In effect, the UN was now sanctioning war against a non-state entity, as well as the state that harbored that entity.

Israel immediately attempted to co-opt the legal framework arising from the U.S. war against Al Qaeda to justify Israel's own use of military force against Palestinians. It tried to frame Palestinian attacks as tantamount to an armed attack within the purview of UNSC Resolutions 1368 and 1373 and as triggering its right to use force in self-defense.[67]

This was not the first time Israel had appealed to the Security Council to justify its use of force against Palestinians. Throughout the late sixties and seventies, Israel had insisted that its attacks against Lebanon and Jordan, sites the PLO was using to launch its attacks, were an exercise of self-defense.[68] In 1968, 1969, and 1970, the Security Council disagreed. It condemned Israel's attacks as "flagrant violation(s) of the United Nations Charter,"[69] and rejected its pleas of self-defense because, under the law, it could not defend territories it illegally occupied.[70] Israel's attempts now to frame the second intifada as an unprecedented war against terrorism were less new than they were a return to something very old. The critical difference was that whereas Palestinians launched their attacks from other states in the sixties and seventies, in 2001, their attacks emerged from territories where Israel exercised exclusive jurisdiction. This also distinguished Israel's claims from those of the United States.

The International Court of Justice highlighted this distinction when it rejected Israel's claims to self-defense in a 2004 advisory opinion on the legal consequences of the construction of a wall in the Occupied Palestinian Territories. The court reasoned that Article 51 contemplates an armed attack by one state against another state, and "Israel does not claim that the attacks against it are imputable to a foreign state." Moreover, the court held that because the threat to Israel "originates within, and not outside" the Occupied West Bank, the situation is different from that contemplated by Security Council resolutions 1368 and 1373 authorizing the United States to use force against Afghanistan.[71] By emphasizing Israel's effective control of the OPT, the ICJ made clear that the law of self-defense and the use of military force were unavailable to Israel in its dealings with Palestinians. The ICJ's decision amounted to a protest about Israel's attempts to change the law. ICJ advisory opinions, however, are not binding. They constitute a significant intervention in the production of knowledge by jurists, yet are a single element of customary law that traditionalists would argue is not as significant as state practice. Plenty of other jurists published responses to the ICJ's decision, arguing both for and against it. In effect, the question whether Israel had a right to self-defense against Palestinians remained unsettled and contested.

Several years before the ICJ issued this opinion, the High Contracting Parties of the Geneva Conventions, literally all the member states of the United Nations, convened to reaffirm the applicability of the Conventions to the OPT. They rejected Israel's attempt to shift the legal framework, and called on Israel to "abstain from exposing the civilian population to military operations."[72] Separately, the European Union and the European Parliament also rebuffed Israel's attempts to shift from occupation law to the law of war.[73] These statements reflected the *opinio juris* of states and added to the register of protest rejecting Israel's claims of exceptionalism. Israel's persistent practice, conducted without legal accountability, also shaped customary law.

Yet the likelihood of accountability dimmed further "as the [Bush] Administration sought to move aggressively against Al Qaeda" and adopted an assassination policy in its so-called Global War on Terror.[74] In 2002, the administration
launched a Hellfire missile from an unmanned Predator drone at a car carrying
Qaed Salim Sinan al-Harethi, while it was in motion in Yemen, killing him and
the other passengers.[75] Al-Harethi was known as the mastermind of the bombing of the U.S. Navy guided-missile destroyer USS Cole and an active member
of Al-Qaeda. Swedish Foreign Secretary Anna Lindh described the attack as "a
summary execution that violates human rights," putting the tactic into dispute.[76]
The adoption of an assassination policy by the United States was helping to ease
criticism of Israel's practices, but the collapse of the position that there was a
difference between the U.S. and Israeli wars was not immediate.

Initially, the United States attempted to distinguish Israel's assassination
policy from its own. For example, U.S. State Department spokesperson Richard
Boucher, responding to questions about the Bush administration's killing of al-
Harethi in light of its previous condemnation of Israel's practices, said:

> Our policy on targeted killings in the Israeli-Palestinian context has not
> changed . . .
>
> Q: . . . Well, so you have one rule for one conflict and another rule for an-
> other conflict?
>
> MR. BOUCHER: I would say that—if you look back at what we have said
> about targeted killings in the Israeli-Palestinian context, you will find that
> the reasons we have given do not necessarily apply in other circumstances.[77]

A rising and robust counterterrorism industry soon eviscerated these nuances
and steadily subsumed Palestinian militancy. U.S. opposition transformed into explicit collaborations with Israel in the production of knowledge on and state practice
of counterterrorism. These collaborations shaped the customary law regulating use
of force against terrorism without regard to the previous consequential distinctions
between the U.S. and Israeli battlefronts. By May 2002, Bush administration officials had begun high-profile meetings aimed at joint counterterrorism operations.

Douglas Feith, the hawkish U.S. Under Secretary of Defense for Policy, traveled to Tel Aviv to meet with then Prime Minister Ariel Sharon and Defense Minister Binyamin Ben Eliezer, where they discussed "war games, intelligence sharing, and other cooperation."[78] The administration continued its bilateral collaboration in the U.S.–Israel Joint Counterterrorism Group that meets annually "to formally review the full range of counterterrorism issues" for both countries.[79]

Even in the face of this increasing synergy, high-level diplomatic protest against Israel's practice continued. Upon the March 2004 assassination of Sheikh Ahmed Yasin, Hamas's founding member and political leader, the European Union, the UN Secretary-General, the United Kingdom, and Norway, among others, condemned the operation as an extrajudicial assassination. Undeterred, one month later, in April 2004, Israel assassinated Abdel Aziz al-Rantisi, who had succeeded Yasin. In response, the Security Council convened a meeting to condemn the attack and, more broadly, extrajudicial assassinations. Nearly all Council members agreed that while Israel had a right to protect its citizens, such operations as these assassinations exceeded the bounds of international law.[80] This opposition was meaningful and constituted protest of Israel's attempts to change the law, but it was not enough to stem the Israeli practice.

Whatever protest existed against targeted killings during the Bush administration all but disappeared during President Barack Obama's tenure. The Obama administration oversaw over 500 drone strikes, nearly ten times the number of strikes authorized by the Bush Administration.[81] However, domestic and international protest about the policy, now deployed by a self-proclaimed liberal administration, was faint and ultimately faded.[82] Meanwhile, and under Obama's leadership, U.S.–Israeli counterterrorism efforts became more robust. In 2011, the Obama administration would cite Israeli jurisprudence in a Department of Justice memo providing legal justification for the targeted killing of Anwar al-Awlaki, a U.S. citizen in Yemen accused of ties with Al Qaeda in the Arabian Peninsula.[83] U.S. and Israeli academics have similarly engaged intensely in producing knowledge about such counterterrorism efforts, indicating not only the synergy between them but also the lack of meaningful distinctions that should have otherwise set them apart.[84] Significantly, these collaborations and publications become part of the state practice and *opinio juris* that constitute customary law, and they have added to the register of acceptance of assassinations as targeted killings.

The United States and Israel also argued that because they are at the forefront of fighting a "war on terror," they are specially affected states. As such, U.S. and Israeli state practice should, they say, be given greater weight and consideration in the formulation of customary humanitarian law.[85] Conversely, the operational practice and legal opinions of other states should bear less weight. In these circumstances, a small number of specially affected states can determine the custom for other countries so long as those states do not object.[86] In other words, the United States and Israel are saying they should determine the law for all other states. This understanding is not widely accepted, but the impact of such a controversy is only as significant as the protest against the practice; and such global protest against the use of assassinations has been neither consistent nor long-lasting.[87]

Had the United States maintained its opposition to targeted killings and to the framework of "armed conflict short of war," Israel's actions might have remained somewhere between a controversial proposition and a violation of international law. However, because of diminishing U.S. protest, which culminated in U.S. adoption of the assassination policy, Israel's violations steadily escaped the zone of brazen violations and moved into the scope of legitimacy. Assassination shifted from being the policy of one rogue state to being a policy of targeted killing by the world's superpower in what it called the Global War on Terror.[88] Together with the production of knowledge by jurists, national jurisprudence, and, significantly, waning protest from other states, extrajudicial assassinations became increasingly tolerated as legitimate tactics in certain theaters of war and recognized as targeted killings.[89] Although a counterfactual analysis is not determinative, in this instance the impact of Al Qaeda's 2001 attacks on the United States on this process cannot be overstated. As put by Reisner:

> It took four months and four planes to change the opinion of the United States, and had it not been for those four planes I am not sure we would have been able to develop the thesis of the war against terrorism on the present scale.[90]

Israel succeeded in making the practice of assassinations, as well as its expanded use of force against Palestinians, a proposition for a new international norm, but it did not stop there. The seeds it planted in the second intifada came into full and lethal bloom in its military operations in the Gaza Strip. There

Israel continued its efforts to change the laws of war, and methods of colonial domination, primarily in its confrontations with Hamas, which increasingly featured rocket and mortar fire against Israel.

Planting the Seeds of Destruction

In 2003, and in the midst of the second intifada, the Israeli army sought to update its military doctrine. It recruited Asa Kasher, Professor of Professional Ethics at Tel Aviv University and the author of the Israeli army's ethical code of conduct established in the mid-nineties, as well as Amos Yadlin, a Major General in the Israeli Army and the head of Military Intelligence, to lead an ethics committee composed of military personnel. In Yadlin's words, they had to "formulate how to fight terror … where the laws and ethics of conventional war did not apply."[91] Whereas in conventional warfare between two states, everyone shares the same values, in this case Yadlin argues, the state has to confront "a people that have totally different values and rules of engagement."[92] Since "[t]he other side is fighting outside the rules [Israel has] to create new ethical rules for the international law of armed conflict, in keeping with the traditional IDF concept of "the purity of arms."[93]

Kasher, Yadlin, and their committee made several sweeping proposals for how to amend existing laws of war in order to ease restrictions on states fighting terrorists. In 2005, they built on this proposal with a more comprehensive article in the *Journal of Military Ethics*, an academic publication highly regarded among the military and political elite and national security law scholars, where it received global attention.[94] Kasher explains that while Moshe Ya'alon, the Israeli army's Chief of Staff, did not formally make the document binding, he and his successors adopted the principles it proposed.[95] Kasher and Yadlin, who intended to re-shape international law through their scholarly interventions and the influence of Israel's military practice, soon saw that happening in the Gaza Strip, following Israel's unilateral withdrawal from that territory of its settler population and military installations in 2005.

Lethal Fruits: Devastating Wars Against the Gaza Strip

Upon its unilateral disengagement, Israel argued that it no longer occupied the territory and, therefore, could no longer conduct police operations there, making necessary the use of military force as a measure of first resort: in effect, Israel declared war on Gaza.[96] To facilitate this shift in the relevant language of law, it modified the analysis of effective control it had used in the early 2000s. Then, and in order to justify assassinations, Israel had argued that its withdrawal from Area A diminished its effective control in that territory, permitting its use of military force. Since it was still in control of the majority of the territory, however, it would have to balance the laws of war and the humanitarian provisions of occupation law to quell unrest.[97] Whereas Israel argued that the Al Aqsa intifada was an "armed conflict short of war," in 2005, it argued that its confrontation with Palestinians in Gaza was explicitly warfare because Israel had ended its effective control when it withdrew from the entire territory (and not just part of it), thus ending its occupation.

Israel equated the presence of its armed forces in Gaza to effective control, the threshold analysis for determining the existence of a military occupation, and the redeployment of those forces as that occupation's cessation.[98] However, according to Article 42 of the Hague Regulations (1907), a belligerent has effective control of a territory so long as it has established its authority and has the ability to exercise it, regardless of the continuous presence of ground troops.[99] The Nuremberg Tribunal[100] and the International Criminal Tribunal for the Former Yugoslavia (ICTY), are among the tribunals that have affirmed that a territory remains occupied so long as an army could reestablish physical control of that territory "at any time."[101]

In its Disengagement Plan, Israel reserved the right to use force against Palestinians living in the Gaza Strip in the name of preventive and reactive self-defense, and it has conducted several military operations in Gaza in the name of such self-defense. Israel has maintained control of its air space, its seaports, its telecommunications network, its electromagnetic sphere, its tax revenue distribution, and its population registry. Israel also has complete control of Palestinian movement as it controls four of its five border crossings with Gaza and therefore the ingress and egress of all the territory's goods and people. Upon announcing Israel's withdrawal, Israel's political elite made clear that Israel did not intend to relinquish control of the Gaza Strip. Dov Weisglass, senior adviser to Prime Minister Ariel Sharon, explained that the disengagement was meant to freeze the peace process by supplying "the amount of formaldehyde that is necessary

so there will not be a political process with the Palestinians."[102] Unilateral withdrawal sought to alter the balance of power by offering a veneer of Palestinian
independence while retaining Israeli control.

The International Criminal Court,[103] the Human Rights Council's Fact-
Finding Mission to the Gaza Strip[104] and multiple international human rights
organizations[105] have acknowledged that Israel remains in effective control of
the Gaza Strip. Accordingly, the laws of occupation should remain in force,
thus obligating Israel to use its law enforcement authority to restore order
and prohibiting it from declaring war upon the territory it occupied. While
these legal findings help to shape the *opinio juris* regarding the territory's
status, absent meaningful sanction they are insufficient to regulate Israel's use
of force against the Gaza Strip; Israel has retained that latitude as a matter
of sovereign right.

Israel insisted its occupation had ended, but it also recognized that Gaza
was not sovereign. It declared Gaza a "hostile entity," which was neither a
state wherein Palestinians have the right to police and protect themselves nor
an occupied territory whose civilian population Israel had a duty to protect.
This meant that it could deny Palestinians the right to fully govern themselves
and simultaneously use military force to thwart their resistance to colonial
domination.

Since winning parliamentary elections in 2006, Hamas has been the legitimately elected leadership of the Palestinian population under occupation.
In June 2007 and in response to a U.S.-supported attempted coup, the party
routed its rival Fatah from the Gaza Strip and assumed control of the territory.
Hamas claims that it represents a nascent Palestinian state still under colonial
domination, and maintains armed struggle as a legitimate form of resistance.
Israel's outstanding rejection of Palestinian claims to sovereignty renders Hamas
a non-state actor, denies its forces belligerent privilege, and regards any use of
force as ipso facto terroristic, even when it is directly targeting Israeli military
installations.[106]

Israel achieves this conundrum by insisting that both Gaza's legal status and
the hostilities against Israel are *sui generis*. Echoing its statements at the start of
the Al Aqsa intifada, Israel argued that as the pioneer in this new military frontier,
it would have to define what the appropriate laws of war should be, based on its

experience and discretion; in other words, it would make up the law.[107] In effect, Israel usurped the right of Palestinians to defend themselves because they did not belong to an embryonic sovereign, relinquished its obligations as an occupying power, and expanded its right to unleash military force, thus rendering Palestinians in the Gaza Strip triply vulnerable. This framework has since become the bedrock of Israel's military campaigns against the coastal enclave.

Since announcing its disengagement in April 2004, Israel has launched twenty-two military campaigns against Gaza, including three massive onslaughts between 2008 and 2014: Operation Cast Lead (2008), Operation Pillar of Cloud (2012), and Operation Protective Edge (2014).[108] In the course of those onslaughts across six and a half years, Gaza's captive population became subject to Israel's deployment of new laws of warfare without external regulation. As put by Uzi Landau, former Israeli Minister of the Interior, Israel became a "laboratory for fighting terror."[109] More accurately, the Gaza Strip became Israel's colonial laboratory for experimentation with weapons and tactics in the so-called Global War on Terror.[110]

Force Protection: Shifting the Risks of Warfare
from Soldiers onto Enemy Civilians

In their 2005 article, Kasher and Yadlin had proposed revising the scope of force protection and considering the military value of protecting soldiers. They argued that, in a war on terror, the lives of a belligerent state's soldiers are worth more than the lives of enemy civilians. Traditional laws of war consider the lives of soldiers last or next to last on the list of priorities during combat. This is because soldiers have the right to kill, are supported by a military and political infrastructure during combat, and assume the risks of death and injury when they enlist—hence why soldiers are considered "brave." In contrast, civilians have no right to kill, have no infrastructure to support them during hostilities, and are not expected to assume the risks of warfare because they are either its victims or its survivors. Therefore the laws of armed conflict demand that soldiers bear the risks of combat in order to protect civilians to the maximum extent possible, and in the case that civilians are harmed, that the harm must be proportional to the military advantage achieved; this is the principle of proportionality. Kasher and Yadlin reject this logic, which they consider to be immoral. A combatant is a citizen in uniform. In Israel, quite often he is a conscript or on reserve duty. His blood is as red and thick of that of citizens who are not in uniform. His life is as precious as the life of anyone else. . . . That fact that persons involved in terror are depicted as noncombatants is not a reason for jeopardizing the combatant's life in their pursuit. He has to fight against terrorists because they are involved in terror. They shoulder the responsibility for their encounter with the combatant and should therefore bear the consequences.[111]

This proposition unduly shifts the risk of warfare from soldiers to enemy civilians in its calculus of proportionality.[112] While all armed forces consider force protection as part of their military advantage, Israel's proposal is radical in that it considers its soldiers' lives to be *more valuable* than the lives of enemy civilians. Therefore, when assessing proportionality, it tolerates greater numbers of civilian deaths and injuries so long as that spares Israel's soldiers from harm. The outcome of this almost ensures devastating results. At the most extreme end of this proposition is permission for a belligerent force to carpet bomb its adversary for the sake of preserving its own soldiers' lives.

Indeed, Michael N. Schmitt, a canonical figure of national security law and an editorial advisory board member for the *Journal of Military Ethics*, together with fellow scholar John Merriam, uncritically notes that the Israeli public's aversion to soldier casualties "leads Israel to liberally apply force, particularly airstrikes and counter-battery fire, in order to 'guarantee force protection.'"[113] The testimonies of soldiers deployed to the Gaza Strip in the summer 2014, during Operation Protective Edge, indicate how this principle was translated into operational state practice. One soldier explains that the rules of engagement became incredibly lenient and his commander had instructed him and the other soldiers that

[a]nything you see in the neighborhoods you're in, anything within a rea-sonable distance, say between zero and 200 meters—is dead on the spot. No authorization needed." We asked him: "I see someone walking in the street, do I shoot him?" He said yes. "Why do I shoot him?" "Because he isn't supposed to be there. Nobody, no sane civilian who isn't a terrorist, has

any business being within 200 meters of a tank. And if he places himself in such a situation, he is apparently up to something."...

... The working assumption states—and I want to stress that this is a quote of sorts: that anyone located in an IDF area, in areas the IDF took over—is not [considered] a civilian.... We entered Gaza with that in mind, and with an insane amount of firepower. I don't know if it was proportionate or not. I don't claim to be a battalion commander or a general. But it reached a point where a single tank—and remember, there were 11 of those just where I was—fires between 20 and 30 shells per day. The two-way radio was crazy when we entered. There was one reservist tank company that positioned itself up on a hill and started firing. They fired lots—that company's formal numbers stood at something like 150 shells per day. They fired, fired, fired.[114]

Israeli society has been supportive of this burden-shifting framework. Compulsory service in Israel means that every family sends its children to the battlefront, thus heightening everyone's sensitivity about the welfare of the armed forces. In 2006, this sensitivity came into sharp relief when Hamas captured Israeli soldier Gilad Shalit in a cross-border raid. The Palestinian parliamentary body and militant force sought to exchange Shalit for Palestinian political prisoners. His capture has been described as "torment" for Israel, "where every newscast would end with how many days Shalit had been in captivity."[115] Israeli society blamed the army for not authorizing the Hannibal Directive, or the use of massive fire, to rescue Shalit before he was captured. This directive encourages the use of indiscriminate force in order to prevent a capture and thus avoid the consequences of negotiating a soldier's release and also to deter soldiers' capture for use as bargaining chips.[116] Three Israeli army officers developed it in the late eighties after Hezbollah captured two Israeli soldiers across the Lebanese border. Upon Shalit's release in 2011, in exchange for 1,027 Palestinian prisoners, the Israeli army modified the directive so that field commanders could initiate a Hannibal operation even without authorization from their superior commanders.

In August 2014, in the course of Operation Protective Edge, the commander of Israel's Givati Brigade, Ofer Winter, initiated a Hannibal operation in Rafah upon news that Second Lieutenant Hadar Goldin was missing. Israeli troops sealed a perimeter with a 1.5 mile radius around the suspected capture point to prevent anyone from fleeing. For the next two days, Israeli soldiers fired 500 artillery shells and launched 100 airstrikes on the area. In late afternoon on the second day of the operation, Israeli soldiers discovered the remains of Goldin's body, and forensics concluded that he had died in a firefight; he had never been captured. By then, the Israeli operation had killed 190 Palestinians, including 55 children, 36 women, and 5 men over the age of sixty. Winter told the Associated Press, "That's why we used all this force. . . . Those who kidnap need to know they will pay a price. This was not revenge. They simply messed with the wrong brigade."[117] Under Israel's new force protection rubric, the carnage borne by Palestinian civilians based on inaccurate intelligence and acted upon without superior orders became acceptable.

Not a Combatant nor a Civilian but Always a Target

In addition to force protection, Kasher and Yadlin's 2005 article also proposed a radical redefinition of who is a direct participant in hostilities, the threshold analysis of when a civilian becomes a legitimate target. Under Article 51(3) of the Additional Protocol I, civilians forfeit their immunity "for such time" as they take up arms.[118] Kasher and Yadlin proposed expanding the temporal scope of this participation beyond the exact time of participation in hostilities so that a civilian involved in hostilities is "presumed to be involved in terror for an additional half year (or some other period, to be determined on professional intelligence grounds)." In effect, a Palestinian civilian who participated in hostilities would be a legitimate target for several months after the direct participation unless there was evidence to definitively rebut the presumption of continued involvement.

In December 2006, the Israeli High Court of Justice adjudicated this issue in its case on targeted killing, *The Public Committee Against Torture in Israel v. The Government of Israel*. While the Court rejected the presumption of future involvement based on past involvement, it also disregarded the temporal scope of Article 51(3). It suggested that

> a civilian who has joined a terrorist organization which has become his "home," and in the framework of his role in that organization he commits a chain of hostilities, with short periods of rest between them, loses his

immunity from attack "for such time" as he is committing the chain of acts. Indeed, regarding such a civilian, the rest between hostilities is nothing other than preparation for the next hostility.[119]

The Court reasoned that membership in a designated terrorist organization as a continuous combat function and therefore sufficient for denying a civilian his immunity. Under this framework, a military commander does not need to ask what the alleged terrorist is doing at the time he is targeted in order to kill him. Instead, he only needs to verify that the target is an active member of a designated terrorist organization. Armed forces can thus kill a civilian designated as a member of a terrorist organization, even when he is not a threat. because his membership status creates a presumption of direct involvement.[120] At the heart of this legal reasoning is a justification for the use of preventive force. Under the previous standard of direct participation in hostilities, no military advantage exists for killing a civilian who is no longer posing a threat. Under this one, because the civilian is presumed to have a continuing combat function, there is a lawful military advantage in killing a dormant alleged terrorist, because the framework considers that inactivity or sleep as "rest between hostilities."[121] Kasher noted after the 2006 Israeli judicial decision that, "there was no need to revise the document that [we] drafted by even one comma. What we are doing [in that document] is becoming the law."[122]

Israel's legal reasoning found support in an International Committee for the Red Cross document, the 2009 Interpretive Guidance on the Notion of Direct Participation in Hostilities Under International Humanitarian Law.[123] Developed out of a series of expert meetings convened between 2003 and 2008, this interpretive guidance came to very similar conclusions about the participation of civilians in hostilities. In his capacity as Special Rapporteur on Extrajudicial, Summary or Arbitrary Executions, Philip Alston noted that the document's conclusions are "questionable" because they are tantamount to a status determination, despite treaty language that temporally limits participation in hostilities.[124] Notably, U.S. and Israeli operational practice, jurisprudence, and scholarly production helped to shape these conclusions. The major distinction, however, is that this Red Cross analysis refers to members of organized armed groups, whereas Hamas is a governing authority with distinct civilian and military branches that should be distinguished.[125] Israel does not make that distinction because it considers Hamas an organized armed group and not an embryonic sovereign. This raises at least two troubling issues. First, because Israel rejects Hamas's legitimate political standing, it categorizes all of its members, regardless of political or military function, as civilians who directly participate in hostilities. Two, even Palestinians in Gaza who are not members of Hamas are at risk because, as the governing authority in the territory, Hamas employs the public sector. This includes law enforcement officers who may have no military purpose and no affiliation to Hamas beyond employment. Israel's revised military doctrine, which has no regard for Hamas's sovereignty claims, risks rendering nearly any Palestinian participation in the public sector in Gaza as presumptively continuous. Therefore, Israel can justify targeting these individuals militarily regardless of the actual threat they pose.

That is precisely what Israel did in late December 2008 when it launched a guided missile at a group of young police cadets in the Gaza Strip. The cadets were marching in their graduation ceremony with their families in audience. Within a few minutes of the attack, sixty Israeli jet fighters similarly targeted Hamas police and security forces across the tiny span of the coastal enclave. Israel killed a total of 200 Palestinians in the attack, which initiated Operation Cast Lead, a military offensive in the winter of 2008 to 2009.[126] The police cadets and the Hamas police officers are civilian law enforcement personnel and therefore not legitimate military targets. Israel defended its attack by arguing that once in a state of conflict, Hamas would absorb the officers within its military ranks. This is highly speculative, because all civilian law enforcement in Gaza falls under Hamas's authority, regardless of police officers' political allegiance. Police officers could be members of Fatah or the communist party rather Hamas, for example, even though they are employed by Hamas by virtue of its governing authority. Although the cadets possessed civilian status, were not definitively members of Hamas, and posed no military threat at the time of their killing, Israel killed them based on their employment by Hamas and to prevent the possibility that they would ever become a threat.

This is a radical reading of humanitarian law. Israel's analysis significantly expands the definition of a legitimate target by working on the basis of unchecked forward-looking speculation and not on incontrovertible evidence of posing a lethal threat. It is a risk-averse analysis that places the brunt of any risk on enemy civilians. The equivalent would be to consider nearly all Israelis aged eighteen or above as legitimate targets because they would eventually be conscripted into the army or called to serve in its reservist troops. Under Israel's revised analysis, this disturbing hypothetical is not plausible because the analysis insists that traditional laws of armed conflict remain intact during conventional warfare. Israel narrowly applies its new military directive to non-state actors, thus shielding states from ever being brutally attacked based upon the same logic.

Moreover, because Hamas members can be targeted at any time and not just when they take up arms, the likelihood increases that they will be surrounded by uninvolved civilians at the time of targeting, as when individual political leaders are sleep in their homes surrounded by their families, or when they eat at a restaurant or walk in the street. When civilians are killed during Israeli assassination attacks, Israel accuses Hamas's leaders of using them as human shields, thereby absolving itself for those civilian casualties.[127] Israel's High Court considered this dilemma in its 2006 decision and demanded that the military advantage gained by assassinating a Hamas operative be proportionate to the civilian casualties and destruction caused.

This call for restraint based on military deference has been negligible precisely because of Israel's radical modifications of proportionality.[128] During Israel's 2008 to 2009 winter military offensive, for example, Israeli aerial and ground attacks killed 1,400 Palestinians, including more than 300 children. Palestinian forces killed 9 Israelis, 3 of whom were civilians.[129] Under a traditional proportionality assessment, these figures create a presumption of Israel's disproportionate and indiscriminate use of force. However, Israel's revised military doctrine regarding force protection upends this logic because it shifts responsibility for Palestinian casualties onto Hamas, and it ascribes a higher value to the lives of Israeli soldiers. In the aftermath of the offensive, Asa Kasher explained that

> the concept of proportionality has ... changed. There is no logic in comparing the number of civilians and armed fighters on the Palestinian side, or comparing the number of Israelis killed by Qassam rockets to the number of Palestinians killed in Gaza.[130]

In its 2006 decision, the Israeli High Court had also imposed a duty upon the army to warn civilians of an impending attack, in order to mitigate harm.[131] Israel's warning procedures include a tactic called "knock on the roof," in which Israeli soldiers launch a submunition at a home or building in order to warn the civilian inhabitants of an imminent strike. The relatively small rocket causes damage, and shocks and often paralyzes its intended civilian beneficiaries. Between forty-five seconds and three minutes later, Israel launches the larger rocket intended to cause significant damage. The time frame is so short that it does not afford the population adequate time to flee and has failed to reduce the high toll of civilian deaths.[132] Israel argues that providing any more time for Palestinians to flee would diminish its military advantage.[133] Worse perhaps, Israel may also have considered civilians who did not flee to be voluntary human shields directly participating in hostilities, and therefore legitimate targets, or involuntary human shields, whose deaths are then Hamas's responsibility. In both approaches, the warning system absolves Israel of the casualties caused by its subsequent attack.

Israel's logic finds no authority in traditional law, since an attacking state maintains a duty to distinguish between civilians and combatants if a warning is ineffective and the population cannot flee or take shelter.[134] This is necessary to balance the anticipated harm against the anticipated military advantage. In most cases investigated during Israel's 2014 offensive, the warnings were gratuitous as Palestinians had no safe shelter. Israeli forces did not consider any designated area as unequivocally immune from target. The UN Office for the Coordination of Humanitarian Affairs reported that

> [t]hroughout the conflict there was a real fear among the population that no person or place was safe, as evidenced by attacks on hospitals, residential buildings and schools designated as shelters. Psychosocial distress levels, already high among the population of Gaza, have worsened significantly as a result of the conflict.[135]

Israel even disregarded the immunity of UN infrastructure, which maintains a civilian status and possesses a presumption of immunity. The rooftops of UN buildings are emblazoned with the organization's blue emblem to ensure visibility and distinction. This apparently did not ensure civilian safety during Israel's

2014 offensive. In the course of fifty-one days, Israel attacked seven UNRWA schools providing shelter to civilians. A 2014 UN investigation found that in one instance in Rafah, UN personnel provided Israel with a school's GPS coordinates thirty-three times to try to avoid harm to nearly 3,000 civilians seeking refuge. Israel struck near the school anyway, killing 15 Palestinians and injuring at least 30 more.[136] In its investigation of the attack, Israel claimed that a Palestinian militant on a motorcycle traveled by the UN school, and in doing so, he was using the civilians as human shields to protect himself and/or to injure Israel's image. Accordingly, Israel shifted responsibility for the deaths in the school to the Palestinian militant, thereby absolving itself of responsibility for the casualties.[137] Such a shift removes the attack on the school as well as the 15 casualties and the dozens injured from the register of harm in Israel's proportionality assessment, making them acceptable in its new language of law.[138] It also justifies targeting the UN shelter.

Muted Protests and Foreseeable Horizons

During Operation Cast Lead, Israel destroyed 2,900 homes, 29 schools, 121 commercial and industrial workshops, 60 police stations, and 30 mosques, in addition to the high number of civilian casualties. During the eight days of Operation Pillar of Cloud, Israel killed 167 Palestinians.[139] In the course of Operation Defensive Shield, in 2014, Israel launched 6,000 airstrikes and fired almost 50,000 artillery and tank shells. It killed nearly 2,200 Palestinians, including 1,462 civilians, of whom 551 were children, orphaned 1,500 children, left 370,000 children in need of psychosocial treatment, completely destroyed 18,000 homes, and, at the height of the onslaught, displaced half a million Palestinians.[140] This carnage becomes acceptable in Israel's proposed military directive, specifically under the enlarged scope of force protection, direct participation in hostilities, and the analysis of proportionality.

Israel's officials, scholars, and military personnel, as well as its legal establishment, have insisted these shifts are necessary to meet the demands of unprecedented warfare against terrorists in the *sui generis* battlefield against a "hostile entity." This does not mean that Israel's lethal propositions advanced in the Gaza Strip are accepted norms; they are not. However, that does not make them unequivocal violations of law either. In the aftermath of the three devastating onslaughts on Gaza and amid projections that the coastal enclave will be unlivable by 2020, these military tactics stand somewhere between a violation and a new customary norm. If not rebuffed legally and politically by other states, they could eventually become accepted as the seed for new custom. Muted protests as well as collusion by Palestinians' traditional allies, and even Palestinians themselves, indicate a troubling horizon.

In the course of Israel's first major onslaught on the Gaza Strip in 2008 and 2009, Fatah, Hamas's rival that is in control of the West Bank, violently quelled Palestinian protests in that territory against the gruesome offensive.[141] Fatah's U.S.-trained security forces did so in coordination with Israel's military forces for the sake of preventing a Hamas takeover of the West Bank similar to the Gaza takeover.[142] Fatah's focus on this internecine rivalry for authority, rather than on Israel's violent domination, has also shaped its quietude in regard to Israel's assassinations of Palestinian leaders in the Gaza Strip.[143] And in the fall of 2009, the Fatah-dominated leadership undermined one of the few legal accountability instruments available to challenge Israel's new military doctrine.

Following Operation Cast Lead, the United Nations Human Rights Council initiated the United Nations Fact-Finding Mission on the Gaza Conflict, which represented the most significant protest against Israel's tactics.[144] The mission's report, popularly known as the Goldstone Report, made a number of recommendations: referring Israel to the International Criminal Court, referring the issue for review by the UN Security Council, convening a conference to reaffirm the applicability of occupation law in the Palestinian territories, and convening a further conference to assess Israel's illegal use of prohibited weapons in urban-based armed conflict. Although none of these tactics sufficed to regulate Israel's behavior, they signaled global resistance to its new means and methods of warfare. As a result of intense U.S. pressure, however, the Palestinian Ambassador to the United Nations in Geneva deferred the Human Rights Council vote on the report to the following session six months later.[145] While the Fact-Finding Mission did not rescind the report, its deferral effectively toppled global momentum for legal accountability in the aftermath of Israel's first large-scale offensive against the Gaza Strip.

Fatah's policies towards Hamas and Israel reflect a broader regional trend that divides the Middle East roughly between a U.S sphere of influence and the political formations that resist it. The resultant political configuration situates Egypt, Saudi Arabia, Lebanon's March 14 Coalition, Jordan, and Fatah, who lean towards U.S. patronage, against Iran, Syria, Hezbollah, and, by default, Hamas. These antagonistic formations compete, by explicit and implicit means, for hegemony in the region, and this contest for power has subsumed and overshadowed the question of Palestine.

Since 2007, Egypt has closed the Rafah border crossing, one of the five points of ingress into and egress out of the Gaza Strip, thus complementing Israel's control of the other four crossings. The closure amounts to acquiescence to Israel's blockade, which is tantamount to an act of war.[146] Egypt's policy reflects a disdain for the Muslim Brotherhood, a rival political party to the ruling government that briefly assumed power in Egypt between 2012 and 2013, and enjoys the support of Qatar; Hamas is an offshoot of the Muslim Brotherhood and has thus come into Egypt's direct line of fire by association.[147] During Israel's 2014 offensive, Egypt and Israel negotiated a ceasefire without Hamas's participation, and publicly blamed the Palestinian party for the civilian casualties when the ceasefire collapsed.[148] In 2016, an Egyptian military delegation visited Israel to strengthen the cooperation between the two states and, in effect, further diluted protest against Israel's destructive military doctrine deployed in the Gaza Strip.[149] In similar vein, Saudi Arabia has accused Hamas of being a regional proxy for Iran for the purpose of destabilizing the Middle East,[150] and has vowed to disarm it and other militant groups in the Gaza Strip.[151] In 2016, a Saudi delegation of academics and businessmen visited Israel in an effort to normalize and strengthen their relations.[152]

Israel's offensives against the Palestinian population in Gaza have been refracted through the regional contest for control. In effect, the concern is no longer about the welfare of Palestinian civilians and their claims for independence but instead about the political balance in the region that has aligned Egyptian, Saudi Arabian, and Israeli interests. These regional trends amount to a quiet approval for Israel's military policies and diminish the protest necessary to put Israel's revised tactics in war into disrepute.

While global protest beyond the region has been significant, it has not offered an effective counterweight to these developments. After Israel's offensive in the summer of 2014, the United Nations initiated two investigations, one carried out by the UN Independent Commission of Inquiry on the 2014 Gaza Conflict (Operation Protective Edge), which looked at the offensive in its entirety, and the other conducted by a UN Headquarters Board of Inquiry convened by the Secretary-General that specifically examined Israel's attacks on seven UNRWA schools.[153] The reports from both these sources have raised serious questions about Israel's practices, but neither has resulted in meaningful consequences. Like the reports before them, they are likely to become marginalized and forgotten.

In a sign of positive development, in late December 2014, Palestine acceded to the Rome Statute, the multilateral treaty that brought the ICC into existence. Palestine referred the situation in Palestine to the ICC, and as a result, the ICC has begun a preliminary investigation of Israel's onslaught. This bid to involve the ICC cannot indefinitely restrain Israel, but in the short run, it works as a deterrent because of the new risks of accountability that court's jurisdiction poses. Nevertheless, that multilateral body, which is highly vulnerable to state interests and interventions, is replete with the trappings of legal technicalities and is likely to yield unsatisfactory outcomes that range from abhorrent to tolerable. Among the most significant challenges to robust legal accountability is the provision of complementarity, which affords the ICC jurisdiction only over cases where a state "is unwilling or unable to genuinely carry out the investigation or prosecution." Complementarity would benefit Israel, which can and has argued that it has the capacity to investigate itself. In contrast, Hamas, which was a party in the conflict, would be unable to make a similar demonstration. While Israel's dismal record of investigating its own war crimes during Operation Cast Lead puts the adequacy of complementarity into question, the demonstration of that inadequacy would require a separate and likely lengthy legal process.[154] The principle of complementarity would, at best, shield Israel from ICC investigation and, at worst, delay the process so severely as to thwart justice. The Palestinian leadership has pursued ICC jurisdiction formulaically, without any appreciation for its political nature. It has not mobilized a popular campaign aimed at delegitimizing Israel and cultivating a base of support for the prosecutor nor has it sought diplomatic partners to help it withstand U.S. sanctions or made moves to contextualize Hamas's militant operations within a frame of armed national liberation. In effect, it has not challenged the geopolitical structure undergirding

Palestinian subjugation and repression. In the long-run, ICC jurisdiction may prove even more detrimental than beneficial to Palestinian interests.[155]

In light of the currently minimal protest at top diplomatic and multilateral levels, Israel, together with the United States, will continue to define its military practices as the "new normal" in asymmetric warfare.[156] Israeli and U.S. military operations, legal jurisprudence, and scholarly interventions will add to the state practice and *opinio juris* constitutive of customary law. This means that as customary law on irregular combat continues to crystallize, Gaza's besieged population, and Palestinians generally, will continue to bear the devastating consequences of its experimentation.

Worse, perhaps, are the implications that these shifts have had on the question of Palestine more generally. Israel's practice of systematic war, together with its framework of unique distinction applied to Gaza, has set the Gaza Strip apart from the question of Palestine. By emphasizing the role of Hamas and diminishing the question of Palestine, Israel has collapsed conditions in Gaza into the kinds of asymmetric conflicts that characterize what has come to be known as the Global War on Terror, thus eliding the consequential distinctions between Palestinians and other non-state actors. By setting Gaza apart from the rest of the Palestinian question, Israel is supplanting a peacemaking, let alone settler-colonial, framework for understanding the conflict with a national security one. The internecine conflict between Fatah and Hamas together with regional polarization only strengthens this paradigm shift and, with it, Israel's colonial domination.

This shift also reflects an Israeli policy goal first publicly articulated by Shimon Peres in 1993. In the initial aftermath of the signing of the Declaration of Principles, Peres told a UNESCO conference that he saw the Gaza Strip progressively evolving into a Palestinian state, while the West Bank would become an autonomous polity of Palestinians and Israeli settlers whose status and borders would eventually be defined.[157] Unlike the West Bank, which Israel covets for its natural resources as well as its religious and security significance, Israel has considered Gaza a "cancer."[158] When Israel unilaterally withdrew from Gaza in 2005, that territory had only 8,000 settlers. compared with 400,000 in the West Bank. The shift to warfare against the coastal enclave, together with the arrangement wrought by the peace process, has helped Israel realize its vision:

separating Gaza from the broader Palestinian question and transforming its indeterminate occupation in the West Bank into a permanent structure.

This is the current phase of the Palestinian-Israel conflict. In many ways it is a return to a bygone era where Palestinian claims for self-determination were severely muted and its resistance efforts framed as terroristic violence. The status quo, however, is not much more favorable for Israeli interests, since Israel's absolute rejection of Palestinian self-determination, together with its stark regime of racial discrimination, are unsustainable. Israel is on the cusp of expanding its sovereignty across nearly all the territory between the Jordan River and the Mediterranean Sea. A significant cross-section of Israel's population, together with a settler-controlled Knesset, supports this policy. If it actually comes to fruition, it means that Israel will not only fulfill its vision for a Greater Israel, it will also enter a phase of unabashed racial discrimination: a de jure apartheid regime.

CONCLUSION

IN 2018, the prospect of a sovereign and independent Palestinian state is obsolete. As of late 2015, the Israeli settler population in the West Bank numbered more than 600,000, a 200 percent increase since the advent of the Oslo peace process in 1993.[1] Israel's settlement enterprise carves the West Bank into more than twenty noncontiguous landmasses separating approximately three million Palestinians into as many groups that stand apart from one another, thus undermining any sense of territorial contiguity or national cohesion. In 2000, Israel began constructing a separation barrier, or wall, allegedly to halt the flow of Palestinian suicide bombers within Israel's undeclared borders.[2] By the time of the wall's completion in 2020, 85 percent of its length will run through the West Bank and effectively confiscate 13 percent of that territory, conveniently where most of Israel's largest settlement blocs are located. Israeli military law prohibits the presence and travel of Palestinians between the West Bank and Gaza, thereby entrenching their political and geographic fragmentation (see the Access Restrictions map). In Gaza, Israel has securitized nearly two million Palestinians and held them captive under a land siege and naval blockade for more than a decade. Palestinians cannot freely travel to East Jerusalem, and that area's 300,000 Palestinians are subject to an aggressive removal campaign.[3] In the years since 1948, nearly two thirds of the Palestinian population has been driven into a global diaspora, including fifty-eight refugee camps in the Arab world, and is being denied the right to return. Having torpedoed the possibility of a Palestinian state, Israel is now the sole source of authority from the Mediterranean Sea to the River Jordan.

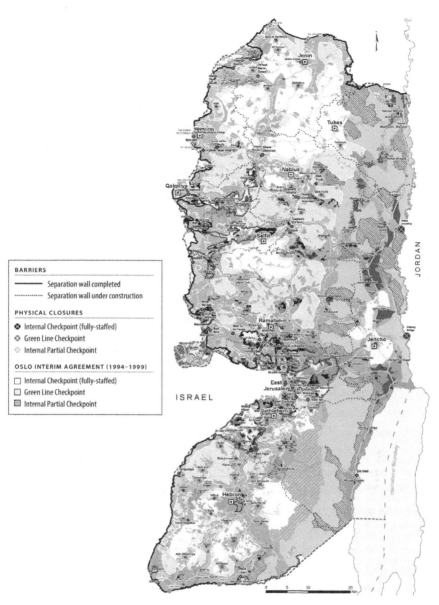

BARRIERS

———— Separation wall completed

·············· Separation wall under construction

PHYSICAL CLOSURES

⊗ Internal Checkpoint (fully-staffed)

⊗ Green Line Checkpoint

⊗ Internal Partial Checkpoint

OSLO INTERIM AGREEMENT (1994–1999)

☐ Internal Checkpoint (fully-staffed)

☐ Green Line Checkpoint

▨ Internal Partial Checkpoint

Access Restrictions, 2017

As of 2017, Israel's separation wall, settlement enterprise, annexation of East Jerusalem, bypass roads, and military installations in the West Bank have destroyed that area's territorial contiguity as well as the national cohesion of the Palestinian population.

SOURCE: Adapted from OCHA West Bank Access Restrictions map, October 2017. For a more detailed, color version of the map please see https://www.ochaopt.org/content/west-bank-access-restrictions-october-2017.

Legal work has been central to Israel's expansionist project. The Israeli judiciary, diplomatic corps, and civil and military legal advisers have understood the law's imbrication with politics and have leveraged the state's diplomatic, military, and economic prowess to perform legal work in pursuit of its political ambitions. Following the First World War, a sovereign exception marking Palestine as a site of Jewish settlement engendered a specialized legal arrangement that justified the juridical erasure of a Palestinian political community. This regime, together with three decades of British imperial sponsorship, enabled Israel to assert its Jewish-Zionist settler sovereignty by force over 78 percent of Mandate Palestine in 1948. Israel used the fiction of Palestinian national non-existence together with the structure of permanent emergency between 1948 and 1966 to transform its native Palestinian population into present-absent individuals, whose lands could be arbitrarily confiscated for Jewish settlement. When it terminated its emergency regime, Israel enshrined the subordination of Palestinians as second-class citizens in civil law. In 1967, Israel deployed a legal-political mechanism, also predicated upon Palestinian national nonexistence, to establish an occupation premised on *sui generis* claims to facilitate its steady land grab within the West Bank and Gaza. The Oslo Accords framework established in 1993 engendered yet another specialized regime that has enabled Israel to continue its settler-colonial expansion, this time under the veneer of peacemaking. Since 2000, also in accord with similar claims of unique distinction, Israel has criminalized all Palestinian use of force. At the same time, the state has expanded its right to use force against Palestinians and in the process has forged new laws of armed conflict.

Israel's success has had an unintended consequence: it oversees an apartheid regime. Without a partition separating Israel from the territories, Israel now has to contend with the reality that its jurisdiction contains a significant native Palestinian population. According to the Israeli Bureau of Statistics, as of October 2012, approximately 5.9 million Jewish-Israelis, including the settler population, and 6.1 million Palestinians were living across Israel, the West Bank, and Gaza.[4] Population projections indicate that by 2035, Jewish-Israelis will constitute only 46 percent of the total population.[5] The inclusion of Palestinians from Gaza and the West Bank as citizens would undermine the Jewish demographic majority inside the 1949 armistice lines (the Green Line). The current arrangement in which Israel rules occupied Palestinians but excludes them from citizenship exemplifies a regime that administers distinct legal systems based on its own racial definitions: in other words, an apartheid regime.[6]

Israeli Prime Minister Benjamin Netanyahu's predecessors knew the dangers of this legal bifurcation. During his tenure as Prime Minister, Ehud Olmert commented that failure to create a Palestinian state would force Israel to "face a South African-style struggle for equal voting rights, and as soon as that happens, the state of Israel is finished."[7] After leaving the Prime Minister's post, Ehud Barak offered this warning: "If, and as long as between the Jordan and the sea, there is only one political entity, named Israel, it will end up being either non-Jewish or non-democratic. . . . If the Palestinians vote in elections, it is a bi-national state, and if they don't, it is an apartheid state."[8]

Not all Israelis are concerned about this reality. Significant sectors of Israeli society have hailed the current status quo as a tremendous victory. Some want to consecrate their accomplishment by officially annexing Area C, which covers 60 percent of the West Bank, where Israel's largest settlement blocs are located.[9] In 2012, a government committee revived the discourse of Palestinian nonexistence when it concluded there is no occupation because the West Bank belongs to no other sovereign, justifying Israel's permanent presence in the territory.[10] While de jure annexation risks absorbing the Palestinian population, an autonomy framework has the capacity to ensure that population's formal exclusion. Under the Oslo framework's terms, Israel has steadily reduced the Palestinian population in Area C and concentrated Palestinians within Areas A and B.[11] Although it was ostensibly an interim arrangement until the achievement of final status talks, the Oslo framework has become interminable. Its continuation would successfully contain Palestinians and suspend them as non-sovereigns in their autonomous regions and non-citizens of Israel, thereby diminishing the demographic challenge they pose.

This political trend is not merely a right-wing phenomenon. Population transfers, land swaps, and annexation for the sake of ensuring a decisive Jewish majority and Palestinian exclusion have become increasingly normalized concepts within Israeli mainstream discourse. A 2012 poll evidenced popular Israeli support for the voluntary or forcible transfer of Palestinian citizens out of Israel.[12] More recent initiatives have proposed providing economic incentives to encourage Palestinian citizens to leave.[13] Still other proposals seek to swap villages with large concentrations of Palestinian-Israelis with the Palestinian Authority in exchange for Jewish-Israeli settlements.[14]

More sympathetic, or at least more politically astute, Israelis deny allegations of apartheid by acknowledging Palestinians' grievances but disaggregating their claims.[15] They emphasize that the treatment of Palestinian citizens of Israel is a matter of domestic concern, whereas controversies in the West Bank reflect the challenges of conflict resolution, and Gaza is a national security issue. By emphasizing the statist legal and geographic demarcations separating and distinguishing Palestinians from one another, liberal Israelis refute claims that Israel oversees a singular discriminatory regime. These exculpatory attempts contradict the lived experience of Palestinians themselves.

As early as 2000, after the collapse of the Camp David talks that precipitated the Al Aqsa intifada, a group of Palestinian scholars issued a statement describing Palestinians' concentration within a "series of small, disconnected areas . . . being posited as the emerging Palestinian state."[16] They referred to those areas as "bantustans," in reference to the model of territorialized subordination of blacks used in apartheid South Africa and Namibia. The statement echoed the Palestinian legal and political analyses that had culminated in the 1975 General Assembly resolution declaring Zionism to be a form of racism (Resolution 3379), and seemed to signal an return to such analyses. However, there are at least two differences distinguishing these 1975 and 2000 articulations and also differentiating case studies looking at Palestine versus South Africa and Namibia.

First, unlike the situation in the mid-1970s when the PLO supported the introduction of Resolution 3379, the Palestinian leadership today has not officially endorsed the anti-apartheid framework. Recognition of a singular legal regime would contravene its ambitions to establish a state. Palestinian officialdom has referred to apartheid and the possibility of a single democratic state only as a threat to compel Israeli compromise in negotiations.[17] Second, in 1976, the international community rebuffed South Africa's attempts to establish black homelands, decrying them as measures aiming to "consolidate the inhuman policies of apartheid, to destroy the territorial integrity of the country, to perpetuate white minority domination and to dispossess the African people of South Africa of their inalienable rights."[18] In contrast, the international community has celebrated Palestinian autonomy as the germ of independence and has contributed tremendous financial and diplomatic support in an effort to uphold an arrangement that is in effect—if not in intention by supporters—oppressive. While Palestinians outside of officialdom have increasingly understood the apparatus of their dispossession and domination as apartheid, the international community has continued to frame it as "interim autonomy," for the sake of peacemaking. Meanwhile, and under the cover of peacemaking, Israel has intensified its eliminatory structures targeting Palestinian natives.[19]

Despite its seeming success in establishing contiguous sovereignty across most of the area that was formerly Mandate Palestine, Israel's settler-colonial frontier remains active. Settler-colonial studies scholar Lorenzo Veracini tells us that the ultimate triumph of settler-colonialism is its extinguishment; it becomes so normalized as to be imperceptible.[20] In Palestine, that project remains explicit and vulgar precisely because of the demographic reality as well as the Palestinians' obstinate refusal to relinquish their claims to native belonging. In a continuation of the policies Israel began in 1947, and which it consolidated into a permanent structure of emergency in 1948, today it and its para-statal institutions remove, dispossess, and concentrate Palestinian natives without regard to legal jurisdictions or geographic demarcations. Israel's aims then and now are the same: to achieve and maintain a Jewish demographic majority and also to acquire the greatest amount of land with the fewest possible number of Palestinians on it. It achieves this through civil law in Israel, a mix of administrative and martial law in East Jerusalem, martial law in the West Bank, and all out warfare in Gaza.[21]

The concentration of Palestinians under Israeli jurisdiction onto small areas of land is most obvious in the West Bank, where they are placed and bounded into Areas A and B. It is also evident in Gaza, which has the largest concentration, as well as within Israel itself, where the government has been shaping legislative policy intended to remove nearly 80,000 Bedouin Palestinians from the Negev region and concentrate them into noncontiguous urban townships under the auspices of development.[22] In Jerusalem, the so-called center of life policy mandating that Palestinian Jerusalemites demonstrate an uninterrupted presence in that city to maintain their residency has steadily reduced the Palestinian population.[23] In the rest of the West Bank and Gaza, Israel has outrightly revoked the residency permits of a quarter of a million Palestinians between 1967 and 1994, shrinking the Palestinian population there by at least 10 percent.[24] Within Israel, a legislative ban on family reunification in certain circumstances denies spouses of Israeli citizens who hail from "enemy states" (where a significant number of Palestinians reside) the right to adjust their status—an explicit effort to diminish their presence.[25] These are only select examples of the matrix of laws and policies aimed at Palestinian removal.[26] Palestinians have increasingly described their condition as constituting an ongoing *nakba* (catastrophe), in reference to the removal and forced exile of 80 percent of the Palestinian population during the 1948 War.[27] The reference recognizes Israel's eliminatory project as an institutionalized policy and a colonial continuity.

Israel's settlement and dispossession policies, together, amount to forced population transfer,[28] a violation of the 1973 International Convention on the Suppression and Punishment of the Crime of Apartheid.[29] An apartheid regime is both the consequence of Israel's settler-colonial ambitions and the modal governance structure for protecting and maintaining its colonial takings. A growing number of international human rights organizations and analysts have scrutinized the resulting conditions, and have come to regard the mal-distribution of natural resources, unequal access to housing, and differential punishments in the West Bank as a racially discriminatory regime.[30] In 2012, the UN Committee on the Elimination of All Forms of Racial Discrimination concluded that the "hermetic character of the separation of two groups" in the Occupied Territories is tantamount to apartheid.[31] In 2017, the UN Economic and Social Commission for Western Asia (ESCWA) caused an uproar when it took this analysis further and concluded that Israel practices apartheid towards all of its Palestinian natives, without regard to legal status or geographic residence.[32] The UN report was the first of its kind to authoritatively make the claim that Israel's holistic legal regime was not being limited to the Occupied Territories. Israel, together with the United States, forced the United Nations to shelve the report.[33] ESCWA's Director resigned in protest; the report was leaked and widely disseminated.[34] The Palestinian Authority issued statements condemning the dismissal of the report but did not officially endorse the critique of Israel's governance as a singular apartheid regime.[35]

It is a cruel, but not unprecedented, twist in the history of co-opted liberation movements and authoritarian postcolonial regimes that the Palestinian leadership has become a part of the Palestinian problem.[36] Today, the buy-in and collaboration of the Palestinian leadership is central both to Israel's apartheid regime and to the enduring denial of its existence. Palestinian participation in U.S.–brokered bilateral talks sustains the false conception that a sovereign state is within reach. Facts on the ground make evident that establishing a Palestinian state today would be as difficult as, if not more difficult than, dismantling Israel's apartheid system. The framework of peacemaking sustains the fiction of parity and diminishes the imperative to exert pressure on Israel. In addition, the Palestinian Authority's representational claims over the Palestinians resident in the West Bank and Gaza, to the exclusion of Palestinian refugees and citizens of Israel, helps uphold the legal and geographic fragmentations separating Palestinians from one another and subverting, in practice but not law, their status as a holistic nation.[37] Historically, the Palestine Liberation Organization (PLO) has represented all Palestinians, but since 1994, the liberation movement has been subsumed into the Palestinian Authority rendering it functionally absent. These fragmentations undergird Israeli claims that its relationship with Palestinians is either a matter of conflict resolution or national security but not of apartheid.

Worse, as part of the Faustian bargain that is the Oslo framework, the Palestinian Authority has internalized the colonial logic that its compliance and good behavior will be rewarded with independence.[38] In fact, its subservience has reified Israel's domination and has significantly benefited a select political and economic Palestinian elite.[39] As part of its pact, the PA diligently polices its own population to protect Israel's settler population as well as the civilian and military infrastructure that sustains the settlers' presence. The PA allocates 31 percent of its national budget to security, which makes up half of its public sector.[40] That is more than it spends on its "health, education and agriculture sectors combined."[41] The PA's security coordination with Israel has become so effective that U.S. General Keith Dayton, who trained several classes of Palestinian security officers, lauded the Palestinians for turning their guns on "real enemies," in reference to Palestinians suspected of posing a threat to Israel's national interests.[42] There is no reciprocal security arrangement to protect Palestinians. In its futile attempt to demonstrate its capacity to govern, the Palestinian leadership has relieved Israel of at least a portion of its military burden as an occupying power and aided it in in controlling the native population.

This approach has severely altered the post-1965 Palestinian national movement and transformed it into a critical part of Israel's settler-colonial machinery, rather than being the primary impediment to that apparatus. In his work on the colonial politics of recognition, Glenn Coulthard highlights how settler-colonialism, as a form of governmentality, makes this perverse outcome predictable. Indigenous nations who have established their sovereignty through formal recognition established a relational structure with the settler states that ensures those states' continued access to their lands and resources. Under the framework of bureaucratic administration, indigenous peoples become "instruments of their own dispossession." Under this arrangement, Coulthard continues, "contemporary colonialism works *through* rather than entirely *against* freedom."[43]

Palestinian officialdom's uncritical adoption of this managerial approach risks confusing what is being offered in terms of limited autonomy with incremental steps towards freedom.[44] This illusory quest, bolstered by the perks of self-autonomy and access to multilateral fora, has shaped the Palestinian leadership's commitment to U.S. tutelage and its reticence to embark on a bolder course based on a politics of resistance.

Politics of Acquiescence and the Phantom State

After the October 1973 War, the PLO's mainstream and moderate elements sought a direct channel to the United States. They finally got it in late 1991 when the United States, together with the Soviet Union, embarked on the Oslo peace process. The cost of abandoning that direct channel would be high and, most likely, irreversible. As condition for entering into a compact with the U.S. and Israeli governments, the PLO willingly relinquished its political claims, even though they were enshrined in UN resolutions and in international treaties. Worse, the PLO naively endorsed an autonomy arrangement without any guarantees of national sovereignty. The Oslo Accords established a new, specialized legal regime that not only made applicable international law misplaced but also made its very invocation a threat to peacemaking. In practice, this *realpolitik* strategy necessitates strict adherence to the U.S.–brokered bilateral process, which is entirely self-referential, lacks external review mechanisms, and is dictated by expedience and pressure.[45] The Palestinian leadership has assented to this realpolitik approach because it has regarded the United States, in its capacity as the world's lone superpower and Israel's primary patron, as the only party capable of delivering a Palestinian state. So long as Palestinians remain compliant with this framework, the value of their legal work will be tenuous at best.

To achieve the law's emancipatory potential, Palestinians must wield it in the sophisticated service of a political movement that targets the geopolitical structure that has rendered their claims exceptional and, therefore, non-justiciable. The United States' massive military, diplomatic, and financial aid to Israel has constituted the primary pillar of that structure since at least 1967. Historically, Palestinians effectively challenged the structure when they revolted against Britain's colonial administration (1936–1939), when they engaged in an armed liberation struggle and consolidated their interests with a counter-hegemonic global coalition to inscribe their juridical status into international law (1968–1988), and when they became ungovernable during the first intifada (1987–1991). These moments are instructive.

Until the 1990s, The PLO had managed, through civil uprisings, irregular combat, political mobilization, and legal work, to successfully challenge and overcome Palestinians' juridical erasure and their exception from the promise of self-determination. The PLO's acceptance of the Oslo framework then stunted and reversed these gains. Since the peace process unraveled at Camp David in 2000, the Palestinian leadership has embarked on several contentious legal campaigns. However, its commitment to achieve independence through U.S. and Israeli acquiescence has diminished the liberatory potential of its most ambitious legal strategies. These efforts include the 2004 International Court of Justice advisory opinion on Israel's wall, the 2011 to 2012 UN statehood bid, the UN General Assembly resolution augmenting Palestine's observer state status, the accession to the Rome Statute and the subsequent admission to the International Criminal Court, and most recently, Security Council Resolution 2334. This is to say nothing of the fact that statehood, as a remedy, does not correspond to the reality and scope of Palestinian grievances today, as discussed earlier. Assuming for the sake of argument that being recognized as a state by the United Nations could remedy Palestinian subjugation, the Palestinian leadership's legal strategies in pursuance of that goal remain strategically insufficient.

In each of the aforementioned instances, the Palestinian leadership pursued a legal campaign aimed at, in the crudest and most rudimentary terms, holding

Israel to account through international law. Simultaneously, it has refused to challenge the United States' unequivocal aid to Israel. Any successful legal strategy should seek to unsettle this pillar of support. Instead, Palestinian officialdom has pursued each of its legal strategies with the policy of maintaining U.S. favor and/or using the legal initiative as a threat to enhance its negotiating leverage in bilateral talks.[46] The outcomes of these initiatives are, by virtue of these circumstances, noncommittal and haphazard. An examination of the Palestinians' UN statehood bid illustrates this point.

In 2011, the Palestinian leadership sought to upgrade the Palestinian territories' status from a nonmember observer entity, achieved in UNGA Resolution 3237 (1974), to a member state at the United Nations. UN membership requires a Security Council recommendation to the General Assembly.[47] It was immediately evident that the United States would veto such a recommendation. Alternatively, the PLO could circumvent the Security Council and upgrade its status to nonmember observer state by garnering the vote of two thirds of the General Assembly.[48]

By 2011, 130 individual states had already recognized the State of Palestine. According to John Quigley, Palestine has enjoyed international recognition as a state since 1988, when the General Assembly endorsed its Declaration of Independence followed by immediate diplomatic recognition by eighty-nine states.[49] Achieving nonmember *state* status in 2011 would officiate this standing and settle any outstanding controversy surrounding Palestine's legal status. Such a step would certainly be significant, although hardly radical.[50] Achieving UN membership would be more difficult than achieving recognition, as it would require U.S. support in the Security Council. However, neither recognition nor membership would alter Israel's behavior or realities on the ground.

International law is not a command. At most, the statehood bid could provide the Palestinian leadership with opportunities to mobilize the international community to exert pressure on Israel to act in accord with its sovereignty claims, or to urge penalties for Israel's failure to do so. To that end, upgrading Palestine's status would be beneficial, since recognition, even without membership, confers the juridical standing of a state with all the duties and privileges that flow therefrom. Upon this basis, Palestinians could, for example, embark on an aggressive diplomatic and grassroots campaign aimed at isolating and shaming

Israel, increasing the diplomatic and financial cost of its gross treatment of Palestinians, as well as enhancing Palestinians' appeals for greater international intervention. The value of the statehood bid was therefore always dependent on the political resolve and strategic vision of the Palestinian leadership to leverage these opportunities. The most significant among them was the chance to directly confront the United States and embark on an international strategy beyond the confines of the Oslo framework. Yet the Palestinian leadership had no such intentions. In fact, the statehood bid seemed to be a means to salvage the PLO's own legitimacy, which was in tatters in 2011, rather than to signal a profound strategic shift.[51]

When the matter came before the Security Council, the Palestinian leadership refused to force a U.S. veto. Doing so could have revealed the peace broker's bad faith and lack of fitness to be a mediator. The Palestinian leadership let Palestine's membership application die quietly. The next year, in December 2012, it brought Palestine's status to a vote in the General Assembly where it easily prevailed.[52] The Assembly's overwhelming vote affirmed the Palestinian cause of self-determination. At that juncture, the Palestinian leadership still had the opportunity to leverage the vote to lobby supportive states to apply pressure on Israel as well as to find an alternative state or group of states to fulfill the United States' mediation role. Instead, in July 2013, the leadership unceremoniously returned to the bilateral talks, where the realpolitik negotiating framework had the capacity to obviate the Palestinians' most recent legal and diplomatic achievement.[53]

Despite damning empirical evidence demonstrating U.S. unwillingness and inability to challenge Israel, the Palestinian leadership has remained hopeful that the global superpower would deliver independence. Perhaps it has had no other choice. The Palestinian Authority's national economy is dependent on international aid and stands to lose significant economic guarantees and perks should it abandon the U.S. sphere of influence.[54] In December 2017, the risk of Palestinian officialdom's conciliatory approach and undue faith in the United States became clear: U.S. President Donald Trump announced that the United States would move its Israeli embassy from Tel Aviv to Jerusalem.[55]

On the surface, the announced move broke with five decades of U.S. policy; it appeared to be a brazen act of a reckless administration. However, every presidential administration, beginning with Lyndon B. Johnson, has maintained a contradictory policy on Jerusalem and on Israel's presence in the West Bank and Gaza more generally. They all have insisted that civilian settlements in occupied territory contravene international law and undermine the prospects of permanent peace. Yet simultaneously and over the decades, the United States has shielded Israel from diplomatic censure and ensured its military prowess in the region while tacitly endorsing Israel's *sui generis* occupation framework that alters the territorial status quo by appropriating Palestinian lands but not the Palestinians on them. Consequently, U.S. Mideast policy has enabled Israel to expand its settlement enterprise without serious consequence. The Trump administration's announcement did not mark an abrupt and ruinous rupture in U.S. policy; it made it unambiguously coherent.

In the same speech, Trump insisted that his decision did not detract from the U.S. commitment to broker a viable peace agreement.[56] Indeed, facts on the ground, which Israel could establish under a rule-of-law framework, have governed the pragmatism upon which the negotiations have been based. Moreover, nearly every Israeli leader who has led negotiations has offered only limited self-autonomy to Palestinians in the Occupied Territories. Even under Ehud Barak's "generous" offer for actual statehood, there would be no return to the 1967 borders, no Palestinian control over external borders, no Palestinian jurisdiction over the most significant water sources in the West Bank, and no right of return for Palestinian refugees. Trump's initiative to move the embassy would remove any possibility of Palestinian jurisdiction over Jerusalem. This was less a departure than a concretization of the steady evisceration of the prospect of Palestinian statehood.

Palestinian officialdom rejected Trump's overtures and rescinded an invitation to U.S. Vice President Mike Pence.[57] The UN General Assembly condemned the U.S. policy by a vote of 128 to 9.[58] For its part, the United States vetoed a Security Council resolution doing the same.[59] Less than a month later, the United States threatened to cut critical aid to the Palestinian Authority as well as to the UN Relief Works Agency—which provides for the humanitarian needs of over five million Palestinian refugees—if the PA did not return to the negotiating table.[60] The peace process is critical to fulfilling Israel's land-grab scheme, and Palestinian participation has been central to its success.

No international law has had the potential to immediately stem the United States' revised Middle East policy. The Palestinian leadership has been partly to blame. In late 2016, the Obama administration punted the question of Palestine onto the international stage, removing it from the backwaters of U.S. bilateralism. The administration abstained on Security Council Resolution 2334 affirming the illegality of Israel's settlement enterprise, including in East Jerusalem. That might have been a moment of opportunity for Palestinians to run a diplomatic marathon. The end goals of the race could have been to establish new terms of reference, isolate Israel, and finally, reject U.S. tutelage. The Palestinians have had this opportunity many times before, not only after the 2012 statehood bid but also in 2004, 2009, 2011, and 2014 when, at each of these junctures, the United States impeded Palestinian efforts to internationalize the conflict.[61] As in those instances, the Palestinian leadership in 2017 and 2018 remained committed to a realpolitik approach and failed to effectively leverage the opportunities afforded by Resolution 2334.

Over the course of two and a half decades of "peacemaking," the United States has made increasingly clear that it is part of the problem.[62] The Trump administration's decision to move the U.S. embassy to Jerusalem only confirmed the dubious role of the United States as an "honest broker." While the Palestinian leadership has failed to respond to this reality, it has incrementally advanced its cause on the international stage. Its efforts have included acceding to dozens of international treaties,[63] requesting that Palestine be placed under an international protection system,[64] and launching a campaign to achieve recognition among European states. There seems to be an inverse relationship between Palestinian faith in U.S.-brokered bilateralism and its internationalization efforts.[65] If accurate, this trend signals a possible pivot away from the Oslo framework and the restoration of a politics of resistance. It could also indicate a floundering leadership increasingly bereft of vision and popular legitimacy. Whatever the case may be, a decisive strategic shift is necessary to leverage the emancipatory potential of any future Palestinian legal initiatives.

Lessons from Namibia

The legal strategy of Namibia during its struggle for liberation and independence provides some lessons on the potential benefits of international law.[66] As with Palestine, the League of Nations placed Namibia under the League's Mandate authority but did not guarantee its independence.[67] Upon the dissolution of the

League of Nations in 1946, South Africa, in its capacity as a Mandatory Power, refused to relinquish its administration of Namibia and deliberately obscured that state's political claims for independence.[68] Namibia became a battleground for a global and ongoing struggle against racial discrimination and colonization.[69] Former colonies and armed national liberation movements, and also the bodies those movements created—like the Non-Aligned Movement and specialized committees within the United Nations—requested a series of advisory opinions from the International Court of Justice (ICJ) and influenced the Security Council to pass a string of binding resolutions addressing the illegality of South Africa's presence. They also constructed the legal infrastructure within the United Nations to shepherd Namibia to independence.

By 1956, the ICJ had issued three advisory opinions in response to procedural questions about Namibia that began to outline a legal blueprint for its independence.[70] The 1950 opinion affirmed South Africa's role as the Mandatory authority of Namibia until an alternative arrangement was established and simultaneously imposed upon it a legal obligation to submit to the supervision of the United Nations.[71] The 1955 and 1956 advisory opinions elucidated the voting procedure over the territory as well as rules regarding appearances before the specialized Committee on Southwest Africa, which functioned much like the Permanent Mandates Commission during the interwar years.[72]

In 1966, the UN General Assembly ended the Mandate and sought to establish a UN trusteeship to usher in Namibia's independence, but South Africa refused to surrender its control. In response, the South West African People's Organization (SWAPO), established in 1964, launched an armed insurrection.[73] The UN General Assembly zealously supported Namibian independence, but the Security Council refused to compel South Africa's withdrawal. The Security Council was nevertheless sympathetic and passed several binding resolutions outlining the basis of a political resolution, including Resolutions 264 (1969) and 276 (1970).[74] Resolution 264 condemned South Africa's presence as well as its establishment of bantustans aimed at autonomous government.[75] The following year, the Security Council passed Resolution 276 and called on "all States, particularly those which have economic and other interests in Namibia, to refrain from any dealings with the Government of South Africa" that sustain its illegal presence in Namibia.[76]

In 1970, the Security Council requested an ICJ advisory opinion that proved to be pivotal in outlining a resolution to the political impasse. It asked: "What are the legal consequences for States of the continued presence of South Africa in Namibia, notwithstanding Security Council resolution 276 (1970)?" In June 1971, the ICJ answered that legal and political developments between the establishment of the Mandate system and 1971 "leave little doubt that the ultimate objective of the sacred trust of civilization was the self-determination and independence of the peoples concerned," rendering South Africa's presence a breach of law.[77]

The legal strides did little to alter South Africa's behavior and by 1986, Namibia, like Palestine, also seemed to signal a failure of international law to topple a discriminatory racial regime and deliver independence. To avoid the pressures of a global consensus, South Africa initiated a political process to discredit the United Nations and arrive at a political agreement that excluded SWAPO.[78] South Africa proposed a limited political and economic autonomy in black homelands that would not lead to statehood.[79] The parallels to Israel's autonomy framework and to the question of Palestine generally are striking.

But there was a unique element in the Namibia case. In 1975, Cuban forces had arrived in Angola to support its transition to independence and resist U.S.– and South African–backed takeovers by right-wing political adversaries.[80] Angola became the site of a proxy civil war with regional implications. The fighting continued through 1988 and shaped U.S. intervention in resolving the Namibian question. In its proposal for Namibian independence, the Reagan administration linked South Africa's withdrawal from Namibia to Cuba's withdrawal from Angola, in accordance with UN Security Council Resolution 435.[81] Passed in 1978, that resolution stipulated a UN process to oversee South African withdrawal and outlined a process for negotiations. In December 1988, South Africa agreed to implement the resolution if it facilitated the withdrawal of Cuban forces, in line with the U.S. linkage policy. Unlike the case of Palestine, the peace process would be established on the basis of hard-won reference to international law. In 1989, Namibians democratically elected SWAPO leader Sam Nujoma as President, but South Africa refused to completely withdraw. Ongoing resistance ultimately pushed South African forces out, and Namibia became independent in 1991.

While Namibians waged a much more strategic and cumulative legal strategy than the Palestinians have, this was not the decisive element in their successful liberation movement. There are three fundamental differences between the cases. First, Namibians rejected South Africa's peace process as an alternative to the international framework. SWAPO refused to enter South Africa's exclusive sphere of influence and thus maintained an adversarial position, unlike the PLO, which has been committed to U.S.-mediated bilateral talks for twenty-five years now. Two, SWAPO never relinquished its right to use of force or ceased its armed struggle until Namibia achieved independence. Cuban troops stationed in Angola significantly enhanced the potential of this armed resistance and ultimately created the requisite negotiating leverage to compel U.S. and South African compromise. In contrast, the PLO relinquished its right to arms as a condition for entering the Oslo Accords. Three, the international context in the late eighties was much more sympathetic to the cause of anticolonial liberation and to the struggle against apartheid than it is now. This enabled SWAPO to wage an effective political battle against the United States and South Africa. Namibia's legal strategy fulfilled the needs of that battle by creating the tools, frameworks, and infrastructure necessary for its success. SWAPO, together with a global alliance, used international law in the service of a political strategy featuring significant coercive pressure that directly challenged the geopolitical structure denying Namibian self-determination. In contrast, the Palestinian leadership has engaged in a politics of diplomatic respectability and has refrained from cultivating or joining a global movement highlighting the justness of its cause and/or Israel's role as an aggressor.

This is not to suggest that Palestinians should rely on armed struggle against Israel. Today, revolutionary violence is out of time and place. Israelis, with U.S. backing, can swiftly delegitimize any use of force by Palestinians as criminal and terroristic regardless of whether Palestinians are targeting military objects or using indiscriminate force. Additionally, Israel's legal work deployed since 2000 significantly expanded Israel's use of force and enables its troops to shoot to kill even unarmed Palestinians with impunity. Although armed resistance remains available to occupied Palestinians as a matter of legal right, as a matter of strategy it is counterproductive and dangerous. But a military option is not the only means of pressure available to Palestinians.

The current status quo has made Israel vulnerable to what former Special Rapporteur to the Occupied Palestinian Territories Richard Falk calls a legitimacy war.[82] A war of legitimacy would challenge the legitimacy of Israel's policies (removal, dispossession, containment, exclusion, and war) and the assumptions on which they are based (security and sovereignty) in the court of public opinion. In particular, it would take aim at the denial of native Palestinian attachment to the land and at the ways in which a sovereignty framework has obscured and conditioned Palestinian claims on Israeli consent. While the peace process masked the reality of settler-colonization, the evisceration of a false partition between Israel and the territories as well as the escalation of Israeli force has created space for the resuscitation of a justice framework.

A Rights-based Alternative: Overcoming the Sovereignty Trap

In 2005 and after nearly twelve years of a counterproductive peace process, Palestinians outside of officialdom launched a campaign that sought to correct their leadership's deleterious policy. On the one-year anniversary of the International Court of Justice's advisory opinion on the separation barrier, declaring its route illegal, a large swath of Palestinian civil society organizations, individuals, and political parties breathed life into the ICJ's recommendation to cease economic and diplomatic relations facilitating Israel's encroachment into the Occupied Territories.[83] The grassroots initiative also significantly expanded that recommendation. The Boycott National Committee (BNC) issued a call for a global solidarity movement to boycott, divest, and sanction Israel until it, first, ends its occupation of Arab lands; second, establishes meaningful equality for its Palestinian citizens; and third, fulfills the right of return of Palestinian refugees.

The 2005 BDS Call, as it is known, also made three fundamental shifts. First, the Call deliberately drew on international law and human rights norms to frame Palestinian grievances in order to transcend the impasse wrought by the peace process. Second, the three demands it issued jointly rehabilitated the Palestinian people as a holistic nation across the juridical and geographic fragmentations that divided them. Third, it deliberately invoked South African legacies to highlight Israel's discriminatory regime by analogy and to deploy the mechanism of boycott, divestment, and sanctions (BDS) that had been central to the global fight against apartheid in South Africa. Together, these shifts have created an impression that the BDS movement's goal is the establishment of a single democratic state for all people in Palestine-Israel and the abandonment of a two-state solution. The BNC, however, is not committed to an explicit political vision.

Omar Barghouti, a founding member of the BNC and the BDS movement, explains that the BNC does not take a position on the one- versus two-state solution.[84] Instead, the movement seeks to establish a rights-based alternative to the Palestinian leadership's realpolitik approach where nearly every Palestinian right is vulnerable to negotiation. The BNC insists that the three rights-based demands should be fulfilled regardless of the nature of a political solution.[85] Given these goals, even with the unlikely establishment of a Palestinian sovereign state and the end of Israel's military occupation, the BDS movement remains salient so long as refugees remain exiled and Palestinian citizens of the state continue to constitute a discriminated minority in Israeli society.

The deliberate refusal to adopt an explicit political program has been the BDS movement's primary strength. Its emphasis on rights highlights the sovereignty trap laid out by Oslo's realpolitik framework, while its appeal to international law and human rights norms imbues it with liberal values of universalism, secularism, and reason.[86] This has enabled it to effectively challenge the self-proclaimed liberalism of North American and European powers, especially, which have supported Israel's Jewish-Zionist settler sovereignty at the expense of Palestinian human rights. The invocation of international law and human rights norms also highlights the contradictions of Israel's self-proclamation as a liberal democracy. A rights-based approach challenges Israel's rule-of-law claims and, therefore, the legitimacy it derives from its supposed adherence. The BDS movement has been quite successful.

Originally perceived as a fringe effort of the radical left, the movement has progressively entered the mainstream.[87] Its cultural boycott victories include the cancellation of concerts in Israel by Roger Waters, Lauryn Hill, Elvis Costello, and Lorde.[88] World-renowned physicist Stephen Hawking refused to attend a conference in Tel Aviv, and National Football League defensive lineman Michael Bennett pulled out of a junket to Israel organized by the Israeli Ministry of Foreign Affairs.[89] In addition, several U.S.-based academic associations endorsed the academic boycott of Israel, while the Presbyterian Church USA and the Methodist Church divested their holdings in companies that profited from the occupation.[90] In April 2018, Dublin became the first city to pledge its support for the BDS movement and discontinue its business dealings with several corporations complicit in Israel's human rights violations.[91]

BDS's reach has led Israel's leaders and most ardent allies to describe the popular movement as the second most significant threat to Israel after a nuclear capable Iran.[92] The Israeli government has responded aggressively in attempts to thwart its impact. In 2011, the Knesset passed legislation enabling civil suits against any individuals who promote BDS, including those merely signing a petition.[93] In 2014, Prime Minister Netanyahu led an effort to establish an anti-BDS task force within the Ministry of Strategic Affairs and allocated a $25.5 million budget to combat the movement.[94] In January 2018, a freedom of information request revealed that Israel has created a "blacklist" of BDS activists and adherents to be barred from entering the country, including members of the U.S.-based organization Jewish Voice for Peace.[95]

The BDS movement has carved out tremendous new political space. It has successfully transformed the conversation about Israel from one about negotiations and sovereignty to one about Israel as a site of gross and systemic human rights violations. It has also cultivated a global and grassroots base eager to support the Palestinian cause. The Boycott National Committee, which leads the movement, has refused to step into that political space to chart a political program and leverage its gains. It insists that only the PLO, or an equivalent institution, possesses the authority to represent all Palestinians and make decisions on its behalf.[96] But since 1993, the PLO has been steadily enfolded within the Palestinian Authority and has refused to endorse the BDS movement in its adherence to realpolitik pragmatism. Moreover, despite several grassroots efforts to resuscitate a representative and accountable Palestinian national body, none of these alternatives has had the requisite global scope and legitimacy to fill the political void left by the PLO's decline.[97] This absence of leadership has created a political vacuum and enlarged the significance of the movement's rights-based nature.

During its struggle to end apartheid, the African National Congress along with other political formations, launched divestment as a tactic of global solidarity to complement and enhance its domestic campaign. That campaign created a vision for the future of South Africa that included a place for white South Africans and catalyzed their political mobilization. The ANC's domestic work was so effective that Nelson Mandela became the symbolic leader of all South Africans and not just its black citizens.[98] The BDS movement, in contrast, has defined itself as a tactic of global solidarity and has purposefully avoided developing a political movement or mantle capable of challenging the Palestinian Authority's dominance. The outcome is dissonance between the official Palestinian leadership's political strategy of achieving sovereignty with U.S.–Israeli acquiescence and the BDS movement's agenda of fulfilling Palestinian rights in direct confrontation with the United States and Israel. More significantly, the aversion to articulating a political program leaves open the question of how to manifest Palestinian demands. The BDS movement—a grassroots, global, and decentralized phenomenon—possesses a radical politics and is itself a politicizing space, but those attributes have been inadequate to fill an outstanding political void. This renders BDS, at best, a necessary but insufficient tactic for overturning Israel's expansionist project and associated violence. The lack of a corresponding political program also enhances the signifying role of international law as a normative framework, which poses some risk.

The movement's potential is remarkable precisely because of its emphasis on universal principles enshrined in law. However, the appeal to universalism can inadvertently depoliticize the question of Palestine by framing it as a movement for equality. It is indeed a struggle to end discriminatory practices, but more fundamentally, it is a struggle against settler-colonial dominance. The question of Palestine is about claims to belonging to a particular land and all that flows from that belonging, including livelihoods and social systems. A discriminatory race-based system is the outcome of a territorial project that seeks to usurp that land and remove the markers of native Palestinian attachment.[99] Striving to dismantle the legal barriers to inequality without addressing the territorial dimensions of the Palestinian struggle is not enough. Palestinian citizens of Israel originally from Ikrit and Kufr Bir'im, for example, do not just want better education, health care, and job opportunities within the state, they seek to return and rebuild their demolished villages.[100] Failing to center these demands has the potential to democratize the settler-colony without upending the "elementary terms of cohabitation" structuring the relationship between Jewish settlers and

Palestinian natives.[101] These terms currently include Jewish-Zionist exclusive claims to belonging to the land as well as a right to rule everything within it. A political program that centralizes settler-colonization requires contending with a history of dispossession. It requires committing to a future that affirms the centrality of native people. A rights-based approach can support this program, but on its own it cannot achieve it.

A rights-based approach also risks setting up a discourse of competing rights. For example, Jewish settlers can and have already claimed that they have a *human right* to remain in their homes in the West Bank settlements.[102] Other Israelis have claimed the right to settler sovereignty as the realization of their human right to Jewish national self-determination.[103] Absent a political framework, these rights lack context and can be framed as competing demands that should be resolved by compromise.[104] This is precisely the logic that has led to partition, and various perverted forms of it, as a solution since 1947. This logic is inadequate and unworkable. A leadership with a political framework can diminish this risk by leading a movement wherein it can assign particular meaning to the law it deploys and/or abandon the law when its terms entrench undesirable outcomes. To leverage the law's emancipatory potential, even in a rights-based approach, Palestinians must shape the meaning of law in the context of a discerning political project.

Legal work is critical to shaping the meaning and application of international law and human rights norms, which are susceptible to strategic deployment and competing interpretive models. The transformation of several legal norms across time and space evidences international law's predisposition to legal work. We can see, for example, how self-determination is initially cast—during the Mandate era—as a tool facilitating colonial governance and penetration under the veneer of a "sacred trust of civilization" to usher a state to independence. Forty years of political, legal, and armed struggle by colonized nations, including Palestinians, ultimately transformed this vague legal norm into a positive right to sovereign self-governance and independence. Similarly, we can see how the legal work of liberation movements and newly independent states in the late 1970s legitimated the use of force by non-state actors as long as that use abides by international legal regulation. Then, between the start of the Al Aqsa intifada, in 2000, and the present, Israel's legal work delegitimized this "right to fight" by defining it as criminal and terroristic in the language of law. We can also trace how UN Security Council Resolution 242 functioned as an oppressive tool of Palestinian dispossession and juridical erasure from 1967 through 1987, but became a primary tool of Palestinian resistance during the Middle East peace process that began in 1991. The value and potential benefit of law is dependent on the political framework, and the legal workers, that give it meaning. In the case of Palestine, a political program is necessary to avoid confusing the equivocating tendencies of a human rights framework with a practice of decolonization.

A Palestinian youth action in November 2011 illustrates this latent tension. On 15 November 2011, six young Palestinians boarded Egged Bus number 148 connecting West Bank settlements to Jerusalem. The bus is normally reserved for Jewish-Israeli settlers, who also possess the distinct privilege of being able to freely enter Jerusalem.[105] The Palestinians who boarded the bus described themselves as "Freedom Riders," in homage to the activists who defiantly sat in the front of buses in the segregated U.S. South during the civil rights movement.[106] The Palestinian organizers explained:

Israelis suffer almost no limitations on their freedom of movement in the occupied Palestinian territory, and are even allowed to settle in it, contrary to international law. Palestinians, in contrast, are not allowed to enter Israel without procuring a special permit from Israeli authorities.[107]

The action generated international attention and praise for highlighting Israel's apartheid system. It also drew controversy from those Palestinians who understood the action as a demand for integration at the expense of liberating the land. In response, the Freedom Riders revised their advisory:

In undertaking this action Palestinians do not seek the desegregation of settler buses, as the presence of these colonizers and the infrastructure that serves them is illegal and must be dismantled. As part of their struggle for freedom, justice and dignity, Palestinians demand the ability to be able to travel freely on their own roads, on their own land, including the right to travel to Jerusalem.[108]

The revision centralized Palestinians' concern with their erasure and dis-possession. Notably it maintained its emphasis on rights, indicating the space available for, and the compatibility between, rights-based claims and a political program. The challenge remains to define that program. Can and should rights-based strategies be pursued in the absence of a political program? On their own, such strategies have tremendous capacity to advance the Palestinian cause even as they fail to command behavior or yield a satisfactory political outcome. Legal and rights-based strategies are critical and beneficial, but we should be none-theless skeptical of their potential. A rights-based approach without a political program that can strategically deploy the law, articulate its meaning, and leverage its yields bears risk and is insufficient to achieve freedom.

Horizons of Freedom Beyond the State

In 2018, the official Palestinian leadership has a clear political vision aimed at establishing a Palestinian state but has abandoned a politics of resistance, thus diminishing the potential of its legal strategies to challenge the geopolitical structure sustaining Palestinian oppression. Worse, officialdom's commitment to statehood is obscuring the reality of settler-colonial removal and inadvertently enabling an apartheid regime. The BDS movement has articulated a rights-based approach that has filled the resistance void left by Palestinians' formal leadership and has successfully carved out a new political space. But due to a commitment to a rights-based approach, it has been unwilling to fill that space and catapult the movement into its next phase. This current juncture in the question of Palestine is a holding position contingent on multiple and unknown vectors, including, most significantly, Palestinian initiative.

During the 1970s, the PLO advanced a combination of a political program and an aggressive legal strategy. It sought to restore native sovereignty in a single democratic state for all people, and it strategically wielded the law in service of that vision. It successfully inscribed the juridical status of Palestin-ian peoplehood in legal instruments, crafted an alternative legal framework for peace in place of Security Council Resolution 242, contributed to the creation of new law (Additional Protocol I) where none existed in order to legitimate its use of force, and established that Zionism is a form of racism akin to apartheid.

The PLO's strategic turn to international law engendered a notable conflict: how can a state-centric legal order that sanctifies the sovereignty of settler states rectify and stem ongoing dispossession and native erasure? That same legal order equivocates between statehood and freedom, thus casting the Palestinian question as a nationalist struggle between two peoples over one land. But the Palestinian struggle has not been merely about the League of Nations' unfulfilled promise of independence; it has equally been about claims to belonging, to being, to existing.[109] Indeed, the loss of Palestine and the desire to return to it, poignantly narrated by Palestinian author and revolutionary Ghassan Kanafani, does not bemoan a lack of self-governance but rather the usurpation of home, memory, and attachment to land.[110] Trump's Jerusalem announcement embodies a similar duality. Palestinian officials have lamented the revised U.S. policy as the end of their statist ambitions.[111] For the vast majority of Palestinians, the affront is not the loss of a would-be capital, but the imperial rejection of Palestinian belonging and the formalization of their erasure. Then as now, there seems to be incongruence between the demand for settler-decolonization and the statist remedy international law affords.

In 1988, Palestinians resolved that tension by embracing a truncated state in the West Bank and the Gaza Strip as the site and scope of their self-determination. That compromise was not inevitable. Although regional and international shifts compelled the PLO to moderate its platform in the 1970s, the liberation movement could not have anticipated its 1982 expulsion from Lebanon nor its steady decline that followed. The PLO's turn to international law was consequential for but not determinative of the two-state solution it ultimately endorsed. The more decisive element was the popular national desire for a state and the possibility that it could be realized through compromising negotiations.[112]

Twenty-five years of the peace process experiment have made clear that Israel is not interested in compromise. In its pursuit of Greater Israel, it extinguished the surest way of ensuring its settler-sovereignty—establishing a Palestinian state in the West Bank and Gaza. Conditions on the ground today constitute a de facto one-state reality, and once again, Palestinians have a decision to make about their political program, this time with more information and certitude. This choice has been cast as being between a "one-state solution" and a "two-state solution," slogans that currently stand in for a multiethnic democracy or an enfeebled autonomy arrangement, respectively. This assumption about the significance of possible solutions requires more scrutiny.

The two-state solution, as proposed and envisioned by Palestinians themselves, was a pathway to freedom. Israel's territorial ambitions severely mutated this possibility and produced the oppressive status quo afflicting the region today. While Israel recognized the juridical peoplehood of Palestinians in 1993, it never accepted, let alone embraced their claims to belonging. Instead, its peace efforts aimed to resolve the Palestinian question by suspending Palestinians in an autonomy framework and pursuing its settler-colonial ambitions by other means. It did not revisit its mythology of righteous conception nor its forced removal and exile of 80 percent of a native population nor its Declaration of Independence that edified a social contract among Jewish settlers to the exclusion of all others.[113] Israel established itself by force and insists on maintaining its settler-sovereignty by force. Jewish-Zionist leaders—primarily from Europe—did not come to the Middle East to reestablish their indigenous attachments there. They came as settlers claiming nativity and as conquerors intent on earning acceptance within Europe by establishing a nation-state beyond its shores.[114] Any possible future necessitates an accounting of this history, not simply for the sake of cathartic truth telling, but for the sake of decolonization.[115]

At its core, a decolonization practice must reorganize the relational terms mediating Israelis—as settler sovereigns—and Palestinians—as natives marked for erasure. The outcome of this practice can vary. Settler-decolonization does not only mean the removal of the settler. That was the case in Algeria. It was not the case in South Africa. Significantly, the demographic realities make the removal of Jewish-Israelis a matter of sensational fancy. In Algeria and South Africa, the native population was the overwhelming majority, whereas in Palestine, the balance, excluding the refugee population, is nearly equal. Moreover, no analogous case of settler-colonialism has featured such a significant exiled native population; Palestinians were removed but not annihilated. They constitute approximately ten million people globally, two thirds of whom live in diaspora and forced exile but who insist on native belonging to Palestine. As Israeli historian Benny Morris laments, "had [David Ben-Gurion] carried out a full expulsion—rather than a partial one—he would have stabilized the State of Israel for generations."[116] Ben-Gurion did not, which is why the demographic balance is such a key issue and why Israel's eliminatory methods include challenging the definition of a Palestine refugee and an insistence that refugees amalgamate into their Arab host states;[117] the Trump administration's threat to defund UNRWA is pointed in this regard.[118] These methods negate the right to return, but more fundamentally, they negate the right to belong.

Without a decolonization praxis, the one-state solution—assumed to be a desirable model to end Palestinian dehumanization and exclusion—can also be severely mutated to engender similar if not more oppressive outcomes. The existence of a majority Palestinian population does not guarantee any particular result; white rule over a black majority in South Africa indicates as much. There is no just solution that does not travel through a direct confrontation with Israel's insistence upon maintaining Jewish sovereignty and the framework of exception that has made that sovereignty an immovable priority. This framework has relegated Palestinian claims as always secondary to, and contingent upon, Israeli prerogative, thereby justifying the cruel costs of that commitment as either necessary or irrelevant. Arriving at a more equitable future requires the centering of Palestinian claims because they have the potential to benefit everyone, not just a select few.

Since his Jerusalem announcement, President Trump has alluded to a "deal of the century" for Palestinians and Israel.[119] Though it has yet to be made public, leaked versions of the deal indicate that it is a modified arrangement of previous proposals of limited and fragmented Palestinian autonomy couched within Israel's overall sovereignty. The deal also offers a new element of formally severing Gaza and placing it under joint Palestinian-Egyptian administration. If implemented, these arrangements will freeze into place Palestinian subjugation and consecrate the forced exile of two thirds of the Palestinian population. Trump's "deal of the century," with the legacy of U.S.–Israeli solutions that it continues, prioritizes Israel's sovereignty and attempts to appease Palestinians with what, if anything, remains.

Because Jewish sovereignty is incommensurable with Palestinian presence, it necessarily engenders fragmentation, partition, separation, and population transfer. The inverse is not true: Palestinian sovereignty does not obviate Jewish belonging. Moreover, Palestinians' primary claim is not to control; it is to belong. The unbending refusal to center Palestinian claims and invert the equation of

Jewish sovereignty equaling Palestinian oppression is preventing us from turning to more fruitful possibilities. This is not about proposing a political solution. The horizon of any such solutions is clear and has acted as a formidable impasse for nearly a century. In contrast, insisting upon centering Palestinian claims is an exercise in visioning a future with the capacity to disrupt the incommensurability of Jewish and Palestinian belonging.[120]

Zionist opposition to Palestinian return and belonging is predicated on a zero-sum view: Israel is if Palestinians are not; Palestinians are not if Israel is. Perhaps instead of asking what it will take to overcome Zionist opposition to Palestinian belonging, we should ask, what possibilities does the return of Palestinians and the recognition of their belonging create? Palestinian refugees, exiled now for seven decades, will return to a memory—in the case of several generations, they will return to their grandparents' memory. The journey will, by definition, be a project of building something new. Returning to Palestine will be literally going back to an unknown future.

The overwhelming majority of Palestinians have not demanded Jewish-Israeli removal in that future, only a relinquishment of their desire to rule. Decolonization demands that the settler reimagine himself or herself in this environment. If, as Zionists insist, their settlement in Palestine is a return to that land rather than a conquest of it, then they must acknowledge the Palestinians on that land on their terms and in their context.[121] Zionists, however, once on that land, have sought to establish a Jewish homeland that is exogenous to the Middle East and closer to, if not an extension of, Europe. Rather than embrace everything indigenous to the Middle East—from language to livelihood and peoples—Zionism rejected them. Israel established itself as the site of in-gathering for the Jewish diaspora; a purpose perpetually driving its removal of Palestinian natives.[122] Gabriel Ash, an Israeli-American analyst, points out that the Jewish nationalist population, because of its commitment to colonial domination, suffers "from a congenital inability to belong to the land it claims as its homeland."[123] He states that an "Israeliness that is at home in the Middle East" must be mediated by Palestinians who were always already home.[124] What possibilities become available when Jewish-Israelis are *made part of the land and the rest of the Middle East* rather than forming a satellite state merely *located in the Middle East*?

The numbers of Jewish-Israelis who are of Middle Eastern origin—from
Iran, Iraq, Algeria, Morocco, Syria, Yemen, and beyond—and whose identities
have been deliberately obscured by Israel, make this consideration even more
pressing and appropriate. In their efforts to liberate Jews from past conditions
of inferiority and oppression, Zionist leaders attempted to create a "new Jew"
modeled on white European values and culture. This revived citizen possessed
qualities in purposeful opposition to cultural markers carried by Middle Eastern
Jews. Moreover, the presence of Palestinian natives, who remained in Israel and
with whom Middle Eastern Jews had more in common than with European
Jews, threatened Zionist efforts to distinguish Israelis as Zionist and assert their
civilizational proximity to Europe.[125] The nascent state embarked on a series of
policies to transform the Eastern Jew into the "new Jew," including the removal
of Middle Eastern children from their families—so they could be acculturated
to the new values—and the supplanting of a Judeo-Islamic cultural geography
with a singular history of European Jews framed as being as universal to all
Jews.[126] This binary framework forced Middle Eastern Jews to choose between
their cultural, ethnic, and linguistic ties and their religion. To become Israeli,
Middle Eastern Jews had to cease being Middle Eastern in anything but name, a
process that scholar Ella Shohat describes as an "exercise in self-devastation."[127]
Today, most Middle Eastern Jewish-Israelis cannot return to their countries of
origin, even if they wanted to, either because of legislation deliberately excluding
them and/or because of wars afflicting those countries. There is no viable future
that does not account for these communities. Middle Eastern Jews belong to
the region, yet Israel's state-building project severed them from it in order to
gain acceptance within Europe. What opens for all of us concerned in the way
of co-existence when Middle Eastern Jews, and Jewish-Israelis generally, are
rehabilitated as part of the region's history and future, when they are not merely
in the Middle East to assert their belonging elsewhere?

It seems, at least in part, that the struggle for Palestinian sovereignty has
similarly been a quest for inclusion in, and recognition from, a world order that
left Palestinians behind. In the middle of the last century, Frantz Fanon entreated
his fellow subjugated peoples to imagine a better horizon for humanity than
Europe was offering in the form of nation-states. Nearly all colonized peoples
pursued self-determination in that form nonetheless. Palestinians joined them

and participated in three monumental periods when oppressed peoples shed the yoke of imperial domination in pursuit of national independence: in the years between the World Wars, during the height of the anticolonial liberation movements, and again in the early nineties with the downfall of apartheid in Namibia and South Africa. None of those efforts yielded a Palestinian state, and now Palestinians are potentially ready to seek out and explore new and uncharted paths toward liberation.

The possibilities are immense and can draw upon various analytical frameworks for a better understanding of the conditions of unfreedom, including race, labor, class, and gender and the intersections they weave.[128] The Palestinian struggle—local/particular and simultaneously global/exemplary—embodies kernels of these possibilities and has proven instructive. Angela Davis, the black, radical scholar-activist and former political prisoner, for example, has drawn on Palestinian steadfastness and resistance to better understand the limits and prospects of prison abolition in the United States.[129] Upon her visit to the region, Wazatayiwan, a Dakota woman and native scholar, noted the value of a resistance spirit for the well-being of oppressed communities. She writes, "I have never lived under conditions in which struggle was celebrated by anything other than a small minority. It is this aspect of Palestine that I found most beautiful."[130] Phenomena, such as these, are piecing together different ways of understanding what it means to exist with dignity in excess of sovereignty.

In any scenario moving forward, more conflict and bloody confrontations are all but certain. No community has ever relinquished its privileges voluntarily, and no community has ever submitted to a condition of perpetual servitude and domination. The question should not be how to avoid such violence, but rather what is the optimal outcome that would make it tolerable? What possible futures can Palestinians build for themselves as well as for the Jewish-Israelis that currently dominate them that would make this tortured history a chronicle of hope rather than one of mourning?

This path is not well-paved; in fact, it does not even exist. Embarking upon it is a commitment to build new possibilities for decolonization and freedom more generally. It is primarily a commitment to ask different questions. The future of Palestine has the potential to provide new models for humanity, including legal orders that can make us whole, ones that Europe has not been able to deliver. Fulfilling this potential requires centering our gaze upon ourselves, to recognize ourselves as free already, in order to forge a path to a future where our liberation is not contingent or mutually exclusive but reinforcing.[131] That is Palestine's promise, still.

ACKNOWLEDGMENTS

This book project has been one of the most difficult and fulfilling endeavors I have embarked upon. It demanded an intense research and writing praxis that challenged me intellectually, emotionally, forcing me to alter my sense of time as well as my commitments. There was no possible way to cross these turbulent channels without the remarkable support of legions of generous and brilliant human beings for whom I am profoundly grateful.

Thank you Kate Wahl of Stanford University Press for your trust in my process and your extraordinary guidance in what felt, at times, like an experiment because of its propensity to shift and adapt to new ideas and approaches. Thanks also to Leah Pennywark of the press for your close reading of the work and excellent remarks.

The book has benefited tremendously from the incisive feedback and unparalleled expertise of many individuals who read varying parts of it. They include Abdel Razzaq Takriti, Andrew Dalack, Anis Fawzi Kassem, Arjun Sethi, Asad Abukhalil, Camille Mansour, Darryl Li, Itamar Mann, Joel Beinin, John Reynolds, K-Sue Park, Nicola Periguini, Nour Joudah, Omar Dajani, Raja Shehadeh, Rashid Khalidi, Richard Falk, Tareq Radi, and Vijay Prashad. Three readers in particular merit distinct mention: Lisa Hajjar, Victor Kattan, and Sherene Seikaly read the entire book, and several drafts of it, providing me with invaluable feedback about the project as a composite whole. Their generosity with their time and collaboration is the most any young scholar can ask for. Sherene, you more than anyone lived through the iterative process of thinking and writing and editing and scrapping and rewriting and disaffection and enthusiasm: growing with you intellectually has been a reward unto its own. Indeed, I am happily indebted to each of my readers, and so very grateful. Any and all mistakes that remain are entirely my own.

In addition to these readers, this book has benefited from the intellectual prowess of individuals who were kind enough to help me wrestle with ideas that consumed me. Thank you Adil Ahmed Haque, Ahmed Ghappour, Ardi Imseis, Carlton Mackey, Chris Tinson, Dana Erekat, David Palumbo-Liu, Dennis Ray Childs, Duncan Kennedy, George Bisharat, Ibtisam Azem, Huda Asfour, Husam Al-Qoulaq, Jumana Musa, Lena Ghannam, Lori Allen, Mazen Masri, Nadia Barhoum, Nadya Sbaiti, Purvi Shah, Robin DG Kelley, Samera Esmeir, Sarah Ihmoud, Seth Azscinka, Shira Robinson, Tareq Baconi, Tareq Radi, and Ziad Abu-Rish. I could not ask for a better team to help me find my way through mazes of my own making. Thank you also to Professor Richard Buxbaum for planting a seed of critical inquiry in 2002 that continues to drive my intellectual curiosity.

Completing this work would not have been possible without the incredible research assistance of Mayss Al-Alami and Nusayba Hammad and their herculean research efforts to help me achieve what initially appeared as impossible. Thank you also to Noor Barakat, Ina Kosova, Lilah Suboh, Shezza Dallal, and Tareq Radi, who helped illuminate new lines of inquiry I had not considered. And thank you to Dalal Hilou and Mohammed Abou Ghazaleh for completing discrete and pressing research tasks. Thank you to each of you. I have no doubt you will continue to blaze new paths in your respective pursuits, and I hope that I can be as helpful to each of you as you have been to me.

Similarly, this book has benefited from the closest attention to detail by the editorial support of Allison Brown, Kenya Moore, Maia Tabet, Nehad Khader, Osama Alkhawaja, and Tammy Hineline. Thank you for your scrutinizing eyes, which are far more adept than my own.

I also extend my thanks to the institutions and individuals who supported my research efforts. These include the Palestinian American Research Center, which funded some of my travels to the region, as well as Charles Anderson, Hala Shoaibi, Husam Al-Qoulaq, Elias Khoury, Khaled Farraj, Rosie Bsheer, and Salim Tamari who introduced me to critical interlocutors, book recommendations, and resources. And a special thank you to the librarians and archivists who waded through materials with me: Jeanette Sarouphim of the Institute for Palestine Studies-Beirut and Hana Sleiman and Kaoukab Chebaro of the American University in Beirut. Finally, thank you to my colleagues at George Mason University for their sustained support in the writing process.

To my heroic friends who tolerated me during my bouts of confusion and loss, who kindly listened to me argue with myself and helped me make amends with my many minds, thank you for walking this path with me. Thank you also to the IG community that allowed me to feel surrounded by people even through long stretches of isolation. #NerdFest

The greatest appreciation is reserved for my family, who in the sincerest terms had to endure me for the past three years. Thank you for believing in me even as I stumbled forward Nahla, Saleh, Subhiyeh, Mohammed, Ahmed, and Yousef Erakat; Asmahan, Naya Asmahan, Carole, Elie, and Michael Haddad; Khalid, Jude, and Julian Namez; and Simina Sattar. Your unconditional love—literally— the homes you cradled me in, the food you made me, and your faith that I would make it out the other end of this endeavor makes this life worth living.

Bassam Haddad, you are *sui generis* in the best way. Your ability to make gold out of straw, to smile in the midst of shit storms, and to give selflessly even in your most challenging moments is so very humbling. Your example alone lit my path. But more, you willingly embarked on road trips with me while know-ing full well I would talk about one idea for nearly five hours, insisted I was on the right track when I insisted I was lost, put off your own writing projects, and supported my writing retreats, sometimes begging me to leave so you did not have to respond to one more request to tell me how a sentence sounded—I am totally down for this kind of love. Thank you B, it's your turn now. . . .

NOTES

INTRODUCTION

1. United Nations Security Council (UNSC), 7853rd meeting, UN Doc. S/PV.7853 (23 December 2016), https://unispal.un.org/DPA/DPR/unispal.nsf/0/9097BDD8E5EFE86785258098 00550E37.

2. UNSC, Resolution 2334, UN Doc. S/RES/2334 (23 December 2016), https://www.un.org/webcast/pdfs/SRES2334-2016.pdf.

3. Majed Bamya, First Counsellor at the Mission of the State of Palestine to the UN, interview by the author, New York, 23 October 2017.

4. UNSC, Resolution 465, UN Doc. S/RES/465 (1 March 1980), https://unispal.un.org/DPA/DPR/unispal.nsf/0/5AA254A1C8F8B1CB852560E50075D7D5.

5. Global Policy Forum, *Subjects of UN Security Council Vetoes*, accessed 12 November 2017, https://www.globalpolicy.org/security-council/40069-subjects-of-un-security-council-vetoes.html.

6. UN News, "United States Vetoes Security Council Resolution on Israeli Settlements," 18 February 2011, http://www.un.org/apps/news/story.asp?NewsID=37572#.WgrkOxNSwWp.

7. Helene Cooper, "Obama Says Palestinians Are Using Wrong Forum," *New York Times*, 21 September 2011, http://www.nytimes.com/2011/09/22/world/obama-united-nations-speech.html.

8. Julie Hirschfeld Davis, "Obama Assures Netanyahu That U.S. Opposes Palestinians' Bid to Join Court," *New York Times*, updated 12 January 2015, https://www.nytimes.com/2015/01/13/world/middleeast/obama-assures-netanyahu-that-us-opposes-palestinians-bid-to-join-court.html.

9. "U.S. and Israeli Intervention Led UN to Reject Palestinian Resolution," *The Guardian*, 31 December 2014, https://www.theguardian.com/world/2014/dec/31/us-israel-un-reject-palestinian-resolution-nigeria-security-council.

10. UNSC, "Divisions over Resolution on Settlements Deemed Illegal Risk . . . ," UN Meetings Coverage and Press Releases, updated 17 January 2017, https://www.un.org/press/en/2017/sc12683.doc.htm.

11. Danny Danon, Israel's Permanent Representative to the United Nations, lamented that the resolution impeded peace because it described Israel's "presence in parts of Jerusalem in 1967 as a flagrant violation of international law." Ibid.

12. Ibid.

13. UNSC, "Israel Markedly Increased Settlement Construction . . . ," UN Meeting Coverage and Press Releases, 24 March 2017, https://www.un.org/press/en/2017/sc12765.doc.htm.

14. League of Nations, The Covenant of the League of Nations (28 April 1919), art. 22.

15. Susan Pedersen, "The Impact of League Oversight on British Policy in Palestine," in *Britain, Palestine, and Empire: The Mandate Years*, ed. Rory Miller (Farnham: Ashgate, 2010), 45; Covenant of the League of Nations, art. 22.

16. Covenant of the League of Nations, art. 22.

17. Victor Kattan, *From Coexistence to Conquest: International Law and the Origins of the Arab-Israeli Conflict, 1891–1949* (New York: Pluto Press, 2009), 107.

18. United Nations General Assembly (UNGA), 207th plenary meeting, Application of Israel for Admission to Membership in the United Nations: Report of the Ad Hoc Political Committee, UN Doc. A/855 (11 May, 1949), https://unispal.un.org/DPA/DPR/unispal.nsf/52b7d0e66142a40e852 56dc70072b982/0b3ab8d2a7c0273d8525694b00726d1b?OpenDocument.

19. See the *Israel Law Review, Palestine Encyclopedia of Law, Palestine Law Review, Palestine Yearbook of International Law*, and *Jewish Law Review*.

20. My concept of "legal opportunity" is based on Robert Knox's definition of "principled opportunism" as the use of international law as "a mere tool, to be discarded when not useful." He continues, "The strategic question of international law's progressive potential is—as a matter of principle—reduced to the tactical, instrumental deployment of legal argument." Knox, "Marxism, International Law, and Political Strategy," *Leiden Journal of International Law* 22, no. 3 (September 2009): 433–34.

21. Duncan Kennedy, "A Left Phenomenological Alternative to the Hart/Kelsen Theory of Legal Interpretation," in *Legal Reasoning: Collected Essays* (Aurora: The Davies Group, 2008).

22. United Nations, Charter of the United Nations and Statute of the International Court of Justice (26 June 1945), art. 38(1), http://treaties.un.org/doc/publication/ctc/uncharter.pdf.

23. Martti Koskenniemi, *The Politics of International Law* (Oxford: Hart, 2011), 158.

24. Antony Anghie, *Imperialism, Sovereignty and the Making of International Law* (Cambridge: Cambridge University Press, 2004), 17.

25. Ibid., 22; This is predicated on an assumption that the native is unmanageable and inhabited by savages who do not organize themselves in the image of a European juridical order. Therefore, they are ineligible for organizing themselves at all: "In the same context, colonies are similar to the frontiers. They are inhabited by 'savages.'" Achille Mmembe, "Necropolitics," *Public Culture* 15, no. 1 (Winter 2003), 24. "To be a State was to hold certain factual, not evaluative properties. If non-European entities did not qualify for statehood this was not because of the existence of a material code which would, for all time, have prevented their qualification as such. It was simply because their subjective essence (degree of civilization) did not correspond to that of European States: they were simply too different. For the classical jurist, this difference was a matter of fact, not political opinion." Martti Koskenniemi, *From Apology to Utopia* (Cambridge: Cambridge University Press, 2005), 199.

26. Anghie, *Imperialism, Sovereignty and the Making of International Law*, 21.

27. Michael Fakhri, *Sugar and the Making of International Trade Law* (Cambridge: Cambridge University Press, 2014).

28. Gil Loescher, *The UNHCR and World Politics: A Perilous Path* (Oxford: Oxford University Press, 2001).

29. John Reynolds, "The Long Shadow of Colonialism: The Origins of the Doctrine of Emergency in International Human Rights Law" (Osgoode CLPE Research Paper 19/2010, 2010), http://digitalcommons.osgoode.yorku.ca/clpe/86.

30. Chris Jochnick and Roger Normand, "The Legitimation of Violence: A Critical History of the Laws of War," *Harvard International Law Journal* 35, no. 49 (1994): 68.

31. See Mark Neocleous, "The Problem with Normality: Taking Exception to 'Permanent Emergency,'" *Alternatives: Global, Local, Political* 31, no. 2 (April–June 2006): 191–213. See, generally, China Mieville, *Between Equal Rights: A Marxist Theory of International Law* (New York: Pluto Press, 2006).

32. Kennedy, "A Left Phenomenological Alternative," 158.

33. "It is precisely because principles are contradictory that we are able to find them countersystemic logics. It is precisely because norms are unstable that we can lead them to 'surpass themselves'. And it is precisely because words are ambiguous that we have the chance to make them mean more than they currently want to mean." Susan Marks, "Afterword: Critical Knowledge," in *The Riddle of All Constitutions: International Law, Democracy, and the Critique of Ideology* (Oxford University Press on Demand, 2000), 144.

34. Kennedy, "A Left Phenomenological Alternative," 158.

35. For Duncan Kennedy's concept of "legal work," see ibid., 158.

36. Ibid.

37. Ibid., 160

38. Ibid.

39. Dale Stephens discusses this example in his work on lawfare and its practice by powerful states. Stephens, "The Age of Lawfare," in *International Law and the Changing Character of War*, ed. Raul A. Pedrozo and Daria P. Wollschlaeger, 327–58 (Newport: Naval War College Press, 2011).

40. Jeffrey P. Fontas, "The Bush Administration Torture Policy: Origins and Consequences," *Inquiries* 2, no. 8 (2010), http://www.inquiriesjournal.com/a?id=276. Here, Derrida's discussion on originary violence is instructive since he suggests that the outcome (national security for the United States against terrorist threats), if conceived as just, can justify the means used to effect its establishment (as in the modified definition of torture as "enhanced interrogation techniques"). Jacques Derrida, *Acts of Religion*, ed. Gil Anidjar (New York: Routledge, 2001), 269.

41. Boumediene v. Bush, 553 U.S. 723 (2008); David Cole, "Closing the Law-Free Zone," *The Guardian*, 13 June 2008, https://www.theguardian.com/commentisfree/2008/jun/13/guantanamo.terrorism1.

42. "'Whether a norm is or is not legal is a function not of its origin or pedigree, but of its effects. Law has an effect—is law—when it persuades an audience with political clout that something someone else did, or plans to do, is or is not legitimate.' . . . In this context, ethical and political corroboration with legal rules becomes inevitable." Stephens, quoting David Kennedy, in "The Age of Lawfare," 66.

43. "The fact is that modern State military forces do legitimately use the law to achieve military objectives. This is done as a substitute for the application of force and hence represents a form of lawfare so defined. . . . [I]t may also be manifested in a formal determination as to whether an armed conflict exists at all, whether it is international or non-international and/or whether an opposition group is to obtain prisoner of war rights or not." Ibid., 50.

44. Balakrishnan Rajagopal, *International Law from Below: Development, Social Movements, and Third World Resistance* (Cambridge: Cambridge University Press, 2003); David Ludden, "A Brief History of Subalternity," in *Reading Subaltern Studies*, ed. David Ludden (New York: Anthem Press, 2002), 7.

45. Coercive pressure is force that can be "direct or indirect, physical or symbolic, exterior or interior, brutal or subtly discursive—even hermeneutic—coercive or regulative" (Derrida, *Acts of Religion*, 232).

46. In his seminal text on the question of Palestine, Edward Said explained that "Zionism's effectiveness in making its way against Arab Palestinian resistance lay *in its being a policy of detail*, not simply a general colonial vision." Said, *The Question of Palestine* (New York: Times Books, 1979), 95. The present book is a humble attempt to unpack and scrutinize that policy of detail concerning the law.

47. Lisa Hajjar, "Human Rights in Israel/Palestine: The History and Politics of a Movement," *Journal of Palestine Studies* 30, no. 4 (Summer, 2001): 21–38.

48. The term itself is attributed to U.S. military colonel Charles Dunlap Jr., who in November 2001 explained that law is hijacked in order to fight the war in another way, in response to European and NGO criticism of U.S. military action. In 2007, he described it as the strategic attempt to use or misuse "law as a substitute for traditional military means to achieve an operational objective." Michael Kearney, "Lawfare, Legitimacy and Resistance: The Weak and the Law," *Palestine Yearbook of International Law* 16, no. 1 (2010): 89.

49. Stephens, "The Age of Lawfare," 51.

50. Israeli Ambassador Danny Ayalon's comments describing UNSC Resolution 2334 are exemplary of Palestinian lawfare, as discussed in Kearney, "Lawfare, Legitimacy and Resistance," 80. See, generally, "UN Security Council Resolution 2334: United Nations Security Council Asserts Illegality," *Harvard Law Review* 130, no. 8 (June 2017), https://harvardlawreview .org/2017/06/u-n-security-council-resolution-2334.

51. The organization defines lawfare as "the exploitation of international legal frameworks and principles, [which] has become a major weapon in the political war against Israel, hoping to delegitimize Israeli responses to attacks on its civilian population." It highlights the following organizations as being primary culprits: the Palestinian Center for Human Rights, Al-Haq, Al Mezan, Adalah, BADIL (Resource Center for Palestinian Residency and Refugee Rights), Defense for Children International–Palestine Section, FIDH (International Federation for Human Rights), and the Center for Constitutional Rights. *Key Issue: Lawfare, International Law, and Human Rights*, NGO Monitor, accessed 4 November 2017, https://www.ngo-monitor.org/key-issues/ lawfare-international-law-and-human-rights/about.

52. See David Luban, "Lawfare and Legal Ethics in Guantanamo," *Stanford Law Review* 60, no. 6 (April 2008): 1981–2026; Stephens, "The Age of Lawfare," 52; and Kearney, "Lawfare, Legitimacy and Resistance," 127.

53. Stephens, "The Age of Lawfare," 54.

54. Asad Talal, "Thinking About Terrorism and Just War," *Cambridge Review of International Affairs* 23, no. 1 (2010): 3–24.

55. Law's existence gives rise to the questions: "What kind of (or whose) law, and what type of (and whose) preference?" Martti Koskenniemi, "The Politics of International Law: 20 Years Later," *European Journal of International Law* 20, no. 1 (2009): 17.

56. Meir Shamgar, "Legal Concepts and Problems of the Israeli Military Government: The Initial Stage," in *Military Government in the Territories Administered by Israel, 1967–1980: The Legal Aspects*, ed. Meir Shamgar (Jerusalem: Hebrew University Jerusalem, 1982), 15.

57. See, generally, Mieville, *Between Equal Rights*; Neocleous, "The Problem with Normality."

58. Richard Falk, "Reframing the Legal Agenda of World Order in the Course of a Turbulent Century," in *Reframing the International: Law, Culture, Politics*, ed. Richard Falk, Lester Edwin J. Ruiz, and R.B.J. Walker, 46–69 (New York: Routledge, 2002).

59. Mark Tushnet, "Some Current Controversies in Critical Legal Studies," *German Law Journal* 12, no. 1 (2011): 290–99, https://dash.harvard.edu/handle/1/10880556. "[International relations (IR)] scholars have generally assumed that the existence of a coercive state able to enforce laws made domestic order very different from international order. A prominent group of legal scholars at the University of Chicago, however, now argue that, even within a domestic setting, making successful law and policy requires an understanding of the pervasive influence of social norms of behavior. This is a particularly compelling insight for IR scholars, since the international system is characterized by law and norms operating without direct punitive capacity." Martha Finnemore and Kathryn Sikkink, "International Norm Dynamics and Political Change," *International Organization* 52, no. 4 (Autumn, 1998): 893.

60. Koskenniemi, *From Apology to Utopia*, 169.

61. Ibid., 162.

62. Ibid.

63. Legal Information Institute, "Jus Cogens," Cornell Law School, accessed 20 October 2016, https://www.law.cornell.edu/wex/jus_cogens.

64. Falk, "Reframing the Legal Agenda of World Order," 48.

65. Koskenniemi, *From Apology to Utopia*, 6.

66. Alexander Wendt, "Anarchy Is What States Make of It: The Social Construction of Power Politics," *International Organization* 46, no. 2 (Spring 1992): 395.

67. Since the Westphalian turn gave rise to a state-centric international system, states have become increasingly interdependent and have cultivated "a new universal conscience" that they apply to themselves as an international community. International law can be ascending or descending; an ascending law emerges from particular state interests and then influences a global system, while descending law flows downwards from a global system upon each state. Koskenniemi, *From Apology to Utopia*, 182. See also Noura Erakat, "U.S. vs. ICRC-Customary International Humanitarian Law and Universal Jurisdiction," *Denver Journal of International Law and Policy* 41, no. 2 (Winter 2013): 238.

68. J. T. Checkel, "The Constructivist Turn in International Relations Theory," *World Politics* 50, no. 2 (January 1998): 324, 326, 327–328.

69. Wendt, "Anarchy Is What States Make of It," 397.

70. Ibid., 395.

71. Finnemore and Sikkink, "International Norm Dynamics and Political Change," 889; J. Goldsmith, "Sovereignty, International Relations Theory, and International Law," *Stanford Law Review* 52, no. 4 (April 2000): 959, 984, 965.

72. Harold Hongju Koh, "Why Do Nations Obey International Law?," *Yale Law Journal* 106, no. 8 (1997): 2602; Dino Kritsiotis, "When States Used Armed Force," in *The Politics of International Law*, ed. Christian Reus-Smit (Cambridge: Cambridge University Press, 2004), 48.

73. Mary Ellen O'Connell, "New International Legal Process," *American Journal of International Law* 93, no. 2 (1999): 334.

74. UNSC, Resolution 2334 asserts that states must "distinguish, in their relevant dealings, between the territory of the State of Israel and the territories occupied in 1967."

75. Bamya, interview.

76. Hugh Lovatt, *EU Differentiation and the Push for Peace in Israel-Palestine* (London: European Council on Foreign Relations, 2016), 2.

77. Ibid.

78. Bamya, interview.

79. Lovatt, "EU Differentiation and the Push for Peace in Israel-Palestine," 5.

80. Ibid., 2.

81. Ibid., 6.

82. See UN ESCWA, *Israeli Practices Towards the Palestinian People and the Question of Apartheid, Palestine and the Israeli Occupation* (Beirut: United Nations, 2017).

83. Ibid., v.

84. Ibid., 54–55.

85. Reuters, "Senior UN Official Quits After 'Apartheid' Israel Report Pulled," Reuters, 17 March 2017, https://www.reuters.com/article/us-un-israel-report-resignation/senior-u-n-official-quits-after-apartheid-israel-report-pulled-idUSKBN16O24X.

86. Carl Schmitt, *Political Theology: Four Chapters on the Concept of Sovereignty*, trans. George Schwab (Chicago: University of Chicago Press, 2005).

87. Giorgio Agamben, *State of Exception*, trans. Kevin Attell (Chicago: University of Chicago Press, 2005), 30.

88. In both cases, the policies are driven by the necessity to achieve a political outcome. Agamben, *State of Exception*, 18. (In both circumstances, neither framework is necessary lawful, "but is rather a proceeding guided essentially by the necessity of achieving a certain end." Schmitt, *Political Theology*, 172, as quoted in Agamben, State of Exception, 18.)

89. Exception may be an expression of necessity that "does not recognize law" or that "creates its own law," in which case, "more than rendering the illicit licit, necessity acts here to justify a single, specific case of transgression by means of an exception." Agamben, *State of Exception*, 24.

90. Dictionary.com, s.v. "sui generis," http://www.dictionary.com/browse/sui-generis.

91. "[T]he state of exception does not apply equally to all since the exclusion of and violence perpetuated against some groups is anchored in the law." Alexander G. Weheliye, *Habeas Viscus: Racializing Assemblages, Biopolitics, and Black Feminist Theories of the Human* (Durham: Duke University Press, 2014), 87.

92. See, e.g., William Peel et al. (1937), Report of the Palestine Royal Commission (London: HMSO), paras. 24, 33, and 42, http://unispal.un.org/pdfs/Cmd5479.pdf.

93. Avi Shlaim, "The Balfour Declaration and Its Consequences," in *Yet More Adventures with Britannia: Personalities, Politics and Culture in Britain*, ed. Wm. Roger Louis, 251–70 (London: I. B. Tauris, 2005).

94. Peter d'Errico applies this concept, drawn from Carl Schmitt's observation that the "rule lives off the exception alone," to explain how in U.S. federal Indian law, "Native sovereignty exists

except to the extent that it does not exist." D'Errico, "Indigenous Lèse-majesté: Questioning U.S. Federal Indian Law," *New Diversities*, 19, no. 2 (2017): 44.

95. Agamben, *State of Exception*, 50

96. As occurred with all cases of settler-colonialism, Britain was able to "establish a new people on settled land by practicing an exception to the law that permits eliminating indigenous people while defining settlers as those who replace." Scott Lauria Morgensen, "The Biopolitics of Settler Colonialism: Right Here, Right Now," *Settler Colonial Studies* 1, no. 1 (2011): 52. Malm discusses the ways in which Palestine bodes the future for all in a warming world in "The Walls of the Tank: On Palestinian Resistance," *Salvage*, last modified 1 May 2017, http://salvage.zone/in-print/the -walls-of-the-tank-on-palestinian-resistance; also see Elizabeth F. Thompson, *Justice Interrupted: Historical Perspectives on Promoting Democracy in the Middle East* (Washington, DC: United States Institute of Peace, 2009).

97. "In the political-juridical structure of the camp, the state of exception ceases to be a temporal suspension of the state of law. According to Agamben, it acquires a permanent spatial arrangement that remains continually outside the normal state of law." Mmembe, "Necropolitics," 13.

98. Patrick Wolfe, "Settler Colonialism and the Elimination of the Native," *Journal of Genocide Research* 8, no. 4 (2006): 387–409; Morgensen, "The Biopolitics of Settler Colonialism," 52.

99. Peter Baker and Julie Hirschfeld Davis, "U.S. Finalizes Deal to Give Israel $38 Billion in Military Aid," *New York Times*, 13 September, 2016, https://www.nytimes.com/2016/09/14/world/ middleeast/israel-benjamin-netanyahu-military-aid.html.

100. Rebecca Savransky, "Pence: 'The Day Will Come' When Trump Moves Embassy to Jerusalem," *The Hill*, 18 July 2017, http://thehill.com/homenews/administration/342471-pence-the-day-will-come-when-trump-moves-embassy-to-jerusalem; Loveday Morris, "US Ambassador Breaks with Policy: 'I Think the Settlements Are Part of Israel,'" *Washington Post*, 29 September 2017, https:// www.washingtonpost.com/news/worldviews/wp/2017/09/29/u-s-ambassador-breaks-with-policy -i-think-the-settlements-are-part-of-israel/?utm_term=.e441fce33869.

101. UNSC, Resolution 2334 (3): "Underlines that it will not recognize any changes to the 4 June 1967 lines, including with regard to Jerusalem, other than those agreed by the parties through negotiations."

102. "We would not have let this resolution pass had it not also addressed counterproductive actions by the Palestinians such as terrorism and incitement to violence, which we've repeatedly condemned and repeatedly raised with the Palestinian leadership, and which, of course, must be stopped." Samantha Powers's statement regarding Resolution 2334, "Read: Full Text of US Envoy Power's Speech Following Abstention at the UN," *Jerusalem Post*, 24 December 2016, http://www.jpost.com/American-Politics/ Read-Full-text-of-US-envoy-Powers-speech-following-abstention-at-the-UN-476370.

103. Barak Ravid, "PA Welcomes Paris Summit Concluding Statement, Calls on France to Recognize Palestine," *Haaretz*, 14 November 2017, http://www.haaretz.com/israel-news/LIVE-1 .764993.

104. "Legal argument resolves specific 'violations,' 'disputes,' or 'instances,' but it never questions the general structural logics that lurk beneath them, and so cannot fully eradicate the problems it addresses." Knox, "Marxism, International Law, and Political Strategy," 430.

105. Knox discusses the types of force that determine the meaning of law. Ibid, 427–28.

106. Richard Falk describes the most recent phase of struggle as a "Legitimacy War" that is focused on a global soft power approach and is waged on "symbolic battlefields." Falk, *Palestine's Horizon: Toward a Just Peace* (New York: Pluto Press, 2017), 9.

107. "What must be pursued is a 'principled opportunism,' where—in order to understand the individualizing, legitimating perspective of the law—international law is consciously used as a mere tool, to be discarded when not useful." Knox, "Marxism, International Law, and Political Strategy," 433.

108. In the context of the European enlightenment, "the human being was directly sorted into the order and context of a political community—namely, the nation—and the right to inalienable rights became dependent on the people's sovereignty . . . the sovereign nation-state was the most powerful and most important political agent and the only authority that could guarantee any sorts of rights." Christian Volk, "The Decline of Order: Hannah Arendt and the Paradoxes of the Nation-State," in *Politics in Dark Times: Encounters with Hannah Arendt*, ed. Seyla Benhabib (Cambridge: Cambridge University Press, 2010), 195.

109. Obergefell et al. v. Hodges, Director, Ohio Department of Health, et al., No. 14-556, 576 U.S. (2015).

110. Frantz Fanon, *The Wretched of the Earth* (New York: Grove Press, 1963), 239.

111. Sherene Seikaly, *Men of Capital: Scarcity and Economy in Mandate Palestine* (Stanford: Stanford University Press, 2015).

112. Zachary Lockman, *Comrades and Enemies: Arab and Jewish Workers in Palestine, 1906–1948* (Berkeley: University of California Press, 1996); Gershon Shafir, *Land, Labor and the Origins of the Palestinian-Israeli Conflict, 1882–1914* (Berkeley: University of California Press, 1996).

113. Judith E. Tucker, *In the House of Law: Gender and Islamic Law in Ottoman Syria and Palestine* (Berkeley: University of California Press, 1998).

114. Nadera Shalhoub-Kevorkian, "At the Limits of the Human: Reading Postraciality from Palestine," *Ethnic and Racial Studies* 39, no. 13 (2016): 2252–60, doi:10.1080/01419870.2016.1202432; Noura Erakat, "Whiteness as Property in Israel: Revival, Rehabilitation, and Removal," *Harvard Journal on Racial & Ethnic Justice* 31 (2015): 69–104.

CHAPTER 1

Several sections of this chapter are based on an article I published in 2015: Noura Erakat, "Whiteness as Property in Israel: Revival, Rehabilitation, and Removal," *Harvard Journal on Racial & Ethnic Justice* 31 (2015): 69–104.

1. League of Nations, The Covenant of the League of Nations (28 April 1919), art. 22.

2. Victor Kattan, *From Coexistence to Conquest: International Law and the Origins of the Arab-Israeli Conflict, 1891–1949* (New York: Pluto Press, 2009), 84–88.

3. Yehoshua Porath, *The Emergence of the Palestinian-Arab National Movement, 1918–1929* (London: Frank Cass, 1995), 44.

4. Ellen L. Fleischmann, "The Emergence of the Palestinian Women's Movement, 1929–39," *Journal of Palestine Studies* 29, no. 3 (2000): 16.

5. Tamir Sorek, "Calendars, Martyrs, and Palestinian Particularism Under British Rule," *Journal of Palestine Studies* 43, no. 1 (2013): 14.

6. This account of Al Qassam and the Great Revolt draws from Elizabeth F. Thompson, *Justice Interrupted: Historical Perspectives on Promoting Democracy in the Middle East* (Washington, DC: United States Institute of Peace, 2009), 5; Mark Sanagan, "Teacher, Preacher, Soldier, Martyr," *Die*

Welt des Islams 53 nos. 3-4 (2013): 332; W. F. Abboushi, "The Road to Rebellion: Arab Palestine in the 1930's," *Journal of Palestine Studies* 6, no. 3 (1977): 23–46; Charles W. Anderson, "From Petition to Confrontation: The Palestinian National Movement and the Rise of Mass Politics, 1929–1939" (PhD diss., New York University, 2013), 647; and Mustafa Kabha, "The Palestinian Press and the General Strike, April–October 1936: 'Filastin' as a Case Study," *Middle Eastern Studies* 39, no. 3 (2003): 170, http://www.jstor.org/stable/4284312.

7. Kabha, "The Palestinian Press," 170.

8. Ibid., 174.

9. On the Peel Commission and the Palestinian response to the proposal of partition, see Penny Sinangolou, "The Peel Commission and Partition, 1936–1938," in *Britain, Palestine, and Empire: The Mandate Years*, ed. Rory Miller, 119–40 (London: Ashgate, 2010); and Anderson, "From Petition to Confrontation," 829, 663.

10. Kabha, "The Palestinian Press," 175.

11. *British White Paper of 1939*, The Avalon Project, http://avalon.law.yale.edu/20th_century/brwh1939.asp.

12. Patrick Wolfe has illuminated how settler-colonialism is a structure of governance and indigenous elimination rather than a singular event of invasion and carnage. I draw on his work to establish that Israeli settler-colonialism constituted a permanent structure of governance aimed at Palestinian elimination. Wolfe, "Settler Colonialism and the Elimination of the Native," *Journal of Genocide Research* 8, no. 4 (2006): 387–409.

13. Two excellent texts that examine this period with great attention to detail and nuance, and upon which this chapter is heavily reliant, are Victor Kattan, *From Coexistence to Conquest: International Law and the Origins of the Arab-Israeli Conflict, 1891–1949* (New York: Pluto Press, 2009); and John Quigley, *The Case for Palestine: An International Law Perspective* (Durham: Duke University Press, 2005).

14. E. L. Woodward and Rohan Butler, eds., "Memorandum by Mr. Balfour (Paris) Respecting Syria, Palestine, and Mesopotamia," in *Documents on British Foreign Policy, 1919–1939*, 1st ser., vol. 4, 340–48 (London: HMSO, 1952).

15. Aziza Khazzoom, "The Great Chain of Orientalism: Jewish Identity, Stigma Management, and Ethnic Exclusion in Israel," *American Sociological Review* 68, no. 4 (2003): 490–91.

16. On ethnographic science and racial hierarchies, see George M. Fredrickson, *Racism: A Short History* (Princeton: Princeton University Press, 2002). Fredrickson comments that the "scientific thought of the Enlightenment was a precondition for the growth of modern racism based on physical typology." On how the triumph of reason made Jews eligible for assimilation but only by the obliteration of any markers of distinction, see Hannah Arendt, *The Jewish Writings*, ed. Jerome Kohn and Ron H. Feldman (New York: Schocken Books, 2007); and Sherene Seikaly and Max Ajl, "Of Europe: Zionism and the Jewish Other," in *Europe After Derrida: Crisis and Potentiality*, ed. Agnes Czajka and Bora Isyar (Edinburgh: Edinburgh University Press, 2013), 120. On the reformulation of Jews' status in Orientalist terms, see Amnon Raz-Krakotzkin, "The Zionist Return to the West and the Mizrahi Jewish Perspective," in *Orientalism and the Jews*, ed. Ivan Davidson Kalmar and Derek Jonathan Penslar (Waltham: Brandeis University Press, 2005), 162; and Ella Shohat, "Reflections of an Arab Jew," *Fellowship*, 64, nos. 5–6 (1998): 4–5.

17. Adam Gopnik, "Trial of the Century: Revisiting the Dreyfus Affair," *The New Yorker*, 28 September 2009, http://www.newyorker.com/magazine/2009/09/28/trial-of-the-century. Albert

Dreyfus, an Alsatian Jew living in Paris and serving in the French army, was accused and wrong-fully convicted of treason in a controversial trial during which the scant evidence against him was kept secret and after which subsequent media coverage and public commentary set off anti-Semitic riots around France and Algiers. For assimilated European Jews, including Herzl, who was covering the Dreyfus affair as a reporter for a Vienna newspaper, the miscarriage of justice and outburst of anti-Semitic rhetoric against Dreyfus, whose life had been dedicated to military service to the na-tion, and his supporters represented the failure and impossibility of Jewish assimilation in France, which had once been its most promising setting, and by extension throughout the rest of Europe.

18. On Zionism's internalization and reproduction of Orientalist tropes, see Raz-Krakotzkin, "The Zionist Return to the West," 170; and Theodor Herzl, *The Jewish State* (New York: Dover, 1988).

19. Zachary Lockman, *Comrades and Enemies: Arab and Jewish Workers in Palestine, 1906–1948* (Berkeley: University of California Press, 1996), 29.

20. Christian Volk, "The Decline of Order: Hannah Arendt and the Paradoxes of the Nation-State," in *Politics in Dark Times: Encounters with Hannah Arendt*, ed. Seyla Benhabib (Cambridge: Cambridge University Press, 2010).

21. Hurst Hannum, *Autonomy, Sovereignty, and Self-Determination: The Accommodation of Con-flicting Rights* (Philadelphia: University of Pennsylvania Press, 1996), 27

22. Ibid., 59, 63, 96.

23. Ibid. The quotation is from Herzl, *The Jewish State*, 23.

24. Quigley, *The Case for Palestine*, 7.

25. Arthur James Balfour, *Balfour Declaration 1917*, The Avalon Project, http://avalon.law .yale.edu/20th_century/balfour.asp.

26. Beshara Doumani, "Palestine Versus the Palestinians? The Iron Laws and Ironies of a People Denied," *Journal of Palestinian Studies* 36, no. 4 (Summer 2007): 49–64.

27. E. J. Hobsbawm, *Nations and Nationalism Since 1780: Programme, Myth, Reality* (Cambridge: Cambridge University Press, 1990), 18–19; Hugh Seton-Watson, *Nations and States: An Enquiry into the Origins of Nations and the Politics of Nationalism* (London: Methuen, 1977), 1; Hannum, *Autonomy, Sovereignty, and Self-Determination*, 24. In the social sciences, this shared sense of history, language, culture, and so forth is known as a *social imaginary*.

28. George Antonius, *The Arab Awakening: The Story of the Arab National Movement* (London: Kegan Paul, 2015), app. A.

29. *The Sykes-Picot Agreement: 1916*, The Avalon Project, http://avalon.law.yale.edu/20th_cen-tury/sykes.asp. See also Sara Pursley, "'Lines Drawn on an Empty Map': Iraq's Borders and the Leg-end of the Artificial State (Part 1)," *Jadaliyya*, 2 June 2015, http://www.jadaliyya.com/Details/32140; and Kattan, *From Coexistence to Conquest*, 99.

30. Thompson, "Justice Interrupted," 5.

31. Timothy Mitchell, *Carbon Democracy: Political Power in the Age of Oil* (New York: Verso, 2011), 87. This issue is not settled, and other reasons for Britain's policy are advanced by various historians, as discussed by Avi Shlaim, "The Balfour Declaration and Its Consequences," in *Yet More Adventures with Britannia: Personalities, Politics and Culture in Britain*, ed. Wm. Roger Louis, 251–70 (London: I. B. Tauris, 2005). Susan Pedersen advances yet another argument, suggesting that this has to do not with interests but rather with the incorporation—and embeddedness—of Chaim Weizmann in the British deliberations. Susan Pedersen, "Writing the Balfour Declaration

into the Palestine Mandate," presentation at the conference "100 Years Since the Balfour Declaration," Israel Academy of Sciences and Humanities, Jerusalem, November 2017.

32. Rashid Khalidi, *Iron Cage* (Boston: Beacon Press, 2006), 37; Shlaim, "Balfour Declaration and Its Consequences."

33. Correspondence with the Palestine Arab Delegation and Zionist Organization, Presented to Parliament by Command of His Majesty, Cmd. 1700/Non-UN document (excerpts), London (1 July 1922), 20; Khalidi, *Iron Cage*, 36.

34. Mitchell, *Carbon Democracy*, 87.

35. Thompson, "Justice Interrupted," 4.

36. Letter from Foreign Secretary Arthur J. Balfour to Prime Minister Lloyd George, 19 February 1919 as cited in a confidential memorandum on the "Arab choice of His Majesty's Government as a mandatory Power for Palestine," Document No. 47756/2117/M.E. 44/1919, National Archives, as quoted in Kattan, *From Coexistence to Conquest*, 121.

37. Doumani, "Palestine Versus Palestinians?," 50.

38. Denis Vovchenko, "Creating Arab Nationalism? Russia and Greece in Ottoman Syria and Palestine (1840–1909)," *Middle Eastern Studies* 49, no. 6 (2013): 901–18.

39. Porath, *Emergence of the Palestinian-Arab National Movement*, 45.

40. But see Kattan, *From Coexistence to Conquest*, 131. Kattan argues that Britain intended to include the political rights of Palestinians even if it failed to mention them explicitly. I disagree with his reading. British administration of Mandate Palestine and the absence of high-ranking Palestinians in the colonial administration, as well as indications that Transjordan would be the sovereign of Arab Palestine, belie this conclusion.

41. Shlaim, *The Balfour Declaration and Its Consequences*, 5.

42. William Peel et al. (1937), "*Report of the Palestine Royal Commission*" (London: HMSO), para. 48, available from http://unispal.un.org/pdfs/Cmd5479.pdf.

43. Khalidi, *Iron Cage*, 37.

44. Susan Pedersen, "The Meaning of the Mandates System: An Argument (League of Nations)," *Geschichte und Gesellschaft* 32, no. 4 (October 2006), 560–82.

45. The recourse to necessity is an extrajudicial evaluation. Giorgio Agamben, *State of Exception*, trans. Kevin Attell (Chicago: University of Chicago Press, 2005), 30.

46. Lori Allen, "Determining Emotions and the Burden of Proof in Investigative Commissions to Palestine," *Comparative Studies in Society and History* 59, no. 2 (2017): 385–414. Palestinians protested Jewish land acquisition as early as 1891, and in 1914, Palestinian candidates for parliament ran on an anti-Zionist platform. In 1918, Palestinians used the first anniversary of the issuance of the Balfour Declaration to deliver a petition to the British Mandate Military Governor of Jerusalem protesting Zionist policy. Kattan, *From Coexistence to Conquest*, 79; See also Porath, *Emergence of the Palestinian-Arab National Movement*, 31.

47. Quigley, *The Case for Palestine*, 9.

48. Ibid.; Ken Grossi, Maren Milligan, and Ted Waddelow, *Restoring Lost Voices of Self-Determination*, King-Crane Commission Digital Collection (August 2011), http://www2.oberlin.edu/library/digital/king-crane/intro.html.

49. Ibid.

50. Mitchell, *Carbon Democracy*, 86–108.

51. Miriam Mckenna, "The Means to the End and the End of the Means: Self-Determination, Decolonization, and International Law," *Jus Gentium: Journal of International Legal History* 2, no. 1 (2017): 94–95. Rupert Emerson argues that even after 1960, the right was not enforceable but rather a claim that could be validated by the use of requisite military force. Emerson, "Self-Determination," *American Journal of International Law* 65, no. 3 (1971): 459–75.

52. United Nations General Assembly (UNGA), Resolution 1514, Declaration on the Granting of Independence to Colonial Countries and Peoples, UN Doc. A/RES/15/1514 (14 December 1960), http://www.un.org/en/decolonization/declaration.shtml. See also McKenna. "The Means to the End and the End of the Means," 94–95; and Emerson, "Self-Determination."

53. *President Woodrow Wilson's Fourteen Points*, The Avalon Project, http://avalon.law.yale.edu/20th_century/wilson14.asp.

54. Allen Lynch, "Woodrow Wilson and the Principle of 'National Self-Determination': A Reconsideration," *Review of International Studies* 28, no. 2 (2002): 419–36, doi:10.1017/S0260210502050204199.

55. Derek Heater, *National Self-Determination: Woodrow Wilson and His Legacy* (London: Palgrave Macmillan, 1994), 8, as quoted in Lynch, "Woodrow Wilson and the Principle of 'National Self-Determination,'" 20.

56. Vladimir Lenin, a leader of the revolution that established the Union of Soviet Socialist Republics (USSR), which supported liberation movements throughout the former imperial colonies, did champion national self-determination, although he insisted that anticolonial independence movements would only succeed if they fought a class struggle against their own oppressive elites and averted the ascendance of bourgeois nationalism. He did not want "to support bourgeois nationalism in oppressed nations." Hannum, *Autonomy, Sovereignty, and Self-Determination*, 32.

57. Hannum, *Autonomy, Sovereignty, and Self-Determination*, 28–29.

58. Covenant of the League of Nations, art. 22.

59. Antony Anghie, *Imperialism, Sovereignty and the Making of International Law* (Cambridge: Cambridge University Press, 2004), 148.

60. Mitchell, *Carbon Democracy*, 69.

61. Anghie, *Imperialism, Sovereignty and the Making of International Law*, 133.

62. Ibid., 146.

63. Kattan, *From Coexistence to Conquest*, 121.

64. Covenant of the League of Nations, art. 22.

65. Mitchell, *Carbon Democracy*.

66. On Faysal's advocacy and the creation of the Syrian Arab Kingdom, see Thompson, "Justice Interrupted," 3–5, 7; and Mitchell, *Carbon Democracy*.

67. Similarly, Peter d'Errico discusses the co-constitutive nature of exception and *sui generis* law as regards U.S. federal Indian law. D'Errico, "Indigenous Lèse-majesté: Questioning U.S. Federal Indian Law," *New Diversities* 19, no. 2 (2017): 41–54.

68. Correspondence with the Palestine Arab Delegation and Zionist Organization, para. 4. Articles 94 to 97 of the treaty provisionally recognize the independence of Iraq and Syria, while Article 95 intentionally avoids making similar reference to Palestine, in order to fulfill the Balfour Declaration.

69. Ibid., 3.

70. Ibid., para. 11(c). The Colonial Office also stated "that the Principal Allied Powers, concerned as they were to ensure the fulfillment of a policy adopted before the Covenant was drafted, were well advised in applying to Palestine a somewhat different interpretation of paragraph 4 of Article 22 of the Covenant than was applied to the neighboring countries of Iraq and Syria." Ibid., para. 5.

71. Samera Esmeir contends that the inclusion of colonial subjects in the body of law served a punitive function without necessarily affording these subjects a rights-bearing agency. Esmeir, *Juridical Humanity: A Colonial History* (Stanford: Stanford University Press, 2012).

72. Correspondence with the Palestine Arab Delegation and Zionist Organization, 13–14.

73. Pedersen, "Writing the Balfour Declaration into the Palestine Mandate."

74. Ibid.; Pederson, "The Impact of League Oversight on British Policy in Palestine," in *Britain, Palestine, and Empire: The Mandate Years*, ed. Rory Miller (Farnham: Ashgate, 2010), 42; Charles H. Levermore, *Third Year Book of the League of Nations* (1922), 137, as discussed in UN Special Committee on Palestine, Report to the General Assembly (Lake Success, NY: 1947), chap. 2, para. 180, https://unispal.un.org/DPA/DPR/unispal.nsf/0/07175DE9FA2DE563852568D3006E10F3.

75. *The Palestine Mandate*, 24 July 1922, The Avalon Project, http://avalon.law.yale.edu/20th_century/palmanda.asp.

76. Khalidi, *Iron Cage*, 33.

77. The one reference to "natives" in the Mandate for Palestine appears in Article 9 and distinguishes natives from foreigners, rather than natives from the Jewish immigrants afforded the legal right to settle the land.

78. Pedersen, "Writing the Balfour Declaration into the Palestine Mandate."

79. Khalidi, *Iron Cage*, 38.

80. Porath, *Emergence of the Palestinian-Arab National Movement*, 51.

81. Khalidi, *Iron Cage*, 40.

82. Ibid., 33.

83. In 1918, 573,000 Palestinians and 66,000 Jews made up the population, and Jews owned only 1 percent of the land. Porath, *Emergence of the Palestinian-Arab National Movement*, 41.

84. Ibid., 44.

85. Khalidi, *Iron Cage*, 33.

86. Porath, *Emergence of the Palestinian-Arab National Movement*, 53.

87. In response to an appeal by the Palestine Arab Congress in 1925, the PMC "decided—and would hold to this decision in the future—that it could not consider petitions that called into question 'the very principle of the Palestine Mandate,'" including the Balfour Declaration. Pederson, "The Impact of League Oversight on British Policy in Palestine," 45. Also see ibid., 51 and 53.

88. Matthew Hughes, "From Law and Order to Pacification: Britain's Suppression of the Arab Revolt in Palestine, 1936–39," *Journal of Palestine Studies* 39, no. 2 (Winter 2010): 6–22.

89. John Reynolds, "The Long Shadow of Colonialism: The Origins of the Doctrine of Emergency in International Human Rights Law," Osgoode CLPE Research Paper 19/2010 (2010), http://digitalcommons.osgoode.yorku.ca/clpe/8; League of Nations, Report by His Majesty's Government in the United Kingdom of Great Britain and Northern Ireland to the Council of the League of Nations on the Administration of Palestine and Trans-Jordan for the Year 1937 (31 December 1937), https://unispal.un.org/DPA/DPR/unispal.nsf/0/7BDD2C11C15B54C2052565D10057251E.

90. It was institutionalized "as a mechanism to protect British interests over those of the native other" during several counterinsurgency campaigns, including the India mutiny (1857), the mass revolt in Jamaica (1865), and the Egyptian and Iraqi revolts (1919–1920), as well as the Irish War of Independence (1919–1921). Laleh Khalili, "The Location of Palestine in Global Counter-insurgencies," *International Journal of Middle East Studies* 42, no. 3 (2010): 422, http://www.jstor.org/stable/40784820.

91. Sovereignty is characterized by a right to identify the other as a mortal threat, whose elimination strengthens a sovereign's ability to live. Achille Mmembe, "Necropolitics," *Public Culture* 15, no. 1 (Winter 2003): 24.

92. Mark Neocleous, "The Problem with Normality: Taking Exception to 'Permanent Emergency,'" *Alternatives: Global, Local, Political* 31, no. 2 (April-June 2006): 207.

93. The state of exception can assume a "permanent spatial arrangement that remains continually outside the normal state of law." Mmembe, "Necropolitics," 13.

94. Khalili, "The Location of Palestine in Global Counterinsurgencies," 422.

95. Ibid., 423. My account of the British suppression of the revolt relies on Khalili, "The Location of Palestine in Global Counterinsurgencies," 422–23.

96. Hughes, "From Law and Order to Pacification," 6.

97. Khalidi, *Iron Cage*, 107.

98. Walid Khalidi, *From Haven to Conquest* (Beirut: Institute for Palestine Studies, 1971), app. 4, 846–49.

99. MacDonald in Permanent Mandate Commission, Minutes, 36th Sess., 8–29 June 1939, 98–99, as quoted in Pederson, "Impact of League Oversight on British Policy in Palestine," 62.

100. Porath, *Emergence of the Palestinian-Arab National Movement*, 277; Victor Kattan argues that protest from Muslims in India, which Britain maintained as a colony, formatively influenced British policy. Kattan, "How India's Muslim Backlash, Led by Jinnah, Thwarted the Balfour Declaration," *Haaretz*, 30 October 2017, https://www.haaretz.com/opinion/how-india-s-muslim-backlash-wrecked-the-balfour-declaration-1.5461135.

101. Porath, *Emergence of the Palestinian-Arab National Movement*, 286.

102. See *British White Paper of 1939*: "His Majesty's Government are unable at present to foresee the exact constitutional forms which government in Palestine will eventually take, but their objective is self government, and they desire to see established ultimately an independent Palestine State."

103. Anderson, "From Petition to Confrontation," 1102.

104. Upon reexamination, Britain modified its earlier position, moving from emphatic opposition to a promise for Palestinian independence. It now adopted a less firm position that stated simply that the "the language in which its exclusion was expressed was not so specific and unmistakable as it was thought to be at the time." This reflected a partial concession to resolve a controversy between the Foreign and Colonial Offices. The Foreign Office was adamant that Palestine was not excluded, while the Colonial Office took the opposite stance. Upon soliciting expert legal advice, they learned that the letter was not unequivocal and remained vague. See Porath, *Emergence of the Palestinian-Arab National Movement*, 284–90. This legal debate and its outcome was also rehearsed in the UN Special Committee on Palestine's Report to the General Assembly, paras. 167–69.

105. Porath, 290.

106. Pederson, "The Impact of League Oversight on British Policy in Palestine," 64.

107. Quigley, *Case for Palestine*, 27.

108. Ibid., 29.

109. Pederson, "The Impact of League Oversight on British Policy in Palestine," 55.

110. Quigley, *Case for Palestine*, 33.

111. UN Special Committee on Palestine, Report to the General Assembly, paras. 176–80.

112. UNGA, Official Records of the Second Session of the General Assembly: Ad Hoc Committee on the Palestinian Question, United Nations Special Committee on Palestine, UN Doc. A/364, sup. no. 11 (3 September 1947), https://unispal.un.org/DPA/DPR/unispal.nsf/0/07175DE9FA2DE5 63852568D3006E10F3.

113. Kattan, *From Coexistence to Conquest*, 148–51; Quigley, *Case for Palestine*, 35.

114. The United States, the most enthusiastic proponent of partition, successfully delayed the UNGA vote on the matter in order to apply coercive financial pressure on smaller states to obtain their support and ultimately secure a majority vote. This pressure included threatening to cut aid to financially dependent countries in order to obtain support for partition; this was done with public knowledge. Kattan, *From Coexistence to Conquest*, 153; Quigley, *Case for Palestine*, 37.

115. Kattan, *From Coexistence to Conquest*, 153; Quigley, *Case for Palestine*, 37.

116. "In its [survey publication] *Village Statistics*, the Mandatory Power estimates the total area of land owned by Jews in 1945 to be 1,491,699 dunams, compared with about 13 million dunams owned by Arabs in Palestine." United Nations Division for Palestine Rights (DPR), *Acquisition of Land in Palestine* (1 January 1980), https://unispal.un.org/DPA/DPR/unispal.nsf/181c4bf00c44e5fd85256cefo 073c426/7d094ff80ff004f085256dc200680a27?OpenDocument.

117. UNGA, Resolution 181 (II), Future Government of Palestine, UN Doc. A/RES/181(II) (29 November 1947), https://unispal.un.org/DPA/DPR/unispal.nsf/0/7F0AF2BD897689B785256C330 061D253. Specifically, see chap. 2 on religious and minority rights; chap. 3(1) on citizenship and rights; chap. 2(2) on the prohibition of discrimination; chap. 2(3) on equal protection; and chap. 2(8) on the prohibition of land expropriation.

118. Walid Khalidi, "Plan Dalet: Master Plan for the Conquest of Palestine," in "Palestine 1948," special issue, *Journal of Palestine Studies* 18, no. 1 (Autumn 1988): 14, http://www.jstor.org/ stable/2537591.

119. Ian J. Bickerton and Carla L. Klausner, *A Concise History of the Arab-Israeli Conflict* (Upper Saddle River: Prentice Hall, 2002), 86–87; Charles D. Smith, *Palestine and the Arab-Israeli Conflict*, 2nd ed. (New York: St. Martin's Press, 1992), 140.

120. Ilan Pappé, *The Forgotten Palestinians: A History of the Palestinians in Israel* (New Haven: Yale University Press, 2011).

121. Smith, *Palestine and the Arab-Israeli Conflict*, 140.

122. The Haganah told the Anglo-American Committee of Inquiry (a commission initiated by the governments of the United States and the United Kingdom in 1946 to examine the situation and help propose a solution), as early as March 1946, that if Britain and the United States were unwilling to enforce partition, they should not interfere and should allow Zionist forces to do it themselves. Khalidi, "Plan Dalet," 13.

123. Ibid., 15; Kattan, *From Coexistence to Conquest*, 183.

124. Khalidi, "Plan Dalet," 16, 20. Appendix A (pp. 20–23) contains the text of the May 1946 Plan Gimmel (Plan C).

125. Gershon Rivlin and Elhanan Oren, eds., *The War of Independence: Ben-Gurion's Diary* (Tel Aviv: Ministry of Defense, 1986), 210–11.

126. David Ben-Gurion, *In the Battle* (Tel Aviv: Am Oved, 1949), 255–72, as cited in Ilan Pappé, *The Ethnic Cleansing of Palestine* (Oxford: One World Oxford, 2006).

127. Pappé, *Ethnic Cleansing*, 48.

128. Central Zionist Archives, 45/1 Protocol (2 November 1947), as cited in Pappé, *Ethnic Cleansing*.

129. Shabtai Teveth, *Ben-Gurion and the Palestinian Arabs: From Peace to War* (Oxford: Oxford University Press, 1985), 189, as quoted in Nur Masalha, "60 Years After the Nakba: Historical Truth, Collective Memory and Ethical Obligations," *Kyoto Bulletin of Islamic Area Studies* 3, no. 1 (2009): 37–88.

130. Khalidi, "Plan Dalet," 11.

131. Ibrahim Abu-Lughod discusses Benny Morris's finding of Ben-Gurion's role in Operation Dani leading to the expulsion of Palestinians from Lydda and Ramleh. Abu-Lughod, "The War of 1948: Disputed Perspectives and Outcomes." *Journal of Palestine Studies* 18, no. 2 (1989): 119–27, doi:10.2307/2537638.

132. Benny Morris, "Revisiting the Palestinian Exodus of 1948," in Eugene L. Rogan and Avi Shlaim, eds., *The War for Palestine*, 37–59. In his review of Morris's *1948 and After: Israel and the Palestinians*, Nur Masalha argues that Morris makes a problematic distinction, which is central to his conclusions, between outright expulsion on the one hand and the (vague or euphemistic) "causing," "promoting," "precipitating," "encouraging," "nudging," and "prompting" people into flight through various military pressures and psychological means on the other. The problem with this distinction is that it leaves glaring discrepancies between the evidence he produces and the conclusions he deduces. Nur Masalha, "'1948 and After' Revisited," review of *1948 and After: Israel and the Palestinians*, by Benny Morris, *Journal of Palestine Studies* 24, no. 4 (1995): 90–95.

133. UNGA, Draft Trusteeship Agreement for Palestine: Working Paper Circulated by the United States Delegation, UN Doc. A/C.1/277 (20 April 1948), https://unispal.un.org/DPA/DPR/unispal.nsf/0/6E8713B260ABA5EE80256473004A2B37; Quigley, *Case for Palestine*, 44; Kattan, *From Coexistence to Conquest*, 190.

134. Khalidi, "Plan Dalet," 17.

135. Ibid., 17 and 24.

136. Appendix B in Khalidi, "Plan Dalet," 29. This appendix contains the text of the March 1948 Plan Dalet (Plan D).

137. In particular, the British recruited and trained armed Jewish settlers to protect the Haifa-Lydda Railway as Palestinian rebels repeatedly targeted and bombed the pipeline delivering oil from Haifa to Kirkuk, Iraq. Mitchell, *Carbon Democracy*, 104.

138. Khalili, "Location of Palestine in Global Counterinsurgencies," 415–16.

139. Kattan discusses some of the most notable operations, including sexual assault against women. Kattan, *From Coexistence to Conquest*, 191–202.

140. Nur Masalha, *The Politics of Denial: Israel and the Palestinian Refugee Problem* (London: Pluto Press, 2003), 33.

141. Daniel A. McGowan, *The Saga of Deir Yassin: Massacre, Revisionism, and Reality* (Geneva, NY: Deir Yassin Remembered, 1999).

142. Pappé, *Ethnic Cleansing*, 90.

143. Khalidi, "Plan Dalet," 19.

144. Ibid., 17–18; Pappé, *Ethnic Cleansing*, 119.

145. The "final outcome of the war was thus not a miracle but a faithful reflection of the underlying Arab-Israeli military balance. In this war, as in most wars, the stronger side ultimately prevailed." Avi Shlaim, "The Debate About 1948," *International Journal of Middle East Studies* 27, no. 3 (1995): 295. The account here of the Arab armies and King Abdullah's command draws on Shlaim, "Debate About 1948"; Avi Shlaim, *Collusion Across the Jordan, King Abdullah, the Zionist Movement, and the Partition of Palestine* (New York: Columbia University Press, 1988); and Bickerton and Klausner, *A Concise History of the Arab-Israeli Conflict*, 89.

146. Shlaim, "Debate About 1948," 299.

147. Spiro Munayyer, "The Fall of Lydda," *Journal of Palestine Studies* 27, no. 4 (Summer 1998): 80–98.

148. Pappé, *Forgotten Palestinians*, 18; Walid Khalidi, *All That Remains: The Palestinian Villages Occupied and Depopulated by Israel in 1948* (Washington, DC: Institute for Palestine Studies, 2006).

149. United Nations Security Council (UNSC), Official Records, 358th mtg., UN Doc. S/PV.385 (17 December 1948), https://unispal.un.org/DPA/DPR/unispal.nsf/0/437DD877E3491 51B052566CE006D9189.

150. UNGA, Resolution 273 (III), Admission of Israel to Membership in the United Nations, UN Doc. A/RES/273(III) (11 May 1949), para. 5.

151. Special Unit on Palestinian Rights (SUPR), *Right of Return of the Palestinian People*, a study prepared for the Committee on the Exercise of the Inalienable Rights of the Palestinian People (CEIRPP) (1 November 1978), https://perma.cc/BJG9-VSZR. Resolution 194 mandates that the Conciliation Commission on Palestine "facilitate the repatriation, resettlement, and the economic and social rehabilitation and the payment of compensation" for Palestine refugees. UNGA, Resolution 194 (III), Palestine: Progress Report of the United Nations Mediator, UN Doc. A/RES/194(III) (11 December 1948), https://unispal.un.org/DPA/DPR/unispal.nsf/0/C758572B78D1CD0085256B-CF0077E51A. For more on the right of return, see Special Unit on Palestinian Rights, *The Right of Return of the Palestinian People*; and UNGA, Resolution 181 (II), chap. 2.

152. UNGA, Resolution 273 (III), para. 5.

153. See the statement of Abba Eban, in UNGA, 45th mtg.: Application of Israel for Admission to Membership in the United Nations, UN Doc. A/AC.24/SR.45 (5 May 1949), https://unispal.un.org/DPA/DPR/unispal.nsf/85255a0a0010ae82852555340060479d/1db943e43c280a2 6052565fa004d8174?OpenDocument.

154. Shlaim, "Debate About 1948."

155. UN Charter (26 June 1945), chap. I, arts. 1 and 2, http://treaties.un.org/doc/publication/ctc/uncharter.pdf.

156. "As this law to come will in return legitimate, retrospectively, the violence that may offend the sense of justice, its future anterior already justifies it. The foundation of all states occurs in a situation that one can thus call revolutionary. It inaugurates a new law; it always does so in violence. *Always*, which is to say even when there have not been those spectacular genocides, expulsions or deportations that so often accompany the foundation of states, great or small, old or new, right nearby, or very far away." Jacques Derrida, *Acts of Religion*, ed. Gil Anidjar (New York: Routledge, 2001), 269.

157. "Founding violence" institutes law and decides what it is; "violence that preserves" maintains and preserves the law (Derrida, *Acts of Religion*, 264).

158. The Jewish-Zionists who established the state produced a Declaration of Independence that, as Mazen Masri demonstrates, was "a conditional offer of inclusion and equality [to Palestinian natives] only if 'the peace' as understood by a settler state is preserved." Moreover, K-Sue Park emphasizes that the "concrete history of the social contract, in fact, is both extremely settler colonial *and* American" in that it embodies a pact among settlers to protect themselves as a unit against the native other and external threats. Mazen Masri, "Israel's Colonial Declaration of Independence," presentation at the Nakba Files online symposium on Masri's book *The Dynamics of Exclusionary Constitutionalism: Israel as a Jewish and Democratic State* (Oxford: Hart, 2017); K-Sue Park, "The Colonial History of Social Contracts," a response presented at The Nakba Files online symposium.

159. On Israel's treatment of Palestinians who remained within the newly formed state, see Erakat, "Whiteness as Property in Israel." On what happens when the exception is the everyday, as is the case for those racialized populations who are suspended in a normalized state of emergency deployed through civil means, see Alexander G. Weheliye, *Habeas Viscus: Racializing Assemblages, Biopolitics, and Black Feminist Theories of the Human* (Durham: Duke University Press, 2014), 86. Denise Ferreira da Silva "introduces a formulation of racial violence that captures how raciality immediately justifies the state's decision to kill certain persons—mostly (but not only) young men and women of colour—in the name of self-preservation. Such killings do not unleash an ethical crisis because these persons' bodies and the territories they inhabit always-already signify violence." Ferreira da Silva, "No-Bodies: Law Raciality, and Violence," *Griffith Law Review* 18, no. 2 (2014): 213.

160. Yoav Mehozay, "The Fluid Jurisprudence of Israel's Emergency Powers: Legal Patchwork as a Governing Norm," *Law & Society Review* 46, no. 1 (2012): 144, http://www.jstor.org/stable/41475256; Moshe Naor, "Israel's 1948 War of Independence as a Total War," *Journal of Contemporary History* 43, no. 2 (2008): 244, http://www.jstor.org/stable/30036505.

161. Mehozay, "Fluid Jurisprudence of Israel's Emergency Powers," 143–44. The British had actually repealed the emergency regulations on 12 May 1948, in the 1948 Order in Council. Thus, "the regulations were not in force on 14 May 1948, and therefore, were not covered by the statute preserving the British law in force." This was known to the Israeli government. Ultimately, it formally canceled or replaced a handful of the 162 sections of the DERs, most notably those restricting Jewish immigration and land purchases. Quigley, *Palestine and Israel: A Challenge to Justice* (Durham: Duke University Press, 1990), 103.

162. The military government was established by the Defense Ministry on 21 October 1948. Shira Robinson, *Citizen Strangers: Palestinians and the Birth of Israel's Liberal Settler State* (Stanford: Stanford University Press, 2013), 35. Naor ("Israel's 1948 War of Independence as a Total War," 244) says the State of Emergency was declared on 19 May, while Mehozay ("Fluid Jurisprudence of Israel's Emergency Powers," 137) says it was 21 May, and Tawfiq Zayyad says that military rule was imposed on Palestinian villages and towns on 12 December 1948 and only formalized into an established set of laws on 20 March 1950. Zayyad, "The Fate of the Arabs in Israel," *Journal of Palestine Studies* 6, no. 1 (1976): 95.

163. Mehozay, "Fluid Jurisprudence of Israel's Emergency Powers," 144.

164. Robinson, *Citizen Strangers*, 41; see also Arnon Degani, "The Decline and Fall of the Israeli Military Government, 1948–1966: A Case of Settler-Colonial Consolidation?," *Settler Colonial Studies* 5, no. 1 (2015): 84–99.

165. Quigley, *Palestine and Israel*, 109.

166. Emergency Regulations (Absentees' Property) Law, 5709-1948, suppl. B, art. 37, Israel (12 December 1948); Hanna Nakkara, "Israeli Land Seizure Under Various Defense and Emergency Regulations," *Journal of Palestine Studies* 14, no. 2 (1985): 18.

167. Geremy Forman and Alexandre (Sandy) Kedar. "From Arab Land to 'Israel Lands': The Legal Dispossession of the Palestinians Displaced by Israel in the Wake of 1948." *Environment and Planning D: Society and Space* 22, no. 6 (2004): 809–30.

168. Absentees' Property Law, 5710-1950, Israel (1948–1987). The law described four categories of persons whose land would be confiscated. It applied to any land held between 29 November 1947 and the time of legislation by a person who (1) was a national or citizen of Lebanon, Egypt, Syria, Saudi Arabia, Jordan, Iraq or Yemen; or (2) was in one of these countries or in any part of Palestine outside the area of Israel; or (3) was a Palestinian citizen and left his ordinary place of residence in Palestine for a place outside of Palestine before September 1948; or (4) was a Palestinian citizen and left his ordinary place of residence in Palestine for a place in Palestine held by enemy forces.

169. "Adalah to Attorney General and Custodian of Absentee Property: Israel's Sale of Palestinian Refugee Property Violates Israeli and International Law," Adalah: Legal Center for Arab Minority Rights in Israel (22 June 2009), http://www.adalah.org/en/content/view/7003.

170. In her work, Samera Esmeir explores how modern law justified violence in the quest for humanity following the demise of colonial rule. Esmeir emphasizes how colonial subjects' visibility within the law, as mentioned earlier, made them eligible for punishment but did not make them rights-bearing agents. See Esmeir, *Juridical Humanity*.

171. Nakkara, "Israeli Land Seizure," 19. On the legal transformation process aimed at seizing the properties of non-absent Palestinians, and the designation of "closed areas," see Forman and Kedar, "From Arab Land to 'Israel Lands,'" 819–20; and Robinson, *Citizen Strangers*, 38. On the Land Acquisition Law, see Nakkara, "Israeli Land Seizure," 19.

172. Robinson, *Citizen Strangers*, 47.

173. Nakkara, "Israeli Land Seizure," 29–31; Letter from His Grace Monseigneur G. Hakim, Archbishop of the Greek Catholic Diocese of Acre, Haifa, Nazareth, and the rest of Galilee, resident in Israel to Dr. Hertzog, The Ministry of Religions, Israel, reprinted in Izzat Tanous, *Persecution of the Arab Minority in Israel*, Haifa, 15 January 1952, 10,12.

174. Quigley, *Palestine and Israel*, 106.

175. Robinson, *Citizen Strangers*, 191. On the dispossession of Palestinians through land administration, see also Forman and Kedar, "From Arab Land to 'Israel Lands,'" 824.

176. Nakkara, "Israeli Land Seizure," 18. See also the Abandoned Areas Ordinance of 1948, the Emergency Regulations (Security Zones) Law of 1949, the Prevention of Infiltration Law of 1954, the Plant Protection Law of 1956, and the Prescription Law of 1958.

177. Zayyad, "The Fate of the Arabs in Israel," 95.

178. Robinson, *Citizen Strangers*, 91.

179. Robinson, *Citizen Strangers*, 232n78. More generally, the description here of Palestinians refugees' attempt to return home and the force used against them draws on Robinson, *Citizen Strangers*, 68–113.

180. The Nationality Law, 5712-1952, also known as the Citizenship Law, was passed by the Knesset on 1 April 1952; see the English translation at http://www.israellawresourcecenter.org/israellaws/fulltext/nationalitylaw.htm.

181. Law of Return, 5710-1950, Israel (5 July 1950), published in *Sefer HaChukkim* (Book of laws), no. 51, 159; Katie Hesketh et al., *The Inequality Report: The Palestinian Arab Minority in Israel*, (Haifa: Adalah, March 2011), 14, 16, https://www.adalah.org/uploads/oldfiles/upfiles/2011/Adalah_The_Inequality_Report_March_2011.pdf.

182. Special Unit on Palestinian Rights, *The Right of Return of the Palestinian People*, UNGA, Resolution 273 (III); Statement of Abba Eban, in UNGA, 45th mtg., Application of Israel for Admission to Membership in the United Nations.

183. The Nationality Law denied Israeli citizenship to "a person having ceased to be an inhabitant of Israel before the coming into force of this Law" (2[c][1]). See also Victor Kattan, "The Nationality of Denationalized Palestinians," *Nordic Journal of International Law* 74 (2005), 67–102, https://ssrn.com/abstract=993452.

184. Nationality Law 2(c).

185. Law of Return, 4(B) and 4(A)(a).

186. *The Discriminatory Laws Database.*

187. Erakat, "Whiteness as Property in Israel."

188. Robinson, *Citizen Strangers*, 143–44.

CHAPTER 2

1. Theodor Meron, Memorandum to Aviad Yafeh [Political Secretary to the Prime Minister], "Settlement in the Administered Territories" (original in Hebrew), Israel State Archives, 153.8/7921/3A (18 September 1967), English translation available at http://www.soas.ac.uk/lawpeacemideast/resources/file48485.pdf, p. 3.

2. Ibid.

3. Proclamation No. 3, IDF Forces Commander in the West Bank, 7 June 1967 as discussed by Meron in Memorandum to Aviad Yafeh.

4. Meron, Memorandum to Aviad Yafeh.

5. Ibid.

6. Gershom Gorenberg, "Israel's Tragedy Foretold," *New York Times*, 10 March 2006, http://www.nytimes.com/2006/03/10/opinion/israels-tragedy-foretold.html.

7. Avi Raz, "Dodging the Peril of Peace: Israel and the Arabs in the Aftermath of the June 1967 War," in *The Oxford Handbook of Contemporary Middle-Eastern and North African History*, ed. Amal Ghazal and Jens Hanssen (Oxford: Oxford University Press, 2015), 4.

8. John Quigley, *Palestine and Israel: A Challenge to Justice* (Durham: Duke University Press, 1990), 158.

9. *Israeli-Syrian General Armistice Agreement, July 20, 1949*, The Avalon Project, http://avalon.law.yale.edu/20th_century/armo4.asp.

10. United Nations Security Council (UNSC), Resolution 93, Question of Palestine, UN Doc. S/2157 (18 May 1951); also see the discussion in Quigley, *Palestine and Israel*, 158.

11. "Public figures . . . used strong language that was widely interpreted in the Arab world as a signal of Israel's intent to overthrow the Syrian regime by force," including Prime Minister Yitzhak Rabin's threatening response to the Syrian regime's support of Palestinian guerilla insurgencies and, earlier, Prime Minister Levi Eshkol's equally threatening comments alluding to meeting the Syrian regime with punitive measures. It was clear, across the board, that "Nasser neither wanted nor planned to go to war with Israel." Avi Shlaim, *The Iron Wall: Israel and the Arab World* (New York:

Norton, 2001), 236–237. Nasser conveyed to the Egyptian military general Abdel Hakim Amer "that there was an American-Israeli plot to destroy the military and overthrow the entire regime." Hazem Kandil, *Soldiers, Spies, and Statesmen: Egypt's Road to Revolt* (London: Verso Books, 2012), 72.

12. CIA intelligence reports confirmed that Egypt did not believe it could militarily defeat Israel. Informal reports from confidants who met directly with Nasser in Cairo confirmed that Nasser sought food aid and did not seek to enter into combat. Olivia Louise Sohns, "Lyndon Baines Johnson and the Arab-Israeli Conflict" (PhD diss., Cambridge University, 2014), 165–167.

13. Ibid.

14. Avi Raz, *The Bride and the Dowry: Israel, Jordan, and the Palestinians in the aftermath of the June 1967 War* (New Haven: Yale University Press, 2012), 265.

15. On the morning of the 5 June 1967 attack, Israel Defense minister Moshe Dayan addressed the nation, stating, "Our purpose is to bring to naught the attempts of the Arab armies to conquer our land and to break the ring of the blockade and aggression which threatens us." Raz, *The Bride and the Dowry*, 267.

16. According to an account put forward by Tom ?egev, the final decision to initiate the attack was motivated by Israel's desire to gain "aerial supremacy" by occupying the Sinai, and by the increased "risk of the Egyptians bombing the [Israeli] reactor at Dimona." ?egev, *Ve-Ha'aretz Shintah et Panehah* (And the face of the land changed), (Jerusalem: Keter, 1967), 804, 812.

17. Walid Khalidi, Palestinian historian and member of the Iraq delegation to the United Nations for the 1967 proceedings, interview by the author, Institute for Policy Studies, Washington, DC, 4 February 2016.

18. United Nations General Assembly (UNGA), Fifth Emergency Special Session, 1558th Plenary Meeting, UN Doc. A/PV.1558 (21 July 1967), para. 2.

19. International law recognizes a customary right to preemptive self-defense if an attack is imminent and inevitable. Therefore, it is left to debate whether Egypt's attack was indeed inevitable. See Noura Erakat, "New Imminence in the Time of Obama: The Impact of Targeted Killings on the Law of Self Defense," *Arizona Law Review* 56, no. 1 (2014): 206–209. Julius Stone discusses the element of intent in the context of a larger debate on the lawfulness of preemptive attack. Stone, *Israel and Palestine: Assault on the Law of Nations* (Baltimore: Johns Hopkins University Press, 1981), 46–53. Ardi Imseis finds historical value in the gap "partially bridging between Arab and Israeli scholars" by new Israeli historiography that illustrates the war as not being wanted by either party. Thus, intent could not be confidently outlined as either preemptive or aggressive. Imseis, "On the Fourth Geneva Convention and the Occupied Palestinian Territory," *Harvard International Law Journal* 44, no. 1 (2003), 71. See also Eugene V. Rostow, "The Illegality of the Arab Attack on Israel of October 6, 1967," *American Journal of International Law* 69, no. 2 (1975), 272–89.

20. "No Egyptian tanks had moved toward the Negev at dawn, nor had the Egyptian aircraft approached Israel's territory. It was Israel that had started the war by launching a meticulously preplanned aerial attack on Egyptian air bases less than half an hour before the broadcast of the announcement. Because of stark warnings from friend and foe—including the United States, Britain, France, and the USSR—not to fire the first shot, the Israelis had been looking for a pretext to justify their assault. On June 1, for example, Chief of Staff [Yitzhak] Rabin and some of his generals had considered staging a mock shelling of an Israeli settlement to create a false pretext for going to war against Egypt." Raz, *The Bride and the Dowry*, 265. Quigley concludes that parties engaged in the conflict "did not expect Egypt to attack in the absence of an Israeli invasion of Syria." Quigley,

Palestine and Israel, 161. Both David Ben-Gurion's and Yitzhak Rabin's statements regarding the matter reflect a shared understanding that the intent and the ability of Nasser to follow up on his threats with military action were absent. Imseis, "On the Fourth Geneva Convention and the Occupied Palestinian Territory," 8–9.

21. Raz, "Dodging the Peril of Peace," 8.

22. Sohns, "Lyndon Baines Johnson and the Arab-Israeli Conflict," 56

23. Memorandum from the President's Special Counsel (McPherson) to President Johnson, 11 June 1967, in *Foreign Relations of the United States, 1964–1968*, vol. 19, *Arab-Israeli Crisis and War*, Document 263. Also discussed in Sohns, Lyndon Baines Johnson and the Arab-Israeli Conflict," 197.

24. Quigley speaks of Israel's alteration of Egypt's communications with Jordan and Syria, in an effort to create the impression of a possible Arab victory so that the combat would be extended. Once militarily engaged, Israel geared its military maneuvers towards the extension of warfare and the acquisition of lands, indicating "that Israel did not plan to limit its attack to Egypt." "Israel apparently wanted the Arab states to believe they had a chance to win, so they would continue fighting." Quigley, *Palestine and Israel*, 162–63.

25. Gershom Gorenberg, *The Accidental Empire: Israel and the Birth of Settlements, 1967–1977* (New York: Times Books, 2006), 37.

26. Ibid.

27. Ibid., 37.

28. Hearings Before the Subcommittee on Immigration and Naturalization of the Judiciary Committee of the U.S. Senate, 95th Cong., 1st Sess., on the Question of West Bank Settlements and the Treatment of Arabs in the Israeli-occupied Territories, 17 and 18 October 1977 (statement of John Ruedy, "Israeli Land Acquisition in Occupied Territory, 1967–77").

29. Avi Raz, *The Bride and the Dowry*, 3.

30. Even when its position was at odds with the global consensus, Israel "continued to insist that it has not occupied anyone's land. How could it when it considered 'Judea and Samaria' as land that belonged, on biblical grounds, to the Jewish people?" Raja Shehadeh, "Human Rights and the Israeli Occupation," *New Centennial Review* 8, no. 1 (2008): 40.

31. See Sharon Korman, *The Right of Conquest: The Acquisition of Territory by Force in International Law and Practice* (Oxford: Clarendon Press, 1996), as discussed in Orna Ben-Naftali, Aeyal M. Gross, and Keren Michaeli, "Illegal Occupation: Framing the Occupied Palestinian Territory," *Berkeley Journal of International Law* 23, no. 3 (2005): 571.

32. UN Charter, art. 2, para. 4, and art. 51, http://treaties.un.org/doc/publication/ctc/uncharter. pdf. "The unacceptability of territorial acquisition on the use, or threat, of force is thus viewed as a corollary of the prohibition on the use of force." Ben-Naftali, Gross, and Michaeli, "Illegal Occupation," 572.

33. Imseis, "On the Fourth Geneva Convention and the Occupied Palestinian Territory," 89.

34. Ibid., 91.

35. International Committee of the Red Cross, Convention (IV) Relative to the Protection of Civilian Persons in Time of War, Geneva, 12 August 1949, art. 49 (75 UNTS [*United Nations Treaty Series*] 287), https://www.icrc.org/applic/ihl/ihl.nsf/Article.xsp?action=openDocument&documentId =77068F12B88857C4DC12563CD0051BDB0.

36. See, e.g., ibid. See also Diplomatic Conference for the Establishment of International Conventions for the Protection of War Victims, *Final Record of the Diplomatic Conference of Geneva of 1949*, vol. II-A, 12 August 1949, 759–60.

37. International Committee of the Red Cross, Convention (IV) Relative to the Protection of Civilian Persons in Time of War, Geneva, 12 August 1949: Commentary of 1958, https://www.icrc .org/applic/ihl/ihl.nsf/Comment.xsp?action=openDocument&documentId=523BA38706C71588 C12563CD0042C407.

38. Imseis, "On the Fourth Geneva Convention and the Occupied Palestinian Territory," 87.

39. See, e.g., International Committee of the Red Cross, "Occupation and International Humanitarian Law: Questions and Answers" (4 August 2004), https://www.icrc.org/eng/resources/ documents/misc/634kfc.htm.

40. Imseis, "On the Fourth Geneva Convention and the Occupied Palestinian Territory," 87.

41. Timothy Mitchell, *Carbon Democracy: Political Power in the Age of Oil* (New York: Verso, 2011), 69.

42. UNGA, Resolution 1514, Declaration on the Granting of Independence to Colonial Countries and Peoples, UN Doc. A/RES/15/1514 (14 December 1960), https://www.un.org/en/ decolonization/declaration.shtml. See also Miriam Mckenna, "The Means to the End and the End of the Means: Self-Determination, Decolonization, and International Law," *Jus Gentium: Journal of International Legal History* 2, no. 1 (2017): 93–130.

43. Ibid.

44. Raz, *The Bride and the Dowry*, 5.

45. Nigel J. Ashton, "Searching for a Just and Lasting Peace?: Anglo-American Relations and the Road to United Nations Security Council Resolution 242," *International History Review* 38, no. 1 (2015).

46. Kent Germany, "Lyndon B. Johnson: Foreign Affairs," University of Virginia, Miller Center, https://millercenter.org/president/lbjohnson/foreign-affairs.

47. Sohns, "Lyndon Baines Johnson and the Arab-Israeli Conflict," 15.

48. P.L. 110-429, Naval Vessel Transfer Act of 2008, as quoted in Jeremy M. Sharp, "U.S. Foreign Aid to Israel" (Washington, DC: *Congressional Research Service*, 2012), 8, http://journalistsresource .org/wp-content/uploads/2012/04/Military-Aid-to-Israel.pdf.

49. Lyndon B. Johnson, Address at the State Department's Foreign Policy Conference for Educators (19 June 1967), The American Presidency Project, http://www.presidency.ucsb.edu/ ws/?pid=28308.

50. Vijay Prashad, *The Darker Nations: A People's History of the Third World* (New York: New Press, 2008), Kindle edition.

51. See also UNSC, Official Records, 1377th mtg., UN Doc. S/PV.1377 (15 November 1967), para. 6, https://unispal.un.org/DPA/DPR/unispal.nsf/o/FAA6138B684A6E8605256724004D8394.

52. Johnson, "Address."

53. Of the approximately 860,000 Arabs who had lived in the area of Palestine now called Israel, 133,000 remained. Charles D. Smith, *Palestine and the Arab-Israeli Conflict*, 2nd ed. (New York: St. Martin's Press, 1992).

54. Johnson, "Address."

55. Yezid Savigh, *Armed Struggle and the Search for a State: The Palestinian National Movement, 1949–1993* (Oxford: Oxford University Press, 1997), 96–98.

56. UNSC, United States of America: Draft Resolution, UN Doc. S/8229 (7 November 1967), https://unispal.un.org/DPA/DPR/unispal.nsf/0/5EDDD417E21187BE8525730F0050FEE3; UNSC, Union of Socialist Republics: Draft Resolution, UN Doc. S/8253 (20 November, 1967), https://unispal.un.org/DPA/DPR/unispal.nsf/0/EF952D6E12538A348525730F006AE06E.

57. UNGA, Fifth Emergency Special Session, 1540th Plenary Meeting (29 June 1967), paras. 78; and 154; and 3rd Plenary Meeting (30 June 1967), para. 157, as discussed in Walid Khalidi, "Israel's 1967 Annexation of Arab Jerusalem: Walid Khalidi's Address to the UN General Assembly Special Emergency Session 14 July 1967," *Journal of Palestine Studies* 42, no. 1 (2012): 71–82.

58. UNGA, Argentina, Barbados, Bolivia, Brazil, Chile, Colombia, Costa Rica, Dominican Republic, Ecuador, El Salvador, Guatemala, Guyana, Honduras, Jamaica, Mexico, Nicaragua, Panama, Paraguay, Trinidad and Tobago and Venezuela: Revised Draft Resolution, UN Doc. A/L.523/Rev. 1 (4 July 1967), https://unispal.un.org/DPA/DPR/unispal.nsf/0/510EF41FAC855100052566C D00750CA4.

59. During the General Assembly discussion, U.S. Representative Arthur Goldberg commented: "It is ironic that the Soviet representative belatedly refers favourably to the Latin American initiative at this Assembly. But the history of the United Nations cannot be rewritten. It shows that the United States supported and voted in favour of the Latin American draft resolution [A/L.523/Rev.1] and that the Soviet Union worked against that resolution and voted against it and . . . castigated its Latin American sponsors." UNGA, Fifth Emergency Special Session, 1559th Plenary Meeting (18 September 1967), para. 61.

60. Michael Lynk, "Conceived in Law: The Legal Foundations of Resolution 242," *Journal of Palestine Studies* 37, no. 1 (2007): 9.

61. Ashton, "Searching for a Just and Lasting Peace?," 30.

62. UNSC, Official Records, 22nd Sess., 1382nd mtg., para. 50 (22 November 1967).

63. Johnson, "Address."

64. Sohns, "Lyndon Baines Johnson and the Arab-Israeli Conflict," 231.

65. Ibid., 198.

66. UNGA, Resolution 2253, Measures Taken by Israel to Change the Status of the City of Jerusalem, UN Doc. A/RES/2253 (ES-V) (4 July 1967), https://unispal.un.org/DPA/DPR/unispal.nsf/0/A39A906C89D3E98685256C29006D4014.

67. Walid Khalidi, "Israel's 1967 Annexation of Arab Jerusalem," 74. See also Nir Hasson, "Wary Israel Tried to Conceal East Jerusalem's Annexation in 1967, Documents Reveal," *Haaretz*, 18 April 2017, http://www.haaretz.com/israel-news/1.783429.

68. UNSC, United Kingdom: Draft Resolution, UN Doc. S/8247 (16 November 1967), https://unispal.un.org/DPA/DPR/unispal.nsf/0/99DCE031BD9697498525730F0068F430.

69. UNSC, Official Records, 1382nd mtg., para. 31.

70. UNSC, United Kingdom: Draft Resolution.

71. John McHugo, "Resolution 242: A Legal Reappraisal of the Right-Wing Israeli Interpretation of the Withdrawal Phrase with Reference to the Conflict Between Israel and the Palestinians," *International & Comparative Law Quarterly* 51, no. 4 (2002): 874–75.

72. Comment by Foreign Minister of Israel and Telegram 3164, UK Mission in New York to Foreign Office, FO 961/24 (12 November 1967), as quoted in McHugo, "Resolution 242," 875.

73. French Representative to the UNSC's 1382nd mtg. (22 November 1967), paras. 108–9.

74. Indian Representative to the UNSC's 1382nd mtg. (22 November 1967).

75. Israeli Representative to the UNSC's 1382nd mtg. (22 November 1967).

76. Mr. Tomeh on behalf of the Syrian Delegation to the UNSC's 1382nd mtg. (22 November 1967), paras. 16–17.

77. Arthur Lall, *The UN and the Middle East Crisis, 1967* (New York: Columbia University Press, 1968), as discussed in McHugo, "Resolution 242," 872.

78. Ashton," Searching for a Just and Lasting Peace?," 37.

79. Yoram Meital argues that this summit meeting marked a departure in Egypt's policy towards Israel, in contravention of a consensus view that it hardened an Arab position of non-reconciliation. Meital, "The Khartoum Conference and Egyptian Policy After the 1967 War: A Reexamination," *Middle East Journal* 54, no. 1 (2000): 64–82, http://www.jstor.org/stable/4329432.

80. Savigh, *Armed Struggle and the Search for a State*, 143.

81. UNSC, Resolution 242, UN Doc. S/RES/242 (22 November 1967), https://unispal.un.org/DPA/DPR/unispal.nsf/0/7D35E1F729DF491C85256EE700686136.

82. Ibid.

83. Walid Khalidi, interview.

84. Yehuda Z. Blum, "The Missing Reversioner: Reflections on the Status of Judea and Samaria," *Israel Law Review* 3, no. 2 (1968): 294.

85. Ibid.

86. Other arguments point out that the "threat to peace clause" nullifies Palestinian claims for self-determination because of the threat they pose to Jewish-Zionist settler sovereignty, that the resolution refers to Arabs and not Palestinians, and that UN resolutions are not legally binding. Liora Chartouni, "70 Years After UN Resolution 181: An Assessment." Jerusalem Center for Public Affairs (11 March 2018), http://jcpa.org/article/70-years-un-resolution-181-assessment. Israel's Declaration of Independence bases the legal validity of Israel's establishment on Resolution 181, and states, "This recognition by the United Nations of the right of the Jewish people to establish their State is irrevocable." Provisional Government of Israel, The Declaration of the Establishment of Israel (14 May 1948). In his 1949 address to the Israeli Knesset, Prime Minister David Ben-Gurion argued that the resolution's stipulations regarding the status of Jerusalem as *corpus separatum* are null and void because "the United Nations did not succeed in implementing its own decisions," and "but for [the Zionist paramilitary's] successful stand against aggressors acting in defiance of the United Nations, Jewish Jerusalem would have been wiped off of the earth." Ben-Gurion's view at once draws Israel's legal legitimacy from Resolution 181 while rejecting its stipulations. David Ben-Gurion, "Jerusalem and the Holy Places": Statement to the Knesset by Prime Minister Ben-Gurion, 5 December 1949, Israeli Ministry of Foreign Affairs, *Foreign Policy—Historical Documents*, vols. 1–2, *1947–1974*.

87. Kattan, *From Coexistence to Conquest: International Law and the Origins of the Arab-Israeli Conflict, 1891–1949* (New York: Pluto Press, 2009), 135.

88. Legal Consequences of the Construction of a Wall in the Occupied Palestinian Territory, Advisory Opinion of 9 July 2004, 2004 ICJ [International Court of Justice] 63, paras. 70–78.

89. Kattan, *From Coexistence to Conquest*, 135.

90. Ibid.

91. Ibid., 189. See also Imseis "On the Fourth Geneva Convention and the Occupied Palestinian Territory."

92. Harvard Program on Humanitarian Policy and Conflict Research (HPCR), International Humanitarian Law Research Initiative, *Review of the Applicability of International Humanitarian Law to the Occupied Palestinian Territory* (Boston: HPCR, July 2004), 7.

93. Arthur Watts, "Israeli Wall Advisory Opinion (Legal Consequences of the Construction of a Wall in the Occupied Palestinian Territory)," in *Max Planck Encyclopedia of Public International Law* (2007) http://opil.ouplaw.com/view/10.1093/law:epil/9780199231690/law-9780199231690-e150; see also Natalino Ronzitti, "Civilian Population in Armed Conflict," in *Max Planck Encyclopedia of Public International Law (2010)* http://opil.ouplaw.com/view/10.1093/law:epil/9780199231690/law-9780199231690-e268.

94. HPCR, *Review of the Applicability of International Humanitarian Law to the Occupied Palestinian Territory.*

95. "It is worth noting that the relevant terminology ('territory belonging to one of the belligerents') present in Article 1 of the ... 1874 Brussels Declaration was dropped from the definition of occupation subsequently set down in Article 42 of the Hague Regulations." Shane Darcy and John Reynolds, "An Enduring Occupation: The Status of the Gaza Strip from the Perspective of International Humanitarian Law," *Journal of Conflict & Security Law* 15, no. 2 (2010): 224.

96. In 1970, the UN adopted the Declaration on Principles of International Law Concerning Friendly Relations and Co-operation Among States, which reiterated the prohibition on the acquisition of territory by force, whether defensive or aggressive. Also see Ben-Naftali, Gross, and Michaeli, "Illegal Occupation," 572–73; and Imseis, "On the Fourth Geneva Convention and the Occupied Palestinian Territory," 97.

97. Hearings Before the Subcommittee on Immigration and Naturalization of the Committee on the Judiciary of the U.S. Senate, 95th Cong., 1st Sess., on the Question of West Bank Settlements and the Treatment of Arabs in the Israeli-Occupied Territories, 17 and 18 October 1977, https://www.loc.gov/law/find/hearings/pdf/00139297647.pdf.

98. John J. Mearsheimer and Stephen M. Walt, "Setting the Record Straight: A Response to Critics of 'The Israel Lobby,'" (12 December 2006), http://mearsheimer.uchicago.edu/pdfs/A0043.pdf. See also Bernard Gwertzman, "Kissinger Fears Peril in Mideast, Looks to Geneva," *New York Times*, 27 March 1975; David Howard Goldberg, *Foreign Policy and Ethnic Interest Groups: American and Canadian Jews Lobby for Israel* (Westport: Greenwood Press, 1990), 51; and Edward Tivnan, *The Lobby: Jewish Political Power and American Foreign Policy* (New York: Simon & Schuster, 1987), 89.

99. Meir Shamgar, *Over but Not Done With: An Autobiography* (2015), 78–87, as quoted in Smadar Ben Natan, "Temporary as Indefinite: Horizons of the Future in 1967," Paper presented at the Center for Middle Eastern Studies panel discussion "1967 and the Politics of Time," University of California, Berkeley, 28 April 2017.

100. Meir Shamgar, "The Observance of International Law in the Administered Territories," *Israel Yearbook on Human Rights* 1 (1971).

101. High Court of Justice (HCJ) 337/71, Christian Society for the Holy Places v. Minister of Defence, 26(1) PD 574 (1971). This case is discussed in David Kretzmer, "The Law of Belligerent Occupation in the Supreme Court of Israel," *International Review of the Red Cross* 94, no. 885 (2012):

212. When hearing cases on issues of justice or constitutional matters, rather than civil or criminal case appeals, the Israeli Supreme Court functions as the High Court of Justice.

102. Kretzmer, "Law of Belligerent Occupation."

103. "A party [to a treaty] may not invoke the provisions of its internal law as justification for its failure to perform a treaty." Vienna Convention on the Law of Treaties (23 May 1969), art. 27, https://treaties.un.org/doc/publication/unts/volume%201155/volume-1155-i-18232-english.pdf. This is also discussed in Imseis, "On the Fourth Geneva Convention and the Occupied Palestinian Territory," 100.

104. Shehadeh, "Human Rights and the Israeli Occupation," 34.

105. International Committee of the Red Cross, Convention (IV) Respecting the Laws and Customs of War on Land and Its Annex, The Hague, 18 October 1907, arts. 43, 46, 55, and 56. Theodor Meron discusses the concept of usufruct, which he claims prohibits the use of public property for Jewish settlements and violates basic human rights of Arabs. Meron, "The West Bank and International Humanitarian Law on the Eve of the Fiftieth Anniversary of the Six-Day War," *American Journal of International Law* 111, no. 2 (April 2017): 357–375.

106. See, e.g., Christian Society for the Holy Places v. Minister of Defence.

107. Nimer Sultany argues that adjudicating Palestinian claims in the Israeli Supreme Court (ISC) has benefited Israel's legitimacy more than it has the Palestinian claimants. He writes that "a review of more than four decades of an elaborate jurisprudence developed in thousands of ISC rulings on the OPT [Occupied Palestinian Territories] shows that the legitimation effects outweigh the benefits of inclusion. The jurisprudence of occupation is one of inclusive subordination." Sultany, "Activism and Legitimation in Israel's Jurisprudence of Occupation," *Social & Legal Studies* 23, no. 3 (September 2014): 315–40.

108. Kretzmer, "Law of Belligerent Occupation," 214

109. HCJ 4481/91 Bargil et al. v. Government of Israel et al., 47(4) PD (1993), as discussed in Kretzmer, "Law of Belligerent Occupation," 37.

110. HCJ 390/79 Dweikat et al. v. Government of Israel et al., 34(1) PD, 1 (1979). Hereinafter Elon Moreh case. Elon Moreh is the name of the settlement that was, for a time, disallowed by this case.

111. In his own words, "according to International Law the exercise of the right of military administration over a territory and its inhabitants had no time-limit, because it reflected a factual situation and pending an alternative political or military solution this system of government could, from the legal point of view, continue indefinitely." Shamgar, "The Observance of International Law in the Administered Territories."

112. Ben-Naftali, Gross, and Michaeli, "Illegal Occupation," 598.

113. Yehezkel Lein with Eyal Weizman, *Land Grab: Israel's Settlement Policy in the West Bank* (B'Tselem, Israeli Information Center for Human Rights in the Occupied Territories, 2002), 47.

114. HCJ 606, 610/78 Ayyub et al. v. Minister of Defense et al., 33(2) PD 113 (1979).

115. Lein, *Land Grab*, 48.

116. Ibid. Although touted as a remarkable decision for halting the steady confiscation of Palestinian private property, the Elon Moreh case did not stem such acquisitions. In fact, the Elon Moreh settlement ultimately built on what Israel declared to be state land. According to Raja Shehadeh, "All [this case] did was to pave the way for a new and (in the Court's opinio n) sounder

legal course for the military authorities to pursue. Since the Elon Moreh case, therefore, the main method for the acquisition of land in the West Bank has been taking place by declaring land to be 'state' land." Shehadeh: *Occupier's Law: Israel and the West Bank* (New York: Institute for Palestine Studies, 1985), 22.

117. Shehadeh, *Occupier's Law*, 26–27.

118. Raja Shehadeh provides a thorough discussion of the legal regime regulating land under Ottoman, British, Jordanian, and Israeli rule. Under the Ottoman Land Code, only land in the actual ownership and possession of the state is state land, while the rest of the land belongs to the registered owner or the user. This remained the case under British and Jordanian authority but changed upon the assumption of Israel's occupation of the Territories. Ibid., 17–49.

119. Ibid., 23.

120. Ibid., 170–171.

121. Order Regarding Abandoned Property (Private Property) (Judea and Samaria) (Number 58) 5727-1967, http://nakbafiles.org/wp-content/uploads/2016/10/military-order-58-en.pdf; also discussed in Lein, *Land Grab*, 59.

122. Even in the Elon Moreh case, the High Court established that it could reverse the seizures of privately owned land but "was not prepared to intervene in any disputes over ownership status of land." This left the status of land to the exclusive discretion of each Military Area Commander, with a recommendation from the Objection Committee, a government-appointed committee set up to receive complaints from Palestinian residents. Shehadeh, *Occupier's Law*, 21, 28.

123. See HCJ 72/86 Zalum v. Military Commander, 41(1) PD (1987); and also HCJ 4363/02 Zinbakh v. IDF Commander in Gaza, Judgment of 28 May 2002, both as referenced in Kretzmer, "Law of Belligerent Occupation," 224.

124. International Committee of the Red Cross, Convention (IV), art. 4(1).

125. HCJ 393/82 Jami'at Ascan et al. v. IDF Commander in Judea and Samaria et al., 37(4) PD (1983), as referenced in Kretzmer, "Law of Belligerent Occupation," 209.

126. Clyde Haberman, "Israel's Highest Court Upholds the Deportations of Palestinians," *New York Times*, 29 January 1993, http://www.nytimes.com/1993/01/29/world/israel-s-highest-court-upholds-the-deportation-of-palestinians.html?pagewanted=all.

127. HCJ 2164/09 Yesh Din v. Commander of IDF Forces in Judea and Samaria et al., Judgment of 26 December 2011, as referenced in Kretzmer, "Law of Belligerent Occupation."

128. Ben-Naftali, Gross, & Michaeli, "Illegal Occupation," 610.

129. See, e.g., Ruth Lapidoth, "The Misleading Interpretation of UN Security Council Resolution 242 (1967)," *Jewish Political Studies Review* 23 (Fall 2011): 7–17.

130. Yigal Allon, "Israel: The Case for Defensible Borders," *Foreign Affairs* 55, no. 1 (October 1976): 38–53, http://www.jstor.org/stable/20039626.

131. International Committee of the Red Cross, Protocol Additional to the Geneva Conventions of 12 August 1949, and Relating to the Protection of Victims of International Armed Conflicts (Protocol I), 8 June 1977, art. 51(7); International Committee of the Red Cross, Customary IHL (international humanitarian law), "Rule 97: Human Shields," https://ihl-databases.icrc.org/customary-ihl/eng/docs/v1_rul_rule97.

132. Government Statement on Recognition of Three Settlements (26 July 1977), Israel Ministry of Foreign Affairs, *Foreign Policy—Historical Documents*, vols. 4–5, 1977–1979, http://www.mfa.gov.il/MFA

/ForeignPolicy/MFADocuments/Yearbook3/Pages/23%20Government%20statement%20on%20
recognition%20of%20three%20se.aspx.

133. U.S. Reaction to Israeli Settlements Announcement, Statement by State Department Spokesman, 26 July 1977, Israel Ministry of Foreign Affairs, *Foreign Policy—Historical Documents*, vols. 4–5, 1977–1979, aspxhttp://www.mfa.gov.il/MFA/ForeignPolicy/MFADocuments/Yearbook3/Pages/24%20US%20reaction%20to%20Israeli%20settlements%20announcement.aspx.

134. Statement to the Knesset by Prime Minister Begin on his Visit to the US 27 July 1977, Israel Ministry of Foreign Affairs, *Foreign Policy—Historical Documents*, vols. 4–5: 1977–1979, http://www.mfa.gov.il/MFA/ForeignPolicy/MFADocuments/Yearbook3/Pages/25%20Statement%20to%20the%20Knesset%20by%20Prime%20Minister%20Begi.aspx.

135. Press Conference with President Carter-28 July 1977, Israel Ministry of Foreign Affairs, *Foreign Policy—Historical Documents*, vols. 4–5: 1977–1979, http://www.mfa.gov.il/MFA/Foreign-Policy/MFADocuments/Yearbook3/Pages/26%20Press%20Conference%20with%20President%20Carter-%2028%20July.aspx.

136. Rashid Khalidi, *Brokers of Deceit: How the U.S. Has Undermined Peace in the Middle East* (Boston: Beacon Press, 2013).

137. Raz, "Dodging the Peril of Peace," 13.

138. Minutes, KFASC (Knesset Foreign Affairs and Security Committee), 16 and 29 April 1969, A-8162/5, Israel State Archives, as quoted in Raz, "Dodging the Peril of Peace," 10.

139. Alain Gresh, *The PLO: The Struggle Within—Towards an Independent Palestinian State* (London: Zed Books, 1988), 69.

140. Raz, "Dodging the Peril of Peace," 9–11.

141. Dean Rusk, *As I Saw It: A Secretary of State's Memoirs* (London: I. B. Tauris, 1991), 332, as quoted in Raz, "Dodging the Peril of Peace," 12.

142. Sohns, "Lyndon Baines Johnson and the Arab Israeli Conflict," 220.

143. For example, in 1975, U.S. President Gerald Ford and Secretary of State Henry Kissinger acknowledged that the Middle East was in "potentially grave danger" and that it was necessary to pressure Israel over the stalled Egyptian-Israeli peace talks. Ford and Kissinger believed they needed a formal implementation of a reassessment of U.S. policy in the Middle East, including the relationship with Israel. The American Israel Public Affairs Committee (AIPAC) mobilized seventy-six senators to send a letter to President Ford demanding that "the White House halt its threatened reassessment of relations with Israel" and that "the Administration maintain its economic and military aid to Israel." David Howard Goldberg, *Foreign Policy and Ethnic Interest Groups: American and Canadian Jews Lobby for Israel* (New York: Greenwood, 1990): 51; and John J Mearsheimer and Stephen M. Walt, "Setting the Record Straight: A Response to Critics of 'The Israel Lobby'" (12 December 2006), http://mearsheimer.uchicago.edu/pdfs/A0043.pdf. Many of the signatories admitted they were pressured by the lobby to take such action and to sign the "Letter of 76." Senator Daniel Inouye stated, "It's easier to sign one letter than to answer five thousand," and Senator John Culver admitted "the pressure was just too great. I caved." Edward Tivnan, *The Lobby: Jewish Political Power and American Foreign Policy* (New York: Simon & Schuster, 1987), 89.

144. Nearly every occupying power (as seen in, e.g., the U.S. occupation of Grenada, the Iraqi occupation of Kuwait, and the Indonesian occupation of East Timor) has attempted to avoid

external legal regulation, but only the most powerful states have been successful. HPCR, *Review of the Applicability of International Humanitarian Law to the Occupied Palestinian Territory*, 7.

145.   Sayigh, *Armed Struggle and the Search for a State*, 157.

146.   Ibid., 172, 175.

147.   Ibid., 179.

148.   Ibid.

149.   "Yasser Arafat Biography," *Biography* (1 August 2014), http://www.biography.com/people/yasser-arafat-9187265#the-plo.

150.   Ian J. Bickerton and Carla L. Klausner, *A Concise History of the Arab-Israeli Conflict* (Upper Saddle River: Prentice Hall, 2002), 158.

151.   Ibid., 168–172.

152.   Mark A. Tessler, *A History of the Israeli-Palestinian Conflict* (Bloomington: Indiana University Press, 1994), 475.

153.   Ibid., 476.

154.   Ibid.

155.   Bickerton and Klausner, *Concise History of the Arab-Israeli Conflict*, 174–175.

156.   Ibid.

CHAPTER 3

Epigraph: Fayez A. Sayegh, *Zionist Colonialism in Palestine*, Palestine Monographs, no. 1 (Beirut: Palestine Research Center, 1965), 27.

1.   United Nations, "Growth in United Nations Membership, 1945–Present," http://www.un.org/en/sections/member-states/growth-united-nations-membership-1945–present/index.html.

2.   Yezid Sayigh, *Armed Struggle and the Search for a State: The Palestinian National Movement, 1949–1993* (Oxford: Oxford University Press, 1997), 195–216.

3.   James R. Stocker, *Spheres of Intervention: US Foreign Policy and the Collapse of Lebanon, 1967–1976* (Ithaca: Cornell University Press, 2016), 96.

4.   Helen M. Kinsella, *The Image Before the Weapon: A Critical History of the Distinction Between Combatant and Civilian* (Ithaca: Cornell University Press, 2011), 127.

5.   "UN Arafat—1974," 5:58-minute video of Yasser Arafat's speech to the UN General Assembly, 13 November 1974, https://www.youtube.com/watch?v=7L10VlbCL8Q.

6.   United Nations General Assembly (UNGA), 2282nd Plenary Meeting, Question of Palestine, UN Doc. A/PV. 2282 and Corr. 1 (13 November 1974), para. 20. Hereinafter, Arafat, speech at UNGA, 13 November 1974.

7.   Arafat, speech at UNGA, 13 November 1974, para. 22.

8.   Nabil Shaath, strategic consultant to PLO Chairman Yassir Arafat, American University in Beirut professor, and Director-General of the Palestine Planning Center, interview by the author, Fatah Political Organization Building, Ramallah, West Bank, 1 August 2016.

9.   Rashid Hamid, "Palestinian National Council, Fourth Summit, Cairo: 10–17 July 1968," in *Resolutions of the Palestine National Assembly, 1964–1974*, Palestine Books no. 64 (Beirut: Palestine Research Center, 1975), 301.

10.   Ibid.

11.   Shaath, interview, 1 August 2016.

12.   Camille Mansour, legal scholar and adviser to the Palestinian Negotiations team in Washington, DC, interview by the author, Washington, DC, 28 April 2016.

13. Shaath, interview, 1 August 2016.

14. Paul Thomas Chamberlin, *The Global Offensive: The United States, the Palestine Liberation Organization, and the Making of the Post–Cold War Order* (Oxford: Oxford University Press, 2012), 220–22.

15. Naveed Ahmad, "The Palestine Liberation Organization," *Pakistan Horizon* 28, no. 4 (1975): 85.

16. Salah, a political leader of the Popular Front for the Liberation of Palestine, interview by the author, Ajyal Youth Center, Beirut, 15 August 2016.

17. UNSC, Resolution 338, UN Doc. S/RES/338 (22 October 1973), https://unispal.un.org/DPA/DPR/unispal.nsf/0/7FB7C26FCBE80A31852560C50065F878.

18. UNSC, 1747th mtg., The Situation in the Middle East, UN Doc. S/PV.1747 (22 October 1973), https://unispal.un.org/DPA/DPR/unispal.nsf/0/AA7207D76EF6191285256E53006AD9C1; see also UNSC, Resolution 338.

19. Stocker, *Spheres of Intervention*, 122.

20. Chamberlin, *Global Offensive*, 244; Salim Yaqub, *Imperfect Strangers: Americans, Arabs, and US–Middle East Relations in the 1970s* (Ithaca: Cornell University Press, 2016), 157–59.

21. Kissinger's personal history in Nazi Germany shaped his affinity to Israel. Henry A. Kissinger, *Years of Renewal* (New York: Simon & Schuster, 1999), 428, as discussed in Yaqub, *Imperfect Strangers*, 157–59.

22. Yaqub, *Imperfect Strangers*, 155–57; see also Memorandum of Conversation, [Henry Kissinger's] Meeting with Jewish Leaders (Philip Klutznik Group), *Foreign Relations of the United States, 1969–1976*, vol. 26, *Arab-Israeli Dispute, 1974–1976*, https://history.state.gov/historicaldocuments/frus1969-76v26/d189.

23. Chamberlin, *Global Offensive*, 225.

24. Ibid., 220–21.

25. *Le Monde*, 15 May 1973, as quoted in Alain Gresh, *The PLO: The Struggle Within—Towards an Independent Palestinian State* (London: Zed Books, 1988), 156.

26. Gresh, *The PLO*, 154.

27. Chamberlin, *Global Offensive*, 222.

28. Stocker, *Spheres of Intervention*, 121.

29. In 1970, the PLO's security chief, Ali Hasan Salame, began security coordination with the CIA to protect the U.S. Embassy and its diplomatic corps in West Beirut. Ibid., 182.

30. Osamah Khalil, "Oslo's Roots: Kissinger, the PLO, and the Peace Process," Al-Shabaka (3 September 2013), https://al-shabaka.org/briefs/oslos-roots-kissinger-plo-and-peace-process.

31. "Palestinian Leaders Discuss the New Challenges for the Resistance," Essay no. 42, trans. Rashid Hamid (Beirut: Palestine Research Center, 1974), 37.

32. Ibid., 35.

33. Ibid., 25, 66–67.

34. Ibid., 40.

35. Ibid., 56.

36. Ibid., 31, 69.

37. These efforts coincided with "cautious attempts" by Arafat and his deputy, Salah Khalaf (Abu Iyad), to indicate their readiness to attend the Geneva Peace Conference. At the same time, Buffum explained, the PLO leadership had to "allay fears among fedayeen rank-and-file" that the

creation of a Palestinian state in the West Bank and Gaza would mean the "surrender or betrayal" of the organization's long-term goals. Khalil, "Oslo's Roots."

38. Abu Iyad [Salah Khalaf] and Eric Rouleau, *My Home, My Land: A Narrative of the Palestinian Struggle*, trans. Linda Butler Koseoglu (New York: Times Books, 1978), 138.

39. Salah, interview.

40. Buffum to Kissinger, "Increase in Public Caution Exercised by Fedayeen Leadership," U.S. Department of State, 3 December 1973, http://al-shabaka.org/wp-content/uploads/2014/05/Khalil_PolicyBrief_BuffumtoKissinger3Dec73.pdf, as quoted in Khalil, "Oslo's Roots."

41. Shaath, interview, 1 August 2016.

42. Gresh, *The PLO*, 147.

43. Ibid.

44. Ibid., 165, 147, 166.

45. "Political Program for the Present Stage Drawn Up by the 12th PNC, Cairo, June 9, 1974," *Journal of Palestine Studies* 3, no. 4 (Summer 1974): 224.

46. Chamberlin, *Global Offensive*, 238.

47. Statement Issued by the Popular Front for the Liberation of Palestine, Beirut, 26 September 1974, http://www.jstor.org.mutex.gmu.edu/stable/pdf/2535859.pdf?refreqid=excelsior%3A1bdd54ac47fcd5abd572d83afeebf40f.

48. Ibid.

49. Rupert Emerson argues that the United Nations has accepted self-determination as "a right of revolution," as demonstrated by the "repeated Assembly injunction that all states should provide moral and material assistance to the struggle for independence of the national liberation movements, some of which are carrying on open warfare." Emerson, "Self-Determination," *American Journal of International Law* 65, no. 3 (1971): 474.

50. Article 3 in each of the four Geneva Conventions, often referred to as Common Article 3, is titled "Conflicts Not of an International Character" and lays out general provisions for the humane treatment of persons who are not active combatants in these conflicts. See, e.g., International Committee of the Red Cross, Convention (IV) relative to the Protection of Civilian Persons in Time of War, Geneva, 12 August 1949, art. 3, https://ihl-databases.icrc.org/applic/ihl/ihl.nsf/Article.xsp?action=openDocument&documentId=A4E145A2A7A68875C12563CD0051B9AE.

51. "Full Text: Mandela's Rivonia Trial Speech," News24 (South Africa), reported 24 January 2011, https://www.news24.com/NelsonMandela/Speeches/FULL-TEXT-Mandelas-Rivonia-Trial-Speech-20110124.

52. Chamberlin, *Global Offensive*, 180–81.

53. UNGA, Resolution 3034, Measures to Prevent International Terrorism Which Endangers or Takes Innocent Human Lives or Jeopardizes Fundamental Freedoms, and Study of the Underlying Causes of those Forms of Terrorism and Acts of Violence Which Lie in Misery, Frustration, Grievance and Despair and Which Cause Some People to Sacrifice Human Lives, Including Their Own, in an Attempt to Effect Radical Changes, A/Res/3034(XXVII) (18 December 1972), http://www.un.org/en/ga/search/view_doc.asp?symbol=A/RES/3034(XXVII); also see Chamberlin, *Global Offensive*, 180–8.

54. UNGA, Resolution 3070, Importance of the Universal Realization of the Right of Peoples to Self-Determination and of the Speedy Granting of Independence to Colonial Countries and Peoples

for the Effective Guarantee and Observance of Human Rights, UN Doc. A/RES/3070(XXVIII) (30 November 1973).

55. UNGA, *Respect for Human Rights in Armed Conflicts: Report of the Secretary-General*, UN Doc. A/7720 (20 November 1969), http://repository.un.org/handle/11176/276648.

56. Georges Abi Saab, legal scholar, former ad-hoc judge of the International Court of Justice, former Judge of the Appeals Chamber of the International Criminal Tribunal for the former Yugoslavia and the International Criminal Tribunal for Rwanda, Skype interview by the author, 24 July 2016.

57. Georges Abi-Saab, *Wars of National Liberation in the Geneva Conventions and Protocols*, Collected Courses of the Hague Academy of International Law, vol. 165 (Leiden: Brill, Nijhoff, 1979).

58. Ibid.

59. Robert A. Mortimer, "Algerian Foreign Policy: From Revolution to National Interest," *Journal of North African Studies* 20, no. 3 (2015), doi:10.1080/13629387.2014.990961.

60. Abi Saab, interview.

61. Kinsella, *The Image Before the Weapon*, 141.

62. Ibid., 135.

63. Abi Saab, interview.

64. Daoud Barakat, former PLO ambassador in Moscow, Geneva, and Vienna, telephone interview by the author, 19 August 2016.

65. Shaath, interview, 1 August 2016.

66. Abi Saab, interview.

67. Miriam McKenna explains, "The growing tension between self-determination, human rights, and sovereignty became increasingly evident throughout the 1960s, as post-colonial States turned to self-determination to support their political integrity. Decolonization transformed the United Nations into a body with unprecedented willingness to question State sovereignty; however, in the application of self-determination to colonial territories, once independence was achieved concerns over the internal make up of these new States receded." Mckenna, "The Means to the End and the End of the Means: Self-Determination, Decolonization, and International Law," *Jus Gentium: Journal of International Legal History* 2, no. 1 (2017): 130.

68. Abi Saab, interview.

69. International Committee of the Red Cross, Protocol Additional to the Geneva Conventions of 12 August 1949, and Relating to the Protection of Victims of International Armed Conflicts (Protocol I), 8 June 1977, art. 1(4), https://ihl-databases.icrc.org/applic/ihl/ihl.nsf/Article.xsp?action=openDocument&documentId=6C86520D7EFAD527C12563CD0051D63C.

70. Gary Solis, *The Law of Armed Conflict* (Cambridge: Cambridge University Press, 2010).

71. International Committee of the Red Cross, Protocol Additional to the Geneva Conventions of 12 August 1949 ... (Protocol I), arts. 1(4), 44(3).

72. Ibid, art. 85(2).

73. International Committee of the Red Cross, Protocols I and II Additional to the Geneva Conventions (1 January 2009), https://www.icrc.org/eng/resources/documents/misc/additional-protocols-1977.htm.

74. *Montevideo Convention on the Rights and Duties of States (inter-American), 26 December 1933,* The Avalon Project, http://avalon.law.yale.edu/20th_century/intam03.asp; Hersch Lauterpacht, *Recognition in International Law* (Cambridge: Cambridge University Press, 1947).

75. Barakat, interview; see discussion of these efforts in Sayigh, *Armed Struggle and the Search for a State*, 319–494.

76. Gresh, *The PLO*, 191.

77. Chamberlin, *Global Offensive*, 251.

78. Gresh, *The PLO*, 191.

79. Ibid.

80. Shaath, interview, 1 August 2016.

81. Ibid.

82 Ibid.

83. Ibid.

84. UNGA, Resolution 3210 (XXIX), Invitation to the Palestinian Liberation Organization, UN Doc. A/RES/3210 (14 October 1974), https://documents-dds-ny.un.org/doc/RESOLUTION/GEN /NR0/738/12/IMG/NR073812.pdf?OpenElement.

85. While other General Assembly resolutions had recognized that Palestinians had a right to self-determination and described the refugees as "Palestinian Arab," none had affirmed the nationhood of Palestinians as this resolution proposed to do. See UNGA, Resolution 2787, UN Doc. A/RES/2787(XXVI) (6 December 1971), https://documents-dds-ny.un.org/doc/RESO-LUTION/GEN/NR0/328/03/IMG/NR032803.pdf?OpenElement. See also UNGA, Resolution 2535, United Nations Relief and Works Agency for Palestine Refugees in the Near East, UN Doc. A/RES/2535 (XXIV) A–C (10 December 1969), https://unispal.un.org/DPA/DPR/ unispal.nsf/0/41F2C6DCE4DAA765852560DF004E0AC8; and UNGA, Resolution 2672, United Nations Relief and Works Agency for Palestine Refugees in the Near East, UN Doc. A/ RES/2672 (XXV) A–D (8 December 1970), https://unispal.un.org/DPA/DPR/unispal.nsf/0/ E7C4B66C913EC0DC852560DE006E8F1B.

86. Ibid.

87. Mortimer, "Algerian Foreign Policy."

88. Karma Nabulsi, scholar in politics and international relations and former PLO representative, Skype interview by the author, 20 August 2016.

89. Final Communiqué of the Asian-African Conference of Bandung (24 April 1955), sec. E, para. 1, http://franke.uchicago.edu/Final_Communique_Bandung_1955.pdf.

90. Chamberlin, *Global Offensive*, 185.

91. Nabulsi, interview.

92. Ahmad, "Palestine Liberation Organization," 101–03.

93. UNGA, Resolution 3151, Policies of Apartheid of the Government of South Africa, UN Doc. A/RES/3151 (14 December 1973), https://documents-dds-ny.un.org/doc/RESOLUTION/ GEN/NR0/282/23/IMG/NR028223.pdf?OpenElement.

94. The First Committee deals with issues of disarmament and security that affect the international community; for more information, see http://www.un.org/en/ga/first.

95. UNGA, 2268th Plenary Meeting, UN Doc. A/PV.2268 (14 October 1974), https://unispal .un.org/DPA/DPR/unispal.nsf/0/2A1CF8A3EA4D1F0385256230005AFFEE.

96. Shaath, interview, 1 August 2016.

97. "The Tripartite Palestinian-Egyptian-Syrian Communique, Issued in Cairo, 21 September 1974," *Journal of Palestine Studies* 4, no. 2 (Winter 1975): 164–80, http://www.jstor.org/ stable/2535859.

98. "The Palestine Resolution of the Seventh Arab Summit Conference, Rabat, October 29, 1974," *Journal of Palestine Studies* 4, no. 2 (Winter 1975): 177–78, http://www.jstor.org/stable/2535859.

99. Arafat, speech at UNGA, 13 November 1974, para. 5.

100. Ibid., para. 72.

101. Shaath, interview, 1 August 2016.

102. For more on these texts, see "Statements by the Late Dr. Fayez Sayegh," in *The Palestine Yearbook of International Law*, 6 (1990/91); these comments were made at the 2134th Meeting of the Third (Social, Humanitarian, & Cultural) Committee of the General Assembly on 17 October 1975. Also see Fayez Abdullah Sayegh, *Zionist Colonialism in Palestine*, vol. 1 (Beirut: Palestine Research Center, 1965).

103. Shaath, interview, 1 August 2016.

104. Arafat, speech at UNGA, 13 November 1974, para. 74.

105. Shaath, interview, 1 August 2016.

106. Arafat, speech at UNGA, 13 November 1974, para. 80.

107. Salah, interview.

108. Nabulsi, interview.

109. Arafat, speech at UNGA, 13 November 1974, paras. 82–83.

110. Chamberlin, *Global Offensive*, 250.

111. UNGA, 2285th Plenary Meeting, UN Doc. A/PV.2268 (14 November 1974), para. 64, https://unispal.un.org/DPA/DPR/unispal.nsf/0/8C323D5263B2F89E852562310069D313.

112. Shaath, interview, 1 August 2016.

113. UNGA, Resolution 3236, Question of Palestine, UN Doc. A/RES/3236(XXIX) (22 November 1974), https://documents-dds-ny.un.org/doc/RESOLUTION/GEN/NR0/738/38/IMG/NR073838.pdf?OpenElement.

114. UNGA, 2296th Plenary Meeting, UN Doc. A/PV.2296 (22 November 1974), paras. 20–21, https://unispal.un.org/DPA/DPR/unispal.nsf/0/7219F7FE733B856485256236005A4700.

115. Ibid., para. 64

116. Ibid., paras. 86–96.

117. UNGA, Resolution 3237, Observer Status for the Palestine Liberation Organization, UN Doc. A/RES/3237(XXIX) (22 November 1974), http://www.un.org/en/ga/search/view_doc.asp?symbol=A/RES/3237(XXIX)&Lang=E&Area=RESOLUTION.

118. UNGA, 2296th Plenary Meeting, UN Doc. A/PV.2296 (22 November 1974), paras. 53–55, https://unispal.un.org/DPA/DPR/unispal.nsf/0/7219F7FE733B856485256236005A4700.

119. Ibid., para. 56.

120. Ibid., para 243.

121. Chamberlin, *Global Offensive*, 236.

122. William Korey, "The PLO's Conquest of the U.N.," *Midstream* 25, no. 9 (November 1979): 11.

123. Sidney Liskofsky, "UN Resolution on Zionism," *American Jewish Yearbook* 77 (1977): 97–126.

124. Enuga S. Reddy, "The United Nations and the Struggle for Liberation in South Africa," in *The Road to Democracy in South Africa*, vol. 3, part 1: *International Solidarity* (Pretoria: Unisa Press, 2008).

125. United Nations, Charter of the United Nations and Statute of the International Court of Justice (26 June 1945), arts. 5 and 6.

126. Spyros Blavoukos and Dimitris Bourantonis, *Chairing Multilateral Negotiations: The Case of the United Nations* (New York: Routledge, 2011), 51.

127. Joshua Muchavnik, "The UN and Israel: A History of Discrimination," *World Affairs Journal* 2 (November/December 2013), http://www.worldaffairsjournal.org/article/un-and -israel-history-discrimination.

128. Associated Press, "Africans Rebuff Arab Call for U.N. to Expel Israel," *New York Times*, 2 August 1975.

129. Ahmad, "Palestine Liberation Organization," 104.

130. Susan Aurelia Gitelson, "Unfulfilled Expectations: Israeli and Arab Aid as Political Instruments in Black African United Nations Voting Behavior," *Jewish Social Studies* 38, no. 2 (Spring 1976): 159–75, http://www.jstor.org/stable/4466923.

131. Associated Press, "Africans Rebuff Arab Call."

132. Ibid.

133. Paul Hoffman, "Nonaligned Bloc Adds 4 Members," *New York Times*, 27 August 1975.

134. Anis Fawzi Kassem, legal scholar and former adviser to the PLO, Skype interview by the author, 16 July, 2016.

135. Chamberlin, *Global Offensive*, 229.

136. Baker to Kissinger, "Senator Baker's Meeting with Yasser Arafat in Beirut," 25 May 1975, http://al-shabaka.org/wp-content/uploads/2014/05/Khalil_PolicyBrief_BakerMtgArafat25May75.pdf, as quoted in Khalil, "Oslo's Roots."

137. "US–"Israeli Memorandum of Agreement Dealing with Future Negotiations, 17 September, 1975," in *The Israeli–Palestinian Conflict: A Documentary Record, 1967–1990*, ed. Yehuda Lukacs (New York: Cambridge University Press, 1992), 60–61, https://israeled.org/resources/documents/us-israeli-memorandum-agreement-dealing-future-negotiations.

138. Interim Agreement Between Egypt and Israel (Sinai II) (4 September 1, 1975), https://www.fordlibrarymuseum.gov/library/document/0331/1553974.pdf.

139. Chamberlin, *Global Offensive*, 254.

140. UNGA, Resolution 3375, Invitation to the Palestine Liberation Organization to Participate in the Efforts for Peace in the Middle East, UN Doc. A/RES/3375 (XXX) (10 November 1975), https://documents-dds-ny.un.org/doc/RESOLUTION/GEN/NR0/000/88/IMG/NR000088.pdf?OpenElement.

141. The question of Palestine was not unique in receiving specialized focus from the United Nations. The General Assembly had previously established other committees aimed at garnering international support to end foreign colonization. The two most prominent were the Special Committee on Apartheid, established in 1962 to end apartheid in South Africa, and the UN Council for Namibia, established in 1967 to act as Namibia's Administering Authority until that state's independence. See UNGA, Resolution 1761, The Policies of Apartheid of the Government of the Republic of South Africa, UN Doc. A/RES/1761(XVII) (6 November 1962), https://documents-dds-ny.un.org/doc/RESOLUTION/GEN/NR0/192/69/IMG/NR019269.pdf?OpenElement; and UNGA, Resolution 2248 (S-V) (19 May 1967).

142. UNSC, Guyana, Pakistan, Panama and United Republic of Tanzania: Draft Resolution, UN Doc. S/12119 (29 June 1976), https://unispal.un.org/DPA/DPR/unispal.nsf/0/F9678DE127E4 81F90525651C0073B022.

143. Convention on the Suppression and Punishment of the Crime of Apartheid, Procedural History, Audiovisual Library of International Law, http://legal.un.org/avl/ha/cspca/cspca.html.

144. Liskofsky, "UN Resolution on Zionism," 100.

145. Shaath, interview, 1 August 2016.

146. Kassem, interview.

147. "Statements by the Late Dr. Fayez Sayegh."

148. Ibid.

149. Ibid.

150. UNGA, Resolution 3379, Elimination of All Forms of Racial Discrimination, UN Doc. A/RES/3379(XXX) (10 November 10 1975), http://www.un.org/en/ga/search/view_doc .asp?symbol=A/RES/3379(XXX).

151. Ibid., para. 158.

152. Ibid., paras. 192, 193.

153. Korey, "The PLO's Conquest of the U.N," 15; Wolff-Moynihan Amendment (1979). This amendment restricted U.S. State Department allocations to the United Nations to a sum equal to 25 percent of spending on pro-PLO activities.

154. Murray Zuokoff, "Lessons of 1975—Challenges in 1976," *Daily News Bulletin* 42, no. 247, Jewish Telegraphic Agency, Dec 31, 1975, http://www.jta.org/1975/12/31/archive/lessons-of -1975-challenges-in-1976.

155. Associated Press, "Jet Attack in Lebanon: U.S–Israeli Rift Reported over Pledge on PLO," *Chicago Tribune*, 3 December 1975, http://archives.chicagotribune.com/1975/12/03/page/18/ article/jet-attack-in-lebanon.

156. Leo Gross, "Voting in the Security Council and the PLO," *American Journal of International Law* 70, no. 3 (July 1976).

157. Henry Kissinger, "The Global Challenge and International Cooperation," Speech delivered at the University of Wisconsin Institute of World Affairs, Milwaukee, 14 July 1975, as quoted in Ronald I. Meltzer, "Restructuring the United Nations System: Institutional Reform Efforts in the Context of North-South Relations," *International Organization* 32, no. 4 (Autumn 1978), https:// doi.org/10.1017/S0020818300032069.

158. Stocker, *Spheres of Intervention*, 196.

159. This notion is often repeated as "strategic parity." Patrick Seale, *Asad: The Struggle for the Middle East* (Berkeley: University of California Press, 1990): 346–47.

160. Bassel Salloukh, "Syria and Lebanon: A Brotherhood Transformed," *Middle East Report* 35, no. 236 (Fall 2005), http://www.merip.org/mer/mer236/syria-lebanon-brotherhood-transformed.

161. Abraham, "PLO at the Crossroads," 9.

162. Khalil, "Oslo's Roots."

163. "Palestinian National Council, Thirteenth Summit, Cairo: 12–22 March 1977," in *The Palestinian Documents, 1977* (in Arabic) (Beirut: Institute of Palestine Studies, 1978), 97–98.

164. Sayigh, *Armed Struggle and the Search for a State*, 420–23.

165. "1977: Egyptian Leader's Israel Trip Makes History," BBC News, 19 November 1977, http://news.bbc.co.uk/onthisday/hi/dates/stories/november/19/newsid_2520000/2520467.stm.

166. Ibid.

167. Sayigh, *Armed Struggle and the Search for a State*, 424–25.

168. For more information on the Secretariat of the Committee on the Exercise of the In-alienable Rights of the Palestinian People (CEIRPP), see United Nations Department of Political Affairs, Division for Palestinian Rights, http://www.un.org/undpa/en/palestinianrights.

169. A Framework for Peace in the Middle East Agreed at Camp David, 17 *International Legal Materials* (I.L.M.) 1466 (1978), http://hrlibrary.umn.edu/peace/docs/campdavid.html.

170. Ibid., 1(c)(ii).

171. Harry Hurwitz and Yisrael Medad, eds., *Peace in the Making: The Menachem Begin–Anwar Sadat Personal Correspondence* (Jerusalem: Gefen, 2011), 85, as quoted in Yair Hirschfeld, *Track-Two Diplomacy Toward an Israeli-Palestinian Solution, 1978–2014* (Washington, DC: Woodrow Wilson Center Press, 2014), 7.

172. Ibid.

173. Gresh, *The PLO*, 218.

174. Ibid.

175. Letters of Understanding with Regard to the Sinai, Jerusalem, West Bank and Gaza, and Airbases, 17 I.L.M. 1471 (1978).

176. Hanan Ashrawi, English scholar and PLO representative, interview by the author, Pal-estinian Ministry of Information, Ramallah, West Bank, 29 December 2015.

177. Gresh, *The PLO*, 221.

178. Ibid., 226.

179. Sayigh, *Armed Struggle and the Search for a State*; Camille Mansour, "The Palestinian-Israeli Peace Negotiations: An Overview and Assessment," *Journal of Palestine Studies* 22, no. 3 (1993): 5–31, doi:10.2307/25375687.

180. Sayigh, *Armed Struggle and the Search for a State*, 545.

181. Shaath, interview, 1 August 2016.

CHAPTER 4

Epigraph: Edward Said, "The Morning After," *London Review of Books* 15, no. 20 (1993).

1. Azzam Tamimi, *Hamas: A History from Within* (Northampton, MA: Olive Branch, 2011), 10.

2. "Intifada Begins on Gaza Strip," History.com, 2010, http://www.history.com/this-day-in-history/intifada-begins-on-gaza-strip.

3. Penny Johnson and Eileen Kuttab, "Where Have All the Women and (Men) Gone? Reflec-tions on Gender and the Second Palestinian Intifada," *Feminist Review*, No. 69 (Winter 2001): 27, doi:10.1080/01417780011007012.

4. "Israel Declines to Study Rabin Tie to Beatings," *New York Times*, 12 July 1990, http://www.nytimes.com/1990/07/12/world/israel-declines-to-study-rabin-tie-to-beatings.html.

5. "25th Anniversary of the First Intifada" (Fact Sheet), Institute for Middle East Understand-ing (December 2016), http://imeu.org/article/25th-anniversary-of-the-first-intifada.

6. Terry Atlas and Uli Schmetzer, "Shultz Outlines Plan For Mideast Peace," *Chicago Tribune*, 27 February 1988.

7. Hanan Ashrawi, English scholar and PLO representative, interview by the author, Palestin-ian Ministry of Information, Ramallah, West Bank, 29 December 2015.

8. Yair Hirschfeld, *Track-Two Diplomacy Toward an Israeli-Palestinian Solution, 1978–2014* (Washington, DC: Woodrow Wilson Center Press, 2014), 62.

9. See, e.g., Saddam Hussein, Interview Session 9, interview by George L. Piro, Baghdad Operations Centre (National Security Archive, 24 February 2004), https://nsarchive2.gwu.edu/NSAEBB/NSAEBB279/10.pdf.

10. "Gulf War Fast Facts," CNN (August 2016), http://www.cnn.com/2013/09/15/world/meast/gulf-war-fast-facts.

11. Yann Le Troquer and Rozenn Hommery al-Oudat, "From Kuwait to Jordan: The Palestinians' Third Exodus," *Journal of Palestine Studies* 28, no. 3 (1999): 37–51, doi:10.1525/jps.1999.28.3.00p0029p.

12. Camille Mansour, "The Palestinian-Israeli Peace Negotiations: An Overview and Assessment," *Journal of Palestine Studies* 22, no. 3 (1993): 5–31, doi:10.2307/2537568.

13. Nabil Shaath, strategic consultant to PLO Chairman Yassir Arafat, American University in Beirut professor, and Director-General of the Palestine Planning Center, telephone interview by the author, 12 June 2016.

14. Hirschfeld, *Track-two Diplomacy*, 96.

15. Thomas L. Friedman, "Israel, Ignoring Bush, Presses for Loan Guarantees," *New York Times*, 7 September 1991, http://www.nytimes.com/1991/09/07/world/israel-ignoring-bush-presses-for-loan-guarantees.html.

16. Letter of Invitation to Madrid Peace Conference (jointly issued by the U.S. and the Soviet Union), 30 October 1991, Israel Ministry of Foreign Affairs, Foreign Policy, http://www.mfa.gov.il/mfa/foreignpolicy/peace/guide/pages/madrid%20letter%20of%20invitation.aspx.

17. U.S Letter of Assurance to Israel, in "Peace Proposals and Ideas," Part 2 of *The Search for Peace in the Arab-Israeli Conflict*, ed. Terje Rød-Larsen, Nur Laiq, and Fabrice Aidan (New York: International Peace Institute, 2015), 439–40.

18. James Baker, Letter of Assurance to the Palestinians, 18 October 1991, Peace Agreements Digital Collection, United States Institute for Peace, http://www.usip.org/sites/default/files/file/resources/collections/peace_agreements/letter_of_assurance.pdf.

19. Ashrawi, interview.

20. Camille Mansour, legal scholar and former PLO adviser, email interview by the author, 3 January 2018.

21. Yezid Sayigh, *Armed Struggle and the Search for a State: The Palestinian National Movement, 1949–1993* (Oxford: Oxford University Press, 1997), 654.

22. Tamimi, *Hamas*, 11.

23. Are Knudsen, "Crescent and Sword: The Hamas Enigma," *Third World Quarterly* 26, no. 8 (2005): 1375.

24. Tamimi, *Hamas*, 44–45.

25. Jean-Pierre Filiu, "The Origins of Hamas: Militant Legacy or Israeli Tool?" *Journal of Palestine Studies* 41, no. 3 (2012): 65–66.

26. Tamimi, *Hamas*, 51.

27. *Hamas Covenant 1988: The Covenant of the Islamic Resistance Movement* (Hamas National Charter), art. 11, The Avalon Project, http://avalon.law.yale.edu/20th_century/hamas.asp.

28. *Hamas Covenant*, art. 27.

29. Hirschfeld, *Track-two Diplomacy*, 59.

30. Rashid Khalidi, "The Resolutions of the 19th Palestine National Council," *Journal of Palestine Studies* 19, no. 2 (1990): 35.

31. United Nations General Assembly (UNGA), Agenda Item 37: Letter Dated 18 November 1988 from the Permanent Representative of Jordan to the United Nations Addressed to the Secretary-General: Annex III: [Palestinian] Declaration of Independence, UN Doc. A/43/827 (18 November 1988), https://unispal.un.org/DPA/DPR/unispal.nsf/0/6EB54A389E2DA6C6852560DE0070 E392.

32. Ibid.

33. "Documents and Source Material," *Journal of Palestine Studies* 16, no. 4 (1987): 189.

34. Tamimi, *Hamas*, 63, 189.

35. Sayigh, *Armed Struggle and the Search for State*, 640–51.

36. Mansour, "Palestinian-Israeli Peace Negotiations, 7.

37. Ashrawi, interview.

38. Ibid.; Clyde Haberman, "Palestinian Says His Delegation Will Assert P.L.O. Ties at Talks," *New York Times*, 22 October 1991, http://www.nytimes.com/1991/10/22/world/palestinian-says-his-delegation-will-assert-plo-ties-at-talks.html.

39. Ashrawi, interview.

40. Address by Dr. Haider Abdul Shafi, Head of the Palestinian Delegation, The Madrid Conference Opening Speeches (31 October 1991), Israel Ministry of Foreign Affairs, Foreign Policy, http://www.mfa.gov.il/mfa/foreignpolicy/peace/mfadocuments/pages/address%20by%20dr%20ohaide r%20abdul%20shafi-%20-%2031-oct-91.aspx.

41. Ashrawi, interview.

42. Ibid.

43. Camille Mansour, interview by the author, 13 December 2015.

44. Mansour, "Palestinian-Israeli Peace Negotiations," 10.

45. Ibid., 10.

46. Ibid., 12.

47. Raja Shehadeh, *From Occupation to Interim Accords: Israel and the Palestinian territories* (London: Kluwer, 1998).

48. Anis Fawzi Kassem, legal scholar and former adviser to the PLO, email interview by the author, 8 September 2016.

49. Shehadeh, *From Occupation to Interim Accords*, 107.

50. Mansour, "Palestinian-Israeli Peace Negotiations," 15.

51. Ibid., 13

52. Ibid, 14.

53. Ibid.

54. Rashid Khalidi, historian and former adviser to the PLO, interview by the author, Columbia University, New York, 3 May 2016.

55. Mansour, "Palestinian-Israeli Peace Negotiations," 17.

56. Shehadeh, *From Occupation to Interim Accords*, 114–16.

57. Hirschfeld, *Track-two Diplomacy*, 106.

58. Shehadeh, *From Occupation to Interim Accords*; Rashid Khalidi, interview.

59. Hirschfeld, *Track-two Diplomacy*, 107; Ashrawi, interview.

60. Mansour, "Palestinian-Israeli Peace Negotiations," 18.

61. Rashid Khalidi, interview.

62. Shehadeh, *From Occupation to Interim Accords*, 121; see also Sayigh, *Armed Struggle and the Search for a State*, 656. "Trojan Horse" refers to the tale of the ancient Greeks offering a wooden horse to the city of Troy as a peace offering. Once inside the city gates, Greek warriors hiding inside the horse, emerged at night to let in more Greek solders. The term has come to be synonymous with acts of subversion.

63. Mansour, "Palestinian-Israeli Peace Negotiations," 22.

64. In his discussion of the role of law in the final status negotiations, Omar M. Dajani draws on contract and negotiations theory to demonstrate that the law can serve two other interrelated functions. First, the "shadow of the law" concerns how negotiating parties may alter their positions in light of the possible remedies imposed by noncompliance. Second, the "shade of the law" concerns law's potential value absent the threat of enforcement—for the purpose of legitimacy, for example. Dajani, "Shadow or Shade? The Roles of International Law in Palestinian-Israeli Peace Talks," *Yale Journal of International Law* 32, no. 1 (2007): 61–124.

65. A Framework for Peace in the Middle East Agreed at Camp David, 17 I.L.M. 1466, 1978, http://hrlibrary.umn.edu/peace/docs/campdavid.html.

66. *United Nations Peacemaker*, Treaty Series, Israel-Jordan Common Agenda (14 September 1993), https://peacemaker.un.org/sites/peacemaker.un.org/files/IL%20JO_930914_Israel%20Jordan%20Common%20Agenda.pdf.

67. Mansour, "Palestinian-Israeli Peace Negotiations," 23.

68. Thomas L. Friedman, "Bush Rejects Israel Loan Guarantees," *New York Times*, 18 March 1992, http://www.nytimes.com/1992/03/18/world/bush-rejects-israel-loan-guarantees.html.

69. Daniel Reisner, head of the Israel Defense Force's International Law Department from 1995 to 2004 and senior member of Israel's negotiating teams since 1994, Skype interview by the author, 12 June 2016.

70. Shehadeh, *From Occupation to Interim Accords*, 107.

71. Rashid Khalidi, interview.

72. Ashrawi, interview.

73. Shehadeh, *From Occupation to Interim Accords*, 2.

74. Mansour, "Palestinian-Israeli Peace Negotiations," 24.

75. Ibid., 26.

76. Tamimi, *Hamas*, 65.

77. Ibid., 66.

78. Clyde Haberman, "Israel Expels 400 from Occupied Lands; Lebanese Deploy to Bar Entry of Palestinians," *New York Times*, 17 December 1992, http://www.nytimes.com/1992/12/18/world/israel-expels-400-occupied-lands-lebanese-deploy-bar-entry-palestinians.html?pagewanted=all.

79. Hirschfield, *Track-two Diplomacy*, 108.

80. Ibid; Ashrawi, interview.

81. Ahmed Qurei, *From Oslo to Jerusalem: The Palestinian Story of the Secret Negotiations* (London: I. B. Tauris, 2008), 41.

82. Hirschfield, *Track-two Diplomacy*, 108.

83. Ibid., 107.

84. Qurei, *From Oslo to Jerusalem*, 92.

85. Hirschfield, *Track-two Diplomacy*, 114.

86. Ibid., 112.

87. Ibid., 117, 127.

88. Ibid., 120.

89. Draft Minutes, Meeting with U.S. State Department Officials, Ana Hotel, Washington, DC, 13 May 1993, http://www.palestine-studies.org/sites/default/files/uploads/files/Minutes Kurtzer, Miller meeting 13 May 93.pdf.

90. Ibid.

91. Camille Mansour, interview by author, Dean and Deluca Café, Washington, DC, 28 April 2016.

92. Qurei, *From Oslo to Jerusalem*, 111–13.

93. Ibid., 143.

94. Hirschfield, *Track-two Diplomacy*, 118.

95. Shehadeh, Raja. "Human Rights and the Israeli Occupation." *The New Centennial Review* 8, no. 1 (2008): 46.

96. Hirschfield, *Track-two Diplomacy*, 122.

97. Shehadeh, *From Occupation to Interim Accords*, 124; Hirschfield, *Track-two Diplomacy*, 121.

98. Qurei, *From Oslo to Jerusalem*, 157.

99. Hirschfield, *Track-two Diplomacy*, 123.

100. Shehadeh, *From Occupation to Interim Accords*, 126.

101. Qurei, *From Oslo to Jerusalem*, 199

102. Chas. W. Freeman Jr., "The Angola/Namibia Accords," *Foreign Affairs*, 68 (Summer 1988): 126–41.

103. But see Dajani, "Shadow or Shade" who takes more issue with the role of law in the negotiations and how it could be more effectively wielded, and is less concerned with the structural asymmetries distinguishing the negotiating parties.

104. Shehadeh, *From Occupation to Interim Accords*, 127.

105. Qurei, *From Oslo to Jerusalem*, 161.

106. Ibid., 235, 238.

107. Shehadeh, *From Occupation to Interim Accords*, 159n3.

108. Qurei, *From Oslo to Jerusalem*, 245.

109. Declaration of Principles on Interim Self-Government Arrangements (13 September 1993), Israel Ministry of Foreign Affairs, Foreign Policy—Peace Process, http://www.mfa.gov.il/mfa/foreignpolicy/peace/guide/pages/declaration%20of%20principles.aspx.

110. Rashid Khalidi, Interview.

111. Declaration of Principles on Interim Self-Government Arrangements, art. IV.

112. Shaath, interview, 12 June 2016.

113. Declaration of Principles on Interim Self-Government Arrangements, art. XV.

114. *United Nations Peacemaker*, Treaty Series, Treaty of Peace Between the Arab Republic of Egypt and the State of Israel (26 March 1979), https://peacemaker.un.org/sites/peacemaker.un.org/files/EG%20IL_790326_Egypt%20and%20Israel%20Treaty%20of%20Peace.pdf; *United Nations Peacemaker*, Treaty Series, Treaty of Peace Between the State of Israel and the Hashemite Kingdom of Jordan (26 October 1994), https://peacemaker.un.org/sites/peacemaker.un.org/files/IL%20JO_941026_PeaceTreatyIsraelJordan.pdf.

115. Reisner, interview.

116. Declaration of Principles on Interim Self-Government Arrangements, art. VI, and Annex II.

117. Shehadeh, *From Occupation to Interim Accords*, 165.

118. Declaration of Principles on Interim Self-Government Arrangements, Preamble.

119. See *A Crisis of Faith*: Second Submission of the Palestine Liberation Organization to the Sharm El Sheikh Fact-Finding Committee (30 December 2000); and Third Submission of the Palestine Liberation Organization to the Sharm El Sheikh Fact-Finding Commission (3 April 2001), https://2001-2009.state.gov/p/nea/rls/rpt/3060.htm.

120. Rashid Khalidi, interview.

121. George Salem, attorney and former PLO adviser, interview by the author, DLA Piper, Washington, DC, 28 April 2016.

122. Ashrawi, interview.

123. Shehadeh, *From Occupation to Interim Accords*, 12.

124. Adam Shatz, "A Poet's Palestine as Metaphor," *New York Times*, 22 December 2001, http://www.nytimes.com/2001/12/22/books/a-poet-s-palestine-as-a-metaphor.html.

125. Edward Said, "The Morning After," *London Review of Books* 15, no. 20 (21 October 21, 1993): 3–5, https://www.lrb.co.uk/v15/n20/edward-said/the-morning-afterhttps://www.lrb.co.uk/v15/n20/edward-said/the-morning-after. Also see Edward Said, *Peace and Its Discontents: Essays on Palestine in the Middle East Peace Process* (New York: Vintage, 1996).

126. Shaath, interview, 12 June 2016.

127. Rashid Khalidi, interview.

128. Hirschfield, *Track-two Diplomacy*, 145.

129. Adam Raz, What Israelis Weren't Told About the Alternatives to the Oslo Accords, *Haaretz*, 7 February 2016.

130. Hirschfield, *Track-two Diplomacy*, 146.

131. Shaath, interview, 12 June 2016.

132. Hirschfield, *Track-two Diplomacy*, 135.

133. Burhan Dajani, "An Alternative to Oslo?" *Journal of Palestine Studies* 25, no. 4 (1996): 6, See the discussion drawing on this article in Shehadeh, "Human Rights and the Israeli Occupation," 129.

134. Ioano E. Matesan, *The Dynamics of "Peace Spoiling" in the Palestinian Territories During the Oslo Years*, Maxwell School, Collaborative Governance Initiative, Syracuse University (2010), https://www.maxwell.syr.edu/uploadedFiles/parcc/eparcc/links/Matesan%20Case%20Study(1).pdf.

135. Tariq Dana, "The Prolonged Decay of the Palestinian National Movement," *National Identities* (2017): 1–17, doi:10.1080/14608944.2017.1343813. In another article, Dana comments: "Palestinian businessmen have struggled with statelessness and sought the security that a state would provide, where their companies and profits would be better protected from regional instability. As a result, many of them supported the Oslo Accords as a key step towards establishing a Palestinian state, some even imagining that Oslo's 'peace dividends' would transform the West Bank and Gaza into the Singapore of the Middle East." Dana, "Palestine's Capitalists," Al-Shabaka (20 February 2014), https://al-shabaka.org/briefs/palestinian-capitalists-have-gone-too-far.

136. "The aid advanced to Palestine in the context of the Oslo Accords' agenda, under prolonged occupation and colonization, is political aid *par excellence*. It has been advanced specifically to force and entice the Palestinian people to acquiesce and submit to an imposed political and economic agenda that is determined, shaped, and dictated by the global neo-liberal strategy of Palestine's occupier." Khalil Nakhleh, "Oslo: Replacing Liberation with Economic Neo-Colonialism,"

Al-Shabaka (10 April 2014), https://al-shabaka.org/commentaries/oslo-replacing-liberation-with-economic-neo-colonialism.

137. Israeli-Palestinian Interim Agreement on the West Bank and the Gaza Strip, Washington, DC (28 September 1995), art. II(2), Israel Ministry of Foreign Affairs, http://www.mfa.gov.il/mfa/foreignpolicy/peace/guide/pages/the%20israeli-palestinian%20interim%20agreement.aspx.

138. Israeli-Palestinian Interim Agreement, art. I(5).

139. Israeli-Palestinian Interim Agreement, art. XII(1), also see arts. XI, XI(2)(f), and XIII(2)(b)(2); Human Rights Council, Report of the Independent International Fact-Finding Mission to Investigate the Implications of the Israeli Settlements on the Civil, Political, Economic, Social and Cultural Rights of the Palestinian People Throughout the Occupied Palestinian Territory, Including East Jerusalem, para. 18, UN Doc. A/HRC/22/63 (7 February 2013), http://www.ohchr.org/Documents/HRBodies/HRCouncil/RegularSession/Session22/A-HRC-22-63_en.pdf.

140. Y. F., "Mourning an Israeli Pragmatist," The Economist (4 November 2015), https://www.economist.com/prospero/2015/11/04/mourning-an-israeli-pragmatist.

141. Rashid Khalidi, interview; Hirschfield, Track-two Diplomacy, 145.

142. Nigel Wilson, "Remembering the Ibrahimi Mosque Massacre," Al-Jazeera, 26 February 2016, http://www.aljazeera.com/news/2016/02/remembering-ibrahimi-mosque-massacre-160225061709582.html.

143. Clyde Haberman, "Arab Car Bomber Kills 8 in Israel; 44 Are Wounded," New York Times, 7 April 1994, http://www.nytimes.com/1994/04/07/world/arab-car-bomber-kills-8-in-israel-44-are-wounded.html.

144. Jonathan Cook, "Netanyahu Admits on Video He Deceived US to Destroy Oslo Accord," The National, 18 July 2010, http://www.thenational.ae/news/world/middle-east/netanyahu-admits-on-video-he-deceived-us-to-destroy-oslo-accord; "Shattered Dreams of Peace: Timeline," Frontline, PBS (n.d.), http://www.pbs.org/wgbh/pages/frontline/shows/oslo/etc/cron.html.

145. "Shattered Dreams of Peace"; Reisner, interview.

146. Robert Malley and Hussein Agha, "Camp David: The Tragedy of Errors," The New York Review of Books 48, no. 13 (9 August 2001), http://www.nybooks.com/issues/2001/08/09.

147. Nigel Parry, "Misrepresentation of Barak's Offer at Camp David as 'Generous' and 'Unprecedented,'" The Electronic Intifada, 20 March 2002, https://electronicintifada.net/content/misrepresentation-baraks-offer-camp-david-generous-and-unprecedented/3991.

148. As put by Noam Chomsky, renowned linguist and analyst of Middle East affairs: "the cantons would be surrounded by territory to be annexed to Israel. The areas of Palestinian population concentration are to be under Palestinian administration, an adaptation of the traditional colonial pattern that is the only sensible outcome as far as Israel and the US are concerned." Parry, "Misrepresentation of Barak's Offer."

149. Ewen MacAskill, "The Real Deal," The Guardian, 13 April 2001, http://www.theguardian.com/world/2001/apr/14/comment.israelandthepalestinians.

150. Tamimi, Hamas, 198.

151. Shaath, interview, 12 June 2016.

152. Dan Rabinowitz, "Belated Occupation, Advanced Militarization: Edward Said's Critique of the Oslo Process Revisited," Critical Inquiry 31, no. 2 (2005): 505–11. doi:10.2307/3651502.

153. Clayton Swisher, The Truth About Camp David (New York: Nation Books, 2004), 255.

154. Rabinowitz, "Belated Occupation, Advanced Militarization."

155. "'Provocative' Mosque Visit Sparks Riots," BBC News, 28 September 2000, http://news.bbc.co.uk/onthisday/hi/dates/stories/september/28/newsid_3687000/3687762.stm.

CHAPTER 5

Epigraph: Quoted in Alan Philps, "Israel Rocket Kills Fatah Militant," *The Telegraph*, 10 November 2000.

1. Graham Usher, "Fatah's Tanzim," *Middle East Report* 30, no. 217 (Winter 2000), http://www.merip.org/mer/mer217/fatahs-tanzim.

2. Khalil Shikaki, "Palestinians Divided," *Foreign Affairs* 81, no. 1 (January- February 2002): 89–105, doi:10.2307/20033005.

3. Ibid.

4. Penny Johnson and Eileen Kuttab, "Where Have All the Women (and Men) Gone? Reflections on Gender and the Second Palestinian Intifada," *Feminist Review* 69, no. 1 (Winter 2001): 27, doi:10.1080/01417780010070102.

5. Ibid., 28.

6. Ibid., 23.

7. Ibid., 31.

8. "Three Dead in Israeli 'Assassination,'" BBC News, 9 November 2000, http://news.bbc.co.uk/2/hi/middle_east/1014595.stm.

9. Alan Philps, "Israeli Rocket Kills Fatah Militant," *The Telegraph*, 10 November 2000, http://www.telegraph.co.uk/news/worldnews/middleeast/israel/1373950/Israeli-rocket-kills-Fatah-militant.html.

10. Ibid.

11. Ibid.

12. John Diamond, "Israel Targets, Kills PLO Official," *Chicago Tribune*, 20 November 2000, http://articles.chicagotribune.com/2000-11-10/news/0011100281_1_sieging-israeli-towns-gen-shaul-mofaz-israeli-army.

13. "Three Dead in Israeli 'Assassination.'"

14. Diamond, "Israel Targets, Kills PLO Official."

15. Gal Luft, "The Logic of Israel's Targeted Killing," *Middle East Quarterly* 10, no. 1 (Winter 2003): 3–13, http://www.meforum.org/515/the-logic-of-israels-targeted-killing; Daniel Byman, "Do Targeted Killings Work?" *Foreign Affairs* 85, no. 2 (March-April 2006): 95, doi:10.2307/20031914.

16. Luft, "Logic of Israel's Targeted Killing."

17. Lisa Hajjar, "Lawfare and Targeted Killing: Developments in the Israeli and US Contexts," *Jadaliyya*, 15 January 2012, http://www.jadaliyya.com/pages/index/4049/lawfare-and-targeted-killing_developments-in-the-i.

18. In the 1960s and 1970s, Portugal, South Africa, and Israel faced controversy for their use of force in neighboring countries against non-state actors in the name of self-defense. The United Nations Security Council rejected this self-defense argument, asserting that self-defense was unavailable to states that sought to defend territories they illegally occupied. Christine Gray, *International Law and the Use of Force* (Oxford: Oxford University Press, 2008). See also Antony Anghie, "On Making War on the Terrorist: Imperialism as Self-Defence," in *Imperialism, Sovereignty and the Making of International Law*, 273–309 (Cambridge: Cambridge University Press, 2004).

19. International Covenant on Civil and Political Rights (23 March 1976), art. 6, https://ohchr.org/EN/ProfessionalInterest/Pages/CCPR.aspx; United Nations General Assembly (UNGA), Resolution 44/159, Summary or Arbitrary Executions, UN Doc. A/RES/44/159 (15 December 1989), https://www.un.org/documents/ga/res/44/a44r159.htm. Gerald Ford was the first U.S. President to ban assassinations (in Executive Order 11905 in 1976), in response to public revulsion over the wave of assassinations in the 1970s. U.S. President Reagan affirmed this ban in Executive Order 12333. See Elizabeth B. Bazan, *Assassination Ban and E.O. 12333: A Brief Summary* (Washington, DC: Congressional Research Service, 2002), http://fas.org/irp/crs/RS21037.pdf.

20. Eyal Benvenitsi, "How Challenges of Warfare Influence the Laws of Warfare," *Military and Strategic Affairs* 4, no. 1 (April 2012).

21. International Committee of the Red Cross, Convention (IV) Respecting the Laws and Customs of War on Land, The Hague, 18 October 1907, Annex to the Convention: Regulations Respecting the Laws and Customs of War on Land – Section III: Military Authority over the Territory of the Hostile State, art. 43.

22. Emphasis added. Sharm el-Sheikh Fact Finding Committee, First Statement of the Government of Israel (28 December 2000), Israel Ministry of Foreign Affairs, http://mfa.gov.il/MFA/MFA-Archive/2000/Pages/Sharm%20el-Sheikh%20Fact-Finding%20Committee%20-%20First%20Sta.aspx. See also United Nations Economic and Social Council, The Response of the Government of the State of Israel to the Report of the UN High Commissioner for Human Rights, U.N. Doc. E/CN.4/2001/114 (11 February 2001), para. 28, https://unispal.un.org/DPA/DPR/unispal.nsf/0/7B2C79ACD500ACD285256A9C0055266E.

23. Darryl Li, "Roundtable on Occupation Law," *Jadaliyya*, 22 September 2011, http://www.jadaliyya.com/pages/index/2705/roundtable-on-occupation-law_part-of-the-conflict-.

24. International Committee of the Red Cross, Protocol Additional to the Geneva Conventions of 12 August 1949, and Relating to the Protection of Victims of International Armed Conflicts (Protocol I), 8 June 1977, art. 1(4).

25. Third Submission of the Palestine Liberation Organization to the Sharm El Sheikh Fact-Finding Commission (3 April 2001), 51, https://2001-2009.state.gov/p/nea/rls/rpt/3060.htm.

26. Ibid.

27. International Covenant on Civil and Political Rights, art. 6; UNGA, Resolution 44/159, Summary or Arbitrary Executions. Also see Bazan, *Assassination Ban and E.O. 12333*.

28. Yotam Feldman and Uri Blau, "Consent and Advise," *Israeli Occupation Archive*, 5 July 2009, http://www.israeli-occupation.org/2009-01-29/consent-and-advise/#sthash.svqAII77.dpuf.

29. Legal Consequences of the Construction of a Wall in the Occupied Palestinian Territory, Advisory Opinion of 9 July 2004, 2004 ICJ [International Court of Justice] 63, paras. 138–42; Noura Erakat, "It's Not Wrong, It's Illegal: Situating the Gaza Blockade Between International Law and the UN Response," *UCLA Journal of Islamic and Near Eastern Law* 11, no. 37 (18 November 2012), http://ssrn.com/abstract=2214163.

30. High Court of Justice (HCJ) 769/02 Public Committee against Torture in Israel (PCATI) v. Government of Israel (GOI), Supplementary Notice by the State (2 February 2003), as cited by Galit Raguan, "Adjudicating Armed Conflict in Domestic Courts: The Experience of Israel's Supreme Court," *Yearbook of International Humanitarian Law* 13 (August 4, 2011): 61–95.

31. Dan Izenburg, "What's a Lawyer Doing in a War Zone?" *Jerusalem Post*, 15 April 2005.

32. M. Finkelstein, "Legal Perspective in the Fight Against Terror—the Israeli Experience," *IDF [Israel Defense Forces] Law Review* 1 (November 2003), 343–44.

33. HCJ 2461/01 Can'an v. IDF Military Commander in Judea and Samaria (2001). (Unpublished.)

34. HCJ 3451/02 Almandi v. Minister of Defense, 56(3) PD 30 (2002).

35. "Since late September 2000, severe combat has been taking place in areas of Judea and Samaria. It is not police activity. It is an armed conflict." HCJ 7015/02, Ajuri v. The Military Commander of the Judea and Samaria Area, 56(6) PD 352, 358 (2002).

36. HCJ 2056/04 Beit Sourik Village Council v. the Government of Israel, 58(5) PD 807 (2004).

37. Raguan, *Adjudicating Armed Conflict in Domestic Courts*, 75.

38. Shira Robinson, *Citizen Strangers: Palestinians and the Birth of Israel's Liberal Settler State* (Stanford: Stanford University Press, 2013).

39. Giorgio Agamben, *State of Exception*, trans. Kevin Attell (Chicago: University of Chicago Press, 2003).

40. Ibid., 59.

41. United Nations, Statute of the International Court of Justice (June 26, 1945), art. 38, 3 TIAS [*Treaties and Other International Acts Series*] 1179.

42. Ibid.

43. Anthea Roberts, "Traditional and Modern Approaches to Customary International Law: A Reconciliation," *American Journal of International Law* 95, no. 4 (27 February, 2017): 757–91, doi:10.2307/2674625. See also Noura Erakat, "The US v. The Red Cross: Customary International Humanitarian Law & Universal Jurisdiction," *Denver Journal of International Law and Policy* 41 (Winter 2013).

44. Stefan Talmon, "Determining Customary International Law: The ICJ's Methodology Between Induction, Deduction and Assertion," *European Journal of International Law* 26, no. 2 (December 2015), doi:10.1093/ejil/chv020.

45. During the World Wars, "law served as a second front, where belligerents sought to mobilize public opinion behind the justice of their cause." Chris Jochnick and Roger Normand, "The Legitimation of Violence: A Critical History of the Laws of War," *Harvard International Law Journal* 35, no. 1 (Winter 1994), 77.

46. UNGA, International Law Commission, 58th Sess., *Fragmentation of International Law: Difficulties Arising from the Diversification and Expansion of International Law*, Report of the Study Group of the International Law Commission, U.N. Doc. A/CN.4/L.682 (August 2006), http://legal.un.org/ilc/documentation/english/a_cn4_l682.pdf.

47. United Nations, UN Charter, chap. VII: Action with Respect to Threats to the Peace, Breaches of the Peace and Acts of Aggression (24 October, 1945), http://www.un.org/en/sections/un-charter/chapter-vii/index.html.

48. Jochnick and Normand, *Legitimation of Violence*.

49. "[E]arly attempts to create laws of war reveal the enduring power of military necessity. When ideals for humanity clashed with military necessity, as inevitably occurred in all areas critical to protecting civilians, they encountered an immovable force. As a result, any weapon or tactic that a major power considered necessary, or even potentially useful was beyond the reach of legal regulation.

Attempts to regulate these areas inevitably collapsed into deliberate vagueness to disguise the tragedy of codification—legalized subordination of humanitarian principles." Ibid., 68.

50. Ibid., 68.

51. UNSC, Resolution 487, UN Doc. S/RES/487 (19 June 1981), https://unispal.un.org/DPA/DPR/unispal.nsf/0/6C57312CC8BD93CA852560DF00653995.

52. Feldman and Blau, "Consent and Advise."

53. *Sharm el-Sheikh Fact-Finding Committee: The Mitchell Plan; April 30, 2001*, The Avalon Project, http://avalon.law.yale.edu/21st_century/mitchell_plan.asp.

54. Tracy Wilkinson, "Palestinians' Mortar Fire May Signal a Deadlier Conflict," *Los Angeles Times*, 10 April 2001, http://articles.latimes.com/2001/apr/10/news/mn-49224.

55. Ibid.

56. *Sharm el-Sheikh Fact-Finding Committee.*

57. This meant that Israel should abandon its shoot to kill tactics and instead "adopt crowd-control tactics that minimize the potential for deaths and casualties, withdrawing metal-cored rubber rounds from general use and using instead rubber baton rounds without metal cores." Ibid.

58. Ibid.

59. See *A Crisis of Faith*: Second Submission of the Palestine Liberation Organization to the Sharm El Sheikh Fact-Finding Committee (30 December 2000); and Third Submission of the Palestine Liberation Organization to the Sharm El Sheikh Fact-Finding Commission (3 April 2001), https://2001-2009.state.gov/p/nea/rls/rpt/3060.htm.

60. "The security organizations of the Government of Israel (GOI) and of the Palestinian Authority (PA) reaffirm their commitment to the security agreements forged at Sharm el-Sheikh in October 2000, embedded in the Mitchell Report of April 2001." *The Tenet Plan: Israeli-Palestinian Ceasefire and Security Plan, Proposed by CIA Director George Tenet; June 13, 2001*, The Avalon Project, http://avalon.law.yale.edu/21st_century/mid023.asp.

61. "The GOI will re-institute military police investigations into Palestinian deaths resulting from Israel Defense Forces actions in the West Bank and Gaza in incidents not involving terrorism. . . . The Israeli Defense Forces (IDF) will adopt additional non-lethal measures to deal with Palestinian crowds and demonstrators, and more generally, seek to minimize the danger to lives and property of Palestinian civilians in responding to violence." Ibid.

62. "Powell: Israel 'too aggressive' in Hamas attack," CNN, 2 August 2001, http://www.cnn.com/2001/US/08/01/powell.mideast/index.html?_s=PM%3AUS.

63. Alan Sipress, "From White House, State: 2 Responses," *Washington Post*, 1 August 2001, https://www.washingtonpost.com/archive/politics/2001/08/01/from-white-house-state-2-responses/835f3d78-a97e-4470-8a70-edofecccc6d1/?utm_term=.0571147bdf8f.

64. "Cheney Discusses Patients' Rights, ANWR, and Kyoto," Fox News, 3 August 2001, http://www.foxnews.com/story/2001/08/03/cheney-discusses-patients-rights-anwr-and-kyoto.html.

65. For an argument that anticipatory self-defense is permissible but must be severely limited, see Michael Walzer, *Just and Unjust Wars: A Moral Argument with Historical Illustrations* (New York; Basic Books, 1977), 74. Also see Hugo Grotius, who argued in 1646 that "[t]he danger . . . must be immediate and imminent in point of time. . . . But those who accept fear of any sort as justifying anticipatory slaying are themselves greatly deceived. . . . [I]f a man is not planning an immediate attack, but it has been ascertained that he has formed a plot, or is preparing an ambuscade, or that

he is putting poison in our way . . . I maintain that he cannot lawfully be killed, either if the danger can in any other way be avoided, or if it is not altogether certain that the danger cannot be otherwise avoided." Grotius, *De Jure Belli Ac Pacis Libri Tres*, vol. 2, ed. James Brown Scott, trans. Francis W. Kelsey (Oxford: Clarendon Press, 1925), 173–75. For the argument that anticipatory self-defense is only permissible where the political alternatives are obsolete, see Louis Henkin, *How Nations Behave*, 2nd ed. (New York: Columbia University Press, 1979), 143–44; and Jordan J. Paust, "Use of Armed Force Against Terrorists in Afghanistan, Iraq, and Beyond," *Cornell International Law Journal* 35, no. 3 (Winter 2002): 533, 554. Furthermore, some scholars believe Article 51 of the UN Charter makes anticipatory self-defense illegal in all cases. See Ian Brownlie, *International Law and the Use of Force by States* (Oxford: Clarendon Press, 1963), 278–79.

66. The White House, Press Briefing by Ari Fleischer, 3 August 2001, https://georgewbush-whitehouse.archives.gov/news/briefings/20010803.html.

67. "According to its statement made before the General Assembly on 20 October 2003, the Government of Israel believes the construction of the Barrier is consistent with Article 51 of the Charter of the United Nations, its inherent right to self-defense and Security Council Resolutions 1368 (2001) and 1373 (2001)." UNGA, Tenth Emergency Special Session, Report of the Secretary-General Prepared Pursuant to General Assembly Resolution ES-10/13: Annex I: Summary Legal Position of the Government of Israel, UN Doc. A/ES-10/248 (24 November 2003), para. 6, https://unispal.un.org/DPA/DPR/unispal.nsf/0/A5A017029C05606B85256DEC00626057.

68. *The Yearbook of the United Nations 1969* (*UNYB 1969*), Part I, sec. 1, chap. 11: "The Situation in the Middle East," 201; *UNYB 1970*, Part I, sec. 1., chap. 11: "The Situation in the Middle East," 228; *UNYB 1978*, Part I, sec. 1, chap. 11: "The Situation in the Middle East," 297; *UNYB 1982*, Part I, sec. 1, chap. 9: "The Situation in the Middle East," 434.

69. This language was used in UNSC Resolutions 265 (1969); 267 (1969); 271 (1969); 262 (1968); 279 (1970); and 280 (1970).

70. Christine D. Gray, *International Law and the Use of Force* (Oxford: Oxford University Press, 2009), 138.

71. Legal Consequences of the Construction of a Wall in the Occupied Palestinian Territory, paras. 138–42.

72. Conference of High Contracting Parties to the Fourth Geneva Convention: Declaration, Geneva (5 December 2001), https://unispal.un.org/DPA/DPR/unispal.nsf/0/8FC4F064B9BE5BAD85256C1400722951.

73. Ellen Margrethe Loj, Statement by the Presidency on Behalf of the EU on the Report of the Secretary-General on Jenin, address to the United Nations, New York, 5 August 2002, http://eu-un.europa.eu/eu-presidency-statement-jenin.

74. James Risen and David Johnston, "Bush Has Widened Authority of C.I.A. to Kill Terrorists," *New York Times*, 14 December 2002, http://www.nytimes.com/2002/12/15/world/threats-responses-hunt-for-al-qaeda-bush-has-widened-authority-cia-kill.html?pagewanted=all.

75. Walter Pincus, "US missiles Kill al Qaeda Suspects," *The Age*, 6 November 2002, http://www.theage.com.au/articles/2002/11/05/1036308311314.html?oneclick=true.

76. "If the USA is behind this with Yemen's consent, it is nevertheless a summary execution that violates human rights. If the USA has conducted the attack without Yemen's permission it is even worse. Then it is a question of unauthorized use of force." Brian Whitaker and Oliver Burkeman,

"Killing Probes the Frontiers of Robotics and Legality," *The Guardian*, 5 November 2002, https://www.theguardian.com/world/2002/nov/06/usa.alqaida.

77. U.S. Department of State, Press Briefing by Richard Boucher, 5 November 2002, http://2001–2009.state.gov/p/nea/rt/14961.htm.

78. David Leigh and Tony Geraghty, "The Name of the Game Is Assassination," *The Guardian*, 18 December 2002, https://www.theguardian.com/world/2002/dec/19/usa.comment.

79. U.S. Department of State, "Annual U.S–Israel Joint Counterterrorism Group Meeting," Press Release (14 July 2015), http://www.2009-2017.state.gov/r/pa/prs/ps/2015/07/244877.htm; *White House, U.S–Israel Joint Statement; April 30, 1996*, White House Press Release, The Avalon Project, http://avalon.law.yale.edu/20th_century/palo2.asp.

80. UNSC, "Security Council Urged to Condemn Extrajudicial Executions Following Israel's Assassination of Hamas Leader," Press Release (19 April 2004), http://www.un.org/press/en/2004/sc8063.doc.htm.

81. Micah Zenko, "Obama's Embrace of Drone Strikes Will Be a Lasting Legacy," *New York Times*, 12 January 2016, https://www.nytimes.com/roomfordebate/2016/01/12/reflecting-on-obamas-presidency/obamas-embrace-of-drone-strikes-will-be-a-lasting-legacy.

82. Ibid.

83. Charlie Savage, "Justice Department Memo Approving Targeted Killing of Anwar Al-Awlaki," *New York Times*, 23 June 2014, https://www.nytimes.com/interactive/2014/06/23/us/23awlaki-memo.html.

84. This effort has included arranging conferences dedicated to counterterrorism as well as publishing articles and books on the topic, and also the work of canonical scholars in U.S. national security law. See Michael N. Schmitt and John J. Merriam, "The Tyranny of Context: Israeli Targeting Practices in Legal Perspective," *University of Pennsylvania Journal of International Law* 37, no. 1 (12 April 2015): 53–139, https://ssrn.com/abstract=2593629.

85. The ICJ articulated the concept of specially affected states in a 1969 decision concerning the North Sea Continental Shelf. Germany, Denmark, and the Netherlands had sought a ruling on a dispute regarding jurisdiction over this mineral-rich area. The ICJ found that these three states alone could determine custom for all other countries because they were the only ones with an interest in the shelf and, so long as other countries did not protest, their practice would reflect customary law. North Sea Continental Shelf (Federal Republic of Germany/Netherlands), Judgment of 20 February 1969, 1969 ICJ 3.

86. The United States captured this concept in Restatement (Third) of the Foreign Relations Law of the U.S., sec. 102 (1997).

87. Unlike the case of a specific interest such as jurisdiction over a coast, in the case of war, all states are affected, regardless of their participation, thereby diminishing the role of specially affected states in war. Erakat, "US v. The Red Cross," 240–42.

88. Victor Kattan argues that it is more difficult to establish new custom when it contravenes an existing norm, especially in the case of a *jus cogens*, or compelling norm, from which no derogation is permitted, such as the prohibition of the use of force. "Accordingly, only by accepting the view that the prohibition of the use of force is not jus cogens, and that the rule in Article 2(4) of the [UN] Charter is dead, notwithstanding arguments to the contrary, can the conceptual leap be made: that a new hegemonic law has arisen, led by the United States, the United Kingdom, Australia and Israel that has

modified the prohibition on the use of force to allow for preventive self-defence." Kattan, "Furthering the 'War on Terrorism' Through International Law: How the United States and the United Kingdom Resurrected the Bush Doctrine on Using Preventive Military Force to Combat Terrorism," *Journal on the Use of Force and International Law* 5, no. 1 (2017), 32–33, doi:10.1080/20531702.2017.1376929.

89. UNGA, Human Rights Council, Report of the Special Rapporteur on Extrajudicial, Summary or Arbitrary Executions, Philip Alston, UN Doc. A/HRC/14/24/Add.6 (28 May 2010), http://www2.ohchr.org/english/bodies/hrcouncil/docs/14session/A.HRC.14.24.Add6.pdf.

90. Feldman and Blau, "Consent and Advise."

91. Amos Yadlin, "Ethical Dilemmas in Fighting Terrorism," *Jerusalem Center for Public Affairs* 4, no. 8 (25 November 2004): http://www.jcpa.org/brief/brief004-8.htm.

92. Ibid.

93. Ibid.

94. Asa Kasher and Amos Yadlin, "Military Ethics of Fighting Terror: An Israeli Perspective," *Journal of Military Ethics* 4, no. 1 (2005): 3–32. doi:10.1080/15027570510014642.

95. Amos Harel, "The Philosopher Who Gave the IDF Moral Justification in Gaza," *Haaretz*, 6 February 2009, https://www.haaretz.com/1.5071578.

96. HCJ 9132/07 Al-Bassiouni v. Prime Minister, Judgment of 30 January 2008, http://elyon1.court.gov.il/Files_ENG/07/320/091/n25/07091320.n25.pdf.

97. HCJ 2461/01 Can'an v. IDF Military Commander in Judea and Samaria (2001). (Unpublished.)

98. The Disengagement Plan—General Outline (18 April 2004), Israel Ministry of Foreign Affairs, Foreign Policy, http://www.mfa.gov.il/mfa/foreignpolicy/peace/mfadocuments/pages/disengagement%20plan%20-%20general%20outline.aspx.

99. International Committee of the Red Cross, Convention (V) Respecting the Rights and Duties of Neutral Powers and Persons During War on Land, The Hague, 18 October 1907, art. 1, https://ihl-databases.icrc.org/applic/ihl/ihl.nsf/INTRO/200?OpenDocument.

100. "In the same decision, the tribunal considered a territory occupied even though the occupying army had partially evacuated certain parts of the territory and lost control over the population, as long as it could 'at any time' assume physical control of any part of the territory." Harvard Program on Humanitarian Policy and Conflict Research, *Legal Aspects of Israel's Disengagement Plan Under International Humanitarian Law*, Policy Brief (Boston: HPCR, 2010), 8.

101. Prosecutor v. Naletilic, International Criminal Tribunal of Yugoslavia Judgment of 31 March 2003, para. 217, as quoted in Elizabeth Stubbins, *Occupation, Armed Conflict, and the Legal Aspects of the Relationship Between Israel, the West Bank, and the Gaza Strip: A Resource for Practitioners*, Policy Brief (Boston: HPCR, 2008), http://eprints.lse.ac.uk/25175.

102. Ari Shavit, "Gaza Plan Aims to Freeze the Peace Process," *Haaretz*, 6 October 2004, http://www.haaretz.com/top-pm-aide-gaza-plan-aims-to-freeze-the-peace-process-1.136686.

103. International Criminal Court, *Situation on Registered Vessels of Comoros, Greece and Cambodia*, art. 53(1) Report (6 November 2014), para. 16.

104. "Israel has without doubt at all times relevant to the mandate of the Mission exercised effective control over the Gaza Strip. The Mission is of the view that the circumstances of this control establish that the Gaza Strip remains occupied by Israel. The provisions of the Fourth Geneva Convention therefore apply at all relevant times with regard to the obligations of Israel towards

the population of the Gaza Strip." UNGA, Human Rights Council, 12th Sess., *Human Rights in Palestine and Other Occupied Arab Territories*, Report of the United Nations Fact-Finding Mission on the Gaza Conflict, UN Doc. A/HRC/12/48, 676 (15 September 2009), para. 276.

105. "The removal of settlers and most military forces will not end Israel's control over Gaza. . . . Israel plans to reconfigure its occupation of the territory, but it will remain an occupying power with responsibility for the welfare of the civilian." "Israel: 'Disengagement' Will Not End Gaza Occupation," Human Rights Watch, 28 October 2004, https://www.hrw.org/news/2004/10/28/israel-disengagement-will-not-end-gaza-occupation.

106. "Although not directly bearing on the issue of Israeli targeting, note that the Israeli position deprives members of national liberation movements of any belligerent immunity for their attacks on Israeli targets, including those that qualify as military objectives." Schmitt and Merriam, "Tyranny of Context," 31.

107. The existing laws of war regulating combat were outdated creating a need to "formulate a Fifth Geneva Convention because the Fourth has lost much of its relevance." Dan Harel, "Asymmetrical Warfare in the Gaza Strip," *Military and Strategic Affairs* 4, no. 1 (2012): 22, http://www.inss.org.il/publication/asymmetrical-warfare-in-the-gaza-strip-a-test-case.

108. "Israeli Military Operations Against Gaza, 2000–2008," *Journal of Palestine Studies* 38, no. 3 (2009): 122, doi:10.1525/jps.2009.xxxviii.3.122.

109. Leigh and Geraghty, "Name of the Game Is Assassination."

110. Samera Esmeir, "Colonial Experiments in Gaza," *Jadaliyya*, 14 July 2014, http://www.jadaliyya.com/pages/index/8482/colonial-experiments-in-gaza-.

111. Kasher and Yadlin, "Military Ethics of Fighting Terror," 17.

112. See the debate between Asa Kasher, Amos Yadlin, and Michael Walzer, "Israel: Civilians and Combatants," in *New York Review of Books* 58, no. 8 (14 May 2009), https://www.nybooks.com/articles/2009/05/14/israel-civilians-combatants; see also "Israel and the Rules of War: An Exchange," *New York Review of Books*, 56, no. 10 (11 June 2009), https://www.nybooks.com/articles/2009/06/11/israel-the-rules-of-war-an-exchange.

113. Schmitt and Merriam, "Tyranny of Context," 8.

114. IDF Soldier #611701, "Anything still there is as good as dead," testimony from Gaza, 2014, in *Breaking the Silence (database)*, http://www.breakingthesilence.org.il/testimonies/database/611701.

115. Ruth Margalit, "Hadar Goldin and the Hannibal Directive," *The New Yorker*, 6 August 2014, http://www.newyorker.com/news/news-desk/hadar-goldin-hannibal-directive.

116. Max Blumenthal, "The Hannibal Directive: How Israel Killed Its Own Troops and Massacred Palestinians to Prevent Soldier's Capture," *Alternet*, 2 September 2014, http://www.alternet.org/hannibal-directive-how-israels-secret-military-doctrine-deliberately-killed-soldiers-and-massacred.

117. William Booth, "The Military Operation in Gaza That Still Haunts Israel One Year Later," *Washington Post*, 4 August 2015, https://www.washingtonpost.com/world/the-military-operation-in-gaza-that-still-haunts-israel-one-year-later/2015/08/03/915859a8-3480-11e5-b835-61ddaa99c73e_story.html?utm_term=.f52983d3229f.

118. International Committee of the Red Cross, Convention (III) Relative to the Treatment of Prisoners of War, Geneva, 12 August 1949, https://ihl-databases.icrc.org/ihl/INTRO/375?OpenDocument.

119. PCATI v. GOI, para. 39.

120. Kristen E. Eichensehr, "On Target? The Israeli Supreme Court and the Expansion of Targeted Killings," *Yale Law Journal* 116, no. 8 (2007): 1873. doi:10.2307/20455778.

121. Ibid., 1879.

122. Harel, "The Philosopher Who Gave the IDF Moral Justification in Gaza."

123. International Committee of the Red Cross, Interpretive Guidance on the Notion of Direct Participation in Hostilities Under International Humanitarian Law (May 2009), http://www.refworld.org/docid/4a670dec2.html.

124. UNGA, "Report of the Special Rapporteur on Extrajudicial, Summary or Arbitrary Executions."

125. International Covenant on Civil and Political Rights, art. 6.

126. Tim Butcher, "Israel Attack on Gaza: Fragile Peace Shattered Again," *The Telegraph*, 27 December 2008, http://www.telegraph.co.uk/news/worldnews/middleeast/palestinianauthority/3981502/Israel-attack-on-Gaza-Fragile-peace-shattered-again.html.

127. Harriet Sherwood, "In Gaza, Hamas Fighters Are Among Civilians. There Is Nowhere Else for Them to Go," *The Guardian*, 24 July 2014, https://www.theguardian.com/world/2014/jul/24/gaza-hamas-fighters-military-bases-guerrilla-war-civilians-israel-idf.

128. In Israel's 2014 assault on Gaza, for example, 7.5 percent of all Israelis killed by Palestinians were civilians while 70 percent of all Palestinians killed by Israel were civilians. Neve Gordon and Nicola Perugini, "Human Shielding and Urban Warfare in Israel/Palestine," *Society & Space* (19 October 2015), http://societyandspace.org/2015/10/19/human-shielding-and-urban-warfare-in-israelpalestine-by-neve-gordon-and-nicola-perugini.

129. "Fatalities During Operation Cast Lead," B'Tselem, The Israeli Information Center for Human Rights in the Occupied Territories (n.d.), http://www.btselem.org/statistics/fatalities/during-cast-lead/by-date-of-event.

130. Harel, "The Philosopher Who Gave the IDF Moral Justification in Gaza."

131. PCATI v. GOI, para. 23.

132. Sanaa Kamel and Zaher Fahim, "Israel's 'Knock on the Roof' Policy: A Three-Minute Race with Death," *Al Akhbar English*, 15 July 2014, http://english.al-akhbar.com/node/20750. A 2014 UN commission investigated fifteen cases of Israeli airstrikes on residential buildings in which 216 people were killed, including 115 children. United Nations Office for the Coordination of Humanitarian Affairs (OCHA), Occupied Palestinian Territory, *Key Figures on the 2014 Hostilities* (23 June 2015), https://www.ochaopt.org/content/key-figures-2014-hostilities.

133. Schmitt and Merriam, "Tyranny of Context," 49.

134. International Committee of the Red Cross, Protocol Additional to the Geneva Conventions of 12 August 1949 . . . (Protocol I).

135. OCHA, *Gaza Initial Rapid Assessment* (27 August 2014), http://reliefweb.int/report/occupied-palestinian-territory/gaza-initial-rapid-assessment-27-august-2014.

136. Letter Dated 27 April 2015 from the Secretary-General Addressed to the President of the Security Council, UN Doc. S/2015/286 (27 April 2015), https://www.securitycouncilreport.org/atf/cf/%7b65BFCF9B-6D27-4E9C-8CD3-CF6E4FF96FF9%7d/s_2015_286.pdf; Chris Gunness, *Response to the IDF Closing the Criminal Investigation into the Shelling Near the UNRWA School in Rafah, Gaza on August 2014*, UNRWA (26 August 2016), http://www.unrwa.org/newsroom/official-statements/record-response-idf-closing-criminal-investigation-shelling-near-unrwa.

137. Isabel Kershner, "Israel Clears Troops in Airstrike Near School in 2014 Gaza War," *New York Times*, 25 August 2016, http://www.nytimes.com/2016/08/25/world/middleeast/israel-gaza-war.html?_r=0.

138. Michael Schwartz, "Israel Warns Gaza Residents to Evacuate Before Strikes," CNN, 13 July 2014, http://www.cnn.com/2014/07/13/world/meast/mideast-tensions. The testimony of Israeli soldiers from the 2014 onslaught similarly evidences the inefficacy of warnings: e.g., "If 'roof knocking' was conducted and no one came out after a few minutes, then the assumption was that there was no one there"; and "Not enough time for everyone to leave," in *Breaking the Silence* (database), http://www.breakingthesilence.org.il/testimonies/database/568083, and http://www.breakingthesilence.org.il/testimonies/database/291321.

139. "B'Tselem's Findings: Harm to Civilians Significantly Higher in Second Half of Operation Pillar of Defense," B'Tselem (8 May 2013), http://www.btselem.org/press_releases/20130509_pillar_of_defense_report.

140. OCHA, *Key Figures on the 2014 Hostilities*.

141. Jim Zanotti, *U.S. Security Assistance to the Palestinian Authority* (Washington, DC: Congressional Research Service, 2010), https://www.fas.org/sgp/crs/mideast/R40664.pdf.

142. "The IDF also felt—after the first week or so—that the Palestinians [the Palestinian security forces] were there and they could trust them. As a matter of fact, a good portion of the Israeli army went off to Gaza from the West Bank—think about that for a minute—and the commander was absent for eight straight days. That shows the kind of trust they were putting in these people now." Speech by Lieutenant General Keith Dayton as quoted in Ibid, 24.

143. David Poort, "The al-Madhoun Assassination," Al Jazeera, 25 January 2011, http://www.aljazeera.com/palestinepapers/2011/01/201112512109241314.html.

144. UNGA, Human Rights Council, *Human Rights in Palestine and Other Occupied Arab Territories*.

145. Dr. Ibrahim Khraishi, Palestinian Ambassador to the United Nations in Geneva, interview by the author, Grand Park Hotel, Ramallah, 31 July 2016.

146. Noga Kadman, *Rafah Crossing: Who Holds the Keys?* (Tel Aviv: Gisha, Legal Center for Freedom of Movement, March 2009), http://www.gisha.org/userfiles/File/publications/Rafah_Report_Eng.pdf.

147. Jean Pierre-Filiu, *From Deep State to Islamic State: The Arab Counter-Revolution and Its Jihadi Legacy* (Oxford: Oxford University Press, 2015), 229–48.

148. Yossi Lempkowicz, "Egypt Blames Hamas for Continuing Bloodshed in Gaza," *Missing Peace*, 18 July 2014, http://missingpeace.eu/en/2014/07/egypt-blames-hamas-for-continuing-bloodshed-in-gaza.

149. "Egyptian Army Delegation Visits Israel," *Middle East Monitor*, 12 April 2014, https://www.middleeastmonitor.com/20140412-egyptian-army-delegation-visits-israel.

150. Adam Rasgon, "Ex-Saudi Intel Chief: Iran Is Using Hamas to Destabilize Region," *Jerusalem Post*, 11 July 2016, http://www.jpost.com/Middle-East/Hamas-and-Saudis-spar-over-Irans-role-in-Middle-East-460077.

151. "Saudi Arabia Vows to Disarm Anti-Israeli Groups in Gaza Strip," AMN News, 7 February 2016, https://www.almasdarnews.com/article/saudi-arabia-vows-disarm-anti-israeli-groups-gaza-strip.

152. "Saudi Delegation Visits Israel in Latest Sign of Growing Ties," Bridges for Peace (25 July 2016), http://www.bridgesforpeace.com/2016/07/saudi-delegation-visits-israel-latest-sign-growing-ties.

153. International Criminal Court, *The Principle of Complementarity in Practice,* (ICC–OTP, 2003), https://www.icc-cpi.int/NR/rdonlyres/20BB4494-70F9-4698-8E30-907F631453ED/281984/complementarity.pdf.

154. United Nations Independent Commission of Inquiry on the 2014 Gaza Conflict, Report of the Independent Commission of Inquiry on the 2014 Gaza Conflict, UN Doc. A/HRC/29/52 (24 June 2015); and United Nations Independent Commission of Inquiry on the 2014 Gaza Conflict, Detailed Findings of the Commission of Inquiry on the 2014 Gaza Conflict, UN Doc. A/HRC/29/CRP.4(24 June 2015), http://www.ohchr.org/EN/HRBodies/HRC/CoIGazaConflict/Pages/ReportCoIGaza.aspx; UNSC, Letter Dated 27 April 2015 from the Secretary-General Addressed to the President of the Security Council, UN Doc. S/2015/286 (27 April 2015), para. 32, https://undocs.org/S/2015/286.

155. Noura Erakat, "Who Is Afraid of the International Criminal Court?" *Jadaliyya,* 12 January 2015, http://www.jadaliyya.com/pages/index/20523/who-is-afraid-of-the-international-criminal-court-.

156. In its 2015 *Law of War Manual,* the U.S. Department of Defense made similar propositions about a revised proportionality assessment that tolerates large numbers of civilian casualties. Adil Ahmad Haque, "The Defense Department's Indefensible Position on Killing Human Shields," *Just Security,* 22 June 2015, https://www.justsecurity.org/24077/human-shields-law-war-manual.

157. Amnon Brazili, "How Peres Sees the Future," *Haaretz,* 28 November 1994, repr. as "For Peres—Yet Another Vision," *Report on Israeli Settlement in the Occupied Territories* 5, no. 1 (January 1995): 2; Chris Hedges, "Arafat and Peres Confer on Accord," *New York Times,* 10 December 1993, http://www.nytimes.com/1993/12/10/world/arafat-and-peres-confer-on-accord.html; Leila Farsakh, "Palestinian Labor Flows to the Israeli Economy: A Finished Story?" *Journal of Palestine Studies* 32, no. 1 (2002): 13–27.

156. Ari Shavit, "The Enemy Within," *Haaretz,* 29 August 2002, http://www.haaretz.com/the-enemy-within-1.35604; Scott Ratner, "'There Is No Co-existence with Cancer:' Right-wing Israelis Demand Gov't Give Military 'Free Hand' to Fight Palestinians," Mondoweiss (9 October 2015), http://mondoweiss.net/2015/10/existence-military-palestinians/#sthash.ej3icDpd.dpuf.

CONCLUSION

1. B'tselem, Statistics on Settlements and Settler Population, http://www.btselem.org/settlements/statistics; also see Hearings Before the Subcommittee on Immigration and Naturalization of the Judiciary Committee of the U.S. Senate, 95th Cong., 1st Sess., on the Question of West Bank Settlements and the Treatment of Arabs in the Israeli-occupied Territories, 17 and 18 October 1977 (statement of John Ruedy, "Israeli Land Acquisition in Occupied Territory, 1967–77"), 124–133. According to Ruedy, 15,000 settlers lived in the West Bank in 1976.

2. Ben White, "Did Israeli Apartheid Wall Really Stop Suicide Bombing?," *The Electronic Intifada,* 10 January 2014, https://electronicintifada.net/blogs/ben-white/did-israeli-apartheid-wall-really-stop-suicide-bombings.

3. "Israel: Jerusalem Palestinians Stripped of Status," Human Rights Watch, 8 August 2017, https://www.hrw.org/news/2017/08/08/israel-jerusalem-palestinians-stripped-status.

4. Akiva Eldar, "The Jewish Majority Is History," *Haaretz*, 16 October 2012, http://www.haaretz.com/israel-news/the-jewish-majority-is-history.premium-1.470233. The Palestinian Central Bureau of Statistics (PCBS) predicts that Palestinians will outnumber Jews by 2020; see DPA, "Palestinians to Outnumber Jewish Population by 2020, Says PA Report," *Haaretz*, 1 January 2013, https://www.haaretz.com/middle-east-news/palestinians-to-outnumber-jewish-population-by-2020-says-pa-report-1.491122. In November 2017, Israel arrested members of the PCBS collecting demographic data, including information from Palestinians in East Jerusalem; see Ibrahim Husseini, "Israel Arrests Palestinians over Population Count," Al Jazeera, 22 November 2017, http://www.aljazeera.com/news/2017/11/israel-arrests-palestinians-population-count-171122151547713.html.

5. Joseph Chamie, "Israeli-Palestinian Population Growth and Its Impact on Peace," *Pass-Blue*, 2 February 2014, http://www.passblue.com/2014/02/02/israeli-palestinian-population-growth-and-its-impact-on-peace.

6. As defined by the UN International Convention on the Suppression and Punishment of the Crime of *Apartheid*, (18 July 1976), 1015 UNTS 14861, https://treaties.un.org/doc/publication/unts/volume%201015/volume-1015-i-14861-english.pdf.

7. Barak Ravid, David Landau, Aluf Benn, and Shameul Rosner, "Olmert to Haaretz: Two-state Solution, or Israel Is Done For," *Haaretz*, 20 November 2007, https://www.haaretz.com/news/olmert-to-haaretz-two-state-solution-or-israel-is-done-for-1.234201.

8. M.S., "Ehud Barak Breaks the Apartheid Barrier," *The Economist*, 15 February 2010, https://www.economist.com/blogs/democracyinamerica/2010/02/israel_demography_democracy_or_apartheid.

9. Jeremy Sharon, "Bennett: We Will Annex Ma'ale Adumim First Then All of Area C," *Jerusalem Post*, 2 January 2017, http://www.jpost.com/Arab-Israeli-Conflict/Bennett-We-will-annex-Maaleh-Adumim-first-and-then-the-rest-of-Area-C-477236.

10. The Levy Commission Report on the Legal Status of Building in Judea and Samaria, 21 June 2012, https://israelipalestinian.procon.org/sourcefiles/The-Levy-Commission-Report-on-the-Legal-Status-of-Building-in-Judea-and-Samaria.pdf.

11. United Nations Office for the Coordination of Humanitarian Affairs (OCHA), Occupied Palestinian Territory, "Area C Humanitarian Response Plan Fact Sheet" (3 September 2010), https://www.ochaopt.org/content/area-c-humanitarian-response-plan-fact-sheet.

12. "In a March 2012 poll commissioned by the Knesset television station, 75 percent of the Jewish public supported the transfer of at least some Arab Israelis as part of a peace deal with the Palestinians, including 28 percent who believed all Arab Israelis should be forcibly transferred." U.S. Department of State, Bureau of Democracy, Human Rights, and Labor, *2008 Country Reports on Human Rights Practices: Israel and the Occupied Territories* (25 February 2009), https://www.state.gov/j/drl/rls/hrrpt/2008/nea/119117.htm.

13. Barak Ravid, "Lieberman's 'Peace Plan': Pay Israeli Arabs to Move to Palestinian State," *Haaretz*, 28 November 2014, https://www.haaretz.com/lieberman-pay-israeli-arabs-to-move-to-palestinian-state-1.5337259.

14. David B. Green, "Rage, Neglect and Transfer: The Israeli Arab Region Lieberman Wants to 'Give' to the Palestinians," *Haaretz*, 11 December 2017, https://www.haaretz.com/israel-news/.premium-neglect-and-transfer-the-israeli-arab-region-lieberman-wants-to-give-to-the-palestinians-1.5628275.

15. Peter Beinart, "Kerry Was Wrong: In Israel, There May Never Be Apartheid. In the West Bank, It's Already Here," *Haaretz*, 1 May 2014, https://www.haaretz.com/opinion/.premium-1.588272; Benjamin Pogrund, "Why Israel Is Nothing Like Apartheid South Africa," *New York Times*, 31 March 2017, https://www.nytimes.com/2017/03/31/opinion/why-israel-is-nothing-like-apartheid-south-africa.html; Ari Shavit, "A Wake-up Call; Celebrating Half a Century of Israeli Occupation," *Haaretz*, 7 April 2016, https://www.haaretz.com/opinion/.premium-1.713117.

16. "An Urgent Statement to the Israeli Public by a Group of Palestinian Academics and Activists," *Palestine-Israel Journal* 7, nos. 3 & 4 (17 November, 2000), http://www.pij.org/details.php?id=267.

17. "PLO: Time to End Dark Chapter of Apartheid," *Middle East Monitor*, 4 October 2017, https://www.middleeastmonitor.com/20171004-plo-time-to-end-dark-chapter-of-apartheid; "Abbas: Israel's Goal, with Trump's Backing Is Consolidation of an Apartheid Regime," *Haaretz*, 1 January 2018, https://www.haaretz.com/middle-east-news/palestinians/1.832445.

18. United Nations General Assembly (UNGA), Resolution 31/6 A, Policies of Apartheid of the Government of South Africa, UN Doc. A/RES/31/6/A-K (26 October 1976), https://documents-dds-ny.un.org/doc/RESOLUTION/GEN/NR0/301/89/IMG/NR030189.pdf?OpenElement. Also see Noura Erakat, "Rethinking Israel-Palestine: Beyond Bantustans, Beyond Reservations," *The Nation*, 21 March 2013, https://www.thenation.com/article/rethinking-israel-palestine-beyond-bantustans-beyond-reservations.

19. The description of Israel's settler-colonial expansion as an eliminatory project draws on Patrick Wolfe's framework of the logic of elimination, discussed at greater length in Chapter 1. See Patrick Wolfe, "Settler Colonialism and the Elimination of the Native," *Journal of Genocide Research* 8, no. 4 (2006): 387–409, http://www.kooriweb.org/foley/resources/pdfs/89.pdf.

20. Settler-colonialism seeks to "supersede the conditions of its operation." Lorenzo Veracini, "Introducing," *Settler Colonial Studies* 1, no. 1 (2011): 3, doi:10.1080/2201473X.2011.10648799.

21. See my discussion of these aims in Noura Erakat, "Whiteness as Property in Israel: Revival, Rehabilitation, and Removal," *Harvard Journal on Racial & Ethnic Justice* 31 (2015): 69–104.

22. Suhad Bishara, "Adalah's Position Paper on 'Prawer II': The Israeli Government's New Plan to Forcibly Displace and Dispossess Palestinian Bedouin Citizens of Israel from Their Land in the Naqab (Negev)," Adalah (January 2017),

https://www.adalah.org/en/content/view/9049; Patrick Strickland, "Negev: Israel Razes Palestinian Village for 113th Time," Al Jazeera, 18 May 2017, https://www.aljazeera.com/news/2017/05/israel-razes-palestinian-bedouin-village-113th-time-170517075143632.html.

23. "Israel: Jerusalem Palestinians Stripped of Status," Human Rights Watch, 8 August 2017, https://www.hrw.org/news/2017/08/08/israel-jerusalem-palestinians-stripped-status; Danielle Jefferis, "The 'Center of Life' Policy: Institutionalizing Statelessness in East Jerusalem," *Jerusalem Quarterly*, no. 50 (2012): 94, http://www.palestine-studies.org/jq/fulltext/78495.

24. "'Forget About Him, He's Not Here': Israel's Control of Palestinian Residency in the West Bank and Gaza," Human Rights Watch, 5 February 2012, https://www.hrw.org/report/2012/02/05/forget-about-him-hes-not-here/israels-control-palestinian-residency-west-bank-and; Akiva Eldar, "Israel Admits It Revoked Residency Rights of a Quarter Million Palestinians," *Haaretz*, 12 June 2012, https://www.haaretz.com/israel-admits-it-revoked-palestinians-residency-since-1967-1.5176492.

25. "Israel: Family Reunification Ruling Is Discriminatory," Human Rights Watch, 17 May 2006, https://www.hrw.org/news/2006/05/17/israel-family-reunification-ruling-discriminatory;

"Israel Must Repeal the Discriminatory Citizenship and Entry into Israel Law," Amnesty International, 19 February 2017, https://reliefweb.int/report/occupied-palestinian-territory/israel-must-repeal-discriminatory-citizenship-and-entry-israel.

26. See *The Discriminatory Laws Database*, Adalah (25 September 2017), https://www.adalah.org/en/content/view/7771.

27. Badil: Ongoing Nakba Education Center, http://www.ongoingnakba.org/en; Gregg Carlstorm, "Palestinians Testify to 'Ongoing Nakba,'" Al Jazeera, 15 May 2014, http://www.aljazeera.com/news/middleeast/2014/05/palestinians-testify-ongoing-nakba-201451561986950.html; Mosheer Amer, "Palestine Commemorates 67 Years of Ongoing Nakba," *Middle East Eye*, 15 May 2015, http://www.middleeasteye.net/columns/palestine-commemorates-67-years-ongoing-nakba-873667795; BDS National Committee (BNC), "BDS: Upholding our Rights, Resisting the Ongoing Nakba," Palestinian Grassroots Anti-apartheid Wall Campaign (15 May 2017), https://www.stopthewall.org/2017/05/15/bds-upholding-our-rights-resisting-ongoing-nakba.

28. A. S. Al-Khasawneh and R. Hatano, "The Realization of Economic, Social and Cultural Rights: The Human Rights Dimensions of Population Transfer, Including the Implantation of Settlers," UN Commission on Human Rights, Sub-Commission on the Prevention of Discrimination and Protection of Minorities, UN Doc. E/CN. 4/Sub. 2/1993/17 (6 July 1993), 6, para. 14, http://www.refworld.org/pdfid/3b00f4194.pdf.

29. International Convention on the Suppression and Punishment of the Crime of Apartheid, arts. II(c) and II(d).

30. "Israel/West Bank: Separate and Unequal," Human Rights Watch, 19 December 2010, https://www.hrw.org/news/2010/12/19/israel/west-bank-separate-and-unequal; Amnesty International, *Troubled Waters: Palestinians Denied Fair Access to Water* (London: Amnesty International, 2009), https://www.amnestyusa.org/pdf/mde150272009en.pdf.

31. UN Committee on the Elimination of All Forms of Racial Discrimination, Consideration of Reports, Comments and Information Submitted by States Parties Under Article 9 of the Convention, UN Doc. CERD/C/SR.2132 (22 February 2012), https://unispal.un.org/DPA/DPR/unispal.nsf/0/CD27F13E032F68A285257AAD005AFAD0.

32. Richard Falk and Virginia Tilley, *Israeli Practices Towards the Palestinian People and the Question of Apartheid: Palestine and the Israeli Occupation*, Economic and Social Commission for Western Asia (2017), https://electronicintifada.net/sites/default/files/2017-03/un_apartheid_report_15_march_english_final_.pdf.

33. "Israel Imposes Apartheid Regime on Palestinians: UN Report," Reuters, 15 March 2017, http://www.reuters.com/article/us-israel-palestinians-report-idUSKBN16M2IN.

34. Ibid.

35. "PLO Condemns UN for Removing Report Accusing Israel of Apartheid," *Iran Daily*, 19 March 2017, http://iran-daily.com/News/189587.html.

36. Osamah Khalil, "'Who Are You?': The PLO and the Limits of Representation," Al-Shabaka (18 March 2013), https://al-shabaka.org/briefs/who-are-you-plo-and-limits-representation.

37. "Abbas Account of Departure from Safed Is Contradictory," *Jerusalem Post*, 18 May 2011, http://www.jpost.com/Diplomacy-and-Politics/Abbas-account-of-departure-from-Safed-is-contradictory; Elhanan Miller, "Why Mahmoud Abbas Is Israel's Best Partner for Peace," *New York Times*, 1 March 2017, https://www.nytimes.com/2017/03/01/

opinion/why-mahmoud-abbas-is-israels-best-partner-for-peace.html?mtrref=www.google. com&assetType=opinion. Tariq Dana comments: "Although the PA was supposed to be subordinate to the PLO, it gradually positioned itself at the center of Palestinian politics. It exercised control over the PLO forces at the expense of their political pluralism, enforcing political fragmentation and autocratic governance." Dana, "The Prolonged Decay of the Palestinian National Movement," *National Identities* (2017): 5, https://doi.org/10.1080/14608944.2017.1343813.

38. Alaa Tartir, "The Evolution and Reform of Palestinian Security Forces 1993–2013," *Stability* 4, no. 1 (2015), https://www.stabilityjournal.org/articles/10.5334/sta.gi.

39. Tariq Dana, "The Beginning of the End of Palestinian Security Coordination with Israel?," *Jadaliyya*, 4 July 2014, http://www.jadaliyya.com/pages/index/18379/the-beginning-of-the-end -of-palestinian-security-c.

40. Ibid.

41. Ibid.

42. Alaa Tartir, "How US Security Aid to PA Sustains Israel's Occupation," Al Jazeera, 2 December 2016, http://www.aljazeera.com/indepth/features/2016/11/security-aid-pa-sustains-israel -occupation-161103120213593.html.

43. Glen Sean Coulthard, *Red Skin, White Masks: Rejecting the Colonial Politics of Recognition* (Minneapolis: University of Minnesota Press, 2014), 156.

44. Ibid.

45. Noura Erakat, "The UN Statehood Bid: Palestine's Flirtation with Multilateralism," in *Land of Blue Helmets: The United Nations and the Arab World*, ed. Vijay Prashad and Karim Makdisi, 95–114 (Minneapolis: University of Minnesota Press, 2016).

46. Khaled Elgindy, former adviser to the PLO Negotiations Affairs Department, telephone interview by the author, 22 March 2018.

47. The 1950 ICJ advisory opinion on Article 4, paragraph 2 of the UN Charter holds that "recommendation of the Security Council is the condition precedent to the decision of the Assembly by which the admission is affected."

48. For a wide range of essays on the context of the UN statehood bid, see Noura Erakat and Mouin Rabbani, eds., *Aborted State? The UN Initiative and New Palestinian Junctures* (Washington, DC: Tadween, 2013).

49. John Quigley, "The Palestine Declaration to the International Criminal Court: The Statehood Issue," in *Is There a Court for Gaza?*, ed. Chantal Meloni and Gianni Tognoni, 429–40 (The Hague: T.M.C. Asser Press, 2011).

50. Marlise Simons, "Court Rejects Palestinians in Their Bid for a Tribunal," *New York Times*, 3 April 2012, http://www.nytimes.com/2012/04/04/world/middleeast/international-criminal-court- rejects-palestinian-bid-for-tribunal.html.

51. On the heels of the Arab Uprisings that began in December 2010 and had already begun to rock Egypt and Tunisia, Al Jazeera published confidential documents leaked from the PLO's negotiations unit. The Palestine Papers, as they came to be known, confirmed what many analysts already knew about the peace talks: in pursuit of an agreement, Palestinian negotiators were willing to make remarkable concessions that further disemboweled popular Palestinian claims enshrined in General Assembly resolutions, customary law, and human rights norms. Palestinians across the diaspora, among Israel's citizens, and within the Territories revolted

against the Palestinian Authority. Their demands ranged from resuscitating the Palestinian National Council for the sake of democratizing decision making on behalf of Palestinians to dissolving the Oslo Accords and the Palestinian Authority they created. The expiration of PA President Mahmoud Abbas's electoral mandate to govern in 2010 exacerbated disdain for the institution. The Palestinian leadership announced the statehood bid in this context. Though it failed to thoroughly appease Palestinian frustrations, the bid managed to provide the PA with a momentary reprieve. The statehood bid captured the attention of the international community and of Palestinians especially, who braced themselves for a potential break in the debilitating status quo. Erakat, "UN Statehood Bid," 10–12.

52. With a vote of 138 in favor, 9 against, and 1 abstention. UNGA, Resolution 67/19, Status of Palestine in the United Nations, UN Doc. A/RES/67/19 (4 December 2012), https://unispal .un.org/DPA/DPR/unispal.nsf/0/19862D03C564FA2C85257ACB004EE69B.

53. Harriet Sherwood and Paul Lewis. "Middle East Peace Talk Negotiators Agree That 'All Issues Are on the Table.'" *The Guardian*, 30 July 2013, https://www.theguardian.com/world/2013/ jul/30/middle-east-peace-talks-livni-erekat-final-agreement.

54. Tariq Dana, "A Resistance Economy: What Is It and Can It Provide an Alternative?," PAL Papers Series (Berlin: Rosa Luxemburg Stiftung, 2014); Tariq Dana, "The Palestinian Capitalists That Have Gone Too Far," Al-Shabaka (14 January 2014), https://al-shabaka.org/briefs/ palestinian-capitalists-have-gone-too-far.

55. "Full Video and Transcript: Trump's Speech Recognizing Jerusalem as the Capital of Israel," *New York Times*, 6 December 2017, http://www.nytimes.com/2017/12/06/world/middleeast/ trump-israel-speech-transcript.html; Peter Baker, "An Embassy in Jerusalem? Trump Promises, but So Did Predecessors," *New York Times*, 18 November 2016, https://www.nytimes.com/2016/11/19/ world/middleeast/jerusalem-us-embassy-trump.html.

56. "Full Video and Transcript: Trump's Speech Recognizing Jerusalem."

57. "Abbas Snubs US Vice President Pence over Jerusalem Move," Al Jazeera, 10 December 2017, www.aljazeera.com/news/2017/12/abbas-snubs-vice-president-pence-jerusalem-move -171210064514836.html.

58. Carol Morello and Ruth Eglash, "U.N. Resoundingly Rejects U.S. Decision on Jerusalem in Pointed Rebuke." *Washington Post*, 21 December 2017, www.washingtonpost.com/world/ national-security/un-begins-debate-on-jerusalem-resolution/2017/12/21/37cf9bf8-e65d-11e7-833f -155031558ff4_story.html?utm_term=.db1a6f50fe7e.

59. Michael Schwirtz and Rick Gladstone, "U.S. Vetoes U.N. Resolution Condemning Move on Jerusalem." *New York Times*, 18 December 2017, www.nytimes.com/2017/12/18/world/middleeast/ jerusalem-un-security-council.html.

60. "US Threatens to Cut UNRWA Funding Unless Palestinians Engage in Peace Talks," *Middle East Eye*, 2 January 2018, www.middleeasteye.net/news/us-may-halt-unrwa-funding-until -palestine-returns-negotiating-table-884720630.

61. See, e.g., the discussion of U.S. obstructionism in the Introduction.

62. Rashid Khalidi, *Brokers of Deceit: How the US Has Undermined Peace in the Middle East* (Boston: Beacon Press, 2013); John J. Mearsheimer and Stephen M. Walt, *The Israel Lobby and U.S. Foreign Policy* (New York: Farrar, Straus and Giroux, 2008).

63. "Palestinians Plan to Join 60 U.N. Bodies, Treaties." Al Arabiya English, 28 April 2014, http://english.alarabiya.net/en/News/middle-east/2014/04/28/Palestinians-plan-to-join-60-U-N-bodies-treaties-.html.

64. Vijay Prashad cites Mahmoud Abbas's letter to UN Secretary-General Ban Ki-moon of July 13 requesting international protection. Prashad, "Holding Out," *Frontline* [India], 19 September, 2014.

65. Erakat, "UN Statehood Bid," 15.

66. See, e.g., Susan Akram, "The Palestinian Statehood Strategy in the United Nations: Lessons from Namibia," *Jadaliyya*, 3 October 2011, http://www.jadaliyya.com/Details/24468/The-Palestinian-Statehood-Strategy-in-the-United-Nations-Lessons-from-Namibia; and Stephanie Koury, "Legal Strategies at the United Nations: A Comparative Look at Namibia, Western Sahara, and Palestine," in *International Law and the Israeli-Palestinian Conflict: A Rights-based Approach to Middle East Peace*, ed. Susan M. Akram, Michael Dumper, Michael Lynk, and Iain Scobbie, 147–83 (New York: Routledge, 2010).

67. U. O. Umozurike, "Law and Self-Determination in Namibia," *Journal of Modern African Studies* 8, no. 4 (December 1970): 585–603.

68. Julio Faundez, "The Relevance of International Law," *Third World Quarterly* 8, no. 2 (April 1986): 541.

69. G. J. Eddy Gouraige, "The United Nations and Decolonization," *The Black Scholar*, 5, no. 7 (1974): 16–23.

70. Ibid., 542.

71. International Status of South West Africa, Advisory Opinion of 11 July 1950, 1950 ICJ 128.

72. Admissibility of Hearings of Petitioners by the Committee on South West Africa, Advisory Opinion of 1 June 1956, 1956 ICJ 23.

73. Faundez, "Relevance of International Law," 543.

74. UNSC, Resolution 539 [Namibia], UN Doc. S/RES/539 (28 October 1983), http://www.refworld.org/docid/3b00f16c2c.html; UNSC, Resolution 385 [Namibia] UN Doc. S/RES/385 (30 January 1976). http://www.refworld.org/docid/3b00f1732c.html; UNSC, Resolution 481 [Israel-Syrian Arab Republic], UN Doc. S/RES/481 (1980) (26 November 1980), http://avalon.law.yale.edu/20th_century/un481.asp.

75. UNSC, Resolution 264, The Situation in Namibia, UN Doc. S/RES/264 (20 March 1969), http://www.refworld.org/docid/3b00f20c14.html.

76. UNSC, Resolution 276, The Situation in Namibia, UN Doc. S/RES/276 (30 January 1970), para. 5, http://www.refworld.org/docid/3b00f2112b.html.

77. Legal Consequences for States of the Continued Presence of South Africa in Namibia (South West Africa) Notwithstanding Security Council Resolution 276 (1970), Advisory Opinion of 21 June 1971, 1971 ICJ 16, para. 53.

78. Faundez, "Relevance of International Law," 552.

79. As explained by one South African Senator, "It stands to reason that when we talk of the Natives' right of self-government in those areas we cannot mean that we intend by that to cut large slices of South Africa and turn them into independent States." Umozurike, *Law and Self-Determination in Namibia*, 596.

80. Christopher Wren, "Namibia Achieves Independence After 75 Years of Pretoria's Rule," *New York Times*, 21 March 1990.

81. UNSC, Resolution 435 [Namibia], UN Doc. S/RES/435 (29 September 1978), https://peacemaker.un.org/sites/peacemaker.un.org/files/NM_780929_SCR435%281978%29.pdf.

82. Richard Falk, *Palestine's Horizon Toward a Just Peace* (New York: Pluto Press, 2017), 9.

83. Its 2004 decision held that the construction of the wall in the West Bank, as opposed to along the 1949 armistice line, violated the Palestinian right to self-determination, contravened the Fourth Geneva Convention, and could not be justified as a measure of Israeli self-defense. It advised Israel to "terminate its breaches of international law; it is under an obligation to cease forthwith the works of construction of the wall being built in the Occupied Palestinian Territory, including in and around East Jerusalem, to dismantle forthwith the structure therein situated." The court also observed that all states had an obligation "not to recognize the illegal situation resulting from the construction of the wall and not to render aid or assistance in maintaining the situation created by such construction." Legal Consequences of the Construction of the Wall in the Occupied Palestinian Territory, Advisory Opinion of 9 July 2004, 2004 ICJ 63, paras. 163, 160.

84. Omar Barghouti, "BDS: A Global Movement for Freedom & Justice," Al-Shabaka (4 May 2010), https://bdsmovement.net/files/2011/02/alshabakaBrief.pdf; see also Noura Erakat, "Beyond Sterile Negotiations: Looking for a Leadership with a Strategy," Al-Shabaka (1 February 2012), https://al-shabaka.org/briefs/beyond-sterile-negotiations-looking-leadership-strategy.

85. Barghouti, "BDS: A Global Movement for Freedom & Justice."

86. Annelien de Dijn, "The Politics of Enlightenment: From Peter Gay to Jonathan Israel," *The Historical Journal* 55, no. 3 (2012): 786.

87. Noura Erakat, "BDS in the USA, 2001–2010," *Middle East Report* 40, no. 255, https://www.merip.org/mer/mer255/bds-usa-2001-2010.

88. Daniel Kreps, "Lorde Cancels Tel Aviv Concert After Calls to Boycott Israel," *Rolling Stone*, 24 December 2017, https://www.rollingstone.com/music/news/lorde-cancels-tel-aviv-concert-after-calls-to-boycott-israel-w514660.

89. Hilary Rose and Steven Rose, "Stephen Hawking's Boycott Hits Israel Where It Hurts: Science," *The Guardian*, 13 May 2013, https://www.theguardian.com/science/political-science/2013/may/13/stephen-hawking-boycott-israel-science; Dave Zirin, "Why Michael Bennett Walked Away from the NFL's Israel Delegation," *The Nation*, 13 February 2017, https://www.thenation.com/article/why-michael-bennett-walked-away-from-the-nfls-israel-delegation.

90. Laurie Goodstein, "Presbyterians Vote to Divest Holdings to Pressure Israel," *New York Times*, 20 June 2014, https://www.nytimes.com/2014/06/21/us/presbyterians-debating-israeli-occupation-vote-to-divest-holdings.html.

91. Ireland Palestine Solidarity Campaign, "Dublin City Council Votes to Support Palestinians BDS Movement & Discontinues HP Contracts," Press Release (9 April 2018), http://www.ipsc.ie/bds/dublin-city-council-votes-to-support-palestinian-bds-movement-discontinue-hp-contracts.

92. See, e.g., "Howard Kohr Remarks on Iran at the American Israel Public Affairs Committee (AIPAC) Conference" (Video), C-SPAN, 5 March 2012, https://www.c-span.org/video/?304740-1/howard-kohr-remarks-iran. In 2014, Israeli Prime Minister Netanyahu closed his address at the AIPAC conference by decrying BDS as a manifestation of anti-Semitism, rather than a grassroots political

tactic aimed at applying pressure on a state where diplomacy has failed. "Netanyahu's AIPAC Speech: The Full Transcript," *Haaretz*, 4 March 2014, https://www.haaretz.com/israel-news/1.577920.

93. "The Anti-Boycott Law: Questions and Answers," The Association for Civil Rights in Israel (17 July 2011), https://www.acri.org.il/en/2011/07/17/the-anti-boycott-law-questions-and-answers.

94. Doron Peskin, "Israel Commits $25 Million to New Anti-BDS Task Force, but What Exactly Will They Do?," *Al-Monitor*, 23 December 2015, https://www.al-monitor.com/pulse/originals/2015/12/boycott-bds-movement-israel-government-office-gilad-erdan.html.

95. Noa Landau and Allison Kaplan Sommer, "Israel Says Jewish Voice for Peace on BDS Blacklist, Activists Will Not Be Allowed Entry," *Haaretz*, 7 January 2018, https://www.haaretz.com/israel-news/1.833385.

96. Barghouti, "BDS"; Erakat, "Beyond Sterile Negotiations."

97. Erakat, "Beyond Sterile Negotiations."

98. Mahmood Mamdani, "The South Africa Moment," *Journal of Palestinian Studies* 45, no. 1 (2015): 67.

99. See Stacy Douglas and Souzan Lennon, Introduction, *Canadian Journal of Law and Society/ Revue Canadienne Droit et Société*, 29(2), 141–143, doi:10.1017/cls.2014.9. "Because settler colonialism is first and foremost a territorial project, elimination is an organizing principle of settler colonial society rather than a one-off occurrence," 142; Patrick Wolfe, *Traces of History: Elementary Structures of Race* (New York: Verso Books, 2016).

100. Nadim Nashef, "Palestinian Youth Assert Right of Return with Direct Actions," *The Electronic Intifada*, 11 September 2013, https://electronicintifada.net/content/palestinian-youth -assert-right-return-direct-action/12760.

101. Jared Sexton, "The Vel of Slavery: Tracking the Figure of the Unsovereign," *Critical Sociology* 42, no. 4–5 (2014): 583–97; also discussed in Erakat, "Whiteness as Property in Israel."

102. Mottle Wolfe, "Jews Living in Judea Is a Civil Right," Israel Forever Foundation (31 March 2018), https://israelforever.org/interact/blog/jews_living_in_judea_is_a_civil_right; Sara Yael Hirschhorn, "If You Can't Say Israeli Settlers Are Civilians Too, You're Propping Up Apologists for Terror," *Haaretz*, 31 March 2018; Avinoam Sharon, "How I Became an Evil Settler," *Haaretz*, 13 September 2010, https://www.haaretz.com/1.5112453; Nicola Perugini and Neve Gordon. *The Human Right to Dominate* (Oxford: Oxford University Press, 2015), 19.

103. Richard Silverstein, "Defending the Indefensible Settlements," *The Guardian*, 13 July 2009, https://www.theguardian.com/commentisfree/cifamerica/2009/jul/13/israel-west-bank-settlements-obama. See the response to this claim by Victor Kattan, *From Coexistence to Conquest: International Law and the Origins of the Arab-Israeli Conflict, 1891–1949* (New York: Pluto Press, 2009), 117–45.

104. Lama Abu Odeh, "The Limits of International Law Legalese," *Jadaliyya*, 5 December 2012, http://www.jadaliyya.com/pages/index/8800/the-limits-of-international-law-legalese-.

105. Amira Hass, "Palestinians Embark on Civil Disobedience Protests Against 'Demographic Segregation,'" *Haaretz* 16 November 2011, http://www.haaretz.com/palestinians -embark-on-civil-disobedience-protests-against-demographic-segregation-1.395820.

106. Linah Alsaafin, "Palestinians Clarify Goal of "Freedom Rides" Challenge to Segregated Israeli Buses," *The Electronic Intifada*, 14 November 2011, https://electronicintifada.net/blogs/linah-alsaafin /palestinians-clarify-goal-freedom-rides-challenge-segregated-israeli-buses.

107. Linah Alsaafin, "Freedom Rides in the 21st Century," *The Electronic Intifada*, 9 November 2011, https://electronicintifada.net/blogs/linah-alsaafin/freedom-rides-21st-century.

108. Alsaafin, "Palestinians Clarify Goal of "Freedom Rides Challenge.""

109. In his work, native scholar Taiaiake Alfred interrogates the relationship between nationhood and sovereignty to draw useful distinctions. He explains that nationhood is about "being . . . being is who you are, and a sense of who you are is arrived at through your relationships with other people—your people. So who we are tied with what we are: a nation." Sovereignty is not a part of being, "it has to be conferred, or granted—it's a thing that can be given and thus can be taken away. It's clearly a foreign concept, because it occurs through an exercise of power— over another." Alfred, *Peace, Power, Righteousness: An Indigenous Manifesto*, 2nd ed. (Oxford: Oxford University Press, 2009), 89. "The Arab people of Palestine lost not only the battle for the *political control* of its own country—it lost its *country* as well." Fayez A. Sayegh, *Zionist Colonialism in Palestine*, Palestine Monographs, no. 1 (Beirut: Palestine Research Center, 1965), 17.

110. Ghassan Kanafani, "Men in the Sun" (1963) and "Return to Haifa" (1970), in *Men in the Sun and Other Palestinian Stories*, trans. Hilary Kilpatrick, (Boulder: Lynne Reiner), 1999.

111. Noa Landau and Jack Khoury, "'Two-state Solution Is Over,'Top Palestinian Diplomat Says After Trump's Jerusalem Speech," *Haaretz*, 7 Dec 2017, https://www.haaretz.com/middle-east-news/palestinians/.premium-1.827369.

112. Walid Khalidi, "Thinking the Unthinkable: A Sovereign Palestinian State," *Foreign Affairs*, 56, no. 4 (1 July 1978), https://www.foreignaffairs.com/articles/palestinian-authority/1978-07-01/thinking-unthinkable-sovereign-palestinian-state.

113. The Nakba Files, "Symposium: Israel's Colonial Declaration of Independence" (2016), http://nakbafiles.org/2016/09/06/symposium-israels-colonial-declaration-of-independence.

114. Sherene Seikaly and Max Ajl, "Of Europe: Zionism and the Jewish Other," in *Europe After Derrida: Crisis and Potentiality*, ed. Agnes Czajka and Bora Isyar, 120–33 (Edinburgh: Edinburgh University Press, 2013).

115. A. Dirk Moses scrutinizes Australia's official apology to its indigenous communities and considers its value to a settler-decolonization process and justice for indigenous communities generally. "The apology is only a moment in the process of negotiation, then, suggesting the opening up rather than closing down of political discourse, as the determination of Indigenous people to insist both on their autonomous agency and participate in the collective 'we' of the Australian political nation indicated." Moses, "Official Apologies, Reconciliation, and Settler Colonialism: Australian Indigenous Alterity and Political Agency," *Citizenship Studies* 15, no. 2 (2011): 155.

116. Baruch Kimmerling, "Benny Morris's Shocking Interview," History News Networks, 26 January 2004, http://historynewsnetwork.org/article/3166.

117. Asaf Romirowsky and Alexander Joffe, "Palestinians: Refugees Forever?" *Haaretz*, 5 January 2012, https://www.haaretz.com/opinion/palestinians-refugees-forever-1.434508.

118. Nicole Gaaouette and Jamie Crawford, "US Cuts Funding for Palestinians Following Trump's Twitter threat," CNN, 16 January 2018, https://www.cnn.com/2018/01/16/politics/us-palestinian-aid-agency-cut/index.html.

119. "Trump-Netanyahu's 'Deal of the Century' Revealed," *Middle East Monitor*, 20 July 2017, https://www.middleeastmonitor.com/20170720-trump-netanyahus-deal-of-the-century-revealed.

120. "Incommensurability is an acknowledgement that decolonization will require a change in the order of the world. This is not to say that Indigenous peoples or Black and brown peoples take positions of dominance over white settlers; the goal is not for everyone to merely swap spots on the settler-colonial triad, to take another turn on the merry-go-round. The goal is to break the relentless structuring of the triad—a break and not a compromise." Eve Tuck and K. Wayne Yang, "Decolonization Is Not a Metaphor," *Decolonization: Indigeneity, Education & Society* 1, no. 1 (2012).

121. Sexton, "The Vel of Slavery."

122. This discussion is based on Erakat, "Whiteness as Property in Israel."

123. Gabriel Ash, "The Meaning of Yair Lapid," *Jadaliyya*, 30 January 2013, http://www.jadaliyya.com/Details/27931/The-Meaning-of-Yair-Lapid.

124. Ibid.

125. Ammon Raz-Krakotzkin, "The Zionist Return to the West and the Mizrahi Jewish Perspective." in *Orientalism and the Jews*, ed. Ivan Davidson Kalmar and Derek Jonathan Penslar, 162–81 (Waltham: Brandeis University Press, 2005).

126. Andrea Blanch, interview with Shlomit Lir, "Mizrahi Jews in Israel," Center for Religious Tolerance (2009), http://www.c-r-t.org/content/research/shlomit.pdf.

127. Ella Shohat, "Reflections of an Arab Jew," *Fellowship* 64, nos. 5–6 (1998): 4.

128. In their struggles, Palestinians have already paved this path in coalitions with peoples and movements globally. These efforts have included articulating solidarity between blacks and Palestinians, solidarity with indigenous nations, and antiracist coalitions at the Durban Review Conference in 2001 as well as anti-imperialist ones at the World Social Forum. See Hamid Dabashi, "Black Lives Matter and Palestine: A Historic Alliance," Al Jazeera, 6 September 2016, http://www.aljazeera.com/indepth/opinion/2016/09/black-lives-matter-palestine-historic-alliance-160906074912307.html; Rachel L. Swarns, "The Racism Walkout: The Overview; U.S. and Israelis Quit Racism Talks over Denunciation," *New York Times*, 4 September 2001, http://www.nytimes.com/2001/09/04/world/racism-walkout-overview-us-israelis-quit-racism-talks-over-denunciation.html; "Solidarity from the South: The World Social Forum Declares Its Support to BDS and to the Palestinian people," Palestinian Grassroots Anti-apartheid Wall Campaign, 3 February 2014, https://www.stopthewall.org/2014/02/03/solidarity-south-world-social-forum-declares-its-support-bds-and-palestinian-people; and Ben Norton, "Palestinians Support Indigenous Dakota Pipeline Protests: 'We Stand with Standing Rock,'" *Salon*, 18 November 2016, https://www.salon.com/2016/11/18/palestinians-support-indigenous-nodapl-protests-we-stand-with-standing-rock.

129. Angela Davis has highlighted how Israel's perversion of the two-state solution is emblematic of the dangers of political reform agendas. This is especially true with regard to the prison-industrial complex that is incapable of reformation. Surveillance mechanisms, such as ankle bracelets, framed as mitigative measures are part of an endemic structure of domination. Davis, remarks during a panel discussion, "Understand Palestine Intersectionally," at the Annual Meeting of the Middle East Studies Association, Washington, DC, 19 November 2017.

130. Waziyatawin, "Malice Enough in Their Hearts and Courage Enough in Ours: Reflections on US Indigenous and Palestinian Experiences Under Occupation," *Settler Colonial Studies* 2, no. 1 (2012): 186.

131. Liberation is to be found in our practices, not merely in our international status. As Glen Sean Coulthard says: "[T]hose struggling against colonialism must 'turn away' from the colonial state and society and instead find in their own *decolonial praxis* the source of their liberation." Coulthard, *Red Skin, White Masks*, 48. In her seminal work, Audra Simpson discusses alternative modes of sovereignty, including nested sovereignty. She is interested in how indigenous citizenships "may move ... from these seductive inducements to perform for the state, and the way they do a different kind of work through a narrative and memory-based process of constructing and affording rights to each other." Simpson, *Mohawk Interruptus: Political Life Across the Borders of Settler States* (Durham: Duke University Press, 2014), 159.

INDEX

Made in the USA
Las Vegas, NV
13 October 2023

79050648R00204